**The Emperor of
Men's Minds**

Rhetoric & Society

General Editor: Wayne A. Rebhorn

The Emperor of Men's Minds

Literature and the Renaissance Discourse of Rhetoric

WAYNE A. REBHORN

CORNELL UNIVERSITY PRESS

ITHACA AND LONDON

First published 1995 by Cornell University Press.

Library of Congress Cataloging-in-Publication Data

Rebhorn, Wayne A., 1943–
   The emperor of men's minds : literature and the Renaissance
discourse of rhetoric / Wayne A. Rebhorn.
      p.   cm.— (Rhetoric and society)
   Includes bibliographical references (p.) and index.
   ISBN 0-8014-2562-X (alk. paper)
      1. European literature—Renaissance, 1450–1600—History.
   2. Rhetoric—History.   I. Title.   II. Series: Rhetoric & society.
   PN721.R43   1995
   809'.03—dc20   94-34553

Printed in the United States of America

⊗ The paper in this book meets the minimum requirements
of the American National Standard for Information Sciences—
Permanence of Paper for Printed Library Materials, ANSI Z39.48-1984.

For Marlette, Matthew, and Rebecca

Beyond rhetoric

Contents

Illustrations

Foreword

Stated simply, the purpose of this series is to study rhetoric in all the varied forms it has taken in human civilizations by situating it in the social and political contexts to which it is inextricably bound. The series Rhetoric and Society rests on the assumption that rhetoric is both an important intellectual discipline and a necessary cultural practice and that it is profoundly implicated in a large array of other disciplines and practices, from politics to literature to religion. Interdisciplinary by definition and unrestricted in range either historically or geographically, the series investigates a wide variety of questions; among them, how rhetoric constitutes a response to historical developments in a given society, how it crystallizes cultural tensions and conflicts and defines key concepts, and how it affects and shapes the social order in its turn. The series includes books that approach rhetoric as a form of signification, as a discipline that makes meaning out of other cultural practices, and as a central and defining intellectual and social activity deeply rooted in its milieu. In essence, the books in the series seek to demonstrate just how important rhetoric really is to human beings in society.

By examining what rhetoricians actually say about the nature and functions of their art, *The Emperor of Men's Minds* offers a revisionary interpretation of Renaissance rhetoric that argues for its historically distinctive character and for its direct engagement with many of the basic concerns of its culture, including political power and authority, social mobility, gender, ethics, and the body. This book also offers a new model for the rhetorical reading of literary works, interpreting them as extensions, elaborations, and critiques of the concepts and issues central to the discourse of rhetoric that is specific to the historical period involved. In the first of its four chapters, *The Emperor of Men's Minds* argues that Renaissance rhetoricians conceive their art in political terms as a matter of power and control, not debate and dialogue, and that they identify orators as absolutist kings and emperors and equate them with the rulers of their contemporary world. Chapter 1 goes on to demonstrate how texts by Machiavelli as well as the second tetralogy of history plays by Shakespeare can be read as critical reflections on this notion of rhetorical rule. The second chapter complicates the thesis advanced in the first by showing how rhetoricians vacillate between identifying orators with actual rulers and seeing them as baseborn outsiders whose verbal skills enable them to climb up the social hierarchy and give them the means to resist or even rebuke the authorities above them. This chapter argues that Renaissance rhetoric is profoundly ambiguous: a conservative instrument that allows rulers to maintain the status quo, it is simultaneously imagined as a subversive force that threatens social stability. This vision is then shown to inform, in quite different ways, George Herbert's "The Method" as well as the anonymous picaresque novel *Lazarillo de Tormes*. Chapter 3 focuses on the sexual politics of Renaissance rhetoric. In response to attacks on an art assumed to be the exclusive province of men, attacks that label it effeminizing and even homosexual, rhetoricians insist on its "masculine" character, imagining it in terms of violent invasion and conquest. Unfortunately, such images wind up equating rhetoric with rape, an equation which Thomas Carew also makes in his elegy on John Donne and which Tirso de Molina criticizes through his satire of Don Juan in *The Trickster of Seville*. Chapter 3 then shows how rhetoricians, thinking of certain aspects of their art as essentially "feminine," render it sexually ambiguous, and how Erasmus embraces and elaborates this ambiguity in his *Praise of Folly*. Finally, the last chapter of the book reveals the conflicted, contradictory vision of the body at the heart of Renaissance rhetoric, a contradiction produced as rhetoricians attempt—and fail—to identify their art with the refined, ethically proper corporal configuration assigned to the upper classes and to disassociate it from its ethically suspect, socially déclassé contrary, what Mikhail Bakhtin calls the grotesque body of the people. This chapter analyzes various works of art, including Rabelais's novels and Shakespeare's *Coriolanus*, as they engage this vision of the body, and it ends by demonstrating how, in the course of the Renaissance, the increasing determination of rhetoricians to purify their art is paralleled by a similar development in literature from Machiavelli's *The Mandrake Root* through Jonson's *The Alchemist* down to Molière's *Tartuffe*.

WAYNE A. REBHORN

Acknowledgments

I have incurred numerous debts in the course of writing this book. First, I thank the Center for Medieval and Early Renaissance Studies at the State University of New York at Binghamton for permission to reuse, in various chapters of this book, portions of my article, "'The Emperour of Mens Minds': The Renaissance Trickster as *Homo Rhetoricus*," which appeared in *Creative Imitation: New Essays on Renaissance Literature in Honor of Thomas M. Greene*, ed. David Quint, Margaret W. Ferguson, G. W. Pigman III, and Wayne A. Rebhorn (Binghamton, N.Y.: Medieval & Renaissance Texts & Studies, 1992), 31–65. I also thank the John Simon Guggenheim Memorial Foundation as well as the University Research Institute of the University of Texas for greatly appreciated fellowships and other financial support which allowed me the free time needed to bring this book to completion. I am especially grateful to those people who willingly wrote letters of support on my behalf: William J. Kennedy, Leah Marcus, Patricia Parker, and David Quint.

My work has profited enormously from having been presented to students and colleagues both at the University of Texas and at other institutions, including the Claremont Graduate School, the California Institute of Technology, the University of California at San Diego, the University of Colorado, Texas Tech University, and the Università Cattolica in Milan. I owe a debt of gratitude to my colleagues Frank Whigham and John Rumrich for having read and commented most helpfully on various portions of the manuscript. Perhaps the greatest debt of this sort is owed to Leah Marcus, who aided me at every stage from the formulation of the project to the reading of final drafts of every chapter; her efforts truly went above and beyond the call of duty and friendship. I am grateful to Patricia Sterling for her careful, thoughtful editing of my manuscript, and I especially thank my editor at Cornell University Press, Bernhard Kendler, whose unwavering support and confidence are very deeply appreciated indeed. Finally, there is my family. My wife, Marlette, has patiently gone through one draft of my manuscript after another, challenging my conceptions, supplying important perceptions of her own (especially in Chapter 3), and generally helping me keep my work clear and free of jargon. To her and to my children I really owe the greatest debt of all, a debt of gratitude for their constant love and support through difficult as well as good times. Dedicating this book to them hardly begins to repay what they have given me.

WAYNE A. REBHORN

Austin, Texas

Abbreviations Used for
Frequently Cited Works

Agricola, *De Inventione*: Rudolph Agricola, *De Inventione dialectica libri tres*, foreword Wilhelm Risse (Cologne, 1528; rpt. Hildesheim: Georg Olms, 1976).

Agrippa, *De Incertitudine*: Henry Cornelius Agrippa, *De Incertitudine et vanitate scientiarum et artium*, in *Opera*, vol. 2 (Lyon, 1600 [?]; rpt. Hildesheim: Georg Olms, 1970).

Alsted, *Rhetorica*: Johann Heinrich Alsted, *Rhetorica* (Herborn, 1616).

Amyot, *Projet*: Jacques Amyot, *Projet de l'Eloquence royale, composé pour Henry III, roi de France* (Versailles: Ph.-D. Pierres, 1805).

Aristotle, *Rhetoric*: Aristotle, *The "Art" of Rhetoric*, trans. John H. Freese (Cambridge, Mass.: Harvard University Press, 1982).

Bacon, *Selected Writings*: Francis Bacon, *Selected Writings*, ed. Hugh G. Dick (New York: Random House, 1955).

Barbaro, *Della Eloquenza*: Daniel Barbaro, *Della Eloquenza*, in *Trattati di poetica e retorica del Cinquecento*, ed. Bernard Weinberg (Bari: Laterza. 1970), 2: 335–451.

Bary, *Rhetorique*: René Bary, *La Rhetorique françoise* (Paris, 1659). Microfilm.

Bulwer, *Chirologia*: John Bulwer, *Chirologia: or the Natural Language of the Hand*, in *Chirologia: or the Natural Language of the Hand and Chironomia: or the Art of Manual Rhetoric*, ed. James W. Cleary (Carbondale: Southern Illinois University Press, 1974).

Bulwer, *Chironomia*: John Bulwer, *Chironomia: or the Art of Manual Rhetoric*, in *Chirologia: or the Natural Language of the Hand and Chironomia: or the Art of Manual Rhetoric*, ed. James W. Cleary (Carbondale: Southern Illinois University Press, 1974).

Caussin, *Eloquentia sacra*: Nicholas Caussin, *De Eloquentia sacra et humana*, 3d ed. (Paris, 1630). Microfilm.

Cavalcanti, *Retorica*: Bartolomeo Cavalcanti, *La Retorica* (Ferrara: Gabriel Giolito, 1559). Microfilm.

Cicero, *De inventione*: Cicero, *De inventione, De optimo genere oratorum, Topica*, trans. H. M. Hubbell (London: William Heinemann, 1949).

Cicero, *De oratore*: Cicero, *De oratore*, trans. E. W. Sutton and H. Rackham (London: William Heinemann, 1959).

de' Conti, *Dialogus*: Anto Maria de' Conti, *De eloquentia dialogus*, in *Trattati di poetica e retorica del Cinquecento*, ed. Bernard Weinberg (Bari: Laterza, 1970), 2:141–61.

Denores, "Breve Trattato dell'Oratore": Giason Denores, "Breve Trattato dell'Oratore," in *Trattati di poetica e retorica del Cinquecento*, ed. Bernard Weinberg (Bari: Laterza, 1970), 3:101–34.

Du Pré, *Pourtraict*: J. Du Pré de la Porte, *Le Pourtraict de l'Eloquence Françoise* (Paris, 1621).

Du Vair, *Traitté*: Guillaume Du Vair, *Traitté de l'Eloquence Françoise*, in *Oeuvres* (Paris: Sebastien Cramoisy, 1641; rpt. Geneva: Slatkine Reprints, 1970), 389–410.

Erasmus, *Ciceronianus*: Desiderius Erasmus, *Ciceronianus*, in *Erasmus von Rotterdam, Ausgewählte Schriften*, ed. Werner Welzig, vol. 7 (Darmstadt: Wissenschaftliche Buchgesellschaft, 1972).

Fabri, *Le grand et vrai art*: Pierre Fabri, *Le grand et vrai art de pleine rhétorique*, ed. A. Héron (Rouen: A. Lestringant, 1890).

Fumaroli, *L'âge de l'éloquence*: Marc Fumaroli, *L'âge de l'éoquence: Rhétorique et "res literaria" de la Renaissance au seuil de l'époque classique* (Geneva: Droz, 1980).

Furetière, *Nouvelle allégorique*: Antoine Furetière, *Nouvelle allégorique, ou Histoire des derniers troubles arrivés au royaume d'Eloquence*, ed. Eva van Ginneken (Geneva: Droz, 1967).

Fuscano, "Della oratoria e poetica facoltà": Giovanni Berardino Fuscano, "Della oratoria e poetica facoltà," *Trattati di poetica e retorica del Cinquecento*, ed. Bernard Weinberg (Bari: Laterza, 1970), 1:187–95.

George of Trebizond, *Oratio*: George of Trebizond (Trapezuntius), *Oratio de laudibus eloquentie*, in John Monfasani, *George of Trebizond: A Biography and a Study of His Rhetoric and Logic* (Leiden: E. J. Brill, 1976), 365–69.

George of Trebizond, *Rhetoricorum*: George of Trebizond, *Rhetoricorum libri V* (Venice: Aldine Press, 1523).

Granada, *Ecclesiastica Rhetorica*: Luis de Granada, *Ecclesiastica Rhetorica* (Cologne, 1582). Microfilm.

Guzman, *Primera Parte*: Joan de Guzman, *Primera Parte de la Rhetorica* (Alcala de Henares, 1589).

Jewel, *Oratio*: John Jewel, *Oratio Contra Rhetoricam*, in *The Works*, ed. John Ayre (Cambridge: Cambridge University Press, 1850), 4:1283–91.

Keckermann, *Systema*: Bartholomew Keckermann, *Systema Rhetorices* (Hanover, 1608).

Le Grand, *Discours*: M. Le Grand, *Discours*, in René Bary, *La Rhetorique françoise* (Paris, 1659). Microfilm.

Melanchthon, *Elementorum*: Philip Melanchthon, *Elementorum Rhetorices Libri Duo* (Wittenberg, 1519). Microfilm.

Melanchthon, *Encomion*: Philip Melanchthon, *Encomion eloquentiae*, in *Werke in Auswahl*, ed. Robert Stupperich (Gütersloh: Gütersloh Verlagshaus Gerd Mohn, 1961), 3:43–62.

Montaigne, *Oeuvres*: Michel de Montaigne, *Oeuvres complètes*, ed. Albert Thibaudet and Maurice Rat (Paris: Gallimard, 1962).

Müllner: Karl Müllner, ed., *Reden und Briefe italienischer Humanisten* (Vienna, 1899; rpt. Munich: Wilhelm Fink, 1970).

Murphy, *Renaissance Eloquence*: James J. Murphy, ed., *Renaissance Eloquence: Studies in the Theory and Practice of Renaissance Rhetoric* (Berkeley: University of California Press, 1983).

Parker, *Literary Fat Ladies*: Patricia Parker, *Literary Fat Ladies: Rhetoric, Gender, Property* (London: Methuen, 1987).

Patrizi, *Della retorica*: Francesco Patrizi, *Della retorica dieci dialoghi* (Venice, 1562). Microfilm.

Peacham, *Garden*: Henry Peacham, *The Garden of Eloquence (1593)*, intro. William G. Crane (Gainesville, Fla.: Scholars' Facsimiles & Reprints, 1954).

Pico, *Epistola*: Giovanni Pico della Mirandola, *Epistola Hermolao Barbaro*, in Giovanni Pico della Mirandola and Gian Francesco Pico, *Opera Omnia*, intro. Cesare Vasoli (Basel, 1557; rpt. Hildesheim: Georg Olms, 1969), 351–58.

Plett, *Rhetorik der Affekte*: Heinrich F. Plett, *Rhetorik der Affekte: Englische Wirkungsästhetik im Zeitalter der Renaissance* (Tübingen: Max Niemeyer, 1975).

Prosatori latini: *Prosatori latini del Quattrocento*, ed. Eugenio Garin (Milan: Riccardo Ricciardi, 1952).

Puttenham, *Arte*: George Puttenham, *The Arte of English Poesie*, intro. Baxter Hathaway (Kent, Ohio: Kent State University Press, 1970).

Quintilian, *Institutio*: Quintilian, *Institutio oratoria*, trans. H. E. Butler (London: William Heinemann, 1963).

Rainolde, *Foundacion*: Richard Rainolde, *The Foundacion of Rhetorike* (London, 1563; rpt. Amsterdam: Da Capo, 1969).

Rainolds, *Oratio*: John Rainolds, *Oratio in laudem artis poeticae*, ed. William Ringler and Walter Allen, Jr. (Princeton: Princeton University Press, 1940).

Rainolds, *Oxford Lectures*: John Rainolds, *Oxford Lectures on Aristotle's "Rhetoric,"* ed. Lawrence D. Green (Newark: University of Delaware Press, 1986).

Ramus, *Attack on Cicero*: Peter Ramus, *Attack on Cicero: Text and Translation of Ramus's "Brutinae Quaestiones,"* ed. James J. Murphy, trans. Carole Newlands (Davis, Calif.: Hermagoras Press, 1992).

Ramus, *Dialectique*: Pierre de la Ramée (Ramus), *Dialectique*, in *Gramere (1562), Grammaire (1572), Dialectique (1555)* (Paris; rpt. Geneva: Slatkine Reprints, 1972).

Regius, *Panegyricus*: Raphael Regius, *De Laudibus eloquentiae panegyricus* (Venice, 1485).

Shuger, *Sacred Rhetoric*: Debora K. Shuger, *Sacred Rhetoric: The Christian*

Grand Style in the English Renaissance (Princeton: Princeton University Press, 1988).

Sidney, *Apology*: Sir Philip Sidney, *An Apology for Poetry*, ed. Forrest G. Robinson (Indianapolis: Bobbs-Merrill, 1970).

Soarez, *De Arte*: Cypriano Soarez, *De Arte Rhetorica Libri Tres* (Verona, 1589). Microfilm.

Speroni, *Dialogo*: Sperone Speroni, *Dialogo della rettorica*, in *Dialogo della lingua e Dialogo della rettorica*, intro. Giuseppe De Robertis (Lanciano: R. Carabba, 1912), 85–140.

Vives, *De Causis*: Juan Luis Vives, *De Causis Corruptarum Artium*, in *Opera Omnia*, vol. 6, ed. Francisco Fabian y Fuero (Valencia, 1745; rpt. London: Gregg Press, 1964).

Vives, *De Ratione*: Juan Luis Vives, *De Ratione dicendi*, in *Opera Omnia*, vol. 2.

Wilson, *Arte*: Thomas Wilson, *The Arte of Rhetorique (1560)*, ed. G. H. Mair (Oxford: Clarendon Press, 1909).

Note on Translations and Quotations

All translations except those from Greek texts are my own. In quoting from foreign languages and from Renaissance English texts, I have normalized spelling, changing i's to j's and u's to v's (and vice versa), when necessary. I have also expanded scribal abbreviations and removed accent marks in the Latin.

The Emperor of
Men's Minds

Introduction

Les maximes de la politique & les mysteres de la religion changent entierement les regles de la Rhetorique, & l'ancienne Rhetorique n'a rien de semblable à la moderne. (The maxims of politics and the mysteries of religion change the rules of rhetoric entirely, and ancient rhetoric has no similarity to its modern counterpart.)

—Le Grand, *Discours*

It would be an understatement to say that rhetoric was important to the Renaissance. From the early Italian humanists down to John Milton, rhetoric was considered an essential part of education, necessary equipment for the well-rounded individual, and it consistently held a place of honor both at the university and as the culminating stage of pre-university training at schools and colleges. Having displaced logic or dialectic from the preeminent position that subject enjoyed in late medieval culture, rhetoric was hailed as the queen of the sciences; despite attacks from hostile critics, debates over correct styles, and the more radical "reformation" recommended for it by the Ramists, it retained its central place in the culture throughout the Renaissance. As an indication of that centrality, James J. Murphy has calculated that more than a thousand treatises, handbooks, commentaries, and the like—texts written in virtually all the languages of western Europe—were produced on the subject in the period.[1] Indeed, this flood of material may actually have been greater than Murphy suggests, for if one considers that significant rehearsals of rhetorical notions and materials can also be found in works not normally considered rhetorics—such as literature and writings on politics and religion—then the scope of Renaissance rhetoric is truly

[1] James J. Murphy, "One Thousand Neglected Authors," in *Renaissance Eloquence*, 20–36. See also Murphy's useful bibliography in *Renaissance Rhetoric*, ed. James J. Murphy with Kevin P. Roddy (New York: Garland, 1981).

enormous, its importance beyond dispute. No wonder at least one prominent scholar, Marc Fumaroli, has argued that the Renaissance could effectively be labeled the *aetas ciceroniana*, the Age of Cicero (*L'âge de l'éloquence*, 40).

Taken together, the hundreds of discussions of rhetoric produced during the Renaissance constitute a distinctive and recognizable *discourse*—but not discourse defined simply as language in its organized written or oral form, meaning roughly what its Latin root *discurrere* suggests: a running, or talking generally, about something. Rather, in this book "discourse" is the equivalent of what J. G. A. Pocock, speaking metaphorically, has called a "language": that is, a specialized idiom that uses only a certain portion of the words and forms of a given language (such as English or French) but, like any language, does have its own distinctive lexicon of terms, its characteristic grammar, and its defining syntax of propositions and relationships.[2] What Pocock means is something like what the French would call a *langage*, the particular language of an individual, group, or profession, as opposed to a *langue*, a language in general such as English. This kind of specialized language constitutes the matrix within which individual texts may be seen to occur as historical events; it is the context which makes those texts possible, comprehensible, and meaningful and which each text necessarily modifies at and by its appearance. In the Renaissance, rhetoric is just such a distinctive discourse, constituted collectively in the huge number of discussions of the subject which appear in individual treatises and handbooks and which surface at times in texts from other domains. It is this discourse, then, with all its ramifications, that is my subject.

To be more precise: this book is concerned with the ways in which Renaissance people represented rhetoric to themselves, with how they thought about or, rather, wrote about it and how they imagined its powers and its limits, its value to the individual and to society, its characteristic uses, its relationship to other disciplines and activities. Although other matters, such as the teaching of rhetoric in schools and universities or its actual employment in political and religious forums, are important and clearly had an impact on how the subject was conceived, it is the expression of that conception in written form that I investigate here. In this connection, the front matter of treatises—prefaces and dedications, initial pages devoted to definitions of rhetoric and

[2] J. G. A. Pocock, "Texts as Events: Reflections on the History of Political Thought," in *Politics of Discourse: The Literature and History of Seventeenth-Century England*, ed. Kevin Sharpe and Steven N. Zwicker (Berkeley: University of California Press, 1987), 21–34.

to its history and purpose—comes in for close scrutiny, although the particular emphases given to different aspects of the subject in the course of those treatises, the characteristic metaphors they summon up to describe it, and the examples provided to show how it could be used effectively also reveal a great deal about what the Renaissance thought of rhetoric and its powers. So, of course, do worries and strictures about avoiding its excesses and failures, for one thing that characterizes rhetoric in the Renaissance, as in virtually all periods of Western history, is its embattled status, its exposure to criticism and attack. Although the vast majority of works that compose the discourse in the period are laudatory, their praise is usually qualified, hedged about with nervous, defensive restrictions. For the discourse also contains a number of texts, such as Giovanni Pico della Mirandola's famous letter to Ermolao Barbaro and John Jewel's *Oratio Contra Rhetoricam* (Oration against rhetoric), which are decidedly hostile: they unfold the doubts and hesitations about rhetoric that one finds expressed often quite vitriolically in literary and political texts and that must have been shared by many people in Renaissance culture. The discourse of rhetoric in the period thus turns out to be richly complex, anything but monolithic in its attitudes and values. As we shall see, although Renaissance rhetoric constitutes a recognizable, definable discourse, it is marked from beginning to end by profound ambiguities, contradictions, and self-divisions.

Throughout the discourse, rhetoric is most frequently identified neither as a matter of supplying stylistic decoration to one's ideas through tropes and figures nor as articulating an implicit philosophy of language, although both notions can be teased out of it. Instead, it is directly defined over and over again as the art of persuasion—or, rather, the art of *verbal* persuasion: it is language (accompanied by supporting looks and gestures) as it is used to move people that constitutes the essential subject of all the works in the discourse. There are of course other means to bring people to do our bidding, a possibility that the Spanish rhetorician Joan de Guzman, in his dialogue on rhetoric from 1589, has one of his speakers acknowledge, noting that one may be persuaded by such things as the beauty of a natural landscape. But Guzman quickly has his other speaker reply that that would not be true persuasion, which must involve reasons and arguments—in other words, language (*Primera Parte*, 14^v–15^v). Occasionally, writers approach the art of rhetoric in a more reflective and Aristotelian manner, analyzing the ways in which persuasion occurs; more typically, their treatises and handbooks are practical and goal-oriented, supplying handy definitions and lists of rules, describing the tools and techniques by means of which we can go about the business of getting others to obey our will. This rhetoric is concerned not only with communication, both oral and written, as it serves to articulate one's thoughts and transmit them to others but also with shaping those of others, determining their ideas and values and ultimately directing their behavior. As the German rhetorician Bartholomew Keckermann puts it succinctly: "The word persuasion is to be interpreted broadly to mean a moving of the heart and emotions, so that the auditor is impelled not only to believe, but also to act [*non tantum ut credat, sed etiam ut agat aliquid*]" (*Systema*, 9). As the Renaissance conceives it, then, rhetoric is no language game; it is a serious business that aims to affect people's basic beliefs and produce real action in the world.

In the thinking of the period, rhetoric is by no means limited to just those three varieties traditionally thought of as defining the art by means of the formal situations in which it is practiced: forensic rhetoric for the law courts, deliberative rhetoric for political discussions, and demonstrative or epideictic rhetoric for speeches of praise and blame. Rhetoric had already migrated into poetics in the Middle Ages, and the Renaissance continues to conflate the two, just as it follows the former period in conceiving letter-writing and preaching as branches of the art.[3] More important, many Renaissance writers take their cue from Aristotle and Cicero and do not limit rhetoric to formal speeches; they conceive of it instead in the widest terms as being present practically wherever communication and persuasion are occurring. In his greatly influential *De Causis Corruptarum Artium* (On the causes of the corruption of the arts), the Spanish humanist Juan Luis Vives begins by defining rhetoric as the use of the three classic genres of speeches—judicial, deliberative, and demonstrative—but then goes on to assert the general usefulness of the art in virtually every sort of human interaction.

> The faculty of speech, like a kind of universal tool, has been diffused through all things, not unlike grammar and dialectic; nor did Cicero and Quintilian omit to mention that there are more genres of which one might speak—in fact, Quintilian unfolded many of them. However, they thought that what was necessary for the other genres could be derived from the precepts given for those three [judicial, deliberative, and demonstrative rhetoric], although the genres all have the most diverse methods of invention, arrangement, and style. For who does not see that invention and elocution are very different in giving

[3] For the transformation of classical rhetoric into poetics (*ars poetica*), letter writing (*ars dictaminis*), and preaching (*ars praedicandi*), see James J. Murphy, *Rhetoric in the Middle Ages* (Berkeley: University of California Press, 1974).

thanks, congratulations, consolations, history, description, and teaching, from what they are in judicial, deliberative, and demonstrative oratory? (*De Causis*, 159)

Nor is Vives alone in regarding rhetoric as a universal tool. George of Trebizond in the fourteenth century stresses the orator's ability to speak in all sorts of situations (*Rhetoricorum*, 80ʳ), and claims that everything people can think or do comes within the purview of *inventio*, or the discovering of one's arguments (*Oratio*, 367). The German Protestant Philip Melanchthon similarly says that to learn eloquence is to learn prudence in all human affairs (*Encomion*, 49), and the Spanish Jesuit Luis de Granada declares that *elocutio*, or style, "is open as wide as possible to all disciplines of all kinds" (*Ecclesiastica Rhetorica*, 40). Granada's countryman Joan de Guzman makes an even more exaggerated claim for rhetoric in comparison with all the other liberal arts: "The others have their fixed boundaries in the same way that water does which does not exceed the point fixed for it by divine commandment, while rhetoric is like the air which . . . has it [i.e., all things] totally surrounded and exceeds and penetrates it and transforms itself into all things created here" (*Primera Parte*, 15ᵛ–16ʳ). Finally, Francesco Patrizi demonstrates just how widespread the notion of rhetoric's universal applicability was in the mid-sixteenth century by devoting the entire second dialogue of his *Della retorica dieci dialoghi* (Ten dialogues on rhetoric) to refuting it.[4]

[4] Alsted makes a claim very similar to Granada's: "This queen [Rhetoric] has no bounded region of any sort whose borders are contained by fences, but it has utensils which all teachers of all subjects can use in adorning letters, dialogues, orations, sermons, consultations, and similar things" (*Rhetorica*, 5–6). For other examples, see Gregorio Tiphernas, "De studiis litterarum oratio," in Müllner, 186; Francesco Filelfo, "Oratio de laudibus eloquentiae," in Müllner, 152; Andrea Giuliano, "Oratio super principio orationum M. Tullii Ciceronis ad auditores," in Müllner, 117; Regius, *Panegyricus*, fviᵛ; Rainolds, *Oxford Lectures*, 250; Cavalcanti, *Retorica*, 9, 12; Ramus, *Attack on Cicero*, 32, 68–69; and Walter Haddon, *De laudibus eloquentiae*, in *Lucubrationes passim collectae*, ed. Thomas Hatcher (London, 1567), 8. Thomas Conley remarks that Rudolph Agricola's redefinitions of rhetoric and dialectic have the effect of extending the domain of rhetoric into all areas; see Conley, *Rhetoric in the European Tradition* (New York: Longman, 1990), 125–27. Maria Luisa Doglio has argued that there was a tremendous expansion of the realm of rhetoric in the second half of the sixteenth century in Italy; see her "Retorica e politica nel secondo cinquecento," in *Retorica e politica*, Atti del II Congresso Italo-tedesco, ed. D. Goldin (Padua: Liviana, 1977), 58–60; however, Conley's observation and the statements by rhetoricians such as George of Trebizond and Vives suggest that the expansion seen by Doglio never really took place, insofar as there was a tendency within the discourse of rhetoric to see itself as a universal phenomenon right from the start. John Monfasani has argued that Jesuits and Calvinists alike made rhetoric a general art of

In an incisive article on Renaissance culture, William J. Bouwsma shows that the breakdown of boundaries between conceptual and social spheres generated both a certain cultural anxiety and a new freedom and mobility for individuals, and he goes on to note how directly this situation affected rhetoric: "Renaissance rhetoric was . . . valued for its plasticity, its ability to flow into and through every area of experience, to disregard and cross inherited boundaries as though they had no real existence, and to create new but always malleable structures of its own."[5] The domain of rhetoric in the period was clearly huge: in addition to formal speeches in law courts and before assemblies, it was seen as potentially including courtship (of one's lord or one's lady), confession and prayer, interventions aimed at the management of the family (which, of course, entailed parents, spouses, children, and domestics), educational interactions ranging from simple catechisms to university debates, and the advising and even occasional rebuking of one's superiors. Polymorphous and ubiquitous, rhetoric could serve practically all individuals and fit practically all situations as it blithely crossed long-established boundaries among disciplines, professions, and social classes. No wonder, then, that Renaissance writers attached so much importance to the art. Although the term "orator" was used in the period to define an actual profession only in the case of diplomats, humanists liked to style themselves thus, choosing the word as an honorific label despite the availability of more suitable words to designate their positions as teachers or secretaries.[6] In a sense, however, almost everyone in Renaissance society could have been dubbed an orator, and, what is more important, Renaissance people knew it.[7]

As it analyzes the ways in which rhetoric was represented in the Renaissance, this book is clearly concerned with historical understanding. It should not be construed, however, as an attempt to compose a com-

---

communication, not just the art of persuasion; see his "Episodes of Anti-Quintilianism in the Italian Renaissance: Quarrels on the Orator as a *Vir Bonus* and Rhetoric as the *Scientia Bene Dicendi*," *Rhetorica* 10 (1992): 137.

[5] William J. Bouwsma, "Anxiety and the Formation of Early Modern Culture," in *After the Reformation*, ed. Barbara C. Malament (Philadelphia: University of Pennsylvania Press, 1980), 234.

[6] See Hanna H. Gray, "Renaissance Humanism: The Pursuit of Eloquence," *Journal of the History of Ideas* 24 (1963): 500.

[7] In general, I refer to the writers of rhetoric texts of whatever sort as "rhetoricians," and use "rhetor" or "orator" to identify those who actually employ the art of rhetoric in real-life situations, whether delivering formal speeches or enagaging in interpersonal interactions, public and private. The two groups are not entirely distinct, since all rhetoricians are necessarily orators in their daily lives, and some include sample orations and conversations within their treatises, thus underscoring their own performance of the rhetor's role.

plete history of those representations, let alone of Renaissance rhetoric in general. First, it is based on an examination of only a restricted set of primary materials, a strategy made necessary by the sheer number of works available; an attempt to read them all would take the better part of a lifetime. James Murphy has not only produced a bibliography listing almost a thousand items based primarily on the holdings of the Bodleian Library at Oxford but, in another place, has observed that such lists must be partial and incomplete, since many less well-known European libraries possess volumes on rhetoric which are not duplicated in the holdings of the main research libraries, such as the Bodleian and the Bibliothèque Nationale, for which catalogues are readily available. Writing an *Ars rhetorica* was something of a growth industry in the Renaissance: there was a good market for such books; the process could be simple, merely involving translating or adapting someone else's work or the notes one had taken in the rhetoric course at the university; and the resulting tome gave one status as an intellectual, a credential for a future career as a teacher or secretary, and, through an artfully crafted dedication, the means to make a bid for patronage from the rich and powerful. Since the sheer volume of material is overwhelming, then, any study of Renaissance rhetoric must necessarily be selective. This one certainly is, although it attempts to counteract the built-in limitation involved by deliberately ranging as widely as possible, both chronologically from the fourteenth to the seventeenth centuries and geographically throughout western Europe. It also bases its conclusions on the works of many more than the twenty authors whom Murphy has identified as constituting a kind of unofficial canon for Renaissance rhetoric because of the frequency with which they are cited by scholars.[8]

This book also differs from traditional histories in that it ignores the issue of diachronic development *within* the Renaissance. I do not attempt to construct a narrative account of the stages through which the discourse of rhetoric develops between what is usually taken as the beginning of the Renaissance in the second half of the fourteenth century and its equally conventional end in the middle of the seventeenth. Such a history might indeed be written, and would no doubt begin by tracing the revival of Ciceronian notions of rhetoric by Italian humanists and proto-humanists such as Petrarch in the late fourteenth and early fifteenth centuries. It might describe the enriching of the discourse through the reacquisition of Greek texts such as that of Hermogenes in the fifteenth century, and then go on to the debate over Ciceronian style

[8] See Murphy, "One Thousand Neglected Authors," 31–32, 23; and his bibliography in *Renaissance Rhetoric*.

which breaks out at the end of that century and continues for at least
another hundred years. It would examine the Ramist revolution in the
mid-sixteenth century, which not only threatens to reduce rhetoric to
style and delivery but also effects a cultural transition, according to
Walter Ong, from an aural to a visual mode of conceiving the world. It
would have to say something about rhetoric in the Reformation and the
Counter-Reformation and about the encyclopedic works on the subject
produced in the early seventeenth century by writers such as Caussin
and Alsted. Finally, it would have to deal with the impact on rhetoric of
Cartesian rationalism and the New Science. Taking a somewhat different approach here, I view the Renaissance discourse of rhetoric as a unified whole.[9] My contention is that that discourse displays important and
striking continuities throughout the period—from the humanist Coluccio Salutati, who was active at the end of the fourteenth century, to the
rhetorician René Bary, who wrote in the middle of the seventeenth—
and that the similarities are sufficiently great to warrant their being
treated as constituent elements in a single, albeit less than monolithic,
reconstructed discourse. To use a proverbial expression, this book is an
attempt at "lumping" rather than "splitting" as far as the Renaissance
is concerned.[10] To be sure, it acknowledges that Salutati and Bary did
not live at the same time and in the same country, and that there
are consequently important historical and cultural differences between
them which one might well choose to focus on. The argument developed in the four chapters of this book, however—and it is, finally, a very
historical argument—is that Salutati and Bary share important notions
and attitudes that link them together and allow them to be fruitfully
distinguished, as representative Renaissance thinkers, from those who
wrote on rhetoric in other periods.[11]

[9] For a diachronic history of at least one segment of Renaissance rhetoric, see
Wilbur S. Howell, *Logic and Rhetoric in England, 1500–1700* (Princeton: Princeton
University Press, 1956). Ong's thesis is to be found in Walter J. Ong, S.J., *Ramus:
Method and the Decay of Dialogue* (Cambridge, Mass.: Harvard University Press,
1958). Most historical accounts take something of the approach I offer: they treat the
subject globally, paying less attention to developments within the period than to the
continuities that allow Renaissance rhetoric to be differentiated from its medieval
predecessor. For examples, see John Monfasani, "Humanism and Rhetoric," in *Renaissance Humanism: Foundations, Forms, and Legacy*, vol. 3, *Humanism and the
Disciplines*, ed. Albert Rabil, Jr. (Philadelphia: University of Pennsylvania Press,
1988), 171–235; and Brian Vickers, *Classical Rhetoric in English Poetry* (London:
Macmillan, 1970).
[10] The *Oxford English Dictionary*, s.v. "lumper," credits Darwin with originating
this distinction, separating "lumpers" from "hair-splitters."
[11] One can, of course, even distinguish among contemporary rhetoricians from the
same country as well as among those who lived during different phases of the Renais-

In other words, the discourse of rhetoric in the Renaissance manifests something like a period style. Writers from the start to the finish conceive their subject in roughly similar terms: rhetoric is not only defined as an art of persuasion directed at producing action in the world but thought of as a particularly political art that repeatedly engages a set of basic social and political concerns and uses much the same conceptual apparatus as it does so. The argument that rhetoric is political in the Renaissance has, of course, been made by a number of scholars, although many, such as Paul O. Kristeller, Hans Baron, and Quentin Skinner, focus on the ways in which rhetoric was *used* and tend to limit the identification between rhetoric and politics just to the earliest phases of the Italian Renaissance; others, such as Marc Fumaroli, stress the affiliation between rhetorical styles and political positions.[12] I contend that rhetoric is political in the Renaissance not because of the uses to which it is put or the styles it engenders but because, in the imagination of the period, the relationship between rhetor and audience is conceived fairly consistently in political terms as one between ruler and subject, and that that conception of rhetoric remains central to the discourse throughout the entire period.

The continuities in the Renaissance discourse of rhetoric are especially manifest in its language, in the particular words and phrases it often adapts from classical sources and reiterates over and over. Thus, as we will see in Chapter 1, writers tirelessly restate, albeit with their own emphases and for their own purposes, Cicero's and Quintilian's notion that rhetoric is a weapon; and, as we will see in Chapter 4, they just as tirelessly repeat their classical predecessors' worried identification of indecorous rhetoric with their own historically distinct vision of theatricality. In Chapter 2 we will encounter Renaissance rhetoricians reworking ancient arguments about the subversive potential of the art, and in Chapter 3 we will see them struggling repeatedly with the notion

---

sance and in different places. Donna B. Hamilton thus contrasts Dudley Fenner, whose work has a decidedly Puritan character, with Thomas Wilson and George Puttenham, who were Fenner's contemporaries in England and who were hostile to Puritanism; see her *Shakespeare and the Politics of Protestant England* (Lexington: University of Kentucky Press, 1992), 16–19. Nevertheless, I stress how much Fenner, Wilson, and Puttenham have in common, rather than what keeps them apart.

[12] See Paul Oskar Kristeller, "The Humanist Movement," in *Renaissance Thought: The Classic, Scholastic, and Humanist Strains* (New York: Harper & Row, 1961), 3–23, and "Rhetoric in Medieval and Renaissance Culture," in Murphy, *Renaissance Eloquence*, 1–19; Hans Baron, *The Crisis of the Early Italian Renaissance* (Princeton: Princeton University Press, 1966); Quentin Skinner, *The Foundations of Modern Political Thought* (Cambridge: Cambridge University Press, 1978), 1:3–40; and Fumaroli, *L'âge de l'éloquence*, and "Rhetoric, Politics, and Society: From Italian Ciceronianism to French Classicism," in Murphy, *Renaissance Eloquence*, 253–73.

that rhetoric is, in some fundamental way, feminine. Moreover, Renaissance rhetoricians like to tell the same stories over and over, such as the myth of the orator-civilizer, the tales of Hegesias and the Egyptians and of Ulysses and Circe, and the fable of the belly, which the Roman Menenius Agrippa used to calm an angry mob of rebellious plebeians. All this material supports the argument that there is indeed a historically distinctive and continuous discourse of rhetoric in the period, a discourse marked by writers' shared sense of the nature and purpose of rhetoric, its particular lexicon of terms and concepts, and the grammar and syntax of functions and narrative structures they use to define it. It is important to recognize, of course, that no single treatise or handbook will provide examples of all the major themes and concepts that characterize the discourse of rhetoric as a whole. Some of the more comprehensive and self-reflexive works, however, engage so large a number of the issues I am concerned with that references to those works appear frequently in the following pages. To be sure, a fair number of works—such as those produced by the Ramists—tend to be schematic and reductive in character, offering little information about the ways Renaissance rhetoricians conceived themselves, their enterprise, and the intellectual, social, and political problems that troubled their age. Yet even these texts demonstrate so remarkable a set of continuities with the other, richer works that it should not seem at all unreasonable to lump them together.

Even though it does not pretend to offer a comprehensive history of Renaissance rhetoric, this book clearly is profoundly concerned with the historical distinctiveness of its subject. In fact, I contend not merely that the conception of rhetoric shared by thinkers from the Renaissance differs significantly from the one held by their medieval predecessors— an argument that scholars have already made convincingly—but also that it differs, albeit in quite subtle and nuanced ways, from the conceptions of classical writers to whom it nevertheless owes so much. Although the Renaissance is often spoken of as a *revival* of classical antiquity—a notion contained in the very label for the period—it will become clear in the course of this book that the discourse of rhetoric in the Renaissance is historically distinct from everything that precedes it.[13] Nor was the distinctiveness of their rhetoric unknown to Renais-

---

[13] For some examples of critics who see Renaissance rhetoric as a revival of classical rhetoric, see Vickers, *Classical Rhetoric in English Poetry*, 117; Monfasani, "Humanism and Rhetoric," 172; John W. O'Malley, *Praise and Blame in Renaissance Rome: Rhetoric, Doctrine, and Reform in the Sacred Orators of the Papal Court, c. 1450– 1521* (Durham, N.C.: Duke University Press, 1979), 5; and William J. Kennedy, *Rhetorical Norms in Renaissance Literature* (New Haven: Yale University Press, 1978), 1–14.

sance writers. Just as Petrarch, in his letters to classical authors, recognizes their historical distance from his age, and Renaissance imitators everywhere write with an awareness of the difference and distance of their works from the ancient texts on which they are based, so Renaissance rhetoricians, especially by the seventeenth century, express a similar historicist awareness about their discipline.[14] In the dedication to his rhetoric textbook, for instance, Gerard Vossius, while claiming that he is going back to the *fontes* of the art in Aristotle, nevertheless blames the contemporary decline he sees in the art on people's tendency to follow the ancients too slavishly: "Some have taught them too superstitiously [*superstitiose*], not realizing that they were giving precepts to our century, not to Rome when it was flourishing."[15] Johann Heinrich Alsted similarly insists that we should not imitate the ancients in too studied a manner: "A studied [*curiosa*] . . . imitation cannot be approved, since now our age is different, as are men [*cum alia nunc sint secula, aliique homines*], and oratorical delivery is also varied on account of the differences among nations" (*Rhetorica*, 422). Like his fellow rhetoricians, Alsted wants to see the ancients as the source of *praecepta universalia* but is forced to realize that those universal precepts, "to be used, must be adapted [*transferenda*], as much as that can be done" (424).[16] Finally, there is M. Le Grand: in his *Discours*, which serves as a preface to René Bary's *Rhetorique françoise* of 1659, he not only expresses a profoundly historicist view of rhetoric but offers an explanation in terms of politics and religion for what he sees. After contrasting the Athenian Areopagus with the Parlement de Paris, Orphic mystagogy with Christian theology, and Philippics with contemporary remonstrances, he concludes with the sentence used as the epigraph for this introduction: "The maxims of politics and the mysteries of religion change the rules of rhetoric entirely, and ancient rhetoric has no similarity to its modern counterpart."

Although many Renaissance rhetoricians did not share the historical self-consciousness of a Vossius, an Alsted, or a Le Grand, they did, in fact, conceive their art very differently from the way that Aristotle, Cicero, and Quintilian conceived theirs. Even if they were merely commen-

---

[14] On Petrarch's historical self-consciousness, see Myron P. Gilmore, "The Renaissance Conception of the Lessons of History," in *Facets of the Renaissance*, ed. Wallace K. Ferguson (New York: Harper & Row, 1959), 71–101. On the historical self-consciousness of Renaissance imitation, see Thomas M. Greene, *The Light in Troy* (New Haven: Yale University Press, 1982), esp. chaps. 1–5.

[15] Gerard Vossius, *Oratoriarum Institutionum Libri Sex* (Leiden, 1606), Dedication, n.p.

[16] For other examples of historical self-consciousness on the subject of delivery, see Keckermann, *Systema*, 508, 527, 536; and Bulwer, *Chironomia*, 239.

ting on, editing, or teaching ancient texts, they necessarily saw those texts not with the eyes of Greeks and Romans but with those of Renaissance Europeans. One cannot deny, of course, that there are significant repetitions of classical materials in their works. It is equally true to say, however, that those materials are "adapted"—*transferenda*, to use Alsted's word—whether consciously or unconsciously, to suit the needs and biases, the assumptions and ideological emphases of their own time.

If this book is historical in its commitment to distinguish Renaissance rhetoric from both classical and medieval antecedents, it is also historical in another and equally important way. It operates on the assumption that the discourse of rhetoric is anything but "pure," detached from other human concerns, merely a set of rules for public oratory or an array of techniques for managing interpersonal communication. On the contrary, it shares the assumption of such scholars as Marc Fumaroli, Nancy Struever, and Patricia Parker that rhetoric is deeply implicated in the social and political order that produces it.[17] It also argues that this relationship assumes two distinct but related forms. First, the discourse of rhetoric can be seen to constitute a site where the work of social self-definition goes on. To put it simply, rhetoric speaks culture, providing a language in which human beings articulate themselves and their world. Upon analysis, the discourse can thus be seen to contain, at the very least, an anthropology, a sociology, a politics, an ethics, and a theology—all of which become visible as one examines its assumptions and assertions, its judgments and evaluations concerning human nature, the social order, the nature of power, and the workings of the universe. Second, the discourse of rhetoric speaks *about* culture; that is, it can be seen as functioning to articulate, clarify, extend, and critique concepts and values at play in the activities and institutions present in the world around it. In either case, whether speaking culture or speaking about culture, the discourse of rhetoric can be seen as both a product and a producer of the social order. In Pocock's terms, rhetoric texts, like all texts, are *events*; they both participate in the discourse or language of rhetoric in their period and contribute their own terms and concepts and strategies, which help construct and, indeed, necessarily transform the discourse to which they belong.

The discourse of rhetoric is "impure" in another sense as well: it is contaminated, interpenetrated, by other discourses. After all, most of its key terms—like many key terms in any discourse—are metaphors, and

[17] See Fumaroli, *L'âge de l'éloquence*; Struever, *The Language of History in the Renaissance* (Princeton: Princeton University Press, 1970); Parker, *Literary Fat Ladies*.

as such they immediately invoke other domains of human experience. For instance, talk about *elocutio*, or style, frequently uses *ornatus*, a word that means, among other things, adornment or dress and consequently summons up the realm of social behavior and etiquette which was the subject of innumerable works, such as Castiglione's *Libro del cortegiano* (Book of the courtier). Indeed, the constant emphasis on *decorum*, on saying and doing what is fitting or proper, has much the same result. Further, discussions of the character of the audience frequently entail a whole range of theological concepts and assumptions about human nature, freedom, and the will, and the ends the rhetor is supposed to pursue are often defined in a specifically political language of power and rule. Perhaps one of the most important discourses present in and helping to shape that of rhetoric is literature. Literary works influence the way rhetoricians characterize the ideal orator as a regal and heroic figure, offer epic or dramatic plot structures to help them imagine the orator's interactions with the world, and provide the persona of the satirist and social critic for the rhetorician. All this does not mean that there is no recognizable discourse of rhetoric with its own proper concepts and shaping principles, no matter how metaphorical they may be, but merely that like all discourses this one does not exist in a linguistic vacuum. To employ Mikhail Bakhtin's helpful notion, although through a process of abstraction and a careful monitoring of borders and boundaries one can produce a monologic model of rhetoric as a unified, self-contained discourse in the Renaissance, its true nature is dialogic, for it is always and everywhere engaged in dialogue with other discourses that are present within it.[18] We will, of course, be talking about the discourse of rhetoric primarily in the more restricted sense I have just specified, but our analysis should also show how other discourses, and particularly that of literature, play a special role in determining its defining features, a role that explains, in part, the particular emphasis in the subtitle of this book: "*Literature* and the Renaissance Discourse of Rhetoric."[19]

As noted earlier, the particular political vision of Renaissance rhetoric

[18] See Mikhail Bakhtin, *The Dialogic Imagination: Four Essays*, ed. Michael Holquist, trans. Caryl Emerson and Michael Holquist (Austin: University of Texas Press, 1981).

[19] One might think of psychological discourse in the twentieth century as being much like rhetorical discourse in the Renaissance. It borrows key concepts, such as *drive*, from other discourses (physics, in this case), and obtains important structuring devices from literature and myth (most obviously, the Oedipus complex). That the discourse of psychology is shot through with other discourses does not mean, of course, that it cannot be described as a unified and self-contained discourse in its own right.

distinguishes it from that of both classical antiquity and the Middle
Ages: the rhetor is imagined as a ruler, his audience become his subjects, and power and control are the central issues.[20] This is not the
usual view of Renaissance rhetoric. For scholars such as Nancy Struever
and Victoria Kahn, Joel Altman and Thomas O. Sloane, the rhetoric of
the period is remarkable for its connections to skepticism, its sense of
the contingency and uncertainty of the world of experience, its recognition of the gap between language and reality, and its resulting commitment to dialogue and debate rather than dogmatic assertion.[21] To those
scholars, Renaissance rhetoric seems particularly contemporary because
of its attempt to grapple with the loss of absolutes and its commitment
to exploratory and interactive styles of life and thought. In their analyses, perhaps the most important aspect of Renaissance rhetoric is its
practice of training students to argue on both sides of issues, the *argu-
mentum in utramque partem*, a practice directly based on the skeptical
epistemology built into the art and leading almost logically to the production of a world view that is necessarily tentative, exploratory, and
dialogic. Hence, it should not be surprising that skeptical works such as
Erasmus's *Praise of Folly*, open-ended dialogues such as More's *Utopia*
and Castiglione's *Book of the Courtier*, and plays such as Shakespeare's,
which debate issues that are unresolved and unresolvable, should all be
celebrated as the ultimate expression of the mentality created by Renaissance rhetoric. Nor should it be surprising that there is an implicit
tendency in the work of some scholars to align that rhetoric with a
democratic or republican form of politics, a tendency made explicit by
Hans Baron, Quention Skinner, and Eugenio Garin, who link the revival
of rhetoric in the Renaissance to the democratic debates and discussions

[20] I speak of the Renaissance rhetor-ruler as "he" advisedly. For rhetoricians in the
period, the figure is invariably male, although, as we shall see in Chapter 3, that
identification is rendered problematic by the fact that many of the attributes assigned
the rhetor are, in fact, conventionally thought of as female or feminine.

[21] Struever, *The Language of History in the Renaissance*; Victoria Kahn, *Rhetoric,
Prudence, and Skepticism in the Renaissance* (Ithaca: Cornell University Press,
1985); Joel Altman, *The Tudor Play of Mind: Rhetorical Inquiry and the Develop-
ment of Elizabethan Drama* (Berkeley: University of California Press, 1978); and
Thomas O. Sloane, *Donne, Milton, and the End of Humanist Rhetoric* (Berkeley:
University of California Press, 1985). For other examples of this view, see Arthur F.
Kinney, *Continental Humanist Poetics: Studies in Erasmus, Castiglione, Marguerite
de Navarre, Rabelais, and Cervantes* (Amherst: University of Massachusetts Press,
1989); Ernesto Grassi, *Rhetoric as Philosophy: The Humanist Tradition* (University
Park: Penn State University Press, 1980); Jerrold E. Seigel, *Rhetoric and Philosophy in
Renaissance Humanism: The Union of Eloquence and Wisdom, Petrarch to Valla*
(Princeton: Princeton University Press, 1968); and Terence Cave, *The Cornucopian
Text: Problems of Writing in the French Renaissance* (Oxford: Oxford University
Press, 1979).

that were the lifeblood of the Italian communes in the twelfth and thirteenth centuries.[22]

Although it is certainly true that Renaissance rhetoricians saw the
world as a place of uncertainty and taught students how to argue cases
from multiple perspectives, the thesis of this book, elaborated in Chapter 1, is that when those rhetoricians define the nature and function of
the art in their treatises and handbooks, they stress its power above all
else, specifically the power it puts in the hands of the orator to control
the will and desire of the audience. They conceive rhetoric as a political
instrument, to be sure, but not one whose main purpose is to enable free
political debate and discussion. Rather, they celebrate rhetoric for giving
its possessor the ability to subjugate others, to place the world beneath
his feet. It is indeed arguable that the actual training students received
in rhetoric during the Renaissance encouraged skepticism and a fundamentally dialogic view of life, and it certainly influenced the endless
debates that mark the period. Nevertheless, the treatises and handbooks
themselves see the student engaged in what is essentially a one-sided
argument in which he does the speaking and his audience, overwhelmed
by his eloquence, agrees to do what he wants them to do. At its core,
then, Renaissance rhetoric is animated by a fantasy of power in which
the orator, wielding words more deadly than swords, takes on the world
and emerges victorious in every encounter. The orator is a conqueror, a
ruler—even, in some treatises, something close to a god. Nor should
this imperial and regal conception of rhetoric as rule really be surprising. Renaissance culture was, for the most part, hierarchical and monarchical or oligarchical, and the period is generally marked by the gradual
centralization of states under single rulers who increasingly controlled
them in absolutist fashion. Granted such social and political realities, it
would be more surprising to find that Renaissance rhetoric did *not* spin
out a fantasy that makes the rhetor, in Henry Peacham's words, an "emperour of mens minds" (*Garden*, iii^v). Revealingly, Renaissance rhetoricians not only frequently direct their treatises to members of the ruling
class and sometimes even to actual rulers but also regularly insist that
the art they celebrate is indispensable for controlling the state. As we
shall see, the father of absolutist political theory, Jean Bodin, views
rhetoric this way, as does the most absolutist of rulers, Louis XIV of
France.

Nevertheless, to say that the Renaissance discourse of rhetoric is ani-

---

[22] See Baron, *The Crisis of the Early Italian Renaissance*; Skinner, *The Foundations
of Modern Political Thought*; Eugenio Garin, *Medioevo e Rinascimento: Studi e
ricerche*, 2d ed. (Bari: Laterza, 1961); and Garin *L'umanesimo italiano: Filosofia e
vita civile nel Rinascimento*, 2d ed. (Bari: Laterza, 1965).

mated by an absolutist fantasy of political power is to tell only part of the story. Chapter 2 thus shows how, in treatise after treatise, the reliance of rhetoric on the passions renders it inherently unstable and unpredictable in its effects, thereby making it a threat to the stability of the social order. More important, the chapter also shows a fundamental ambiguity about the identity of the rhetor that renders the entire discourse contradictory and self-divided. Although frequently equated with legitimate rulers, rhetors are at least as often social inferiors who will use the advantages of their training in rhetoric to improve their lot while protecting themselves from attack by those on high. The fantasy of imperial power at the heart of Renaissance rhetoric thus becomes a fantasy of social mobility in which the baseborn rise up and even come to dominate those above them in the social hierarchy as well as those below. If the identification of the rhetor with the actual ruler makes rhetoric a conservative instrument whose essential function is to maintain the status quo, his identification as baseborn has just the opposite effect. It makes the art a radical means to resist authority, perhaps even a source of sedition and rebellion, which are among the most frequent charges made against rhetoric by its critics throughout the Renaissance. The political ambiguity of rhetoric may be correlated directly with the ambiguous social and political position of the rhetoricians themselves. Men on the make who came from the lower classes, they obviously had no choice but to be deferential to authority. Nor would they have wanted to appear otherwise, for they clearly had a stake in the existing hierarchy, in which they wished to advance and which consequently led them to identify their lot with that of the ruling classes. At the same time, however, they stood outside the corridors of power and could not help but feel resistance to the existing order of things, could not help but see it as an impediment to their advancement, could not help but spin out complex fantasies in which commoners like themselves used their rhetorical skill to enhance their social position, to check the powerful, even to control kings.

If the first two chapters of this study, taken together, unfold the complex and contradictory nature of Renaissance rhetoric, the third and fourth do so too, although they approach the subject from quite different directions. Chapter 3 is concerned with the issue of gender: it shows how Renaissance rhetoricians, living in an intensely patriarchal culture that parallelled rulers with men and subjects with women, attempt to valorize their art—which its critics attack as feminine, effeminate, and even homosexual—by defining it in "masculine" terms as a matter of violent invasion and conquest. Identified as a kind of phallic aggression, rhetoric is characterized by images that are completely consistent with and reinforce the fantasy of imperial, absolutist power at the heart of the discourse. A close reading of that discourse, however, once again reveals its fractured nature, for rhetoricians are unable to resist imagining important aspects of their art in what their culture would have thought of as "feminine" terms such as procreation and bodily adornment. As a result, they produce a double image of the rhetor as both male and female, thus actually raising the very specter of effeminacy and homosexuality they are attempting to exorcise. That double image may also be correlated, once again, with the complex, self-divided condition of the rhetoricians themselves, who both fantasized that their art was capable of making them "masculine" rulers and had to confront the fact that they were in reality baseborn, relatively powerless, "feminine" subjects.

Finally, Chapter 4 turns to the human body as one last locus of self-contradiction in the Renaissance discourse of rhetoric. Again, in order to defend themselves, this time from denunciations of rhetoric as morally, socially, and aesthetically degraded and repugnant—in short, as deformed and monstrous—rhetoricians insist on metaphors identifying their art with a body that is ethically proper, socially elevated, and aesthetically attractive. They thus link rhetoric to the bodily ideal embraced by the upper classes, the ruling classes, of Renaissance Europe, who defined themselves in that way in order to distance themselves from the common people and the grotesque body with which, Mikhail Bakhtin has argued, the people was associated.[23] Nevertheless, from the start of the Renaissance to the end, rhetoricians cannot seem to prevent grotesque elements from appearing in their characterizations of their art, with the result that the "body" of rhetoric is always double, imagined as both a harmonious, well-proportioned entity and a perverse and monstrous one. Thus, one last time, the rhetoricians play out the deep, unresolved contradiction of their condition: identifying themselves with the ruling classes whose ranks they fantasize they can join, they imagine rhetoric in terms of an ethically correct, socially distinguished human body; but in keeping with their actual condition as subjects they cannot help but associate the art they teach with the grotesque body of the people.

Although this book is primarily concerned with rhetoric in the Renaissance, it has an almost equal concern with the literature of the period, for that literature was produced by writers who all received some degree of formal training in rhetoric and were taught to think of rhetoric

[23] See Mikhail Bakhtin, *Rabelais and His World*, trans. Helene Iswolsky (Cambridge: MIT Press, 1968). See also Peter Burke, *Popular Culture in Early Modern Europe* (New York: Harper & Row, 1978).

and "poetry" (no concept of "literature" being then available) as virtually identical in character.[24] Since both arts were seen as employing stories and arguments as well as the refinements of style in order to persuade an audience to embrace an author's views, it should hardly be surprising to discover a significant rhetorical dimension in literary texts from the period. But what is more important than, say, Shakespeare's use of certain rhetorical strategies or tropes and figures—something fairly well studied in the past—is the fact that his works, like those of countless other Renaissance writers, frequently represent rhetorical processes, whether that means a lyric speaker's attempt to move his or her beloved to reciprocal affection, a narrative depicting characters engaged in passionate debate, or a drama portraying a complex set of interchanges and intrigues. Literature does, in other words, what rhetoric treatises and handbooks are prevented from doing, except intermittently, by their form: it presents a direct modeling of rhetorical situations. Literature is a privileged discourse, in a sense, for it opens up the equivalent of a liminal space, a site adjacent to but separate from the space of the real world, in which authors can represent that world in such a way that while often merely rehearsing conventional ideas and arrangements, they also have the freedom to analyze, refine, and critique them. By doing so, they are able not only to dramatize the ideas and perspectives of the rhetoricians but also to elaborate them in ways that clarify what sometimes remains obscure and expose to the light of contemplation what is often submerged or repressed within the discourse of rhetoric. Through the kind of hypothetical extrapolation it necessarily practices, its use of feigning to create a world of "as if," literature refines concepts, exposes contradictions, criticizes assumptions, and revises conclusions from the discourse of rhetoric. It has, in short, an active and critical relationship to that discourse. By contrast, most of what traditionally have been considered "rhetorical" readings of literary texts have tended to view literature as a passive reflection, a simple continuation or repetition, of various aspects of rhetoric. Thus, the latter have been seen as providing a set of tools, such as structures

---

[24] See, among others, Kees Meerhoff, *Rhétorique et poétique au XVIe siècle en France: Du Bellay, Ramus et les autres* (Leiden: Brill, 1986), 282; Kahn, *Rhetoric, Prudence, and Skepticism*, 37; and Brian Vickers, *In Defence of Rhetoric* (Oxford: Clarendon Press, 1988), 50–51. Rhetoric treatises and handbooks frequently take their examples from poetry; works on poetics insist that their art has the same goal as rhetoric, to move or persuade its audience; both arts lay claim to the same mythological progenitors, Orpheus and Amphion; and both see eloquence as the highest achievement of their practitioners. Of course, differences were recognized, but here I emphasize, as did the Renaissance, the congruence rather than the divergence of the two arts.

and devices of style, by means of which the literary works were produced, and those works have been studied in turn in order to demonstrate the presence of rhetorical materials in them and the extensive-
ness of their authors' dependence on that art.[25] While not denying that
literature often serves, especially in the Renaissance, as a demonstration
of authors' rhetoric-centered education and as a rehearsal of rhetorical
materials from it, I want to revise the idea of the "rhetorical" reading by
showing how rhetorical situations are modeled in the liminal spaces of
literary texts. That modeling allows authors to scrutinize the discourse
of rhetoric even as they repeat it; it enables them to analyze and evaluate its assumptions, assertions, and judgments about human beings and
the social and political world in which they live. The literary text consequently becomes a representation not only of the world but of the
discourse of rhetoric as well. By reading literature as a self-conscious
extension of the discourse of rhetoric, I am obviously suggesting that it,
too, is "impure," although its impurity, its dialogic character, is very
different from that which characterizes rhetoric. Literary texts fore-
ground their impurity in a way rhetorical texts do not: they actively
invite the reader or viewer to contemplate their relationship to other
discourses as well as to the social reality they model; they invite us to
see literature as an "allegory" whose relationship to other discourses
and to social reality must be interpreted as an essential part of its meaning.

I want to revise traditional "rhetorical" readings of literature in another way as well. Most of those readings tend to be ahistorical: the
"rhetoric" to which they relate a particular literary text or set of texts is
often not the specific rhetoric contemporary to them but rather a trans-
historical rhetoric, presented as though it were free from all period de-
terminations. Ironically, the literary work may be seen as the product of
a specific era, but the rhetoric it supposedly rehearses belongs to no
time or place; what such rhetorical readings have entailed in practice is
the relating of literary texts to a rhetoric that is usually an amalgama-
tion of Aristotle, Cicero, and Quintilian, or whose characteristics make
it indistinguishable from theirs.[26] To be sure, those authors do have the

[25] An example is the now classic work by Sister Miriam Joseph, *Shakespeare's Use
of the Arts of Language* (New York: Columbia University Press, 1947). To suggest
that such a work is conceptually insufficient is not, of course, to deny its value as
scholarship or to claim that one has nothing to learn from it.

[26] For an example, see Brian Vickers, "'The Power of Persuasion': Images of the
Orator, Elyot to Shakespeare," in Murphy, *Renaissance Eloquence*, 411–35. The first
part of this suggestive essay notes how often Renaissance rhetorics stress the power
and goodness of rhetoric while ignoring its many defects and dangers, and the second
part reviews plays by Shakespeare which unfold the evil potential of the discipline.

virtue of having been studied fairly continually throughout the history
of Western culture, so that a reasonable claim could be made that they
are indeed the primary sources of particular structural principles or figures of speech for authors in a wide variety of historical periods. But to
make such a claim is to ignore the fact that those ancient rhetoricians
have been interpreted quite differently from period to period: the sage
Cicero of the Middle Ages is hardly the political Cicero of the Renaissance, just as the rhetoric of the Middle Ages is generally quite different
from that of the following period. It is consequently essential for a truly
historicized "rhetorical" reading of literature to interpret poems and
plays and stories in conjunction with the specific discourse of rhetoric
produced within their contemporary world.

It is, of course, just such a fully historicized set of "rhetorical" readings that this book offers in its analyses of texts that respond in particularly active and interesting ways to the Renaissance discourse of rhetoric. In order to unfold the complex relationships involved, each of the
four chapters provides readings of literary texts that rehearse many of
the major themes and issues to be found in the rhetorical writings of the
period. Those texts not only elaborate rhetorical themes and issues but
subject them to evaluation and, through that process, critique the contemporary discourse of rhetoric from which they derive. I have attempted to include a variety of works written in several languages and
representing something like the full length of the Renaissance. Thus,
there are analyses of lyric poems and plays, a mock oration and several
novels, texts written in Latin, Italian, English, French, and Spanish,
ranging from Erasmus's *Moriae Encomium* (*The Praise of Folly*) of 1509
to Molière's *Tartuffe* of 1658. All these analyses are, it must be stressed,
partial and suggestive rather than exhaustive. They are meant to be exemplary, to show how one might perform a "rhetorical" reading of a
literary text by relating it to the contemporary discourse of rhetoric—or,
to be more precise, to the particular themes and issues of that rhetoric
as I have separated them from one another for purposes of analysis.

Each chapter treats at least two different literary texts, offering dis-

---

The problem with Vickers's article is twofold. First, he makes no distinction between
what classical writers such as Cicero say about the power and goodness of rhetoric
and what Renaissance writers are claiming. Second, he ignores the presence of attacks
on rhetoric within the discourse itself during the Renaissance, for not only are there
critical works such as John Jewel's *Oratio Contra Rhetoricam*, but many treatises
defending rhetoric give ample play to criticisms of it—even though they do so, in
order to answer the objections raised. In the terms of Vickers's argument, Iago is thus
not so much Shakespeare's *reply* to the positive image of rhetoric in the discourse as
a modeling of the negative image already available within it, though never so fully
realized—unfolded and developed—as in Shakespeare's text.

cussions of them at those points where they seem to interact most interestingly with the aspects of the discourse of rhetoric which that chapter is investigating. The first chapter, concerned with rhetoric as rule, thus looks at works that identify the ruler as an orator. In particular, it examines works by Machiavelli and Shakespeare which elaborate rhetorical theories of kingship but do so in ways suggesting the limitations of rhetorical theory because of its primary focus on the power of language. Texts such as *Il principe* and Shakespeare's second tetralogy of history plays reveal that the ruler's ability to control his subjects depends on an unstable mix of verbal and physical or military power, rather than on one or the other exclusively.

In the second chapter, concerned with the subversive potential of rhetoric, literary texts similarly focus on problems that rhetoric treatises and handbooks either minimize or ignore. In unfolding the different ways in which rhetoric treatises oppose or subvert the established order, the chapter examines George Herbert's "The Method" and the anonymous picaresque novel *Lazarillo de Tormes*, both of which give us rhetors who are *not* rulers but who use their rhetorical skills in what may be considered potentially subversive ways in order to deal with the authorities who rule over them.

The third chapter, where gender is the issue, shows how rhetoricians, by creating the image of an aggressively phallic rhetor, make his behavior look disturbingly similar to rape, an equation that undergirds Thomas Carew's elegy on the death of John Donne and informs the satire that Tirso de Molina directs against the protagonist of his *El burlador de Sevilla* (The trickster of Seville). This chapter also shows how rhetoricians finally wind up creating a sexually unstable—both male and female—vision of the good rhetoric they cherish, a vision with which Erasmus plays wittily in his satirical masterpiece, *The Praise of Folly*.

Finally, the fourth chapter explores the way the kingly rhetor of the Renaissance is haunted by his double, the deceitful, socially debased, grotesque, and indecorous clown, a figure that the discourse consistently tries in various ways to exorcise. This chapter begins by looking at a text that might be classified as either a rhetoric book or a work of literature, Antoine Furetière's *Nouvelle allégorique, ou Histoire des derniers troubles arrivez au royaume d'Eloquence* (Allegorical novella, or History of the late troubles that occurred in the Kingdom of Eloquence). In addition to analyzing examples of "monstrous" rhetoric in the novels of Rabelais and Thomas Nashe, I also examine various versions of Menenius Agrippa's fable of the belly (including the one in Shakespeare's *Coriolanus*) which not only present an ideal vision of the state as a decorous human body but also show how the orator, in serving as the source of those notions, writes—or, rather, speaks—himself into the political order. The chapter goes on to consider how the discourse of rhetoric fails to separate definitively the art it would defend from its demonic double, thus leaving the rhetor always exposed to the charge that he is a grotesque, a clown or trickster, a charge that literary works concerned with orator-tricksters repeat relentlessly throughout the Renaissance. By looking at a number of those works—including Machiavelli's *La mandragola* (The mandrake root), Jonson's *The Alchemist*, and Molière's *Tartuffe*—we can chart an increasing intolerance of the grotesque which leads writers throughout the course of the period to want to banish clowns and tricksters altogether, just as rhetoricians increasingly take offense at the more "monstrous" aspects of their art. What we are witnessing here is less a qualitative transformation than a kind of clarification, a working out to its logical conclusion, of the opposition between the ideal and grotesque bodies and the systems of values associated with them, an opposition that inhabits both rhetorical and literary works in some form from the very start.

In this final chapter, as in all the others, the literature of the period reveals its active engagement with the contemporary discourse of rhetoric. It articulates the intellectual assumptions of that rhetoric, as it models in concrete detail the characters, modes of interaction, and themes that rhetoric treatises and handbooks describe. Most important, Renaissance literature subjects the issues presented in the discourse to a process of examination, clarification, and evaluation, a process which, if nothing else, exposes its many contradictions, evasions, and mystifications for all to see.

1 Bound to Rule

When theorizing about eloquence, Renaissance writers like to begin at the beginning. Thus, in an early chapter of *The Arte of English Poesie*, George Puttenham declares: "Poets were the first priests, the first prophets, the first Legislators and polititians in the world." He wants to make two claims, the first one for the antiquity of poetry, for its existence "before any civil society was among men," and the second—and more important—one for the crucial role it played in bringing that civil society about. "For it is written, that Poesie was th'originall cause and occasion of their [men's] first assemblies, when before the people remained in the woods and mountains, vagarant and dispersed like the wild beasts, lawlesse and naked, or verie ill clad, and of all good and necessarie provision for harbour or sustenance utterly unfurnished: so as they litle diffred for their maner of life, from the very brute beasts of the field" (22). Puttenham elaborates this assertion by identifying the mythical Orpheus and Amphion as primitive poets and interpreting their activities allegorically. The former's taming wild beasts with his music is equated with bringing "rude and savage people to a more civill and orderly life," and the latter's building the walls of Thebes by means of the music of his harp becomes "the mollifying of hard and stonie hearts by his sweete and eloquent perswasion" (22). Puttenham also claims that poets inaugurated religious worship, served as the first priests, and, thanks to their chaste lives and deep meditation, received divine visions so that they became the first prophets as well. He concludes the chapter by asserting that because of their age and gravity, their wisdom and experience, "they were the first lawmakers to the people, and the first polititiens, devising all expedient meanes for th'establishment of the Common wealth, to hold and containe the people in order and duety by force and vertue of good and wholesome lawes, made for the preservation of the publique peace and tranquillitie" (23). In short, *The Arte of English Poesie* opens by detailing a myth of the origin of civilization, and in that myth the eloquent man is the hero.

Puttenham is not the only one in the Renaissance to recount a myth of the orator-civilizer. In 1589, the very year his treatise appeared, the same claim is made by the Spaniard Joan de Guzman, who recounts how human beings once went wandering about the fields "in the manner of savages, sustaining themselves in the same manner as wild beasts, governing themselves not according to the dictates of reason, but according to what each could do by force" (*Primera Parte*, 31ᵛ). What could have brought such people to live in towns and cities? Guzman's answer: eloquence. Across the channel just six years later the French *parlementaire* Guillaume Du Vair, in his *Traitté de l'Eloquence Française* (Treatise on French eloquence), celebrates the eloquence of his native country and argues for the cultivation of rhetoric. Like Puttenham and Guzman, he writes: "Eloquence first softened the manners [*moeurs*] of men, mollified their savage affections, and united their different wills in civil society. It is she without a doubt that built cities, established kingdoms and empires" (395). Perhaps the most extensive version of the myth of the orator-civilizer was produced in the otherwise momentous year 1492 by the Italian Raphael Regius in a panegyric he composed on his art. He begins by agreeing with all those who see eloquence as "the author of all civilization and the parent of all noble arts" (*Panegyricus*, fiᵛ–fiiʳ). Eloquence, he continues, distinguishes men from beasts and enables them to come together in civil society; it is the source of religion, marriage, and reverence for parents. Without it there would be no justice, no recognition of children, no charity to one's neighbors, no contemplation of the heavens or love of God. Finally, in what might seem a surprising move to students of Plato, Regius identifies Socrates as the wellspring of both philosophy and oratory and credits him with being the first to teach that the reins of government (*reipublicae gubernacula*) were to be managed by means of rhetoric (fiiiᵛ). Puttenham, Du Vair, Guzman, and Regius all recount the myth of the orator-civilizer at approximately the same moment in the Renaissance, but they are preceded by many others, including Petrarch, the great Florentine chancellor Coluccio Salutati, and the Paduan Andrea Brenta, who taught rhetoric at Rome in the mid-fifteenth century. And the myth keeps getting retold down to the very end of the Renaissance, as when M. Le

Grand writes in 1659 that eloquence "polished stupid and savage men, and made people civilized [who were] wandering and homeless in the forests and on the mountains" (*Discours*, n.p.).[1]

These Renaissance tellings of the myth of the orator-civilizer can be traced back to passages found in texts written by Isocrates, Cicero, Horace, and Quintilian.[2] The most important and extensive of the ancient versions occurs at the start of Cicero's *De inventione*, and its general outline parallels what one finds in Renaissance texts. In the beginning, says Cicero, men wandered like animals guided only by brute strength, not reason. Lacking religion, marriage rites, and laws, they satisfied their desires, their *cupiditas*, through the abuse of physical force (1.2.2). Then a great man appeared who brought men together from the fields and woods and, through reason and eloquence, tamed them and taught them to observe justice, to work for the common good even at the cost of personal sacrifice, and to accept their social equality with others. Such a man is identical with Cicero's ideal orator, one who combines wisdom with eloquence and stands forth as the most useful and devoted citizen in the state (1.1.1).

All these stories about the orator's founding of civilization, whether ancient or Renaissance, are intensely ideological pronouncements in two quite different senses.[3] In the first place, they are ideological insofar as they define a set of social and political values through explicit, ethically charged oppositions between barbarism and civilization, between the savage and the domesticated, between unruly wandering in the country and an ordered, settled existence in the city. These values in turn are based on a specific vision of an original human nature which is in general fairly negative, for without the civilization the orator stands

---

[1] See Francesco Petrarca, *Le familiari*, ed. V. Rossi (Florence 1933–42), bk. 1, no. 9, to Tommaso da Messina; Coluccio Salutati, *De Laboribus Herculis*, ed. B. L. Ullman (Zurich: Artemis Verlag, 1951), 1:7–8; and for Andrea Brenta, *In disciplinas et bonas artes oratio Romae initio gymnasii habita*, Müllner, 76. For other examples of the myth, see Federico Cerutus, Dedication, in Soarez, *De Arte*, A3ʳ; Johann Sturm, *De universa ratione elocutionis rhetoricae libri III (De Elocutione)* (Strassburg, 1576), ivʳ; Bacon, *Wisdom of the Ancients*, in *Selected Writings*, 412; de' Conti, *Dialogus*, 159–60; Angelo Poliziano, "Oratio super Fabio Quintiliano et Statii Sylvis," in *Prosatori latini*, 882; Melanchthon, *Elementorum*, 460; Caussin, *Eloquentia sacra*, 7; and Rainolds, *Oratio*, 44. Plett, *Rhetorik der Affeckte*, 182, notes that the myth is used, as does Vickers, "The Power of Persuasion" (in Murphy, *Renaissance Eloquence*), 412–16, but neither analyzes it in any detail.

[2] Isocrates, *Antidosis*, in *Works*, trans. George Norlin (Cambridge, Mass.: Harvard University Press, 1929), 254–56; Cicero, *De oratore* 1.8.33; Horace, *Ars poetica*, 391–401, in *Opera*, ed. Edward C. Wickham and H. W. Garrod, 2d ed. (Oxford: Clarendon Press, 1901); and Quintilian, *Institutio*, 2.16.9.

[3] For these two and other senses of "ideology," see Raymond Williams, *Marxism and Literature* (Oxford: Oxford University Press, 1977), 55–71.

for and provides, human beings are assumed to be animals by nature: hard, uncharitable, irrational creatures driven by savage appetites and separated from one another by antisocial indifference or mutual hatred. At the same time, the myth of the orator-civilizer balances this pessimism with an optimism about the power of eloquence to transform human beings. It assumes that their negative traits can be neutralized by the orator's art, which will take a passive people and reshape them as the orator wishes. They are helpless beasts whom Orpheus tamed merely by playing his lyre, blocks and stones out of which Amphion once effortlessly built Thebes. Characterized as "hard," they are easily softened, "mollified," by the orator's magical words; dispersed and "erring" in the wilds, they are easily "led" by him into the city and "unified" as a people in the process. As their fundamental capacity to become passive instruments not only makes their civilizing—indeed, civilization itself—possible, it also clearly testifies to the power and identifies the supreme value of the orator's art.

The myth of the orator-civilizer is also ideological in the sense that it is a mystification of the real power relations that obtain in society. If it defines human beings as possessing a defective nature, it does so in order that their wildness will both require and justify their taming at the orator's hands. The assumed inadequacies of human beings render the orator indispensable and make his activities appear unmitigated blessings. Note how the myth presents the orator as the master of language and depicts the people, by contrast, as essentially mute. It does not dramatize a conflict between his voice and theirs but rather seeks to celebrate the magical power of his words, which can levitate utterly silent stones and control animals who seem deprived of even the capacity to growl or bark. What such a reading of the myth ignores, of course, is the possibility not only of the people's active resistance but of interpreting the orator's behavior as coercion and domination, as a matter of his serving his own interests rather than those of the people he tames.

Even though virtually all versions of the myth attempt to suppress such an interpretation, the very terms they use to define both the orator's and the people's behavior allow that interpretation to emerge. What Cicero says, for instance, is that the orator *forced (De inventione, 1.2.2: compulit)* men into a unity, *turned (1.2.3: converteret)* them away from their former way of life and made each one willing to *endure* or *suffer (pateretur)* equality with others. Cicero's language here is echoed throughout the Renaissance. In the fifteenth century Andrea Brenta writes of how eloquence brings men together (Müllner, 76: *congregavit*) and turns (*convertit*) them from barbarism to humanity. In the preface to the Counter-Reformation *De Arte Rhetorica* of Cypriano Soarez, Federico Cerutus speaks of how eloquence brings and holds people together, "so that, if they should desire to separate because of the perverseness of their spirits, it would tie them down [*devinciat*] . . . by its excellence" (A3ʳ). In his allegorical reading of the myth of Orpheus in *The Wisdom of the Ancients*, Francis Bacon makes the idea of coercion even more insistent when he says that civil philosophy uses persuasion to make the people "assemble and unite and take upon them the yoke of laws and submit to authority" (*Selected Writings*, 412). Most dramatic of all, the Milanese rhetoric professor Anto Maria de' Conti turns Bacon's declaration about the yoke of the laws into a rhetorical question: "Of its own free will [*sponte sua*] did a rough people most desirous of living freely place the laws, like a yoke, upon its neck?" De' Conti answers his question with a most revealing statement, for he says that only a most eloquent man could have persuaded people to live together in a city and make use of the laws, that only such a man "by means of a most eloquent speech could have softened and changed the spirits of people so as to force them to obey his will" (*Dialogus*, 160). What de' Conti's metaphors, like those of all the other treatises, reveal is that if human beings in their natural state are creatures of violence, the orator, too, in taming them, visits a kind of violence upon them, and his doing so may be interpreted as serving his own interests, his own *will*, no matter how much it supposedly serves theirs. In such a light, the rhetoricians' myth becomes a story about civilization as coercion and imperialism, about civilization as the colonization not of distant peoples but of the ones with whom the civilizer lives.

As they unfold their different versions of the myth, Renaissance writers—especially those of the sixteenth and seventeenth centuries—tend to deviate from Cicero and the other ancients in two small but significant respects. First, they offer a more consistently negative view of human nature than the ancients do, a view clearly influenced by Christianity. Cicero may say that humans lived like savages initially, but he claims that they possessed a capacity for civilized behavior which eventually allowed them to rule themselves. By contrast, Renaissance treatments of the myth ignore or downplay such a notion: not only do human beings need to be led into civilization, but their natural depravity requires their constant monitoring lest they return to their natural, postlapsarian condition. Renaissance writers' insistence on human brutality evokes the notion of the Fall, and their emphasis on wandering, on "erring," conjures up the endless journeying visited upon Adam and Eve and their descendants after the expulsion from the Garden. Thomas Wilson presents the most thoroughly Christianized version of the myth. Writing from a strongly Protestant viewpoint, he begins the preface to his *Arte of Rhetorique* of 1560 with the creation of man in the Garden as the rational lord over all things. He goes on: "But after the fall of our first Father, sinne so crept in that our knowledge was much darkned, and by corruption of this our flesh, mans reason and entendement were both overwhelmed" (vi^v). As a result, humans in Wilson's account behave much as they do in other versions of the myth of the orator-civilizer: they live like animals, treat others with violence (which he calls "manhood"), and ignore customs such as marriage, the upbringing of children, and the worship of God. Wilson completes the story when he says that God took pity and stirred up "his faithfull and elect, to perswade with reason all men to societie. And gave his appointed Ministers knowledge both to see the natures of men, and also graunted them the gift of utteraunce, that they might with ease win folke at their will, and frame them by reason to all good order" (vii^r). Writing in the early seventeenth century the Jesuit Nicholas Caussin, hardly to be accused of Protestantism, shares Wilson's division of humanity into the vast mass that must be tamed by eloquence and the select few, the orators, who do the work of civilizing the rest (*Eloquentia sacra*, 7). Moreover, because of the human proclivity to wickedness resulting from the Fall, orators must create laws and governments; as Puttenham puts it, they must "hold and containe the people in order and duety by force and vertue of good and wholesome lawes. . . . The same . . . greatly furthered by the aw of their gods, and such scruple of conscience, as the terrors of their late invented religion had led them into" (*Arte*, 23–24). Whereas Cicero envisages the creation of a republic in which men, once turned into citizens, *cives* (*De inventione*, 1.1.1), rule themselves as orators in their own right, Renaissance writers emphasize the need for the control of the many by the few.

This last consideration marks the second difference between Cicero's and later versions of the myth of the orator-civilizer. Cicero, the republican, envisages a state in which an entire class of human beings rule themselves, competing with one another for preeminence by means of rhetoric. Renaissance writers instead think of the original orator as a prototype of the ruler, who continues to guide the people long after the initial taming involved in civilizing them is done. Like Puttenham, they consequently identify orators as the "first Legislators and polititians in the world" (*Arte*, 22). Nicholas Caussin speaks of them as "Princes of counsel, leaders of the people" (*Eloquentia sacra*, 8); M. Le Grand in his *Discours* (n.p.) says that for their work in guiding others the sophists were appropriately named "Orators of the State, defenders of the nation, masters of the people, and fathers of the country." Although the orator is credited in the Renaissance with teaching the people many different things, what appears central in virtually all accounts is the teaching of obedience. De' Conti, in the passage already cited, captures this notion perfectly when he speaks of how the orator forced the people to obey his will (*suae . . . parere voluntati*). The passage continues: "But after they came together within a single city wall, they certainly began to be ruled no less by eloquence than by the laws they had received. For once they heard the most prudent men speaking of equity and right, they thought, softened by eloquence as they were, that they ought to obey [*parendum esse*] those things which seemed best to them" (*Dialogus*, 160). In de' Conti's conception, the people metaphorically become children who will continually obey (*parere*) those who, thanks to the key verb being used, are their (implicitly male) *parents*, their fathers and the fathers of their country. For Renaissance writers, eloquence thus creates paternal authority and bespeaks paternal rule. It makes men accept not their equality as citizens, as in Cicero's version of the myth, but their inequality, their subjection beneath a supreme orator who benevolently continues to guide them long after they have come together as a people in the city. This slight difference in emphasis that separates Renaissance versions of the myth of the orator-civilizer from their chief model in Cicero's *De inventione* thus turns out to be not so very slight after all. For Cicero, the people, once tamed, compete freely as orator-citizens in the state; for the Renaissance, eloquence transforms them into ideal subjects who continually, as well as initially, need control and direction. It also makes the orator their seemingly perennial ruler, makes him, as Henry Peacham so strikingly puts it in his *Garden of Eloquence*, "the emperour of mens minds" (iii^v), someone who is, by his nature and training, bound to rule.

The prominence of the myth of the orator-civilizer in Renaissance rhetoric confirms what scholars writing on the history of that art have long claimed about it for this period: rhetoric has become political with a vengeance.[4] From the beginning of the Renaissance to the end, writers celebrate the power of language, define oratory as an essential aspect of civil life, and emphasize the role rhetoric plays in the dialogue of power

[4] For some examples, see: Gray, "Renaissance Humanism," 502; Kristeller, "Rhetoric in Medieval and Renaissance Culture" (in Murphy, *Renaissance Eloquence*), 1–19, and "The Humanist Movement," 3–23; Baron, *The Crisis of the Early Italian Renaissance*; Skinner, *The Foundations of Modern Political Thought*, 1:3–40; Monfasani, "Humanism and Rhetoric," 171–235; Struever, *The Language of History in the Renaissance*, esp. 35, 125–27. Although scholars often refer to the "revival" of rhetoric in the Renaissance, it would be more appropriate to speak of a reorientation or redeployment of it, for as Murphy, *Rhetoric in the Middle Ages* (among others), has shown, rhetoric was by no means absent from the landscape of medieval culture.

called politics. They admire Cicero not as a model of style or of wisdom removed from worldly matters, as he was seen to be in the Middle Ages, but as an orator deeply involved in public affairs.[5] Writing in the mid-fifteenth century the Paduan professor Andrea Brenta stresses the many political functions of rhetoric: "It alone and first among all other arts could found cities, arm people against their enemies, repress those who are armed, settle the tumults and discords of citizens, and preserve justice and laws in cities" (Müllner, 76). Brenta's notions are repeated and elaborated over and over throughout the next two centuries: the Italian Sperone Speroni sees eloquence as playing an essential role in the *vita civile* (*Dialogo*, 88); the Frenchman Pierre Fabri defines rhetoric as a *science politique* (*Le grand et vrai art*, 15); the Spanish humanist Juan Luis Vives claims that speech plays an essential role in holding society together (*De Ratione*, 89–90); and the English rhetorician Richard Rainolde declares that nothing is more excellent than eloquence, "by the which the florishyng state of commonweales doe consiste: kyngdomes universally are governed, the state of every one privatlie is maintained" (*Foundacion*, i^r).[6] Perhaps the most extreme example of this identification of rhetoric and politics occurs in the work of the fifteenth-century Greek emigré to Italy, George of Trebizond (Trapezuntius), who asserts that rhetoric is not one of many civil sciences, as most writers claimed, but all the civil sciences in one. He argues that since the part of rhetoric known as invention, or the "finding out" of arguments for one's speech, takes as its province everything that has ever been said or done, invention—and hence, rhetoric—actually includes all of political science within it: "Rhetoric alone has undertaken the management [*gubernationem*] of private as well as public affairs. For what could be said or thought up in matters of action which would not require the power of oratory?" (*Oratio*, 366). In short, whereas the Middle Ages characteristically bound Aristotle's *Rhetoric* next to his *Politics*[7] but failed to

---

[5] Fumaroli, *L'âge de l'éloquence*, 40–43. Cf. Struever, *The Language of History in the Renaissance*, 115.

[6] For other examples of the political nature of rhetoric, see Fuscano, "Della oratoria e poetica facoltà," 190; Du Pré, *Pourtraict*; and Le Grand, *Discours*. Even as early as the 1260s, in the late Middle Ages, Brunetto Latini, following the lead of the pseudo-Ciceronian *Rhetorica ad Herennium*, begins this trend toward identifying rhetoric as the science of governing cities; see his *Li Livres dou Trésor*, ed. Francis J. Carmody, University of California Studies in Philology 22, (Berkeley: University of California Press, 1948), 319. Latini addresses the Italian version of his work to someone he labels as "a good Roman Cicero" who excells at speaking in council or public debate; see *Il Tesoretto*, ed. and trans. Julia B. Holloway (New York: Garland, 1981), lines 47, 45. But Latini does not develop this notion, nor does he consider rhetoric political in the way Renaissance writers would do 150 years after him.

[7] See Murphy, *Rhetoric in the Middle Ages*, 100.

develop a full-fledged concept of rhetoric as political, the Renaissance sees the two volumes, and the sciences they contain, as virtual equivalents.

Scholars such as Eugenio Garin, Quentin Skinner, Paul Oskar Kristeller, and Jerrold Seigel have argued that the political reconceptualization of rhetoric occurs for the first time in northern Italy in the thirteenth century, specifically as a result of the appearance in that region during the preceding century of urban communes, free city-states that enjoyed republican liberty and traditions of political discussion and debate.[8] Their interest in and need for public speaking stimulated a new appreciation of the oratorical culture of antiquity and a concern for both classical rhetoric and classical orations, and it prompted significant modifications in one of the most important forms rhetoric took during the Middle Ages: the art of letter-writing, or *ars dictaminis*. Created in the eleventh century, this art became increasingly classical in style over the next two centuries, and at the same time its model letters began to include political advice. In the thirteenth century the *ars dictaminis* was joined by the new art of public speaking, or *ars arengandi*. The rhetorician Boncompagno of Siena, for instance, grudgingly devoted a chapter of his *Rhetorica novissima* in the early thirteenth century to public speaking, which he condemned as being beneath the dignity of the learned and associated with what he saw as excessive political liberty. Jacques de Dinant wrote an *ars arengandi* at Bologna a little later, summarizing the *Rhetorica ad Herennium*, and the two arts, of letter-writing and public speaking, were fully combined for the first time in the work of Guido Faba (c. 1190–1240). By the mid-thirteenth century, then, rhetorical theory clearly included a significant public and political component. Equally important, it also acquired a specifically political purpose, whether it was to be practiced by the notary, the lawyer, or the letter writer (the *dictator*). Typically, the thirteenth-century *Flore del parlare* explains that rhetoric is useful for those who rule as well as for merchants, thus linking politics to the class that actually did dominate the cities of northern Italy in the period. About the same time Fra Guidotto da Bologna, who translated Cicero, pronounces rhetoric an art of civil importance, and Giovanni del Vergilio praises its dignity, because "only the small part of it called letter-writing calls forth rustics to

[8] The following discussion of the rebirth of rhetoric in Italy draws on the works referred to in note 4 above and on Garin, *L'umanesimo italiano*, and *Medioevo e Rinascimento*; Nancy Struever, "Lorenzo Valla: Humanist Rhetoric and the Critique of the Classical Languages of Morality," in Murphy, *Renaissance Eloquence*, 191–206; Seigel, *Rhetoric and Philosophy*; and Fabio Cossutta, *Gli umanisti e la retorica* (Rome: Ateneo, 1984).

the councils of kings, enriches the needy with wealth, and adorns the dishonorable with honors." Another anonymous *dictator* declares: "Rhetoric, by the grace of God, is the universal mediator of the state, the general teacher of consuls, orators, and judges." Finally, Brunetto Latini, who was employed as a notary, was called both *dittatore* (*dictator*) and *arringatore* (public speaker) by his contemporaries; he not only became the chancellor of Florence (1272–74) but was later praised by the chronicler Giovanni Villani as the first person to have instructed the Florentines in politics.[9]

According to the thesis advanced by Garin, Skinner, and others, the *dictatores*, who overlap with the notaries, were the immediate ancestors of the humanists. Both groups held up classical Latin language and culture as ideals to be imitated; both gained social and political advancement through their learning; both worked principally as secretaries or as teachers of rhetoric; both were dedicated to some version of the active life in society, the *vita civile*, and saw the orator as occupying a position of central importance within it. Indeed, they came to see themselves in classical terms, and although humanists such as Salutati and Bruni were trained as notaries, they came to prefer the honorific, classical *orator* to the traditional *notarius* or *dictator* as a title. Notaries and humanists alike were deeply immersed in the public, political world especially after 1300 and eventually came to dominate the bureaucracies of the Italian towns where they worked. Earlier, notaries had primarily composed documents for businessmen, but as the latter became generally better educated in the later Middle Ages and had less need of such services, public employment offered itself as an important alternative, especially as the administrative bureaucracies of towns were also expanding in this period. Considering, then, the actual social roles that notaries and humanists played, as well as the ideology of political service they were exposed to in the writings of treasured authors such as Cicero and Quintilian, it should hardly be surprising that they would themselves develop such an ideology in their works and see rhetoric as a primarily political instrument essential for the active life in society.

Although the thesis of the revival of a particularly political rhetoric by *dictatores*, notaries, and humanists in the communes of northern

---

[9] For the quotation from Giovanni del Vergilio, see Paul O. Kristeller, "Un 'ars dictaminis' di Giovanni del Vergilio," *Italia Medievale et Umanistica* 4 (1961): 193. The anonymous *dictator*'s comment is cited in John Monfasani, *George of Trebizond: A Biography and a Study of His Rhetoric and Logic* (Leiden: E. J. Brill, 1976), 260. On Latini, see Seigel, *Rhetoric and Philosophy*, 209–11 and the introduction to Latini, *Il Tesoretto*, xvi–xvii.

Italy has much to recommend it, it is problematic in several ways. First, it is mistaken in recognizing no difference between the conception of rhetoric shared by the late medieval *dictatores* and notaries, and that of the humanists and their followers. Second, it misleads in seeing political rhetoric as being *revived*, for it thus implicitly accepts without question a presumed identity between the rhetorical theories of classical authors and those of their Renaissance successors. Third, it posits a necessary connection between republican liberty and the rise of rhetoric in the Renaissance, whereas in fact most northern Italian city-states had become despotisms by 1300, precisely at the time when many late medieval writers were just beginning to assert the essentially political character of rhetoric. The thesis fails to explain why rhetoric would continue to be thought of as political throughout the Renaissance, both inside and outside Italy, in states which were anything but republics and many of which were becoming increasingly absolutist in character. In essence, what Garin, Skinner, and the others cannot account for is the insistence of a Peacham that rhetoric is the "emperour of mens minds."

In the first place, although notaries and *dictatores* are clearly the ancestors of the humanists, the two groups have rather different notions of rhetoric as a political instrument. For the first group, rhetoric is concerned in a general way with "civil matters"; it enables the individual to enter into political discussion, to participate in the dialogue of power occurring in the state. By contrast, for the humanists, as for those who came after them in Italy and throughout western Europe, rhetoric is identified in the political terms we have already discussed: it is seen as an *instrument of rule*. By most accounts, Petrarch is a liminal figure, half medieval and half Renaissance, but when he writes a letter to Tommaso da Messina in praise of rhetoric, he sounds like the medieval notaries and *dictatores*: although he does allude to the myth of the orator-civilizer, he speaks not of the political role of the orator in ruling the city but merely of the pleasure that eloquent writing provides.[10] By contrast, the notary, humanist, and Florentine chancellor Coluccio Salutati, writing less than a half-century after Petrarch, says: "For how [can one] dominate more than by means of the emotions, bend the listener where you might wish and lead him off with grace and desire where you would move him? Unless I am deceived, this is the force of eloquence; this its effort; to this goal all the force and power of rhetors labor."[11] Whereas Petrarch thinks only in general terms about the civic role of oratory,

---

[10] See Petrarca, *Le familiari*, no. 9.
[11] Coluccio Salutati, *Epistolario* (Rome, 1891–1905), 3:15.

Salutati thinks of it specifically as a means to dominate others through their emotions, a conception of the art as a means of ruling others which will mark it throughout the Renaissance. Obsessed with their cultural program of recovering classical antiquities—Poggio Bracciolini, for instance, discovered a complete Quintilian in 1416, and Bishop Gerardo Landriani of Lodi found Cicero's *Brutus, De oratore,* and *Orator* in 1421—the Italian humanists do not initially produce original rhetorics. When the first one does appear, however, in Venice in 1433 or 1434, George of Trebizond's *Rhetoricorum Libri V* (Five books of rhetoric), it opens in a way that confirms the conception we have seen in Salutati. By means of rhetoric, it proclaims, one establishes laws, protects others with counsel, and frightens off enemies, "nor could the state be governed [*gubernari*] without it" (1^r). George of Trebizond is profoundly innovative here: by identifying rhetoric as the instrument of government, he defines the art as it would be defined by all the most important rhetoricians who succeed him in the Renaissance.

Although there are profound similarities between this rhetoric and that of the ancient world, a comparison of the two will show that they contain really quite different political visions. According to M. L. Clarke, the ancient Greeks and Romans essentially regarded rhetoric as a tool for political persuasion.[12] The first rhetoricians, the Sophists, offered their art as education in persuasive speaking for prospective leaders, and they saw themselves as performers—in the tradition of the poets and rhapsodes—engaged in battles of words.[13] Roman rhetoric is equally political, although the forensic variety carries the most weight with both Cicero and Quintilian, who were the chief transmitters of rhetorical theory to the Renaissance. Inscribed in their rhetoric is a particular political model, a republican one in which orators, all theoretically equals, engage in a free competition in the public arena, aiming for victory over their fellow orators.[14] To present this model, both Cicero and Quintilian have recourse to related metaphors of military combat, gladiatorial contests, and athletic games. Antonius, for instance, in Cicero's *De oratore,* sees the orator not as ruling the wills of others but as capturing (*excipiendas*) them (2.8.32) and using weapons to do so (2.72.293; cf. 1.8.32, 1.32.147, 1.34.157, 2.20.84, 3.54.206). Quintilian,

---

[12] M. L. Clarke, *Rhetoric at Rome* (New York: Barnes & Noble, 1963), 2.

[13] George B. Kerferd, *The Sophistic Movement* (Cambridge: Cambridge University Press, 1981), 24–25; W. J. Verdenius, "Gorgias' Doctrine of Deception," in *The Sophists and Their Legacy,* ed. George B. Kerferd (Wiesbaden: Franz Steiner, 1981), 118–22; and W. K. Guthrie, *The Sophists* (Cambridge: Cambridge University Press, 1971), 42–43.

[14] See James L. Kinneavy, *Greek Rhetorical Origins of Christian Faith: An Inquiry* (New York: Oxford University Press, 1987), 35, 39.

similarly, refers on numerous occasions to the "battle in the forum," the *pugnam forensem*, or to some equivalent idea (*Institutio*, 5.12.17, 22; 4.3.2; 10.1.33, 79). Both writers prefer the orator to be a warrior rather than an athlete, just as they prefer the grand style to the more polished one associated with Isocrates (see Shuger, *Sacred Rhetoric*, 22). Speaking of digressions at one point, Quintilian remarks that it is permissible to use in them a certain grace or elegance of style as long as the orator remembers that in the portions of the speech dealing with the main topic he should display not the swollen body of an athlete but the sinews of a soldier, and that he should not wear a multicolored cloak (that is, use a flowery style) little suited to the dust of the forum (10.1.33). For these ancient Roman writers, then, oratory is essentially combat or contest, a fight (*pugna*), a notion that Tacitus would later insist on in his *Dialogus*, even as he believed that the art was degenerating into mere spectacle, and that Saint Augustine would reiterate in his *Confessions*, where he identifies rhetoric as possessing *arma*.[15] It is significant that the word *ornamenta*, which the Latins used for the tropes and figures of speech of rhetoric, also had the sense of "soldier's gear."[16]

In the Roman conception of rhetoric the contest involved always takes place before a *iudex*, the judge in a courtroom, or before *iudices*, the judges who are the people or the orator's fellow senators (see Cicero *De oratore*, 2.29.128–29; Quintilian *Institutio*, 6.2.1–7). Aristotle similarly sees all rhetoric as performance before a judge (*krites*), and he includes even epideictic speeches in this generalization, for that sort of speech, he says, "is put together with reference to the spectator as if he were a judge" (*Rhetoric*, 2.18.1). Reinforcing the notion of oratory as contest, Cicero places the judge metaphorically above the competing speakers: he is the *dominus*, or "lord," and his irrational hostility or bias often defeats the orator's finest efforts (*De oratore*, 2.17.72). Thus, the judge cannot be left completely *hors de combat*; the orator must defeat him, just as he does the other orators he faces. Such triumphs, in which one is able to sweep away (*rapere*) the judges and lead (*perducere*) them to adopt the attitude of mind one wishes, so that one truly dominates (*dominetur*) them, are rare, according to Quintilian (*Institutio*, 6.2.3–4), but his premise, like Cicero's, is that in the endlessly repeated contest of oratory such triumphs can at least sometimes be engineered by the skillful.

---

[15] Tacitus, *Dialogus de oratoribus*, in *Agricola, Germania, Dialogus*, trans. M. Hutton et al. (Cambridge, Mass.: Harvard University Press, 1970), 31–33; Saint Augustine, *Confessions*, trans. William Watts (Cambridge: Harvard University Press, 1960), 9.2.

[16] Ong, *Ramus*, 277.

If Cicero and Quintilian think of rhetoric in republican terms as a competition among equals, the Renaissance, as already indicated, tends to see it instead as a matter of *ruling*. The political model inscribed in this rhetoric is hierarchical, not republican: it does not pit the rhetor against his equals but implicitly sets him above his auditors, who are presented as his inferiors and whom he aims to dominate by means of his art. These auditors are seldom conceived as and even less frequently labeled judges, for that would suggest their superiority to the orator; it would make them, in a sense, his rulers, whereas he practices oratory precisely in order to make himself the ruler over those he addresses. It is particularly revealing, for instance, that George of Trebizond essentially identifies rhetoric as the art of rule in his *Rhetoricorum Libri V*, the first full-scale secular rhetoric produced in the Renaissance. Ironically, this Greek humanist was associated with the Venetian republic, but rather than present rhetoric in republican terms as a means for equals to enter the free, competitive arena of government, he addresses himself to the ruling class of the state as a whole and repeatedly uses forms of the verb *gubernare* to identify the chief function of rhetoric and to define the relationship between the ruling class and the rest of the citizens of the state. Thus, after speculating on the difficulty of joining philosophy and eloquence, he says that if one wishes to know the truth of things, one should pursue the former, "but if one seeks the glory of governing the state [*reipublicae gubernandae*], one should apply oneself to rhetoric" (60^r). George makes similar claims in his *Oratio de laudibus eloquentie* (Oration in praise of eloquence), a speech he delivered at about the same time that he wrote his rhetoric, and he even plays on the literal sense of *gubernator* as "steersman" when he declares: "But just as no ship ever sailed correctly without a steersman [*sine gubernatore*], so no state has ever been well governed [*gubernata*] if eloquence has been expelled from it" (368). Fittingly, he then flatters his Venetian audience by telling them that their flourishing state exemplifies the truth of his idea, since it is governed by eloquence.

George is hardly alone in voicing such sentiments in the Renaissance. Citing the many good things rhetoric can accomplish, the Milanese professor de' Conti, writing in the mid-sixteenth century, speaks of how it governs cities (*Dialogus*, 152), and Stephen Hawes "Englishes" these ideas in his *Pastime of Pleasure* of 1517: "rethorycyans—founde Justyce doubtles / Ordenynge kynges—of ryghte hye dygnyte / Of all comyns—to have the sovereinte."[17] More important, some writers do not speak

[17] Stephen Hawes, *The Pastime of Pleasure*, in *Works*, intro. Frank J. Spang (Delmar, N.Y.: Scholars' Facsimiles and Reprints, 1975), Cviii^v. For other examples of rhetoric as rule, see Christopher Thretius, Dedication, in Sturm, *De Elocutione*, iv^r;

just in general terms of rhetoric as rule but present the specific political model of autocratic, imperial government which informs the thinking of most Renaissance rhetoricians. Thus, when Guillaume Du Vair turns into French the idea of rhetoric's political power, he uses language that makes it the source of empire: rhetoric, he says, "reigns among peoples, and establishes for itself a violent empire over the spirit of men" (*Traitté*, 393). Reviewing the impact that eloquence has on the minds of those exposed to it, the German Johann Heinrich Alsted has recourse to similar language when he asks whether it would not be appropriate to say that rhetoric enjoys an *imperium* over men. He then answers his own question affirmatively: "Because if it makes a great difference whether those whom one commands [*imperatur*] do something of their own free will or unwillingly, I see that the power [*potestatem*] of orators is greater than that of the greatest kings" (*Rhetorica*, Dedication, 8ʳ). Finally, at the very end of the Renaissance, in his *Discours* of 1659, M. Le Grand defines eloquence as "that imperious habit which reigns absolutely in hearts, exercises a legitimate power over wills, and is no less the foundation of empires than the source of triumphs."

Just as rhetoric is imagined in political terms that bespeak Renaissance culture, so the rhetor is appropriately presented as someone, by nature and training, bound to rule—a lord, a king or an emperor. In the fifteenth century, for instance, Lorenzo Valla sees him as the "guide and leader of the people [*rector et dux populi*],"[18] and in the sixteenth Daniel Barbaro calls him the "lord [*signore*] and possessor of each person's spirit" (*Della Eloquenza*, 356). Eloquence itself is often imaged as a lofty lady or a queen, and Antoine Furetière builds an entire allegory on the basis of this very traditional image.[19] The Spanish humanist Juan Luis Vives reveals how such a personification of rhetoric helps define the orator as a royal ruler: "He clearly reigns [*regnat*] among men who is best equipped to speak; and rightly the tragedian Euripides named eloquence a queen" (*De Ratione*, 93). If, for some, rhetoric makes men kings, for Henry Peacham it gives them an even loftier position: it makes the orator "in a maner the emperour of mens minds & affections,

---

Caussin, *Eloquentia sacra*, 757; Vives, *De Causis*, 152–53, and *De Ratione*, 89; Poliziano, "Oratio super Fabio Quintiliano et Statii Sylvis" (in *Prosatori latini*, 882–84); Ramus, *Dialectique*, 134, and *Attack on Cicero*, 6; Rainolds, *Oratio*, 44; Alsted, *Rhetorica*, Dedication, 2ᵛ, 7ᵛ, and *Rhetorica*, 1; Granada, *Ecclesiastica Rhetorica*, 5; and Keckermann, *Systema*, 126.

[18] Lorenzo Valla, *Dialecticae Disputationes*, in *Opera Omnia* (Turin, 1962), 694, cited in James R. McNally, "*Rector et Dux Populi*: Italian Humanists and Relationship between Rhetoric and Logic," *Modern Philology* 67 (1969):171.

[19] See Fuscano, "Della oratoria e poetica facoltà," 190; Fabri, *Le grand et vrai art*, 6; and Furetière, *Nouvelle allégorique*.

and next to the omnipotent God in the power of perswasion" (*Garden*, iii^v). Antonio Llull of Mallorca, vicar general of the diocese of Besançon in the mid-sixteenth century, goes one step beyond Peacham and actually accords the orator quasi-divine status, declaring that eloquence lets the orator rule (*regnare*) among men as if he were a kind of god (*veluti Deum quemdam*).[20]

This Renaissance insistence on rhetoric as rule is not without classical precedents. The notion that Eloquence could be divine goes back to the Greek goddess Peitho, "Persuasion,"[21] and Tacitus in his *Dialogus* laments the decline of that eloquence which was once the mistress, the *domina* (32.4), of Roman life. Moreover, both Quintilian and Cicero do refer to some notion of rhetoric as ruling or dominating. Quintilian defines the perfect orator as one "who can guide [*regere*] cities by his counsels, establish laws, and purge vices by his decisions as a judge" (*Institutio*, 1.Pr.10), and he claims that when the orator's emotional power dominates the court, this form of eloquence rules (6.2.4: *haec eloquentia regnat*). Because of its enormous power, Cicero, citing the words of Pacuvius, celebrates rhetoric as a queen, *regina*, and a "commander," *imperator* (*De oratore*, 2.44.187). In another place he asks rhetorically what is "so . . . kingly, so worthy of a free man" (1.8.32: *tam . . . regium, tam liberale*) as the power that helps suppliants, gives security, and maintains men in the city. Nevertheless, despite such occasional references to rhetoric as rule, both Roman writers chiefly imagine the art, using metaphors of combat, as a contest among free citizens. One should remember that Cicero was a staunch republican and defender of his city-state run by free men (*liberi*)—hence his praise for rhetoric as "worthy of a free man" (*liberale*) in the last quotation. Since he was unable to abide kings, one can only conclude that his calling it "kingly" (*regium*) as well must be a matter of mere metaphor: the rhetor's power over others is so great that it makes him resemble a king in that regard, even though he otherwise remains a citizen like all the other free men in the state, competing in the contest that is their political life.

The different emphases given to the politics of rhetoric between Cicero and the Renaissance leaps from the page when one compares statements they make about the power of rhetoric to rule peaceful cities.

---

[20] Antonio Llull, *De oratione libri septem* (Basel, n.d. [1554–58?]), 12, cited in Antonio Martí, *La preceptiva retórica española en el siglo de oro* (Madrid: Editorial Gredos, 1972), 132. On the issue or the orator's quasi-divinity, see also Wilson, *Arte*, 161; and Gabriel Harvey, *Rhetor* (London, 1577), who praises rhetoric because it makes "men seem divine and most similar to immortal God" (n.p.).

[21] On the Greek goddess Peitho, see Kinneavy, *Greek Rhetorical Origins of Christian Faith*, 34–35.

Cicero writes that eloquence "has especially always flourished and ruled [*dominata*] in every free people, and especially in peaceful, tranquil cities" (*De oratore*, 1.8.30). By contrast, although Giovanni Tuscanella, a professor at Bologna in the 1420s, praises the subject in his inaugural lecture in phrases very close to Cicero's, there are small but significant differences. "Eloquence," he says, "always obtained sovereignty [*principatum*] and has always dominated in every peaceful and free city" (Müllner, 196). Whereas in Cicero the people are free, in Tuscanella it is the city-state, and whereas the former says eloquence *flourishes*, the latter says it obtains *sovereignty*; his word *principatum* can simply mean something like "the first place" but cannot be divorced in its fifteenth-century, Bolognese context from association with princely rule. Later in the Renaissance, Federico Cerutus rewrites Cicero's sentence in his dedicatory letter to the 1589 edition of Cypriano Soarez's *De Arte Rhetorica*, declaring that eloquence "always flourished and ruled in a well established state" (A4^r). Philip Melanchthon similarly, writing in his *Encomium eloquentiae* (Praise of eloquence) about the city depicted on Achilles' shield, claims that eloquence always has a place "in a peaceful city" (52). What separates these two Renaissance writers (one a Counter-Reformation Catholic and the other a founding father of Protestantism) from Cicero is what they omit: neither makes any reference to a free people. For them, as for the Renaissance in general, rhetoric does not mean rule in the sense of an entire class of orators competing with one another in the political arena; it means control by one man or one class over all those below it. Instructively, although the Venetian Raphael Regius does associate rhetoric with republican liberty, he does not identify it with the parry and thrust of debate or the openness of dialogue. Instead, he characterizes it as rule and dominion, and remarkably, he praises Cicero for having reigned in Rome as the most eloquent man of his age (*Panegyricus*, fv^v). Likewise, the Englishman Walter Haddon praises the great Roman republican for his rhetorical prowess by recalling how he was famed as the "king," the *rex*, of Rome.[22] In the Renaissance, the persistant identification of rhetoric with rule ironically turns the arch-republican Cicero into a version of what he most opposed: a Julius Caesar, a would-be king of Rome! Perhaps it would be best to conclude here that rhetoric as it has been defined from antiquity on is neither completely republican nor monarchical/absolutist in character; rather, it is *both*, at least potentially. In Cicero and Quintilian, what counts is the competition among orators in the forum or Senate, although there is a clear recognition—a kind of "minority

---

[22] Haddon, "De laudibus eloquentiae," 5.

view"—as well that rhetoric means power and dominance over others. In the Renaissance, just the reverse is true: even though a connection between rhetoric and republicanism may be occasionally acknowledged, the emphasis really falls on the power that rhetoric gives the orator to control his audience and that makes him a king, a Caesar—as Cicero appeared to be, even in a free state.

As might be expected, Renaissance rhetoricians stress that Caesar himself was an ideal orator, as was his double, Alexander the Great, along with many other ancient kings and emperors. Andrea Benzi, for instance, a doctor who taught in northern Italy in the early fifteenth century, praises rhetoric in a speech he delivered in Florence in 1421, declaring that kings and princes (*reges ipsi ac principes*) have never thought they could accomplish great things without eloquence and that many men achieved the greatest political positions (*maximos magistratus*) and glory thanks to it (Müllner, 111). As examples he then names Peisistratos, Pericles, Philip, Alexander, and Caesar. In a similar vein, George Puttenham, generally equating poets, orators, and rulers, says that Julius Caesar, "the first Emperour and a most noble Captaine, was not onely the most eloquent Orator of his time, but also a very good Poet" (*Arte*, 33). And Jacques Amyot recalls that the great Roman general, his army having revolted, had recourse not to his sword but to "the cutting edge of his tongue," which made his soldiers submit to him of their own accord (*Projet*, 6). Other writers go even further and claim that the very expansion of the Roman empire paralleled, if it was not caused by, the flourishing of eloquence. Thus, Guillaume Du Vair claims that eloquence reached a high point in imperial Rome, for when it "was used even by the emperors and by the Great, it breathed a loftier and fuller majesty" (*Traitté*, 399). He then goes on to cite a somewhat surprising list of Roman leaders and emperors whom he admires for their eloquence, including Pompey, Augustus, Antony, Caligula, Claudian, and Titus. The Italian friar Antonio da Rho, in a work written in 1431, directly identifies rhetoric as an instrument of empire, declaring that virtually the entire world became part of the Roman empire "no less by eloquence than by arms" (Müllner, 165), a sentiment with which the English rhetorician Richard Rainolde clearly concurs when he says that "the state of Rome could by no meanes have growen so mervailous mightie, but that God had indued the whole line of Cesars, with singuler vertues, with aboundaunt knowlege & singuler Eloquence" (*Foundacion*, ii[r]).[23]

[23] For other identifications of kings or emperors as ideal orators, see Francis Bacon, *Advancement of Learning*, in *Advancement of Learning and Novum Organon*, intro. James E. Creighton, rev. ed. (New York: Willey, 1900), 33; Thretius, Dedication, in

If Renaissance writers consider rhetoric an instrument of empire, it should hardly be surprising to find them conceiving it as a weapon: words are swords. This equation runs right through Henry Peacham's *Garden of Eloquence*, which introduces it in the dedicatory epistle by declaring that figures of speech "are as martiall instruments both of defence & invasion, and being so, what may be either more necessary, or more profitable for us, then to hold those weapons alwaies readie in our handes" (iv^r; cf. 48, 57, 81–83, 106, 117, 137, 174). Although Peacham may be more insistent than most, he is far from alone in the period. Bartholomew Keckermann, for instance, declares that a good argument is like an *aries*, or "battering ram" (*Systema*, 144), and the right disposition of one's arguments like an *acies*, a battle formation (121). Similarly, Raphael Regius proclaims that nothing is so "kingly" (*regium*) or necessary for an eminent man than "always to be equipped with these arms so that he does not fear the calumnies of the wicked" (*Panegyricus*, fvi^r).[24] Other writers go beyond this equation of words and swords by arguing that eloquence is actually superior to arms. Andrea Benzi, for instance, who identifies Peisistratos, Pericles, Philip, Alexander, and Caesar as great orators, declares that such men could "accomplish greater and more illustrious deeds by means of eloquence than arms" (Müllner, 111). The Greek king Pyrrhus, according to Jacques Amyot, "confessed freely to have acquired more cities by the eloquence of his ambassador Cyneas than he had conquered by arms" (*Projet*, 4–5). This same anecdote, somewhat amplified, appears at the start of the dedicatory epistle to Thomas Wilson's *Art of Rhetorique*. Wilson recounts that Pyrrhus used to send the "noble Orator, and sometimes Scholer to Demosthenes" to persuade opponents to surrender, so that "Cineas through the eloquence of his tongue, wanne moe Cities unto him [Pyrrhus], then ever himself should els have been able by force to subdue." Wilson then concludes by praising eloquence for its ability "to winne Cities and whole Countries . . . without bloudshed" (ii^{r-v}). What is at issue here is not just the superiority of words to swords in terms of force but their superiority in terms of something like humanity. Thus, Federico Cerutus, in his dedicatory letter to Cypriano Soarez's rhetoric, says: "What wise men know is that whatever can be accomplished with hostile steel can be accomplished with eloquence, because it is more proper to man [*magis hominis est proprium*]" (*De Arte*, A4^v). And M. Le Grand

---

Sturm, *De Elocutione*, iii^v; Vives, *De Ratione*, 95; and Caussin, *Eloquentia sacra*, 39, 170.

[24] Other examples are Fabri, *Le grand et vrai art*, 6; Alsted, *Rhetorica*, Dedication, 3^v; Granada, *Ecclesiastica Rhetorica*, 5; Guzman, *Primera Parte*, 148^v; and George of Trebizond, *Oratio*, 369.

says that Alexander was taught to be a good orator by a teacher who believed that it was less honorable for a conqueror to march over broken scepters and severed heads than "to erect trophies to himself in the spirit of the captains and in the heart of peoples by harangues" (*Discours*, n.p.). All these writers are essentially rehearsing a version of the great Renaissance debate over arms and letters, replacing the latter with oratory, and in every case they conclude that the word is not only mightier than the sword but nobler and more humane as well.[25]

In their insistence that rhetoric is a weapon like, or superior to, actual arms, Renaissance writers are clearly influenced by the identification of the orator as a warrior which runs throughout the works of Cicero and Quintilian and other Roman rhetoricians. Nevertheless, it is crucial to note how the model of oratorical activity has changed. If the Romans imagined the rhetor as engaging in a free competition with other rhetors under the watchful eyes of judges who also had to be manipulated successfully for victory to be achieved, Renaissance writers seem virtually to ignore the idea that the orator faces other orators as opponents, and they seldom refer to judges at all. Instead, thinking in terms of a hierarchical political model, they imagine the orator as opposed by his *audience*, who do not sit above him, as judges might be supposed to do, but are implicitly below him and identified as his subjects either literally or figuratively. Although the Renaissance orator, like his classical counterparts, is a fighter, what differentiates him from them is that he fights and triumphs over his very listeners.[26]

Writing toward the end of the Renaissance, the English Puritan William Chappell spells out quite directly this Renaissance conception of oratorical combat when he says that "because the heart or will hath a great influx into the mind," it is lawful for a speaker "to insinuate something either hiddenly or openly, whereby we may possess the hearers affections, and by them, as by setting scaling ladders invade the

[25] For examples of the rhetoric-arms debate, see Caussin, *Eloquentia sacra*, 6; Du Vair, *Traitté*, 396; Angel Day, *The English Secretary*, intro. Robert O. Evans (Gainesville, Fla.: Scholars' Facsimiles and Reprints, 1967), 33. For classic statements of the arms-letters debate in the Renaissance, see the discussion of the ideal courtier's profession in Castiglione's *Il libro del cortegiano*, ed. Bruno Maier, 2d ed. (Turin: Unione Tipografico-Editrice Torinese, 1964), bk. 1, chaps. 45–46; and the argument that takes place in Cervantes's *Don Quijote*, ed. Martín de Riguer, 10th ed. (Barcelona: Editorial Juventud), pt. 1, chap. 38.

[26] In arguing the historical difference between the Renaissance and classical antiquity, despite the continuity of imagery of combat, I clearly disagree with Brian Vickers, who baldly asserts the absence of any such difference from classical antiquity to the eighteenth century: "The figures [described in Pope's *Essay on Criticism*] are not ornaments but weapons, and Pope is here at one with Peacham or Martianus Capella or the *Ad Herennium*" (*Classical Rhetoric in English Poetry*, 117).

fort of the mind."[27] George Puttenham similarly asserts that the orator who "hath vanquished the minde of man, hath made the greatest and most glorious conquest" (*Arte*, 207). Luis de Granada attributes that result to a combination of rhetoric and dialectic: "The latter conquers, while the former persuades the one who has been conquered to follow and obey" (*Ecclesiastica Rhetorica*, 43). The Frenchman Guillaume Du Vair directly identifies the imperialism—admittedly an imperialism directed at the subjects of one's own state—that is implied by all this emphasis on oratory as conquest: "What greater honor can one imagine in the world than to command without arms and forces those with whom you live? to be the master not only of their persons and goods, but of their very own wills? It is a perpetual empire which does not need guards and attendants [*il ne faut point de gardes ny de satellites*]" (*Traitté*, 395). The Spanish humanist Juan Luis Vives goes even further: he combines the ideas of conquest and rule by imagining the orators in Republican Rome as *tyrants* whose eloquence constituted, metaphorically speaking, the guards who helped them rule: "They exercised a kind of tyranny, protected by the forces of speech as by a force of attendant guards [*satellitio*], by means of which they might aid their friends and tire out their enemies" (*De Causis*, 154).

The idea of conquest appears in Renaissance rhetorics whenever they treat tropes—in particular, that trope of tropes, metaphor. For metaphor, *translatio* in the Latin treatises of the period, means literally a "bearing across or going over"; defined by Puttenham as "an inversion of sence by *transport*" (*Arte*, 166), it involves a necessary crossing of boundaries and movement beyond limits. In the rhetorical transaction those boundaries are the ones between selves, between the orator and the auditor, and what gets transported through the space separating the two is the mind or will of the former, which impresses itself on the mind or will of the latter. As Luis de Granada puts it, the spirit of the multitude must be "bent" (*Ecclesiastica Rhetorica*, 46: *flectendus*) by the orator "so that it will perform what we want [*volumus*]" (44). Even more strikingly, Johann Heinrich Alsted declares that the orator's speech serves as the index to his mind and that "it flows, as it were, into the spirits of others and . . . remarkably impresses its own image in them" (*Rhetorica*, 5). Granada's countryman Joan de Guzman deals more specifically with the particular effect of rhetorical figures (the "flowers" of rhetoric) on the spirits and wills of others: "The little flowers of Rhetoric . . . awaken the spirit and wound it, and they prepare

---

[27] William Chappell, *The Preacher, or The Art and Method of Preaching* (London, 1656), 145.

wills in such a manner as when, by hammering, workmen soften and
render hard iron malleable in order to make their objects out of it"
(*Primera Parte*, 65ʳ). In essence, then, every time a rhetor uses a figure of
speech, every time he has recourse to metaphor or some other trope (and
it would be hard to think of a time when he would not), he both expresses his identity and impresses that identity on his auditor. It
amounts to a *translatio imperii*, an imperial sallying-forth beyond the
boundaries of the self in order to occupy the alien terrain of the Other
and to plant one's banner there as conqueror and ruler. Figures and
tropes constitute mini-dramas of invasion and domination, dramas that
define the relationship between the orator and the auditors and supply
the former with his fundamental political identity as king or emperor.[28]

A figure or trope also supplies the auditors with their identity as the
orator's *subjects* who must be conquered, brought to accept willingly
their politically inferior position. Using a pun that runs through Renaissance rhetorical writing, Alsted speaks of how the orator makes the
heart, like the will and feelings, of the auditor *subjectum Rhetorices*
(*Rhetorica*, 5), "the subject of Rhetoric": that is, both the subject matter
for rhetoric and the (political) subject of rhetoric. Even more forcefully,
Nicholas Caussin opens his *De Eloquentia sacra* by declaring that sacred eloquence, "having inflamed their deepest senses with a certain
celestial ardor, has subjected [*subiecit*] men to itself; it has tamed [*dom-
uit*] kings; having repudiated errors, it has forced under the yoke of
Christ [*ad Christi iugum*] cities, provinces, finally the entire world" (2).
In stressing the way rhetoric creates subjects, Caussin uses a telling image, the yoke, which recurs in works by other Renaissance writers. In
de' Conti's *Dialogus*, for instance, after summoning up the myth of the
orator-civilizer, the author's spokesman asks rhetorically: "Of its own
free will did a rough people most desirous of living freely place the laws,
like a yoke [*tanquam iugo*], upon its neck?" For de' Conti the creation
of civilization here involves an opposition between freedom and subjection, between free will and the yoke. Nor do the citizens merely wear
the yoke of the laws, for as the passage continues, de' Conti's spokesman goes on to say that once inside the city walls, they "began to be
ruled certainly no less by eloquence than by the laws they had received"
(160). Even more categorically, Du Vair declares that nothing is more
useful than speaking well "to contain the people under the yoke of obe-

---

[28] My argument here is indebted to Parker's analysis of metaphor as constituting, in
miniature, the plot of romance (*Literary Fat Ladies*, 36–53). For a different but related
analysis of metaphor as a symbol and an instrument of imperial conquest, see Eric
Cheyfitz, *The Poetics of Imperialism: Translation and Colonialization from "The
Tempest" to "Tarzan"* (New York: Oxford University Press, 1991).

dience [*pour contenir les peuples soubs le joug de l'obeïssance*], to content the Great, to treat with other princes, and to handle successfully all sorts of affairs" (*Traitté*, 396). Andrea Brenta; writing in the third quarter of the fifteenth century, offers something of the same idea, though with a less telling metaphor, when he says that princes have always judged rhetoric the best means by which people could be contained *sub imperio* (Müllner, 77).

The image of the yoke not only implies a political hierarchy in which the orator-ruler occupies a position on high while the audience-subject is kept below but specifically identifies the auditors in the same way that the myth of the orator-civilizer does: they are wild animals who must be tamed in and by the rhetorical transaction. Most important, such images suggest that Renaissance rhetoricians regard that transaction in a very special light, as the very *paradigm of rule*, for if the rhetor's eloquence makes subjects subjects, it necessarily makes him their ruler at the same time and in the same act, thereby bringing into existence the political hierarchy that connects them. As Henry Peacham says, by using his art the properly equipped orator "may prevaile much in drawing the mindes of his hearers to his owne will and affection: he may winde them from their former opinions, and quite alter the former state of their mindes, he may move them to be of his side, to hold with him, to be led by him, . . . and finally *to be subject to the power of his speech* whither soever it tendeth" (*Garden*, 121; emphasis added). If rhetoric means rule, to be subject to the power of speech means, for the Renaissance, to be a subject politically.

The common notion that Renaissance rhetoric constitutes a revival— a repetition—of ancient rhetoric is clearly inadequate, then, given the very different politics inscribed in the two discourses. Moreover, as indicated earlier, the Renaissance insistence on rhetoric as rule, as the subjecting of others to the will of the orator, makes it difficult to accept the equation of rhetoric, humanism, and republican liberty that lies at the heart of Garin's, Skinner's, and others' interpretations of the early Italian Renaissance. Those interpretations also mislead because they tend to ignore the fact that humanism and rhetoric did not bloom exclusively on Florentine soil. Bologna, Ferrara, Milan, and especially Padua were centers of humanism in the fourteenth and fifteenth centuries, and all those city-states were signorial despotisms, when they were not under the control of other states during the period. Indeed, because of the importance of northern Italian cities for the early development of humanism, scholars such as Lauro Martines have gone back to the Burckhardtian notion that humanism and despotism, not republicanism, made the best bedfellows in the early Renaissance. A more reasonable position has been advanced by the Italian scholar Fabio Cossutta, who notes that there were really *two* humanisms, one in Florence and one in Lombardy, although he also argues that what humanism tended to exalt everywhere was *personal* freedom, which would enable one to achieve individual excellence, rather than communal liberty.[29]

The mistaken identification of rhetoric with republicanism in the late fourteenth and fifteenth centuries in Italy has also led scholars to see a "decline" in rhetoric as a political instrument during the course of the Renaissance. Their argument really constitutes a version of Tacitus's thesis in his *Dialogus* concerning the decline of rhetoric in Rome, and it does have antecedents in the Renaissance itself. According to Tacitus, oratory was used to rule during the days of the Republic (32.4); it was a source of power and influence and effectively enabled the advancement of merit. By the end of the first century, however, when the *Dialogus* was most likely written, Tacitus's spokesmen claim that rhetoric has been thrust from the forum and the Senate into the triviality of mere performances in schools of declamation, that men get ahead not by their mastery of the art of speaking but by currying favor with Caesar. Although Tacitus then concedes that in a state where the wisest of men, the emperor, decides matters, there is no need for oratory, which is really necessary only in countries suffering from licence and sedition, this concession seems largely ironic, an attempt to avoid reprisals because of his implicit criticisms directed at the Rome of Domitian.

Various versions of Tacitus's thesis are reproduced by Renaissance writers, especially in the sixteenth century. In *La Retorica* of 1559, for instance, Bartolomeo Cavalcanti identifies the art as being essential for life under a *governo . . . popolare* (3–4); Sperone Speroni writes that rhetoric is particularly suitable for republics because of the variability of judgments within them (*Dialogo*, 136); and both writers suggest that the art is largely irrelevant in their contemporary world. Similarly, Juan Luis Vives says that rhetoric is stronger in a popular government than in a state where one man rules, since eloquent speech will have little effect in the latter case, and he observes that it really flourished only in fifth-century Athens and republican Rome (*De Causis*, 152–54). Davy Du Perron agrees, and in his *Avant Discours du Rhétorique ou traitté de l'Eloquence* (Prefatory discourse on rhetoric or treatise on eloquence), written in the 1580s for the French king Henri III, he claims that eloquence, though essential for uniting a people in a republic, has a much smaller role to play in a monarchy. And the great classical scholar Marc

---

[29] Lauro Martines, *Power and Imagination: City-States in Renaissance Italy* (New York: Random House, 1979), 191–206; Cossuta, *Gli umanisti*, 45–49, 80–90.

Antoine Muret, teaching Tacitus and Cicero in Rome in the 1580s, echoes Du Perron in mourning the decline of eloquence in an age of monarchies that accord at most only epideictic oratory a place in the courts of princes.[30] Offering the most elaborate and dramatic version of the Tacitean thesis in the Renaissance, Francesco Patrizi in 1562 addresses the seventh dialogue of his generally skeptical philosophical work, *Della retorica dieci dialoghi* (Ten Dialogues on Rhetoric), to the question whether rhetoric can flourish only in a free state (38ᵛ). He answers in the affirmative, but his notion of the kind of state in which rhetoric can rule is highly problematic. Rhetoric, declares Patrizi, is an art associated with deception, violence, disorder, and crisis, not at all with orderly government, with government by laws. Orators are essentially rabble-rousers; interested only in their own ends rather than justice or the public good, they seek tyrannical power as each strives to dominate all others in the public arena (39ᵛ–40ʳ). As a result, they naturally have no place in monarchies, tyrannies, or oligarchies, since everything in such states is carried on by small councils, where all is done "in a low voice and among just a few" (41ʳ). Only in popular governments do orators play an important political role, and even there only when those states are not being governed by laws. The orator can rule in such states because the people are "a wild beast," *una fiera*, whose passions he "tickles" in order to get what he wants (42ᵛ). Patrizi concludes his analysis by stating that all the contemporary interest in oratory is due to Petrarch's concern to revive antiquity, but that the old oratorical spirits have still not really come out of their tombs and will not do so until there is true popular government. Of course, Patrizi's debunking notion of the nature of the free society in which orators will rule is hardly consistent with Cicero's Rome and constitutes a brutal mockery of classical republican ideals.

The Tacitean thesis has attracted a number of present-day scholars of the Renaissance. Eugenio Garin, for instance, writing on Patrizi, argues that after the Council of Trent (1545–63) secular oratory had no place in European governments. Marc Fumaroli declares that Tacitus's conception spoke to the Europe of the Age of Absolutism in which oratory had yielded to poetry as the preferred mode of self-expression, but that it did so only after the Plantin edition of his works in 1574. For Vasile Florescu and for George Kennedy, rhetoric became a mere ornament of the prince's court as the Renaissance evolved, and was finally limited to mere philological culture, to the cultivation of style. And Debora Shu-

---

[30] I owe these references to Du Perron and Muret to Fumaroli, "Rhetoric, Politics, and Society" (in Murphy, *Renaissance Eloquence*), 255–58.

ger asserts that secular rhetoric had little place in absolutist states, although sacred rhetoric continued to flourish throughout the period. Even Fabio Cossutta, who wisely recognizes that there is a despotic or absolutist version of rhetoric flourishing in *quattrocento* Lombardy to match the supposedly republican rhetoric of Florence, accepts at face value the humanists' lament that they could not speak publicly and concludes that rhetoric had no place where signorial rule was the norm.[31]

There are at least two basic flaws in such arguments. The first is that even if one agrees with the notion that deliberative rhetoric yielded the palm to epideictic after the death of the Italian communes, it does not mean that rhetoric ceased to be political. After all, epideictic oratory is what courtiers practiced, and courtiers, though admittedly not engaging in debates like the senators of republican Rome, nevertheless did have political roles to play in relationship to the monarchs they served: they offered advice, served on councils of state, and pursued their own political advancement. Second, and more important, the Tacitean thesis fails to come to grips with the fact that most Renaissance writers on rhetoric continued to think that their art was political, concerned with ruling, right down to the end of the period. After stressing the associations of rhetoric and politics for the Italian humanists of the late fourteenth and fifteenth centuries, John Monfasani declares: "There cannot be any doubt that by and large sixteenth-century Italian authors continued to believe, teach, and preach that, in Conti's words, 'eloquentia civitates gubernari'" ("cities are governed by eloquence").[32] What Monfasani says about Italy, of course, can and must be extended to the rest of Europe. It is quite revealing that even if such writers as Cavalcanti, Vives, and Patrizi insist that rhetoric is essentially associated with republican rule and free states, things that scarcely obtained in the Europe in which

[31] Garin, *Medioevo e Rinascimento*, 148; Fumaroli, *L'âge de l'éloquence*, 63–70; Vasile Florescu, *La retorica nel suo sviluppo storico* (Bologna: Il Mulino, 1971), 84–85; George A. Kennedy, *Classical Rhetoric and Its Christian and Secular Tradition from Ancient to Modern Times* (Chapel Hill: University of North Carolina Press, 1980), 200–203; Shuger, *Sacred Rhetoric*, 12; and Cossutta, *Gli umanisti*, 112–19. Tzvetan Todorov, in his *Theories of the Symbol* (trans. Catherine Porter [Ithaca: Cornell University Press, 1982], 60–81), applies the Tacitean thesis to the entire history of rhetoric from ancient Greece through the nineteenth century. Ignoring Roman and Renaissance republicanism, he claims that rhetoric was chiefly useful for epideictic display from the end of Greek democracy to the French Revolution and, elsewhere, that there is no essential difference in rhetoric between antiquity and the eighteenth century: "Quintilian and Fontanier [a rhetorician of the eighteenth century], had they been able to communicate with each other across the centuries, would have understood each other perfectly" (69).

[32] Monfasani, "Humanism and Rhetoric," 209.

they lived, that sad fact did not stop them from producing handbooks and treatises in order to teach the subject to contemporaries who lived under signorial or monarchical governments. Moreover, no matter what their political persuasion, Renaissance writers on rhetoric generally identify their art with ruling. Virtually all of them would have agreed unhesitatingly with M. Le Grand's proclamation, at the height of absolutist rule in France, that "the art of speaking well, and the sovereign eloquence of which I speak, is the most important part of politics [*la plus importante piece de la politique*]" (*Discours*, n.p.).

The identification of rhetoric and politics in Renaissance minds is dramatically underscored by the fact that most rhetorical texts were addressed to members of the ruling class, occasionally to actual monarchs, and that they often presented their doctrines as essential weapons in the arsenals of actual rulers. Going back to the earliest phase of *quattrocento* humanism, we find the Sienese doctor Andrea Benzi, in an oration composed about 1421, claiming that kings and princes have never thought they could rule without rhetoric (Müllner, 111). A century and a half later, in 1574, writing once again in the same region, the Paduan professor Giason Denores begins his "Breve Trattato dell'Oratore" (Brief treatise on the orator) with the statement that although this art of speech is fit for all, it is especially appropriate for those "who legitimately have occasion to rule and govern peoples and cities" (103). Luigi Carbone, a Jesuit and professor of theology at Perugia in the sixteenth century, proclaims rhetoric the monarchical art par excellence, for it is able both to guarantee the authority of the prince and to make it manifest to all. And Sir Balthazar Gerbiers, writing during the troubled period of the Interregnum in England, thinks along similar lines: "This Science may be properly compared unto Justice in Monarchs, and Princes, as being most powerfull to keep Subjects in a due obedience, and absolutely necessary in the great Body of the State; for that well speaking in a Princes mouth, is that which above all other things captivates the hearts and affections of his Subjects." Jean Brèche goes even further in his *Premier livre de l'honneste exercice du Prince* (The first book of the honest exercise of the prince) of 1544, which he dedicated to ·François I, when he declares that only kings possess true eloquence.[33]

That Jean Brèche should have addressed to an actual king a treatise specifying the regal nature of oratory is quite revealing. We have already noted that George of Trebizond and Raphael Regius directed their works

[33] For the reference to Luigi Carbone, see Fumaroli, *L'âge de l'éloquence*, 183; Sir Balthazar Gerbiers, *The Art of Well Speaking: A Lecture* (London, 1650), 5; for Jean Brèche, see Marc-René Jung, *Hercule dans la littérature française du XVIe siècle* (Geneva: Droz, 1966), 79–80.

to the *gubernatores* of the Venetian state. English authors in particular dedicated their rhetorics to noblemen who may not have been kings but who did enjoy positions of authority that allowed them to rule others: Richard Rainolde's *Foundacion of Rhetorike* of 1563 is addressed to Elizabeth's favorite, Robert Dudley; Henry Peacham's 1593 edition of his *Garden of Eloquence*, to John Puckering, Lord Keeper of the Great Seal; Charles Butler's *Rhetoricae Libri Duo* of 1598, to Thomas Egerton, Lord Keeper of the Privy Seal; and Angel Day's 1599 edition of his manual of letter writing, *The English Secretary*, to Edward de Vere, Earl of Oxford. Perhaps the most dramatic example of the tendency to see rhetoric as the art, if not the sport, of kings is provided by two treatises intended for Henri III of France: the *Rhetorique françoise faicte particulierement pour le Roy Henry 3* (French rhetoric expressly composed for King Henri III), probably written by Germain Forget in 1580–83; and Jacques Amyot's *Projet de l'Eloquence royale, composé pour Henry III, roi de France* (Project for royal eloquence, composed for Henri III, king of France).³⁴ At the start of his work, Amyot actually summons up the Tacitean thesis by noting that ancient republics gave the greatest rewards as well as the reins of government to eloquent men, whereas in monarchies, where one man rules and distributes honors and dignities as he chooses, there is generally little concern for eloquence (3). Amyot goes on, however, to declare that it ought to be sought out in monarchies nevertheless, for it is "greatly recommendable, profitable, indeed necessary to the ministers of a great king and principally to the king; and if he knows how to use it with dexterity and appropriately, he will establish, maintain, and augment his state with it, as much as or more than by any other means by which kingdoms and great signories are maintained" (4). Amyot then provides a list of rulers, including Pyrrhus and Julius Caesar, who did more by means of eloquence than by arms, and he concludes by praising the kings of Persia who spoke to the people themselves rather than through their ministers, since they knew that "the word of a King is a principal part of his power" (7).

The identification of rhetoric and politics, of orators and kings, is not restricted to rhetoric manuals and treatises in the Renaissance. It is reproduced and developed by both political theorists and literary writers as well, the latter not merely repeating the idea of an imperial rhetoric but also exploring and critiquing some of its basic aspects. Varied texts demonstrate directly that the discourse of rhetoric was not limited to just those works that self-consciously proclaimed themselves to be con-

---

³⁴ I owe the reference to Forget's work to Meerhoff, *Rhétorique et poétique*, 257.

cerned with the art but extended into other discourses which it helped
to shape and which in turn helped to shape—and often complicated—it.
Collectively, these texts give us a fuller idea of what Renaissance people
thought about the rhetoric that was so central to their culture. They
reveal that those people saw the art as regal because they recognized
what historians and critics have pointed out for some time: namely,
that monarchical rule in the period was indeed a matter of rhetoric, of
rulers' use of language and spectacle to generate and maintain the allegiance of their subjects.[35] What these texts also confirm is the important
role of the discourse of rhetoric in providing a language to shape and
define this notion of politics.

Let us start with the *Politicorum sive civilis doctrinae libri sex* (Six
books of politics or civil doctrine) of Justus Lipsius. This classic statement of political theory declares monarchy to be the preferred form of
government and, following Sallust, claims that human nature desires to
be ruled (2.2,4).[36] Men are normally wild beasts, however, who must be
tamed, and the best way to tame them is to use prudence rather than to
rely on force—prudence, of course, being the key faculty of judgment
operative in rhetoric, according to both classical and Renaissance
thinkers. Speaking here of prudence much as rhetoricians speak in their
writings of the power of eloquence, and using the image of the bridle,
which is often implied when rhetoricians talk of how the orator controls the auditor, Lipsius concludes that "in government," prudence "is
clearly the stronger, because it alone is the gentle bridle, by which those
who are free [*voluntarii*] are brought within the compass of obedience"
(3.1.46). Lipsius devotes the last of his six books to the problem of civil
war, obviously a burning issue in the Europe of the late sixteenth century, and he recommends dealing severely with factions and sedition by
any means, fair or foul. He suggests keeping people disunited, corrupt-
ing opponents with money, and, most of all, using fair words, for "it is
said that you cannot hold the wolf by the ears; but we may most easily
lead the people and whole cities by them" (6.4[186]). To draw the people
by the ears is, of course, to practice oratory, as Fray Luis de Granada
knows when he translates the same passage, which comes from Plutarch: "They say that the wolf cannot be held by the ears, but it is very

---

[35] On Renaissance rulers' use of rhetorical spectacles, see, e.g., Roy Strong, *Splendour at Court: Renaissance Spectacle and Illusion* (London: Weidenfeld & Nicolson,
1973); and Stephen Orgel, *The Illusion of Power: Political Theater in the English
Renaissance* (Berkeley: University of California Press, 1975).

[36] References are to book and chapter (and, where needed, page number) in Justus
Lipsius, *Politicorum sive civilis doctrinae libri sex*, in *Opera Omnia*, vol. 4 (Wesel,
1675).

fitting that the people be led in that way" (*Ecclesiastica Rhetorica*, 5).
For Lipsius, then, rhetoric is the art of kings; in the troubled times of
the late sixteenth century it transcends other means for maintaining the
peace of the state.

Lipsius's recognition of the importance of rhetoric for monarchical
rule is matched by that of Jean Bodin, the thinker usually considered the
chief theoretician of Renaissance absolutism.[37] Bodin could be mistaken
for one of the rhetoricians whose texts we have been citing when he
declares that "the armies and powers of kings and monarchs are not so
strong as the vehemence and ardor of an eloquent man who burns and
inflames the most cowardly to vanquish the most brave, who makes
weapons fall from the hands of the most fierce, who turns cruelty into
gentleness, barbarity into humanity, who changes states, and plays with
peoples at his pleasure."[38] Although Bodin does not retell the myth of
the orator-civilizer here, many of his phrases recall elements of it. Nevertheless, it is important to note that he does not share the positive
evaluation of the orator which most rhetoricians offer. In Bodin's view,
to practice rhetoric is to lie; among fifty orators, he says, it would be
difficult to find a single good one. In fact, he spends most of the short
section on rhetoric in his treatise recounting stories to show that eloquence, wrongly used, is "a very dangerous knife in the hand of a madman" (661). Making a final turnabout, however, Bodin states that for all
its dangers, it is the means "to bring back peoples from barbarity to
humanity: . . . to reform manners, correct laws, chastise tyrants, ban-
nish vices, maintain virtue: and just as one charms . . . serpents with
certain words, so orators charm the most savage and cruel men through
the sweetness of eloquence"; there is no better means, he concludes, to
"pacify sedition and contain subjects in obedience to their princes"
(662).

[37] On Renaissance absolutism, see Perry Anderson, *Lineages of the Absolutist State*
(London: Verso, 1974); Fritz Hartung and Roland Mousnier, "Quelques problèmes
concernant la monarchie absolue," in *Relazioni del X Congresso Internazionale di
Scienze Storiche*, vol. 4, *Storia Moderna* (Florence: Sansoni, 1955), 1–55; Ellery
Schalk, "Under the Law or Laws unto Themselves: Noble Attitudes and Absolutism
in Sixteenth- and Seventeenth-Century France," *Historical Reflections/Reflexions
Historiques* 15 (1988): 279–92; J. H. Shennan, *The Origins of the Modern European
State: 1450–1725* (London: Hutchinson Universal Library, 1974), 9–68; Donald R.
Kelley, *The Beginning of Ideology: Consciousness and Society in the French Refor-
mation* (Cambridge: Cambridge University Press, 1981), 181–99; and Skinner, *The
Foundations of Modern Political Thought*, vol. 2. For Bodin's importance, see also
Julian H. Franklin, *Jean Bodin and the Rise of Absolutist Theory* (Cambridge: Cam-
bridge University Press, 1973).

[38] Jean Bodin, *Les six Livres de la République* (Paris, 1583; rpt. Aalen: Scientia,
1961), 660; subsequent page references are included in the text.

It is particularly fitting that Bodin should come to such a conclusion, because the Renaissance conception of rhetoric as rule may be said actually to prefigure—indeed, to determine—his model of the absolutist state. One essential feature of his model is the reduction of the complex social hierarchy to a system involving just two positions, those of ruler and ruled. As Quentin Skinner has noted, the hallmark of absolutism is that everyone, noble and commoner alike, has become equally the king's subject: "The feudal pyramid of legal rights and obligations is dismantled, the king is singled out as the holder of complete *Imperium*, and all other members of society are assigned an undifferentiated legal status as his subjects."[39] The oratorical transaction, as it is described in Renaissance rhetoric texts, does not merely serve the king's interests in power but, as indicated earlier, constitutes a paradigm of rule itself, presenting an exchange that defines the subject as subject and the ruler as ruler. That paradigm, with its reduction of the social order to just two positions, is clearly the paradigm of absolutism, which was well developed in Renaissance rhetorical writings long before Bodin set pen to paper. Under the circumstances it should hardly be surprising that he would see rhetoric, despite his suspicions of it, as playing an especially important role in the state his treatise describes.

The most absolutist of monarchs agrees with Bodin about the role of rhetoric in government. Louis XIV, writing in the various *mémoires* he composed for his son, declares himself an absolute ruler, stating point-blank that "kings are absolute lords [*seigneurs absolus*] and naturally have the full and free disposition of all the goods" of their subjects.[40] Thinking of a social order reduced to just two essential positions, Louis insists that he maintains an equality of justice between himself and his subjects, keeping them "as it were in a sweet and honest society, despite the almost infinite difference [between him and them] of birth, rank, and power" (*Mémoire de 1662*, 121 [85]). Although he proclaims his right to make people submit to him by force, Louis recognizes that "it is more advantageous for him [the prince] to persuade his subjects than to constrain them" (*Mémoire de 1661*, 2.403 [86]). This rhetorical conception of rule meant for Louis not only the use of speeches and persuasive language generally but, as it did for virtually all Renaissance rulers, the necessity of making brilliant public appearances in spectacles designed to serve as propaganda. In a passage from his *Mémoire de 1662*

---

[39] Skinner, *The Foundations of Modern Political Thought*, 2:264.

[40] Louis XIV, *Mémoire de 1666*, 197, as cited in Jean-Louis Thireau, *Les idées politiques de Louis XIV* (Paris: Presses Universitaires de France, 1973), 73. Louis's works are hereafter cited in the text by title, page, and the page number from Thireau's book in brackets: e.g., *Mémoire de 1666*, 197[73].

he writes: "People . . . like spectacle, where one basically always has as one's goal pleasing them; and all our subjects in general are ravished to see that we like what they like. . . . By that [means] we hold their spirit and their heart, sometimes perhaps more strongly than by rewards and benefits" (122–23 [98]). Louis's language here is that of the rhetoric manuals with their constant insistence on the rhetor-ruler's manipulation of his subject-auditors, on his ability to hold their hearts in his hand. Louis thus demonstrates his intimate awareness of the equation between rhetoric and rule that runs through the discourse of rhetoric in the Renaissance. He knows that if he behaves as a master rhetorician, he will reign secure; more than the Sun King, he will be "the emperour of mens minds & affections, and next to the omnipotent God in the power of persuasion."

The notion that politics is a matter of rhetorical manipulation is written across the face of Machiavelli's works. His princes are creators of shows, of *spettacoli*,[41] a procedure based on the deeply rhetorical assumptions that the world is a place of appearances, that all truths are provisional and contingent, and that one can impose one's will on others by manipulating the image one projects—one's *ethos*, to use the appropriate term from Aristotle. Revealingly, Machiavelli has recourse to *colore* and *colorire* to describe princely behavior, words that can refer to "color" or "pretext" but carry with them as well the common meaning of "rhetorical ornament." Thus, in *Il principe (The Prince)*, he says that the prince must know how to *colorire* his ambitious nature by making it seem virtuous (18.73), and he praises the Roman emperor Septimus Severus as a sly fox who persuades his troops to capture Rome under the *colore* of avenging the death of the previous emperor (19.81). Indeed, Machiavelli's central injunction to the prince to be both a lion and a fox is really an injunction to *play the parts* of those two animals (18.72–73). Essentially, he sees the prince's presentation of his *ethos* as analogous to the rhetor's creation of his speeches: one uses the right ornaments, the right *colori*, the right masks in order to engage others in a rhetorical exchange that leads them to do one's bidding.

What is striking about Machiavelli's presentation of the rhetoricality of politics is the often very restricted role he assigns to language in the prince's performance. To be sure, he insists in the *Discorsi* that leaders should have the ability to use words to inspire their followers (3.33.475); he praises the great Luccan *condottiere* Castruccio Castracani for his mastery of verbal arts; and he recounts in his *Istorie fiorentine* (The

[41] *Il principe*, 7.57 and *Discorsi*, 1.15.172 in Niccolò Machiavelli, *Il principe e Discorsi*, ed. Sergio Bertelli (Milan: Feltrinelli, 1960). References to *Il principe* cite chapter and page number in this edition; those to *Discorsi* cite book, chapter, and page.

Florentine histories) a speech that Lorenzo de' Medici delivered to the Florentines, noting that Lorenzo's eloquence reduced his audience to tears.[42] Nevertheless, Machiavelli spends relatively little time detailing how his princes will acquire the art of using words. In fact, he stresses that their education will be more a matter of learning how to act the soldier than to study rhetoric, which, as part of the trivium and one of the arts of culture in general, he tends to associate with princes' loss of dominion and with the degeneration of the state (see *Istorie fiorentine*, 325). By contrast, in his comedy *La mandragola* (The mandrake root), Machiavelli has his protagonist Callimaco use language to persuade the chief dupe of the play, Nicia, to accept him as a doctor and thence to follow his advice in adopting a "cure" for the supposed sterility of Nicia's wife. Impressed by Callimaco's verbal powers at their initial meeting, Nicia shows himself the rhetor's ideal audience as he exclaims, "This is the worthiest man one can find" (2.2.71).[43] Later, Nicia uses a striking expression to declare that Callimaco has obtained from him precisely what rhetors throughout the Renaissance sought from their auditors—belief. Asked by Callimaco for his *fede*, his "faith" or "trust," Nicia responds with enthusiasm: "Go ahead and talk, for I am ready to honor you in everything and to believe in you more than in my confessor" (2.6.75). The rhetor Callimaco clearly rules his unwitting dupe by means of language, but the words he uses are Latin rather than Italian, and it is likely that Nicia simply does not understand what is being said. Thus, if he is persuaded to accept Callimaco as an authority, he does so not because the particular tropes and figures, the stylistic niceties, of Callimaco's speech persuade him to do so but simply because that speech is uttered in an exotic, prestigious—and barely comprehensible—language. Callimaco's words, in short, are almost not language at all; they are objects like articles of dress, symbolic counters constituting a rhetorical show or spectacle that impresses because of what they are, not what they mean or say.

If, for Machiavelli, the rhetoric of politics clearly extends beyond words, it is important to note that writers of rhetoric manuals and treatises also recognize a significant nonverbal element in their art. Specifically, whenever they write about *actio*, or delivery, they acknowledge that personal appearance, facial expressions, and gestures all play a role, often a decisive role, in the act of persuasion. In fact, the English rheto-

---

[42] Niccolò Machiavelli, *La vita di Castruccio Castracani*, 36–40, and *Istorie fiorentine*, 525–28. Both texts are in *Istorie fiorentine*, ed. Franco Gaeta (Milan: Feltrinelli, 1962).

[43] *La mandragola* is cited by act, scene, and page number from Niccolò Machiavelli, *Il teatro e tutti gli scritti letterari*, ed. Franco Gaeta (Milan: Feltrinelli, 1965).

rician John Bulwer, who composed an entire treatise on the use of the hand in delivery, insists that gestures are more universal and important than words in expressing the speaker's ideas, that the mouth is useless without the hand, and that by means of the latter, ancient orators "extorted approbation from their auditors, and, . . . invading the mind through the eye, with easy accesses put themselves into the possession of the people" (*Chironomia*, 160). Machiavelli does not go so far as Bulwer, but his rhetoric of politics often seems more heavily weighted in favor of the persuasive effect of appearances than most rhetorical treatises are. In one passage from the *Discorsi* he recounts how Francesco Soderini, then bishop of Volterra, stopped a mob in its tracks when they were about to sack his family's home and did so primarily by means of the splendid visual impression he created: "Having heard the noise and seen the crowd, and having put his most honorable clothes on and over them his bishop's chasuble, he approached those armed men and stopped them with his presence and his words" (1.54.253). Words do have a place in this scene, but they come *after* the bishop's careful, actorlike preparation of the show he puts on. Perhaps the extreme example of a persuasive princely spectacle that completely privileges the eye over the ear is the one involving Cesare Borgia's lieutenant, Remirro de Orco, who is betrayed and executed by his master. Machiavelli writes: "He [Borgia] had him placed one morning in two pieces in the piazza at Cesena, with a piece of wood and a bloody knife beside him. The ferocity of that spectacle made the people at the same time both satisfied and astounded" (*Il principe*, 7.37). The silent spectacle arranged by Borgia is gripping, powerfully persuasive, and full of meaning for both the citizens of Cesena and the readers of Machiavelli's text. It is an example of a rhetoric that has transcended its very nature by leaving behind any association with language whatsoever.[44]

Shakespeare shares a similarly enlarged view of rhetoric which goes beyond that of the rhetoricians to stress the enormously persuasive force of visual displays, for his Machiavellian kings and princes also know that silent spectacles can often accomplish as much as a torrent of words. Richard III, for instance, works on the lord mayor and citizens of London by appearing before them silently reading a prayerbook between two bishops (*Richard III*, 3.7). Even more striking is Henry IV's decision to parade his army back and forth in front of Flint castle: "Let's march without the noise of threat'ning drum, / That from this castle's tottered battlements / Our fair appointments may be well perus'd"

---

[44] For a fuller account of this spectacle, see Wayne A. Rebhorn, *Foxes and Lions: Machiavelli's Confidence Men* (Ithaca: Cornell University Press, 1988), chap. 3. For Machiavelli's rhetorical manipulation of his readers, see chap. 5.

(*Richard II*, 3.3.51–53).[45] As Henry goes on to say, his ostensible purpose is to avoid appearing to threaten King Richard, although that, in fact, is just what such a show of force is designed to do. A show that *persuades* without any need for words at all, it is far more powerful than the nonexistent legion of troops that Richard earlier insisted the king's *name* alone could call forth to fight on his side (*Richard II*, 3.2.85–88). Henry's tactic thus confirms what the episode concerning Cesare Borgia and Remirro de Orco suggests: although words may be an important source of a ruler's hold over his people, the silent display of physical force often constitutes a far more potent rhetoric. *Richard II* dramatizes the way that, in the arena of power politics, a calculating awareness of the rhetorical nature of the game being played is essential for success. Ironically, the voluble Richard is defeated in part precisely because he believes in language. Specifically, he believes in the magic of words, but that magic, although creating a wonderful spectacle for everyone watching it, is not directed at persuasion. For Richard, language is a ritual performance rather than a battlefield maneuver or an instrument of conquest and rule. By contrast, the laconic Henry recognizes that if he is to maintain his "name," he must defend it by the rhetorical manipulation of the world, including, of course, the rhetorical manipulation involved in staging silent spectacles of force.

That Henry sees politics in terms of rhetoric is made clear in the climactic scene of *Henry IV, Part 1* (3.2), during which he is reunited and reconciled with the supposedly prodigal Hal. In this scene Henry accuses his son of many failings, including a failure to understand the nature of politics. To explain what he means, Henry offers his own behavior as a model, and as he does so, he elaborates a decidedly rhetorical theory of kingship. He tells Hal how he manipulated "Opinion" (3.2.43) by appearing only occasionally in public.

> By being seldom seen, I could not stir
> But like a comet I was wond'red at,
> That men would tell their children, "This is he!"
> Others would say, "Where, which is Bolingbroke?"
> And then I stole all courtesy from heaven,
> And dress'd myself in such humility
> That I did pluck allegiance from men's hearts,
> Loud shouts and salutations from their mouths,
> Even in the presence of the crowned King.
> Thus did I keep my person fresh and new,

[45] All quotations from Shakespeare's plays cite act, scene, and line from *The Complete Works*, ed. David Bevington, 3d ed. (Glenview, Ill.: Scott, Foresman, 1951).

> My presence, like a robe pontifical,
> Ne'er seen but wond'red at.
>
> (3.2.46–57)

In this theory Henry, like the rhetoricians, assumes that the realm of politics is the realm of custom and contingency, where "Opinion" rather than inherited rights, let alone truth, determines who will be king. This is a realm in which, as Henry imagines it, *sight* is the chief sense: one's "presence" affects the "eyes of men" and must be shaped so that it produces wonder as a response. Indeed, Henry's language makes the king a showman and an actor: he *dresses* himself in humility, maintains the newness of his *person*—that is, his *mask* (*persona* in Latin)—and identifies his *presence* as a "robe pontifical." Renaissance rhetoricians normally equate the ornaments of style with clothing, so that when Henry employs such terms to talk about his personal appearance, he is, in effect, treating it as something that can be turned into a trope. In Henry's theory of rhetorical kingship, personal appearance thus constitutes a compelling means of persuasion.

What is striking in Henry's theory is what is omitted: he says absolutely nothing about *words*. The king's performance, like Richard III's silent reading and the dead body of Remirro de Orco, convinces without the benefit of language. Henry's king operates on the world from a great symbolic distance, no matter how close he may literally come to the crowds that turn out to cheer him. Henry himself knew how to put his theory into practice, at least if one is to accept York's account in *Richard II* of Henry's performance upon his entry into London after the deposition of Richard.

> Then, as I said, the Duke, great Bolingbroke,
> Mounted upon a hot and fiery steed
> Which his aspiring rider seem'd to know,
> With slow but stately pace kept on his course,
> Whilst all tongues cried, "God save thee, Bolingbroke!"
> You would have thought the very windows spake,
> So many greedy looks of young and old
> Through casements darted their desiring eyes
> Upon his visage, . . .
> Whilst he, from the one side to the other turning,
> Bareheaded, lower than his proud steed's neck,
> Bespake them thus: "I thank you, countrymen."
>
> (*Richard II*, 5.2.7–15, 18–20)

In York's speech, as in Henry's own theory, the emphasis falls on the visual spectacle the king creates, on the "greedy looks," the "desiring eyes" of the crowd, as well as on the actorlike (see 5.2.23–24) demeanor and gestures of Bolingbroke. York finally notes that the latter did speak, but what he says hardly counts as much of a rhetorical display; Bolingbroke's "thank you" is just a tiny note in the great visual show he has been orchestrating.

The end such a show aims to bring about is spelled out quite precisely by Henry in his speech to Hal: he wants to *persuade* the people to transfer their loyalty from Richard to him. Although Henry never once utters the word "persuasion," he does employ a phrase that recalls the highly charged language used by Renaissance rhetoricians to define the orator's goal: they conceived persuasion as a violent act, an invasion, conquest and possession of the auditor which works on him in the most intimate way imaginable. Henry repeats this notion when he proclaims that he "did pluck allegiance from men's hearts, / Loud shouts and salutations from their mouths." For Henry, persuasion affects the very organ that Renaissance rhetoricians singled out as well. Consider Bartholomew Keckermann, for example, who declares: "The orator especially looks to the heart [*cor*] that he may excite and move it with varied emotions" (*Systema*, 4). That such affecting of the heart amounts to a violent assault on it is clear not only from the general insistence on the ideas of invasion and conquest running through the Renaissance discourse of rhetoric but from specific passages such as the following one from Nicholas Caussin's *De Eloquentia sacra et humana*: "The entire force of persuasion is carried by emotion as by a vehicle and penetrates hearts [*permeat in pectora*]" (3). Henry presents his own rhetoric as having just such a devastating effect on those exposed to it. But there is a difference: whereas the rhetoricians all talk about the power of words, Henry's theory defines a sheerly visual assault. Ironically, the success of that silent spectacle is underscored precisely by the fact that it makes the crowd speak, makes them shout and cheer and ask with wonder "Where, which is Bolingbroke?"

Unlike his father, Hal is a talker. From his experiences in the tavern with Falstaff and his cronies, Hal has learned to "drink with any tinker in his own language" (*Henry IV, Part 1*, 2.4.18–19), a sentiment with which the Earl of Warwick later concurs when he reassures the sick and dying Henry that the "Prince but studies his companions / Like a strange tongue" (*Henry IV, Part 2*, 4.4.68–69). Fittingly, Hal is the only character in the *Henriad* who can move freely through all locales, a physical freedom doubled by the linguistic virtuosity that allows him to jest with Falstaff, utter high-sounding, martial sentiments on the battlefield like Hotspur and Douglas, and talk the language of Machiavellian political calculation with his father. Such linguistic skill would by itself tend to identify Hal as a version of the ideal orator as the Renaissance conceived the figure: someone capable of handling any audience by adapting his performance to the circumstances involved, the master of figures and tropes and of all styles, high, middle, and low. Shakespeare makes Hal's identification with the orator quite explicit in *Henry V* by having him deliver speech after speech, from the tennis ball rebuff of the French ambassadors in Act 1, through the Saint Crispin's Day oration before Agincourt, to the wooing of Katherine at the play's end. These speeches vary in style from regal, ironic, and angry, through martial and uplifting, to the simplicity and directness of a "plain soldier" (5.2.151). Like his father, Hal clearly regards kingship as a matter of staging spectacles, of performing a public role, but unlike Henry he sees that role not only as centrally concerned with words but as far more various and nuanced than the distanced behavior, the "sun-like majesty" (*Henry IV, Part 1*, 3.2.79), that Henry recommends.

Hal's virtuosity with language elevates him above his father when they are judged from the viewpoint of tactics: that is, from the viewpoint of their success in manipulating other human beings. Or, at least, that is what the great reconciliation scene between Henry and Hal in the middle of *Henry IV, Part 1* suggests, as the prince, in the short space of just thirty-one lines, is able to shift his father's opinion of him 180 degrees. Shakespeare constructs the scene to give Henry the lion's share of the dialogue, in fact to turn it into a virtual monologue; he rebukes Hal for almost ninety lines before giving him a real opportunity to reply. In those ninety lines Henry details his theory of kingship, then attacks Hal for behaving like Richard and running the risk of losing the crown, and finally comes to the bitter conclusion that Hal is likely to fight against him on Hotspur's side. Hal's reply is masterly. He affirms his love for his father, promises to compensate for his youthful misdeeds, and vows to defeat Hotspur or die in the attempt. The effect on Henry is dramatic as he completely reverses his earlier estimate of his son: "A hundred thousand rebels die in this! / Thou shalt have charge and sovereign trust herein" (3.2.158–59). Hal's persuasive words gain what persuasion always seeks to gain according to the rhetoricians: belief, the transformation or conversion of the auditor, as Henry himself suggests when he speaks of "sovereign trust."

What provokes this sudden conversion is less *what* Hal says than *how* he says it, for he both echoes the concepts and style of Henry's theory of kingship and matches the emotional intensity of Henry's denunciation. Hal begins by insisting upon his relationship to Henry, promising to demonstrate publicly that "I am your son" (3.2.134) and that he will redeem the reputation of "*your* unthought-of Harry" (141; emphasis added). But Hal demonstrates that he is his father's child most dramatically through his diction, for no sooner has he promised to avenge himself on Hotspur than he declares: "I will wear a garment all of blood / And stain my favors in a bloody mask, / Which, wash'd away, shall scour my shame with it" (135–37). Here Hal deliberately echoes his father's presentation of politics as rhetorical performance, a matter of dress if not a masquerade, which sometimes requires one to put on the cloak of humility, as Henry did in entering London, and sometimes to don the armor of the battlefield hero, as Hal promises to do. Later, Hal adopts the tones Henry employed earlier in the scene, mingling the martial bravado Henry seemed to admire in Hotspur with the tone of contempt that Henry, the powerful and cunning rhetorician, manifested toward the hapless victims of the spectacles he created. Thus, Hal proclaims: "Percy is but my factor, good my lord, / To engross up glorious deeds on my behalf; / And I will call him to so strict account / That he shall render every glory up, / Yea, even the slightest worship of his time, / Or I will tear the reckoning from his heart" (147–52). Hal's boastfulness and vehemence here respond to the image of Hotspur the warrior, the "Mars in swathling clothes" (112), whom Henry seemed to admire just a few lines earlier. At the same time, Hal turns the heroic Hotspur into a figure of contempt, reducing him to a mere "factor," a merchant's agent, who works unwittingly for Hal's benefit (Henry, of course, saw the public, the king's subjects, as just so many contemptible dupes). Hal's promise to defeat Hotspur ends with an image central to Henry's theory of kingship, the image of the heart. Just as Henry bragged of being able to "pluck allegiance from men's hearts" (52), so Hal declares, literalizing the image, that he will "tear the reckoning from his [Percy's] heart" (152) in mortal combat. Imitation—in this case, a carefully calculated imitation—is the sincerest form of flattery, and in consequence, Henry, who is aching to be reassured of the love and devotion of his son, immediately banishes all doubts and proclaims his complete trust in Hal. What the latter has done is to exercise a form of rhetorical kingship—and to succeed with it against his father!

By conflating the tones of heroic bragging and kingly contempt in his speech, Hal actually does more than merely echo his father, however; he subtly corrects him. Henry has a double and partially incorrect view of Hotspur's character. Although he rightly sees Hotspur as a figure out of epic, he is wrong when, in predicting that Hal will become another Richard, he assigns to Hotspur his own role of cunning, kingly rhetorician. The play makes clear that Hotspur is totally unlike the crafty

Henry; indeed, with his volubility and almost magical belief in language, he seems far closer to Richard than to his Machiavellian adversary. Hal recognizes that his father is mistaken about Hotspur, and while he does duplicate Henry's tone of admiration for Hotspur as martial hero, he simultaneously treats Hotspur to the kind of contempt Henry reserved for Richard as well as for the public. In this way, not only does Hal undercut Henry's admiration for Hotspur as a heroic figure, but he recasts the parts Henry assigned Hotspur and himself, identifying Hotspur as a Richard figure and himself, as we have noted, with Henry. Although such a move clearly flatters Henry, it also constitutes an implicit rebuke, a suggestion that the clever, supposedly clear-eyed king is not so clear-eyed after all. In doing so, it also confirms for us what Henry's conversion confirms in other ways: Hal, not his father, is the real master of rhetorical kingship.

Hal's performances can be read as virtual reproductions of the notion from the Renaissance discourse of rhetoric that eloquence is power. In particular, Shakespeare constructs *Henry V* so that Hal's famous victories seem to result from his command of language even more than from his personal bravery and mastery of tactics—not to mention the technical superiority given the English by the long bow and the good fortune that made the battlefield at Agincourt a quagmire for the heavily armored French knights on horseback. Fluellen and his comrades may debate whether Hal's operations at Harfleur are done "according to the disciplines of the war" (3.2.58), but the play makes such considerations seem almost irrelevant. For Hal appears to maintain the siege not by strategical maneuvers but by the compelling speech that forces his men "unto the breach" and urges them to match their fathers, to be heroes "like so many Alexanders" (3.2.1, 19). In fact, he wins the victory in this case, as Henry IV won his over Richard, not by defeating his opponent in battle but by using rhetoric to persuade him to surrender. Moreover, although the great battle of Agincourt constitutes a genuine military victory, Shakespeare shapes his play to make it seem due to Hal's rhetorical masterpiece, the Saint Crispin's Day speech, as much as to battlefield heroics. For after the speech what we see is a French soldier surrendering to Pistol; the French commanders lamenting that all is lost; Hal instructing his troops to kill their prisoners; and finally, Hal learning from Montjoy that the English have in fact been victorious. What the audience does not see, at least according to Shakespeare's text, is any sort of battle, such as the fighting at Shrewsbury we were treated to in *Henry IV, Part 1*. That Hal actually did participate in that battle and defeat Hotspur shows that he is not all talk, but what *Henry V* suggests is that talk is mostly what he needs.

And indeed, the play ends with one final, stunning rhetorical performance on Hal's part, the performance by means of which he woos Katherine of France by playing the clearly false role of plain, blunt soldier. His rhetorical move here is to adopt a consciously anti-rhetorical posture that enables him to project an *ethos* of sincerity and to dramatize the presumably genuine affection he feels for his future bride. Of course, the play reveals that she really has no choice but to marry the victor of Agincourt, a fact to which Hal himself alludes in passing (5.2.249–50). What Hal accomplishes with his rhetoric is precisely what Renaissance rhetors all wanted to accomplish with theirs: by using persuasion as a kind of force superior to actual force, he brings his auditor to subject herself to him of her own free will, to believe in his arguments and in him, ultimately to love the one who commands her destiny.

Although Hal's virtuosity with language makes him superior to his father as a rhetor-ruler, and *Henry V* can be read at least in part as a celebration of his verbal mastery, Shakespeare does not let the matter rest at this point. In other words, he does not simply reproduce (with elaborations and extensions) the equation of rhetoric with power and rule which one can find in Renaissance handbooks and treatises. After all, both Henry and Hal also possess real force, whether one identifies that as personal prowess on the battlefield, an army under their command, or the legal power and authority granted by a treaty in which the French king agrees to give his daughter to Hal in marriage. Rhetorical displays of spectacular images and words may enable a ruler to terrorize his enemies and gain the allegiance of his subjects, but those displays are always, finally, connected to that ruler's possession of genuine force. In the end, for all that Shakespeare makes rhetoric alone appear to guarantee the famous victories of the English in France, he never lets us forget that other forces are also at work, forces that have nothing to do with rhetoric at all. The *Henriad* may stage the triumph of eloquence in many different ways, but it stubbornly refuses to allow eloquence to have the last word.

If the political conception of rhetoric as rule in the Renaissance is extended—and even critiqued to some extent—in the discourses of politics and, especially, literature, it also has a special relationship with another discourse: the discourse of mythography, which appears in mythological fables, iconographical collections, pictures and illustrations, and emblem books. This discourse provides rhetoric with pictorial images that represent its essentially political character and, in some instances, go well beyond the discourse of rhetoric in critiquing some of its most compelling political claims. For even as some images strive to represent the irresistible power of rhetoric, they can be read simultaneously in ways that undercut that notion. Contrived to body forth the deepest fantasy the Renaissance entertained about the art, the representations they make of it suggest that that fantasy may be just wishful thinking.

From antiquity through the Renaissance several standard figures are used to represent rhetoric. One of the most significant is Lady Rhetoric, the *domina*, a figure that had various forms in the ancient world and was elaborated by Martianus Capella in his allegory of the seven liberal arts, the *De nuptiis Philologiae et Mercurii* (On the marriage of philology and mercury), a work that codified the iconography of the arts right down to the Renaissance.[46] As she appears in frescoes and tapestries and even on playing cards, Lady Rhetoric usually wears a dress covered with flowers ("flowers" are, of course, figures of speech) and is given other attributes that identify her as a queen or a great court lady. Sometimes she holds a dagger or sword and a rod, implements that indicate both the force of rhetoric and its elevated social status. In his *Iconologia* published in Rome in 1603, for instance, Cesare Ripa describes no fewer than three different images of Eloquenza, as well as two of Rettorica and one of Persuasione, all of whom are female and are associated with force and dominance. One of the images of Eloquenza in particular reveals the special emphasis the Renaissance gave to rhetoric: "A beautiful young woman with her breast armored and her arms bare will have on her head a helmet surrounded by a crown of gold and at her flank a staff, in her right hand a rod, in her left a lightning bolt, and she will be dressed in purple." Ripa allegorizes these attributes, relating her being armed to the forcefulness of her persuasive ability, and the implements she carries and her clothing to aspects of style. Finally, he underscores the political nature of rhetoric when he discusses the color of her dress as a sign that "she holds dominion over human spirits, it being the case that, as Plato says in Pol. [*The Republic?*], *Oratorical dignity is conjoined with regal dignity since it persuades what is just and thereby governs Republics.*" Ripa later reinforces this notion by describing the scepter held by one of the images of Rettorica as "a sign that rhetoric is queen of people's spirits, and spurs them on, reins them in, and bends them in that way which pleases her most."[47] One last example: the title page of J. Du Pré de la Porte's *Pourtraict de l'Eloquence Françoise* features the

[46] My discussion of Lady Rhetoric in this paragraph is based on Samuel C. Chew, *The Pilgrimage of Life* (New Haven: Yale University Press, 1962), 196–98; and Plett, *Rhetorik der Affekte*, 144–52.

[47] Cesare Ripa, *Iconologia* (Rome, 1603), 126, 127, 433.

statue of the goddess of eloquence who is crowned and seated on a throne; she has the scepter of Saint Louis at her feet, while two famous contemporary orators, the Duc de Longueville and Guillaume Du Vair, stand at either side slightly beneath her. To emphasize the notion that rhetoric means rule, not only has the artist responsible for this illustration, Michel Lasne, identified it with the French monarchy and with representatives of the *Noblesse de l'Epée* (Longueville) and the *Noblesse de la Robe* (Du Vair), but he stresses the issue of *service* by depicting little angels above the head of Eloquence with a banner reading "Il fait bon la servir" (It is good to serve her) and by placing another banner behind her head reading "Je ne tiens mes sujets qu'aux gages de l'honneur" (I use only the wages of honor to hold my subjects).[48] If rhetoric is represented as a queen throughout the Middle Ages, in the Renaissance that image is taken very seriously indeed.

The Renaissance also had available to it from antiquity and the Middle Ages various male deities that could be used to represent rhetoric. Orpheus and Amphion, each credited with being the father of poetry, are sometimes assigned to rhetoric, although both play a distinctly secondary role to the classical messenger of the gods, Mercury.[49] In the Renaissance, that god frequently appears on title pages to works of rhetoric, music, and poetry, and humanist mythographers take pains to identify him specifically as the god of eloquence. Gabriel Harvey's *Rhetor* (London, 1577), for instance, has a caduceus held by a pair of hands on its title page and identifies Mercury firmly as the *Deus eloquentiae*. In his emblem book, Johannes Sambucus equates Mercury with the "force of speech," and Claude Mignault, in his commentary on Andrea Alciati's *Emblemata*, labels him the "lord of speech." Even more in keeping with the Renaissance identification of rhetoric as rule, the mythographer Giovanni Piero Valeriano characterizes the caduceus Mercury carries as the means by which he "rules spirits by means of words," *regat dictis animos*. Revealingly, another mythographer, Vincenzo Cartari, recounts how Jupiter, at the bidding of Prometheus, sent Mercury to earth in order to teach men eloquence "so that they, once instructed, might persuade others to live a civil and social existence."[50]

---

[48] My attention was first drawn to this illustration by Marc Fumaroli's comments on it in his "Réflexions sur quelques frontispices gravés d'ouvrages de rhétorique et d'éloquence (1594–1641)," *Bulletin de la Société de l'Histoire et de l'Art Français* 101 (1975):28–29.

[49] For Orpheus, Amphion, and Mercury, see Plett, *Rhetorik der Affekte*, 166–70, 172–81.

[50] Johannes Sambucus, *Emblemata* (Antwerp, 1566), 111; Andrea Alciati, *Emblemata*, 4th ed., commentary Claude Mignault (Leiden, 1591), 359; Giovanni Piero Valeriano, *Hieroglyphica* (Leiden, 1579), 116; and Vincenzo Cartari, *Imagines Deorum*,

A similar version of the myth of the orator-civilizer is also told by Nicholas Caussin (*Eloquentia sacra*, 7). Finally, if we extend our analysis into literary works again, we may note that Christopher Marlowe identifies his conqueror Tamburlaine with Hermes, thereby underscoring the fact that his hero achieves as much by his eloquence as by his sword.[51]

Both Lady Rhetoric and Mercury were well known in the Renaissance. By a stroke of luck, however, the period acquired yet another and even more suitable mythological figure to represent its conception of rhetoric as power and rule when, in 1496, a complete edition in Greek of Lucian's works was published in Florence. The figure found there was Hercules or, to be more precise, the so-called Hercules Gallicus, who is described in the *Herakles*—a text which, like the rest of Lucian's works, had been unknown in western Europe from antiquity until that time. According to Lucian's account, there was a depiction of Hercules in a temple at Marseille in which he was identified with Mercury, the god of eloquence, and represented as leading his followers by means of slender chains of gold and amber connecting his tongue to their ears. This text was translated into Latin by Erasmus in 1506 and by the French humanist Guillaume Budé in 1508, and together they gave the figure a wide exposure in European culture, an exposure made all the wider when Geoffroy Tory translated Erasmus's Latin into French in 1529. Because this was the *Gallic* Hercules, it appealed especially to the French, who sometimes conflated it with the Lybian Hercules supposedly responsible for the founding of France and used it in celebrations of their monarchy. As a result, the Hercules Gallicus became a symbol of both inspired eloquence and political power, and, according to Marc-René Jung, it seems to have been known nationwide toward the middle of the sixteenth century. Nor was knowledge of it restricted to France. In the first place, representations of Hercules appeared in French festivals that foreigners attended. When Charles V, for example, came to Paris in 1539–40, the city erected a giant statue of Hercules, and the poem attached to it compared Charles to the Lybian Hercules, who relied on the force of arms, while François I was labeled the Hercules Gallicus, who used eloquence to achieve the willing obedience of his subjects.[52] More impor-

---

Qui Ab Antiquis Colebantur (Leiden, 1581), 219–20, cited in Plett, *Rhetorik der Affekte*, 169.

[51] Christopher Marlowe, *Tamburlaine, Part One*, 1.2.209–10, in *The Complete Plays*, ed. Irving Ribner (New York: Odyssey Press, 1963).

[52] On the Hercules Gallicus, see Plett, *Rhetorik der Affekte*, 166–73; Robert G. Hallowell, "L'Hercule gallique: Expression et image politique," in *Lumières de la Pléiade* (Paris: Vrin, 1966), 243–53; Edgar Wind, "'Hercules' and 'Orpheus': Two Mock-Heroic Designs by Dürer," *Journal of the Warburg Institute* 2 (1938–39): 206–18; and Jung, *Hercule dans la littérature française*, esp. 80.

tant for the European diffusion of the image, however, were illustrations in mythological collections and emblem books. These are worth pausing over a moment.

The wellspring of images of the Hercules Gallicus is the collection of emblems produced by Andrea Alciati, which first appeared in Latin in 1531 in Augsburg and was reissued and translated many times after that. In his collection Alciati includes a graphic rendering of the figure accompanied by a poem and captioned "Eloquentia fortitudine praestantior" (Eloquence is more efficacious than force). In the Paris edition of 1534 and the Padua edition of 1621 for instance, Hercules is depicted wearing his traditional lion skin (from his conquest of the Nemean lion) and holding a club and a bow, but leading others by means of a set of chains extending from his mouth to their ears (see Figures 1 and 2). Stressing the difference from the more conventional Hercules, the accompanying poem asks initially whether this figure seems like him ("Herculis haec igitur facies?"), because he is old and has his tongue pierced by chains. It then answers its own question: "Is it not because the Gauls say Hercules, excelling by means of his tongue, not his strength, gave laws to the peoples? Arms yield to the toga [of peace], and he who is strong in speech draws even the hardest hearts to his wishes."[53] The association here of Hercules with the force of eloquence rather than with that of arms is seconded in Alciati's collection by the particular inflection it gives to another emblem: "Duodecim certamina Herculis" (The twelve labors of Hercules). For the poem accompanying that emblem downplays Hercules' physical prowess in general and stresses instead his intellectual qualities and his eloquence. In fact, as it opens, it allegorizes his first two labors specifically in ways that link him to rhetoric: it declares that the first one represents the triumph of eloquence (*facundia*) over unconquered strength (the Nemean lion) and the second, the defeat of sophistry (the Hydra).[54] Revealingly, commenting on this emblem in the Leiden edition of Alciati's work from 1591, Claude Mignault conflates the Hercules of the twelve labors with the Hercules Gallicus, stressing the superiority of words to swords just as most rhetoricians did. This Hercules, he says, possessed both prudence and eloquence and "triumphed over all the greatest difficulties by means of the dexterity of his genius, something which all of Greece, lying like anything, preferred to turn into the glory of arms" (503).

Sometimes the emblem of the Hercules Gallicus is read as merely

---

[53] Andrea Alciati, *Emblemata*, ed. Christian Wechel (Paris, 1534), 81.

[54] Andrea Alciati, *Emblemata* (Venice, 1546), 15ʳ. This emblem is summarized in a later, Latin-French edition: "By Hercules (who was a magnanimous and eloquent man) is signified virtuous eloquence together with wisdom" (Andrea Alciati, *Emblemes en Latin et Francois* [Paris, 1574], 202).

Eloquentia fortitudine præstantior.

Arcum læua tenet,rigidam fert dextera clauam,
  Contegit & Nemees corpora nuda leo.
Herculis hæc igitur facies?non conuenit illud
  Quòd uetus & senio tempora cana gerit.
Quid quod lingua illi leuibus traiecta cathenis,
  Queis fissa facili allicit aure uiros?
An ne quòd Alciden lingua non robore Galli
  Preſtantem populis iura dediſſe ferunt?
Cedunt arma togæ,& quamuis duriſſima corda
  Eloquio pollens ad sua uota trahit.

1. "Eloquentia fortitudine praestantior." From Andrea Alciati, *Emblemata* (Augsburg, 1531), 97. (Courtesy of the Harry Ransom Humanities Research Center of the University of Texas at Austin)

2. Hercules Gallicus. From Andrea Alciati, *Emblemata* (Padua, 1621), 751.
(Courtesy of the Harry Ransom Humanities Research Center of the University of Texas at Austin)

indicating the force of eloquence, as it is by Filippo Picinelli and Gio-vanni Piero Valeriano.[55] In the 1628 Padua edition of Vincenzo Cartari's *Imagini de gli Dei delli Antichi* (Images of the ancient gods), for in-stance, he is identified as the "God of eloquence and of the military" (*Dio della eloquenza, & dell'essercitio*), and the image is said to denote "force and military discipline" (283).[56] By contrast, a late sixteenth-cen-tury French edition of Alciati's collection identifies the Hercules Gal-licus as a ruler, interpreting the emblem to mean that "Hercules had placed so many people under his obedience."[57] An implicit equation of Hercules with the ruler can also be found in the passage from the 1534 edition of Alciati, quoted above, in which he is credited with giving laws to the nations and is thus presented as a version of the orator-civilizer who leads people out of savagery. This is precisely one of the interpretations Claude Mignault offers of the emblem in the French edi-tion of 1591: "Hercules, excelling in eloquence and force, led the Gauls, once dissipated and wild, to justice and a tamer life by the force of his living eloquence" (632). More significant for the thesis I have been argu-ing concerning Renaissance rhetoric is the illustration that appears in the 1574 edition of Achille Bocchi's *Symbolicarum quaestionum libri* (Books of symbolic questions). This image, the forty-third symbol of Bocchi's second book, is rather wittily entitled: "HIC HERCULES EST GAL-LICUS: INTELLEGAT, QUI AURES HABET" ("Here is Hercules Gallicus: Let him understand who has ears") (see Figure 3).[58] What is striking about the image, however, is not its title but the manner in which Hercules is represented. He has on the traditional lion skin and holds his club, but instead of standing and leading his followers, he is seated atop a cart that is pulled by two oxen ridden by two naked boys whose ears are attached with chains to Hercules' tongue. The cart may also be pulled by the host of men who walk on both sides of it and whose ears are likewise connected to Hercules' tongue by means of chains. Here the image of Hercules may be read as that of a conqueror, the cart being a triumphal wagon, a reading the accompanying poem would seem to sup-port: "He sits in a lofty chariot, and triumphing over the huge crowd of men, he drags them away, conquered, by their ears" (xciiii). The image also allows us, however, to see it as that of a ruler sitting on his throne, transported by his subjects—and it must be remembered in this context

[55] Filippo Picinelli, *Mundus Symbolicus* (Cologne, 1687), 158; and Giovannia Piero Valeriano, *Hieroglyphica*, 239.
[56] Cartari is cited in Plett, *Rhetorik der Affekte*, illus. 4.
[57] Alciati, *Emblemes en Latin et Francois*, 272.
[58] Achille Bocchi, *Symbolicarum quaestionum, de universo genere, quos serio ludebat, libri quinque* (Bologna, 1574), xcii.

HIC HERCVLES EST GALLICVS:
INTELLEGAT, QVI AVRES HABET.

Symb. XLIII.

3. "HIC HERCULES EST GALLICUS." From Achille Bocchi, *Symbolicarum Quaestionum . . . Libri quinque* (Bologna, 1574), bk. 2, symbol 43. (Courtesy of the Harry Ransom Humanities Research Center of the University of Texas at Austin)

that actual rulers in the Renaissance often saw themselves as conquerors and sometimes staged entries into the cities of their realms on just such triumphal carts. In this view, the image can be seen as capturing with dramatic force the exact notion of rhetoric as rule defined by Renaissance rhetoric texts, for not only does it show Hercules controlling his followers by means of his eloquence, which appears so powerful that the club he holds is rendered irrelevant, but it also represents the idea of hierarchy, since Hercules is placed well *above* his followers. Most strikingly, it renders visual a familiar image for subjection from the rhetoric books: it allows the reader to equate Hercules' followers with the oxen, who are *yoked* together as they pull the cart behind them.

The tremendous diffusion of the image of the Hercules Gallicus in France, which has been well documented by historians, explains why writers there would invoke him repeatedly. He appears, for instance, in political works by Jean Brèche (1544) and Jean Le Blond (1546), in a mid-sixteenth-century poem by Mellin de Saint-Gelais, and in Robert Garnier's "Au Roy de France et de Pologne" (To the King of France and Poland).[59] The image had become so commonplace late in the century that Jacques Amyot is content simply to allude to it in his *Projet de l'Eloquence royale*. After invoking a series of kings who relied on eloquence in order to rule and asserting that a king's word is a principal part of his power, Amyot declares: "I will not mention here our famous Hercules Gallicus whom the people followed drawn by the cord from his tongue" (7). It is precisely this figure of whom Jean Bodin thinks when he contemplates the problem of sedition in *Les Six Livres de la République*, a problem which he feels has been caused by the eloquence of *harangueurs*: "For there is nothing which has more force over souls than the grace of speaking well: as our ancient fathers figured the Celtic Hercules as an old man who dragged the people after him, chained and led by the ears with chains which came out of his mouth, to show that the armies and power of kings and monarchs are not so strong as the vehemence and ardor of an eloquent man" (660).

That Hercules was not on the minds only of French thinkers, however, George Puttenham's *Arte of English Poesie* makes abundantly clear. To buttress his contention that eloquence is "violent and forcible," he cites the "pretie devise or embleme" of Lucian's Hercules: "a lustie old man with a long chayne tyed by one end at his tong, by the other end at the peoples eares, who stood a farre of and seemed to be

---

[59] Jung, *Hercule dans la littérature française*, 79–81, 168. Jung provides many other references as well.

drawen to him by the force of that chayne fastned to his tong, as who would say, by force of his perswasions" (154). Puttenham then goes on to stress the fact that Hercules is an old man, thus linking eloquence to experience and wisdom rather than to the physical force of youth. By contrast, Thomas Wilson emphasizes not the orator's age and wisdom but the supreme control he exercises over others. The "power of Eloquence," he writes, is so great "that most men are forced, even to yeeld in that which most standeth against their will. And therefore the Poets doe feine, that *Hercules* beeing a man of great wisedome, had all men lincked together by the eares in a chaine, to drawe them and leade them even as he lusted. For his witte was so great, his tongue so eloquent, and his experience such, that no one man was able to withstande his reason, but every one was rather driven to doe that which he would, and to will that which he did" (*Arte,* vii^r). No matter where the stress falls, however, the Hercules of Puttenham and Wilson is a conqueror and a ruler over the people who are "led" and "drawne" and "driven" to act by his eloquence, even against their own desires. Finally, in his *Third Prolusion,* John Milton alludes to the Hercules Gallicus as he asserts the supreme power of rhetoric, which "so ensnares men's minds and so sweetly lures them with her chains that at one moment she can move them to pity, at another she can drive them to hatred, at another she can fire them with warlike passion, and at another lift them up to contempt of death itself."[60]

As rhetoricians and political thinkers utilize the figure of Hercules, they invariably stress one single theme: the power of rhetoric to rule people. But even though mythographers, the writers of emblem books, and the producers of festivals all attempted to restrict interpretation thus, their task was made complicated by the fact that they worked with a visual representation joined to a verbal description, rather than with a verbal description alone. A picture is not only worth a thousand words but often produces in the minds and mouths of onlookers words that run counter to everything the image maker intended.[61] Thus, in 1549, Henri II made a triumphal entry into Paris and was represented as Hercules leading the four estates by chains attached to their ears. The official, written proclamation addressed him as you "who, without mace, beat down vices, true monsters, and lead rebels back to obe-

[60] In John Milton, *Complete Poems and Major Prose,* ed. Merritt Y. Hughes (New York: Odyssey Press, 1957), 605.
[61] On the possible ambivalence of response to illustrations in the Renaissance, see David Kunzle, "World Upside Down: The Iconography of a European Broadsheet Type," in *The Reversible World,* ed. Barbara A. Babcock (Ithaca: Cornell University Press, 1978), 39–94.

dience"; however, the appropriately named imperial agent Simon Renard reported that the Parisians varied the interpretation considerably by saying that the image showed "that the king was eating the four estates."[62] In the minds of at least some on-lookers, a picture that is supposed to celebrate imperial rule can thus turn into one of depredation and internal colonization and serve to provoke, or at least give form to, popular discontent.

The image of the chain stretching between Hercules' tongue and the ears of his followers can be given yet further twists. It can, for instance, be taken not as an indication of Hercules' dominance but as a sign of linkage, of mutual attachment, between the hero and his people, an indication that neither Hercules nor his subjects can maintain their positions and identities independent of one another. Or, carrying such an interpretation even further, in a move that goes against the grain of most rhetoricians' pronouncements, one can read the chain as signifying the fundamental and necessary dependence of the ruler upon the ruled, the master upon the slave, thus ironically undercutting the supposed power and independence ostensibly enjoyed by Hercules. In this interpretation, what the chain indicates is that the orator-ruler, no matter how powerful or how absolute a monarch, is still constrained. Ironically, one who is bound to rule because of his mastery of the art of rhetoric may well appear bound to rule in a different sense, the sense that he is bound to and by his subjects. Although rhetoricians seldom acknowledge such a notion, since it would completely compromise their fantasy of the supreme power of eloquent speech, it does occasionally surface in their works. Bartolomeo Cavalcanti, for instance, notes that the orator often fails to attain his goal simply because doing so lies not in his power but in that of his auditors (*Retorica*, 9). More subtly, Jacques Amyot declares that the king can say whatever he wants to, but that if his words are to maintain his authority and gravity, there must be some *contentement* in them for his subjects (*Projet*, 15). While such remarks are few and far between in the discourse of rhetoric, the chain of Hercules—with all that it implies—is ubiquitous. It dramatizes the thesis advanced by Norbert Elias in *The Civilizing Process*, the notion that if the centralization of the state through monopolies on taxes and military power meant an increase in the power of the monarch, it also ironically meant his increased dependence on those below him, on

[62] The proclamation excerpt comes from *Registres des délibérations du bureau de la ville de Paris*, ed. P. Guérin (Paris, 1886), 3:169, the Renard quotation from the *Bull[etin de la] soc[iété de l']hist[oire]* (Paris, 1878), 144; both are in Jung, *Hercule dans la littérature française*, 90, 91.

the large numbers of people who paid the taxes and served in the army.[63] Tellingly, the most absolutist monarch of the age, Louis XIV, recognized that his rule, his authority, was based on *l'estime générale* (*Supplément au Mémoire de 1667*, 2.302 [97]). He tells his son: "Whatever you propose to do or order, you must not consider only if the matter is pleasing to you or if it is useful, but you must examine what effect it will be able to produce in the world for or against your reputation" (2.302 [96]). Even the Sun King recognized that his power over others was inseparable from a fundamental dependence on them.

Yet another way of reading Hercules' chain against the grain of interpretation offered by Renaissance rhetoricians is to see it as symbolizing not the dependence of the orator on the auditor but the very constraints of rhetoric itself upon its practitioner. In other words, when the rhetor-ruler exercises his powers of speech to control his subject-auditors, his activity can to some extent be said to be dictated and controlled by the very art he practices; he may use it to rule others, but he is bound to it in the sense of being dependent on it as a result. The mythographic tradition offers at least one example of an image that points to this limitation. In his *Iconologia*, Cesare Ripa describes Persuasione (see Figure 4) as a matron holding a three-headed beast—the auditor—on a leash, but also as being bound herself by "many cords and laces of gold." Ripa explains their significance: "The laces of gold around her waist show that persuasion is nothing other than a being captured by others [*un'esser cattivato ad altri*], and bound with the dexterity and sweetness of eloquent speech" (395). Ripa's explanation is really double: the first part is quite consistent with the previous reading of Hercules' chains, with the notion that the rhetor-ruler is really held captive by those over whom he seems to rule; the second part, however, says that eloquence itself has captured the speaker, who is held in thrall to the very art he practices. What Ripa is getting at here may be what Philip Sidney, for instance, means when he defines poetry as "heart-ravishing knowledge" (*Apology*, 10), knowledge that ravishes the heart of the poet even as it ravishes that of his auditor. Luis de Granada suggests the same notion when he says that an orator should always keep his main end in sight, "no matter where the force of his argument may have carried [*rapuerit*] him in speaking" (*Ecclesiastica Rhetorica*, 409). Or perhaps George of Trebizond identifies Ripa's meaning when he discusses the part of rhetoric called *elocutio* and says it is appropriate for adolescents because

---

[63] See Norbert Elias, *Power and Civility*, vol. 2 of *The Civilizing Process*, trans. Edmund Jephcott (New York: Random House, 1978), 104–16.

4. "La Persuasione." From Cesare Ripa, *Iconologia* (Rome, 1603), 394.
(Courtesy of the Harry Ransom Humanities Research Center of the University of Texas at Austin)

"nothing attracts and allures that age more than rhythmically unfolded discourse" (*Rhetoricorum*, 59ᵛ).

Jacques Amyot offers yet another gloss when he discusses the way that language itself constrains its user. He opens the thirteenth chapter of his *Projet* by saying that the king should be careful to choose only proper words that are good French. In this way, his power, which his skill as an orator supposedly ensures, actually places him in an inferior, subject position vis-à-vis the language he speaks. Amyot dramatizes this inversion by means of an anecdote concerning the Emperor Tiberius, who, he says, always used proper Latin and at one point rejected the word *strena* ("omen," "prognostication") because he doubted its correctness. Amyot continues: "When the lawyer Capito, in order to please him [Tiberius], had said that this word was good Latin and that even if it were not, it would become so if it was pleasing to Caesar, then a certain grammarian, rising up, said, 'No, no, Caesar. You certainly have the power to give the right of citizenship and to naturalize men, but you cannot naturalize a word'" (45). Abruptly ending the anecdote at this point without drawing a conclusion, Amyot lets the nameless grammarian, rather than the lawyer, who practices a profession closely associated with rhetoric, have the final word. Ironically, in a book arguing for the power that rhetoric can give a king, Amyot here demonstrates that even the most rhetorically adept of emperors remains bound by the rules of the language he employs. In a similar way, one might interpret Ripa's image of Persuasione with the cords about her waist to mean that the rules and operations of rhetoric, like those of the language it employs, bind the orator even when he seems most powerful, even when he holds his subject-auditor literally on a leash.

The significance of this paradoxical view of the rhetor-ruler has been spelled out in social terms by Norbert Elias in his study of the court of Louis XIV, for he notes that Louis, though clearly able to dominate the lives of his people in a way few kings before or after him could, nevertheless was bound as tightly by the rhetorical mechanisms he used to control them as they were.[64] Although—or perhaps because—he was equal to the state, he was forced always to display himself as king, always to behave according to the rules of etiquette and ceremony which he himself had established. That constraint can be seen also in the literature of the Renaissance, specifically in Shakespeare's second tetralogy of English history plays, which we examined earlier as a celebration of the power of regal eloquence. Although both Henry and Hal, in their

---

[64] Norbert Elias, *The Court Society*, trans. Edmund Jephcott (New York: Random House, 1969), 117–56.

different ways, act out the rhetoricians' fantasy of conquest and rule through language, Hal especially experiences kingship as restriction. His activities in the tavern, however much he may rationalize them as merely a prelude to the rhetorical show of reformation he will stage, constitute an interlude of freedom from social rules and official roles, an interlude that makes kingship look more like loss than gain. Henry, of course, sees it as a burden that robs him of the sleep enjoyed by a simple "sea-boy" (*Henry IV, Part 2*, 3.1.27), and Hal shares this view: "O majesty! / When thou dost pinch thy bearer, thou dost sit / Like a rich armor worn in heat of day, / That scald'st with safety" (4.5.27–30). In Hal's image, rule is oppressive, stifling; the majestic greatness and richness it entails ironically bear down upon its possessor and threaten asphyxiation rather than offering either freedom or pleasure.

Hal's most forceful presentation of this idea—that kingship is an oppressive burden—occurs in *Henry V* in the famous soliloquy on ceremony, which, of course, means nothing less than the rhetorical display of kingship. Hal initially defines it simply as "place, degree, and form, / Creating awe and fear in other men" (4.1.243–44), but he later expands his definition to present it as entailing the entire range of spectacular objects and devices Renaissance kings had at their disposal to control their subjects: "the balm, the scepter, and the ball, / The sword, the mace, the crown imperial, / The intertissued robe of gold and pearl, / The farced title running 'fore the king, / The throne he sits on" (257–61). Much of this speech can be read, of course, as a self-serving argument that Hal deserves his throne because he alone is willing to put up with all the hard work involved in maintaining it, and that he receives as a reward not the pleasures of power but only empty Ceremony, a god that ironically "suffer'st more / Of mortal griefs than do thy worshipers [i.e., his subjects]" (238–39). But although one is tempted not to take Hal completely at his word here, his speech can also be read as a genuine expression of his feeling of being overwhelmed by the role he has elected to play. Kingship is—or at least could be, in the rhetorical form it had during the Renaissance—a paranoid life-style, as Machiavelli dramatizes throughout his political writings: it demands that one constantly be on the alert, that one play one's role with total and unremitting self-consciousness, that one never drop one's guard. The king can never take the "heart's-ease" (233) for which Hal yearns in his soliloquy. This warrior-king—the supreme version of the rhetor-ruler, one whose performances are ideally designed to confirm his power, make his subjects into subjects, and secure his own identity as king—actually experiences his performance in quite the opposite terms: "O hard condition, / Twin-born with greatness, subject to the breath / Of every fool, whose sense no more can feel / But his own wringing!" (230–33). The ultimate irony here is that from Hal's viewpoint the king and the clown have changed positions: the rhetorical performance of rule actually makes the monarch the "subject" of his subjects—and of his performance itself.

Hal's thoughts here seem to justify the Stoic pessimism of a Pierre Charron, who emphasizes the miseries, rather than the supposed pleasures, of ruling. People desire sovereignty, he says, because they see only its outside, which appears good. Looked at more closely, it is wretchedness, for kings "are less free and masters of their wills than all others; for they are constrained in their proceedings by a thousand considerations." Charron sums up: "There is honor [in ruling], but little or no rest and joy: it is a public and honorable slavery, a noble misery, a rich captivity, *golden and shining shackles, lustrous wretchedness.*"[65] Charron's image of the ruler's golden and shining shackles, his *aureae et fulgidae compedes*, brings us back to the image of the Hercules Gallicus and his chains. It also confirms for us the conclusion that reading the image as an *ambiguous* presentation of the ruler's power would not have been inconceivable for Renaissance thinkers. Such a view is not, of course, what the discourse of rhetoric wished to advance as it exalted the rhetor and his power over his audience of subjects. That view becomes available, fully visible in a quite literal way, only when we examine the modeling to which it is subjected in the discourse of mythography and in literary texts such as Shakespeare's plays. To be sure, these other discourses primarily rehearse what the rhetoric handbooks and treatises insist upon. Nevertheless, although the texts that accompany all the different versions of the image of the Hercules Gallicus strive to limit interpretation, insisting that it celebrates him as a ruler and conqueror who leads the people by their ears, the picture itself clearly escapes such a constricting embrace. It remains open to alternative readings, as does Shakespeare's representation of the burdened, sleepless Hal and Henry. What such texts show, no matter what gloss they give to the Herculean rhetor, is that this emblematic orator-ruler, this divine emperor of men's minds, is, no less than his subjects, a creature in chains.

[65] Pierre Charron, *De la Sagesse, Trois Livres*, ed. Amaury Duval (Paris, 1824), 1:379, 388, 381.

2 Rulers and Rebels

At approximately the same period in the Renaissance, the 1580s, both Jacques Amyot and George Puttenham recount the same striking anecdote about the minor Hellenistic philosopher Hegesias of Cyrene in order to dramatize the power of eloquence. Amyot's version appears in his *Projet de l'Eloquence royale* and comes in the midst of a series of allusions to stories from Greece and Rome, all of which celebrate the orator and his skill. Amyot begins that series by recounting how Cicero completely transformed the hatred of the Roman populace for Lucius Otho by means of a harangue and how Antony, during the wars of Marius and Sulla, saved himself from death by charming his murderers with his speech. At this point, Amyot turns from examples of eloquence fending off death and summons up the quite different tale of Hegesias. By way of transition he remarks: "There is nothing so hard which is not annealed and softened [*destrempé & amolli*] by eloquence" (9), and this observation leads him—almost as if he were responding to his own imagery of softening and dissolution—to declare that if eloquence would desire us to sacrifice our lives, "it would not be in us to refuse" (10). After such an assertion one might expect a story about how some valiant general convinced his followers to make the ultimate sacrifice of their lives in some noble cause. Instead, Amyot documents the supreme power of rhetoric over human life in a quite different way:

Witness the auditors of the philosopher Hegesias, who, unfolding his eloquence in order to recount and put before their eyes all the miseries to which our life is subject, kindled [*allumoit*] such a desire for death in their spirits that many killed themselves of their own will, and King Ptolomy was constrained to forbid him very strictly from speaking any more of such a matter. (10)

George Puttenham rehearses the same story in the third book of his *Arte of English Poesie* in a chapter advancing the notion that speeches and writing ought to be "figurative": that is, ornamented by figures of speech. In this version, Hegesias becomes "a notable Oratour . . . who inveyed so much against the incommodities of this transitory life, and so highly commended death the dispatcher of all evils; as a great number of his hearers destroyed themselves." It was feared that even more people would have died "if king *Ptolome* had not made a publicke proclamation, that the Oratour should avoyde the countrey, and no more be allowed to speake in any matter" (153–54). Attempting to demonstrate the value of figurative speech, Puttenham has recourse to this anecdote for the same reason that Amyot does: it testifies to the supreme power of rhetoric over the human mind. Puttenham sums it up memorably: "Whether now perswasions, may not be said violent and forcible to simple myndes in speciall, I referre it to all mens judgements that heare the story."

Not only do Amyot and Puttenham recount the Hegesias story in similar ways but, although they derive it from classical sources, their recounting of it demonstrates the historical distance between the Renaissance discourse of rhetoric and its ancient antecedents. There is only one place from which knowledge of Hegesias and the Egyptians could have been obtained in the late sixteenth century: Cicero's *Tusculan Disputations*. In the initial book of this philosophical dialogue, Cicero argues that we should not fear death as an evil, first, because the soul is immortal, and second, because life on earth is filled with so much pain. This last observation leads him to invoke Hegesias who, he tells us, wrote a book recommending suicide through starvation and justifying it by means of a dialogue on the incommodities of human life. Death leads us away from evils, not from good things, says Cicero, "and the Cyrenaic Hegesias disputed about this so copiously that it is said he was prohibited by King Ptolomy from saying such things in the schools, since many committed suicide after having heard them."[1] Although there is no significant difference in the outlines of the anecdote in Cicero and in his Renaissance followers, the contexts drastically alter its meaning. For Cicero, it is adduced as evidence for the correctness of his

[1] Cicero, *Tusculan Disputations*, trans. J. E. King (Cambridge, Mass.: Harvard University Press, 1950), 1.34.83.

opinion that life is so filled with evils that humans could easily be led to terminate their own existence. For Amyot and Puttenham, the power of the anecdote—its "shock value"—depends precisely on the contrary view: it is the tenacity with which people cling to life that makes Hegesias's eloquence so awe inspiring. Although Cicero might have used this anecdote in one of his works on oratory and presented Hegesias as a model of eloquence, there is no mention of him outside of the *Tusculan Disputations*, where he has only a bit part to play as a minor authority. In the Renaissance, by contrast, Hegesias is appropriated for rhetoric. He is featured in works concerned with that discipline, is labeled an orator by Puttenham, and, although initially called a philosopher, is offered by Amyot as a master of persuasive speech. More important, for both writers what Hegesias said was not an example of a convincing, rational, philosophical argument; rather, his discourse made manifest the overpowering force of eloquence which, in Puttenham's terms, worked "violence" on the minds of those who listened and, in Amyot's, "kindled [*allumoit*: lit] . . . a desire for death in their spirits." His eloquence made Hegesias the "emperour of mens minds" with a vengeance.

Although both Amyot and Puttenham may have intended the Hegesias anecdote as an illustration of the admirable power of rhetoric, what they show about that art makes it deeply disturbing. First, it inspires an enormously violent and destructive reaction. Revealingly, although both writers use the anecdote to celebrate rhetoric, they also express reservations about what Hegesias has done: Puttenham qualifies the eloquence involved with irony by saying it is "violent and forcible to *simple* myndes" (154; emphasis added); Amyot offers the anecdote as an example of what he calls *eloquence vulgaire* (8), which he says is inferior to the royal—and, by implication, less destructive—eloquence of kings. In both cases the story demonstrates how audience reaction, although certainly produced in some sense by the orator's words, nevertheless exceeds his intentions and control. More important, it also dramatizes the way in which the effects of rhetoric are anything but consistent with social order and thus undercuts the vision shared by so many Renaissance writers—including both Amyot and Puttenham—that rhetoric is an essential tool of civilization. If the anecdote is troubling because it presents audience reaction as excessive and destructive, it is also troubling for another reason. Like many of their fellow rhetoricians, both Amyot and Puttenham generally see their art as the means by which a speaker can control the minds and wills of his subject-auditors; in other words, they both share the Renaissance vision of the rhetor as ruler. But the Hegesias anecdote does *not* identify the rhetor with the ruler; it sets the two at odds. Hegesias may have a regal ability to control his listeners, but his oratory threatens the status quo by inducing mass suicide, and it puts him on a collision course with the legitimate ruler in Alexandria, Ptolomy. Hegesias may be a king metaphorically, but he is not *the* king of Hellenistic Egypt, and from the viewpoint of that figure his oratory threatens the state. It is, consequently, a *subversive* force, not a socially conservative one; its power disrupts the order of society and requires Ptolomy's active intervention to counteract it. Hegesias's eloquence may allow him to control the lives of others, but it must be controlled itself, silenced if not expelled, in order to preserve the kingdom. For both Amyot and Puttenham, the orator may thus be seen as the king's opponent just as readily as his ally or his alter ego.

The Hegesias anecdote dramatizes the two major concerns of this chapter. The first involves the disturbing, mysterious, unstable, and potentially destructive reaction that the rhetor is able to provoke in others. He can do so, as we shall see, because according to Renaissance writers oratory is an art that works on and through the passions, and the passions are fundamentally unstable, unpredictable, always potentially destructive. The second concern of this chapter is the ambivalence and unpredictability not of audience response but of the orator himself. In the Renaissance discourse of rhetoric, as the preceding chapter has shown, the orator is identified over and over again as a ruler, one who, it is assumed, necessarily acts to create civilization and, by implication, supports the status quo. Indeed, writers on rhetoric insist on the socially conservative function of the orator, and many identify him with the legitimate ruler. Just as frequently, however, the discourse of rhetoric disjoins the orator from the prince or king in a variety of ways, and as a result he often appears a distinctly subversive figure. Not surprisingly, critics of rhetoric in the Renaissance attack the rhetor for such things as sedition and antisocial behavior, but even his defenders seem unable to avoid characterizing their hero as a rebel and a danger to the established order, despite their fervent desire to proclaim his orthodoxy. Note how, in offering the Hegesias anecdote, the texts of Amyot and Puttenham behave, at least momentarily, like Hegesias himself: they go out of control. Although both writers explicitly indicate throughout their works their interest in preserving the status quo, this example of oratorical power actually undermines the elevated social function they would assign to the art, making rhetoric seem a threat rather than a blessing. The Hegesias anecdote suggests that both Amyot and Puttenham were, at the very least, deeply conflicted about the art they cherished. Nor were they the only rhetoricians in the Renaissance to feel that way.

To understand the unstable nature of audience response to oratory, let us consider Aristotle's analysis of the rhetorical interaction. In his conception, it has three interrelated aspects, three focal points: *logos*, or the substance of the argument; *ethos*, or the character the speaker creates in the course of the oration; and *pathos*, or the effect of that oration on its audience. Although Aristotle declares at one point that "moral character [*ethos*], so to say, constitutes the most effective means of proof," he generally argues for the importance of all three aspects of the rhetorical act (*Rhetoric* 1.2.4). For other ancient rhetoricians, however, and especially Cicero, the third aspect of rhetoric, its ability to move those who listen, is clearly the most important. This perspective is the one that writers in the fifteenth, sixteenth, and seventeenth centuries adopted. As Debora Shuger puts it: "The Renaissance tends to make emotional power, Cicero's *movere*, the aim of all rhetorical discourse" (*Sacred Rhetoric*, 120). This trend, says Shuger, is anticipated by the *ars praedicandi* in the Middle Ages, but by extending the aim of moving the audience from preaching to every kind of rhetoric, the Renaissance breaks away from the preceding period and aligns itself with the ancients. It even makes letter-writing a matter of moving the addressee, largely thanks to Erasmus's reformulation of that art (see Plett, *Rhetorik der Affekte*, 59–60). To be sure, not every rhetoric from the period names the moving of the audience as its end. Stylistic rhetorics influenced by the Ramist reorganization of the discipline—which assigned invention and disposition to logic, leaving just ornamentation, delivery, and memory for rhetoric—tend to present simple, schematic discussions, definitions, and examples but almost no commentary on the effect such things have on an audience, an omission perfectly in keeping with Ramus's lack of interest in the psychological and affective function of the art and his explicit offering of his work as a response to rhetoric's power to deceive.[2] Moreover, some writers on rhetoric, contemplating the Ciceronian threefold definition of its goals as teaching, delighting, and moving (*docere, delectare*, and *movere*), occasionally single out one of the other two as the orator's chief concern. Sperone Speroni, for instance, says that *diletto* is the *vertù dell'orazione* (*Dialogo*, 90), although he hastens to explain that it is so because the orator cannot move his audience without delighting it. By contrast, Rudolph Agricola says that the function of speech is to teach, but he defines it thus when discussing dialectic; as soon as he comes to rhetoric, he stresses *movere* and posits as an ideal some combination of it with teaching (*De Inventione*, 1–3, 328–32). Thus, even the seeming exceptions sometimes turn into confirmations of the rule. The moving of the audience, the manipulation of *pathos*, is the main preoccupation of Renaissance rhetoric.

What the rhetor aims to move is either the emotions or the will.[3]

---

[2] See Ong, *Ramus*, 211.

[3] See Vickers, *Classical Rhetoric in English Poetry*, 83–121, and *In Defence of Rhetoric*, 256–339; Plett, *Rhetorik der Affekte*; and Conley, *Rhetoric in the European*

Saint Augustine identified will, or love, as the source of the emotions, and his conception, Debora Shuger has suggested, strongly influenced Renaissance and especially Protestant thinkers. She also notes, however, that Saint Thomas Aquinas saw the will as an intellective appetite distinct from the emotions, so that Catholic rhetoricians tended to keep the two apart (*Sacred Rhetoric*, 46–48, 133–35, 143). In most cases, Renaissance rhetorics seem to prefer to elide the problem involved in specifying the exact nature of the relationship between the emotions and the will. Although they focus on the former, they often speak as though the two were virtually identical, or as though moving the emotions would inevitably affect the will and, through its agency, produce action in the world.[4] Thus, in the early *quattrocento*, George of Trebizond insists that since the emotions determine the auditor's judgment, the orator must move his listeners "so that they will speak as their emotions [*ipsa motione animorum*] dictate" (*Rhetoricorum*, 44ᵛ). Later in the fifteenth century Rudolph Agricola similarly stresses the rhetorical end of moving (*movere*) others and defines it as a "disturbing of the emotions [*affectibus perturbare*]" (*De Inventione*, 159). And Juan Luis Vives, writing in 1531, complains that contemporary orators are failures because they are lacking in experience, ignorant of life, and, especially, "entirely unaware of what the emotions [*affectus*] are or how to drive them on or restrain them" (*De Causis*, 170). Cypriano Soarez insists that although appeals to the emotions are especially pertinent in a peroration, they should really be used throughout one's speech (*De Arte*, 179), and Nicholas Caussin devotes an entire and lengthy book of his *De Eloquentia sacra et humana* to the passions (bk. 8, *De Affectibus*), declaring at its start: "The empire of that eloquence is greatest which rules over the emotions [*affectibus*]: for it holds the crowd, allures minds, impells wills [*voluntates*] to go where it wants and leads them away where it wants" (459).[5]

Tradition, 151–87. Plett's argument that the moving of the passions becomes a primary concern for English rhetoric only in the last years of the sixteenth century seems untenable; it ignores Thomas Wilson, who was writing in the middle years of the century, and certainly does not fit those rhetorics written in other languages (particularly Latin) but used in England as well as on the continent. Conley's argument that only in the seventeenth century do the passions become a central concern is also problematic; though earlier rhetorics have no elaborate lists of passions and the ways to move them, they certainly insisted on the importance of the passions and the will. Neither Vickers nor Plett nor Conley discusses the will, which comes up almost as often as the passions do in Renaissance treatises.

[4] Cf. Struever, who emphasizes that for the humanists, as for the Sophists, the will is essential (*The Language of History in the Renaissance*, 59–60).

[5] Other texts defining the end of rhetoric as the moving of the emotions are Guzman, *Primera Parte*, 129ᵛ; Keckermann, *Systema*, 4; Granada, *Ecclesiastica Rhetorica*, 82; and Bartholomew Latomus, *Summa totius rationis disserendi* (Cologne, 1527), D6ᵛ.

That last quotation illustrates the slippage, typical of Renaissance thought, between the emotions and the will, for although Caussin starts out by speaking of dominating the emotions, he quickly turns it into a matter of commanding wills. A similar slippage occurs in Bacon as he defines the office of rhetoric in his *Advancement of Learning*: rhetoric ideally seconds reason by using imagination "for the better moving of the will," a process he redefines a page later as using that faculty to make the "affections in themselves" something they normally are not: namely, "pliant and obedient to reason" (*Selected Writings*, 309–10). Even Johann Heinrich Alsted, who is a rarity among Renaissance rhetoricians in that he strives to keep the two concepts apart, actually winds up blurring any real distinction between them: "the emotions," he says, "are the daughters of the will [*voluntatis filiae sunt affectus*]" (*Rhetorica*, 5).

Renaissance rhetoricians describe two specific ways in which the orator moves his auditors. The first is truly a technique, a matter of *techne* or art; it is the use of style in all its aspects—figures and tropes, rhythms and vivid descriptions—as well as delivery in order to provoke an emotional response. Although classical rhetoric recognized the connection between linguistic effects and *movere*, this technique receives full-scale development in Renaissance treatises, a development that becomes increasingly extensive and systematic in the seventeenth century.[6] For instance, in his widely influential stylistic rhetoric, the *Epitome Troporum ac Schematum* (Epitome of tropes and schemes), Johann Susenbrotus not only provides definitions and examples for the various tropes and figures but also indicates the specific emotional effects they produce. Thus, of *prosopopeia* (a figure involving the speaker's impersonation of someone else) he says: "It adds much to the variety and gravity of the speech and excites the spirit of the auditor vehemently, provided that the magnitude of the subject requires a fiction of this sort." In a rhetoric of 1569, a work in verse which epitomizes tridentine values, the Spaniard Arias Montano declares: "Speak the greatest words you can, those which move rage and anger, quiet grief, or lead souls to piety."[7] Fray Luis de Granada especially emphasizes the need for stylistic vividness, the use of what was called *evidentia* in Latin (*enargeia* in Greek). "It is well known," he writes, "that all the emotions are very greatly excited once the greatness of the matter has been placed before

---

[6] For the connections between style and emotional impact, see the works referred to in note 3.

[7] Johann Susenbrotus, *Epitome Troporum ac Schematum* (Zurich, 1540), 64. Arias Montano, *Rhetoricorum libri IIII* (Antwerp, 1569), 49, cited in Martí, *La preceptiva retórica española*, 120.

our eyes" (*Ecclesiastica Rhetorica*, 132). Granada also notes that amplification similarly excites (*concitari*) the listener (46–47).[8] An English example is Henry Peacham's review of all the tropes and figures, presenting in almost every case the specific "use" to which each one may be put, which often involves the moving of the emotions. Metaphors, for instance, have a number of distinct "fruits," including the ability to move the hearer's affections and to make "such a firme impression in the memory, as is not lightly forgotten" (*Garden*, 13).[9] And even the Ramists, though far more interested in schematizing and defining the tropes and figures than in describing the psychological and emotional effect they produce, do not entirely ignore this subject. In his French-language *Dialectique* of 1555, Ramus himself tells the orator to play on the emotions of the auditor, especially by means of style and delivery: "All the tropes and figures of elocution, all the graces of delivery . . . serve no other purpose than to lead this troublesome and stubborn auditor" (134).

The other technique for moving the passions which the orator has at his disposal is not necessarily distinct from the use of style and delivery, but its focus is on the production and display of emotion rather than on language and gestures. This technique is what may be called the process of "contagion" and derives from various ancient authors, including Cicero (*De oratore* 2.45.189–90) and Quintilian (*Institutio* 6.2.27–36). Essentially, the contagion theory claims that for the orator to move someone else, he must first be moved himself; his emotion, reproduced effortlessly in his words, then directly affects the feelings of the listener, spreading from the one to the other like a contagious disease. This theory is rehearsed endlessly in the Renaissance rhetorics. In the 1430s, George of Trebizond declares that "he will not speak correctly who is not moved, nor, untouched by emotion, will he affect others" (*Rhetoricorum*, 59ᵛ; cf. 78ᵛ). Rudolph Agricola, writing at the end of that century, similarly insists that the speaker's display of emotion will arouse a comparable emotional response in others (*De Inventione*, 335). And Guillaume Du Vair, a full century later, provides one of the most complete definitions of the process, one of the few actually to mention the word "contagion":

> The entire force and excellence of eloquence consists truly in the movement of the passions. By this instrument, as by a strong militia,

[8] Keckermann says the same thing; see *Systema*, 75, 109.

[9] For other statements stressing how tropes and figures affect the emotions, see Fabri, *Le grand et vrai art*, 157; Soarez, *De Arte*, 84; Rainolde, *Foundacion*, iᵛ; Alsted, *Rhetorica*, 31–33 (all of his third book is devoted to the subject); Granada, *Ecclesiastica Rhetorica*, 168–70, 224–30; and Guzman, *Primera Parte*, 65ʳ.

it rules its sovereign empire, turns and bends the wills of men, and makes them serve its designs. For passion, being conceived in our heart, is formed straightway in our words [*se forme incontinent en nostre parole*], and issuing from us by means of our words enters into others and there makes an impression just like the one we have in ourselves by means of a subtle and lively contagion [*par une subtile & vive contagion*]. (*Traitté*, 403)

Luis de Granada not only shares his fellow rhetoricians' naive conception of the equivalence between language and feeling but finds language so unproblematic that it simply disappears from his formulation of the theory. Our first concern in speaking, he writes, "ought to be that emotions and feelings are in us, for then they will burst out by their own natural force, and as they are true feelings, they will truly affect the auditors" (*Ecclesiastica Rhetorica*, 359).

The contagion theory assumes not only that language is unproblematic but that the orator's subjects are essentially passive and will either be voiceless or simply replicate his speech. All these assumptions are implied by the imagery often employed to define the process involved, such as that of one fire serving to ignite another. Using a particularly revealing metaphor, Juan Luis Vives writes that the auditor's emotions are like a lyre that vibrates in response to the cords plucked on another instrument (*De Ratione*, 166); and Daniel Barbaro, after proclaiming that to move others one must first be moved oneself, uses the image of two cords vibrating in response to each other to describe the occult sympathy between the passions of the speaker and the auditor, a sympathy that guarantees the *vittoria* of the former over the latter (*Della Eloquenza*, 376). Like Vives, Barbaro wants to suggest not only that the auditor cannot avoid responding to the sounds made by the orator but that the process is good, a matter of harmony rather than strife or domination. Somewhat later in the sixteenth century, Jacques Amyot represents the process of contagion by means of a rather unusual bird image. Speaking of delivery, he says that the orator's eyes will "imprint on those who look at them passions identical with those of the person who speaks. . . . In this what happens to them is like what happens to the bird which we call the oriole, which in looking at those who have jaundice takes on that same sickness directly" (*Projet*, 50–51). Amyot's image not only stresses once again the passivity and helplessness of the auditor but also suggests that the process is as "natural" as the oriole's changing its color in response to what it sees. One cannot help but note, however, that what is natural here is not especially positive: oratory is equated with disease, an impression which Amyot probably had no intention of creating but which, like the Hegesias story, simply slipped out beyond his control.[10]

Although the Renaissance emphasis on moving the affections and, through them, the will owes much to classical antiquity, the conceptions involved are by no means identical. Ancient writers oppose reason to the passions and deeply distrust the latter: the Greeks see emotion— as their word for it, *pathe*, might suggest—as a disease and a disorder of the soul, and Cicero directly defines emotion or passion (*affectus*) as a "commotion of the soul [*animi commotio*] turned away from right reason and against nature" (*Tusculan Disputations* 4.11). Thus, Aristotle tolerates *pathos* in forensic oratory but only because the audience is too weak to engage in rational disputation (*Rhetoric* 1.1.4–6, 3.1.5–6, 3.7.4– 5), and Cicero and Quintilian essentially agree with his assessment. Augustine, however, takes a more positive view of affectivity, love being an essential part of human nature in his theology, and according to Debora Shuger (*Sacred Rhetoric*, 44–50) his view shaped Renaissance notions of the importance of the emotions, especially, though not exclusively, in sacred oratory. Thus, Francis Bacon, in the section on rhetoric from *The Advancement of Learning*, claims that "the affections themselves carry ever an appetite to good, as reason doth" (*Selected Writings*, 311). In his *Oxford Lectures on Aristotle's "Rhetoric,"* John Rainolds defines emotion in Ciceronian terms as an *animi commotio* but adds that it was "imparted by God for following good and fleeing evil" (142). In this definition, emotion is both divinely sanctioned and essential to one's moral existence, a perspective with which Nicholas Caussin agrees. Citing a certain D. Nemesius, he says that the passions are "commotions of the sentient soul generated by one's opinion of good or evil" (*Eloquentia sacra*, 460) and that they were implanted in human nature by God. Thus, for these Renaissance writers, unlike their classical forebears, the passions have both a divine origin and an important role to play in leading the individual in the direction of the good.

Nevertheless, the Renaissance response to the emotions is more a grudging acceptance than an ecstatic embrace. Though Bacon, for instance, speaks of an "appetite to good," he also stresses the rebelliousness of the emotions and their resistance to the right rule of reason (*Selected Writings*, 310–11). Similarly, for every page John Rainolds devotes to the positive value of the passions (*Oxford Lectures*, 142–52), he spends at least another page on their negative characteristics (124–42).

---

[10] For a more purely positive image, see Fuscano, "Della oratoria e poetica facoltœa": "This thing [eloquence] makes the will in men dry up and become green again, as spring is accustomed to do with flowers and autumn with fallen leaves" (191).

Moreover, when he follows Cicero and defines emotion as an *animi commotio*, that phrase can be translated simply as a "commotion of the soul," but it can also be rendered as an "agitation" or "disorder," thus suggesting that emotion for him is inherently unstable and potentially antisocial. Even more suggestive is the definition of the emotions as *perturbationes* by Bartholomew Latomus (*Summa*, E4ʳ) and Gerard Vossius.[11] And although Nicholas Caussin describes the passions as God-given and credits them with causing us to pursue the good, he devotes much of his discussion of them to their negative features, emphasizing the idea of disorder in the notion of *commotio*, identifying the emotions as unstable and dangerous, and at one point even connecting them to evil, to *Daemones* (461).[12]

Caussin's linking of the emotions to the demonic points to another important difference between classical and Renaissance writers: the latter frequently frame their discussions in Christian terms. As we have seen, they anchor their positive assessment of passion in the fact that it is implanted in humans by God, and in a complementary move they link their negative assessment of it to the Fall. Caussin himself is quite explicit: in order to explain why the emotions are so destructive, why they play such savage games (*feroces ludos*), he says, "the witness is human nature, [which is,] through the fall of our first parent, carried away violently by the most troublesome tyranny of the various emotions" (*Eloquentia sacra*, 460). Caussin's fellow Jesuit Luis de Granada takes a similar line when he insists that the preacher must move the feelings of the auditor, "since men sin more because of corrupted emotion than ignorance of the truth" (*Ecclesiastica Rhetorica*, 82). Caussin's and Granada's views are shared by Renaissance Protestants. Alluding to the Bible (Matthew 26.41: "The spirit indeed is willing, but the flesh is weak"), Thomas Wilson suggests that the postlapsarian nature of man necessitates and justifies the orator's manipulation of emotion: "Though their spirite bee apt, and our will prone, yet our flesh is so heavie and humours so overwhelme us, that we cannot without refreshing, long abide to heare any one thing" (*Arte*, 4). Bartholomew Keckermann actually repeats Granada's words, applying them not just to preaching but to rhetoric in general: "The special function of the orator has been placed in moving the emotions more than in teaching the in-

[11] Vossius, *Oratoriarum Institutionum Libri Sex*, 88. See also Cavalcanti, *Retorica*, 78.

[12] Giason Denores, who held the chair of moral philosophy at Padua from 1570 to 1590, advocates the use of the passions in oratory and has little or nothing negative to say about them; however, he does label them *perturbazioni* (perhaps in order to translate the Ciceronian *animi commotio*), and his word directly emphasizes their disturbing, dangerous, and potentially destructive nature ("Breve Trattato dell'Oratore," 113, 115).

tellect of the auditors, since men sin more because of corrupted emotion
than ignorance of the truth" (*Systema*, 5).[13]

Renaissance rhetoricians repeatedly have recourse to certain key images to describe the emotions and their effects, and an examination of
those images underscores just how ambiguous their thinking is about
the emotions. Caussin identifies the passions as wild beasts feared for
their violence and aggression (see *Eloquentia sacra*, 460–62). Although
he uses this image to characterize human emotion negatively, the notion that passion is an animal does not impose such a characterization
necessarily. If animals may threaten humans, they may also provide
food, and some species may be tamed to serve human needs. Let us
illustrate the positive version of the beast image by pausing for a moment to consider three passages from sixteenth-century writers in Italy,
Spain, and France. In his "Della oratoria e poetica facoltà" of 1531, Giovanni Berardino Fuscano, who lived and worked in the Kingdom of Naples, imagines the orator as taming an animal, a quite specific one, a
horse, using an image for the passions that goes back at least to Plato
and has quite positive connotations: "A swift horse has never moved so
quickly at the touch of the spur or the reins, as, at its every whim, this
[eloquence] removes the gay affections and the sad passions of our
spirits" (191). Like Fuscano, the Spaniard Joan de Guzman also thinks of
the passions, the orator's own passions, as a horse whose impetuous
course will utterly conquer the will of the auditor. That part of a speech
called the confirmation, he says, requires "that we go into it furious,
like a swift lightning bolt, running sometimes with more vehemence
than a runaway horse, principally when it is not clear that we have
already gained any part of the will of the auditor and that our spirit is in
any manner predominant over theirs" (*Primera Parte*, 136ʳ–136ᵛ). And
the Frenchman Jacques Amyot has recourse to the same imagery when
speaking of the orator's listeners on the first page of his *Projet de l'Eloquence royale*. By means of eloquence, he claims, the orator can "manipulate a multitude of people, tickle their hearts, master their wills
and passions, to wit, push them on and hold them back at his pleasure,
and, in a manner of speaking, use the spur and the bridle on them which
are hung from the tip of his tongue."[14] Not only does Amyot identify the

[13] There are two quite different reasons for thinking Keckermann a Protestant. First,
his work includes a satirical attack on friars (*Systema*, 529). Second, and more important, he spent his entire life in German Protestant cities (Danzig, Wittenberg,
Heidelberg, Leipzig), and his collected works were published posthumously in Geneva—places associated with either Lutheranism or Calvinism. For a brief biography,
see Johann Heinrich Zedler, *Grosses vollständiges Universal-Lexikon* (Graz, 1961–
64).

[14] For other references to the passions as a horse or to the spur and bridle, see Granada, *Ecclesiastica Rhetorica*, 16; and Ramus, *Attack on Cicero*, 35.

passions—and hence the auditor who experiences them—as a horse, but he also alludes fleetingly to the figure of the Hercules Gallicus when he speaks of the orator's tongue from which the spurs and the bridle are hung. Fuscano, Guzman, and Amyot all use their imagery to stress the superior power of eloquence to master the animal passions, but what is equally important in the passages is that those passions, for all the danger they potentially represent, are clearly valuable. Their energy can be destructive, but it can just as easily serve the interests of those who can control it as well as of the society they represent. Further, both the danger and the nature of the animal serve to elevate and ennoble the orator, for they identify him implicitly as courageous, even heroic, nothing less than an ideal *cavaliere, caballero,* or *chevalier.*

If animals are ambiguous images for the passions in the Renaissance discourse of rhetoric, so is another image that occurs especially in passages defining the contagion theory: the image of fire. In fact, whereas Guillaume Du Vair speaks of "contagion," most writers have recourse to the image of fire to describe how the orator affects the auditor. Thomas Wilson, for instance, says: "There is no substaunce of it selfe, that wil take fire, except ye put fire to it. Likewise, no mans nature is so apt, straight to be heated, except the Oratour himselfe, be on fire" (*Arte,* 133). In a similar vein, Cypriano Soarez writes that the orator's emotions will move others easily, just like fire encountering fuel (*De Arte,* 180), and Nicholas Caussin declares: "Those emotions which orators have impressed upon them they can quite easily pour forth into the hearts of their auditors. You must burn, if you wish to set others on fire" (*Eloquentia sacra,* 462).[15] A particularly striking example appears in Richard Rainolde's *Foundacion of Rhetorike:* by means of rhetoric, he says, "the moste stonie and hard hartes, can not but bee incensed, inflamed, and moved" (1ᵛ). As the fire of the orator's words transforms human beings out of their hard, stony state, restoring life and vital movement to them, he becomes a version of Orpheus or Amphion, mythical figures for the orator-civilizer. In this context, then, fire is quite positive: it suggests human warmth and life and all the benefits of civilization. Yet the image also possesses less attractive connotations which the rhetorician cannot keep from entering the reader's head: it can suggest anger and fury, violence and madness, the destruction of homes and cities. To be specific, in the context of Renaissance Europe the image of fire cannot help but raise the specter of the pyres on which thousands of religious dissenters were executed across the continent. Rhetoricians seldom suffered such a fate themselves—although the

---

[15] For other examples, see Du Vair, *Traitté,* 400, 403; and Sidney, *Apology,* 49.

most famous one in the period, Peter Ramus, was murdered by Catholic
fanatics during the Saint Bartholomew's Day massacre in 1572, his body
was thrown into the Seine rather than burned—but it should be remembered that virtually all educated people during the Renaissance were
trained in rhetoric and could, with some justice, have styled themselves
orators, and that some of them doubtless had real reasons to fear burning at the stake. The polymath François Rabelais is one such figure. In
the prologue to his first book, *Pantagruel,* as he unfolds his new and
potentially "heretical" ideas, he jokingly declares that he will defend his
book "just up to the pyre [*jusques au feu exclusive*]," and he later has
his protagonist refuse to stay in the city of Toulouse once he learns that
the people there have had "their regents burned alive, like red her-
rings."[16] In this passage Rabelais is probably alluding to the death of Jean
de Cahors, a professor of law, in 1532—and law and rhetoric were, of
course, virtually synonymous in many people's minds throughout the
Renaissance.

If for Renaissance rhetoricians both the emotions of the auditor and
the fire that symbolizes them are profoundly ambiguous, so too is the
will. Specifically, it is ambiguous because it is imagined as being both
free and enslaved, for whereas rhetoricians claim that the auditor *freely*
gives his assent to the orator's words, they insist just as vehemently
that he has no choice but to do so, being compelled by the speaker's
rhetorical prowess. Jacques Amyot, for example, speaks of how wonderful it is to lead men as one wishes by means of force, but how much
better "to lead them willingly [*de gré*], without injury, loss, or danger,
and to their contentment" (*Projet*, 2). Such a passage leaves a significant
question in the reader's mind: are the auditors really free, really going
along "willingly" with the orator, or are they "led" and hence not in
control of their own actions at all? Such a question might also occur
when one reads the following statement in Rudolph Agricola's *De Inventione*: "We create faith . . . in one who believes, and we lead him as
if following us by his own will [*velut sponte*]" (2). The crucial word here
is "as if" (*velut*), for clearly the orator's will, not his auditor's, determines what is happening, although a kind of fiction is created which
enables the auditor to feel *as if* his will were in charge. The paradoxical
nature of the orator's verbal mastery of his free subjects may be understood as a special case of the way power works in general, at least according to the analysis of Michel Foucault.[17] For a person to have the
real experience of power, argues Foucault, he must feel it, and for that to

[16] François Rabelais, *Oeuvres*, ed. Jacques Boulenger and Lucien Scheler (Paris: Gallimard, 1962), 168, 188; see also 354, 733.
[17] Michel Foucault, "The Subject and Power," *Critical Inquiry* 8 (1982): 777–95.

happen, the people over whom he rules must be free and independent enough so that he will have to overcome their active resistance in order to dominate them. In Foucault's analysis, it is the overcoming of resistance that gives the ruler the actual experience identified as power. What that implies, however, is that the ruled must, of necessity, have a will of their own, an independence that prevents their ruler's control over them from ever being perfect and complete. Ironically, the ruler can gain the experience of power only at the price of ensuring the freedom and thereby enabling the resistance of his subject. What one sees in descriptions of the oratorical interaction in Renaissance treatises is exactly this paradox of subjection and freedom, or of subjection that necessitates freedom in order to exist and that will always possess a degree of instability and impermanence as a result.

The strongly political conception of rhetoric in the Renaissance inevitably leads writers to think of the emotions and the will in political terms and to allegorize the relationship between the rhetor's eloquence and the emotions or the will as that between a ruler and his subjects. In his lectures on Aristotle, John Rainolds argues both for and against appealing to the emotions. He starts out by faulting them not only for clouding the minds of the judges but also for being politically dangerous: "Let us avoid thinking that the emotions, the guardians of injustice and the subverters of states [*rerumpublicarum eversores*], can be rightly moved in good states" (*Oxford Lectures*, 130). Nevertheless, Rainolds does defend the emotions by asserting that God created humans with a higher and a lower faculty, which he identifies as reason and appetite, respectively, and then labels with the politically charged terms of "master" and "servant," "guide" and "wayfarer," "leader" (or "ruler") and "fighter" (140: *dominum* and *famulum*, *ducem* and *viatorem*, *imperatorem* and *bellatorem*). Although he never denies the dangers involved, Rainolds concludes that the emotions are acceptable because the orator can, in fact, manage them: "The exciting of the emotions, it seems, is not to be prohibited because they are harmful but to be mastered [*imperanda*] because they are useful" (146). "To be mastered," *imperanda*, here means both that the rousing of emotion is to be commanded in the sense of being "ordered up" and that those emotions, once roused, are to be commanded in the sense of being "put under the orator's control." More important, the word Rainolds uses cannot be dissociated in Renaissance Latin from *imperator*, which means not only "commander" or "general," as it does in classical antiquity, but "emperor" as well. What Rainolds produces, in effect, is a political allegory in which the emotions are the restive subjects who may be essential to the state but are dangerous and must be commanded by the rhetor-ruler, whose control prevents them from acting out their normally subversive and rebellious tendencies. A similar political allegory is implied by Nicholas Caussin when he juxtaposes the *summum . . . imperium* (*Eloquentia sacra*, 459) of eloquence to the *summum . . . imperium* (462) claimed by the emotions as they resist their necessary subjection. Even more striking is Johann Heinrich Alsted's labeling of the intellect as the king (*rex*) and the will as the queen (*regina*) and his identification of the latter rather than the former as the appropriate subject, the *subjectum*, of rhetoric (*Rhetorica*, 5). Finally, there is Bacon who imagines the situation in thoroughly political terms:

> If the affections in themselves were pliant and obedient to reason, it were true there should be no great use of persuasions and insinuations to the will, more than of naked propositions and proofs; but in regard of the continual mutinies and seditions of the affections, . . . reason would become captive and servile, if Eloquence of Persuasions did not practise and win Imagination from the Affection's part, and contract a confederacy between the Reason and Imagination against the Affections. (*The Advancement of Learning*, in *Selected Works*, 310–11)

When Renaissance rhetoricians allegorize the passions and the will as the lower classes and reason and rhetoric as the upper ones, they create an enormous problem, for they open up a gap between reason, which is the nominal ruler, and rhetoric, which actually does the work of persuading the lower faculties to be obedient subjects. As the passage from Alsted and the quotation from Bacon's *Advancement* indicate, reason is generally seen as incapable of ruling the passions and the will by itself; it must depend on rhetoric to aid it. The result is that rhetoric, not reason, becomes the true *imperator* and thus acquires, at least potentially, the ability to displace reason and rule by itself. Ideally, as the quotation from Bacon indicates, rhetoric would simply be the willing servant of the reason-ruler, but in another passage from the Latin version of the *Advancement* Bacon spots the danger: "When the mind is soothed, enraged, or any way drawn aside by the artifice of speech, all this is done by raising the imagination; which, now growing unruly, not only insults over, but in a measure, offers violence to reason, partly by blinding, partly by incensing it."[18] In both passages Bacon imagines reason and eloquence as independent entities, and in both the latter, not the former, has the real power. That eloquence is, moreover, politically unstable: if it is capable of making the unruly passions and the will—

---

[18] Bacon, *The Advancement of Learning and Novum Organon*, 134.

the lower classes—submit to the rule of the reason, it can just as easily, working through the imagination, lead them into rebellion. In other words, the orator may be the agent of civilization and use his powers to serve the interests of the legitimate ruler, as so many Renaissance rhetoricians proclaimed in their works; but because he is by no means identified with that ruler in those works, he may also be a Hegesias, a potential rebel, whose eloquence poses a threat to the realm in Ptolomy's eyes and requires his active intervention to counteract its effects.

The notion that rhetoric and the rhetor are, or may be, subversive is actually widespread in the Renaissance, dominating that fraction of the discourse of rhetoric which, rather than celebrating the art, attacks and condemns it. The Englishman John Jewel, for instance, produced his *Oratio Contra Rhetoricam* sometime between 1544 and 1552, and although one may wish finally to conclude that the work is ironic, it nevertheless does review commonplace arguments that condemn rhetoric explicitly on both moral and political grounds.[19] Jewel's opening move is to identify rhetoric with lying and to turn against the rhetoricians their own boast that the god Mercury is their patron: "They rejoice that they have him as the inventor and chief of studied speech, but, good gods, what a god! One who first introduced frauds, deceptions, robberies, thefts, lies, perjuries into people's behavior" (1286). As Mercury's children, rhetors trick and flatter, confuse right and wrong, and avoid truth in favor of emotional pleas. What is worse, their oratory leads to the overturning of states and the transformation of great empires "into a great desert waste" (1287–88). Jewel says he will not dwell on the seditions, factions, plots, betrayals, wars, and conflagrations caused by rhetoric but stress instead how Athens was leveled because of Demosthenes and Rome because of Marcus Cato and Cicero. He then tells an anecdote about a Kentish woman who lamented the fate of her country when she saw all the law students in London, since a single lawyer back home had done enormous damage there; Jewel adds that the situation would have been even worse if those students had been orators as well. As he finally brings his oration up to date at this point, however, one begins to feel that he may be speaking tongue in cheek, especially when he waxes nostalgic for the days before Cicero was recovered. Since Jewel is writing classical, Ciceronian Latin, he can hardly be yearning for a time when Cicero—in particular, Cicero's letters—had not become the staple of the humanist curriculum, and since he can only be referring to the fifteenth century as the time before Cicero was

[19] For the possibility that Jewel's work may be ironic, see Hoyt H. Hudson, "Jewel's Oration against Rhetoric: A Translation," *Quarterly Journal of Speech* 14 (1928): 374–92.

recovered in England, it is inconceivable that he is not being ironic in celebrating a period that opened with the deposition and murder of Richard II, continued through the War of the Roses, and ended with the reign of Richard III. Nevertheless, even if Jewel's argument seems to self-destruct toward the end, the charges he has made against rhetoric are precisely the ones his contemporaries took seriously.

To see that Jewel's moral and political arguments against rhetoric were cultural commonplaces, one needs only to look to Italy and the almost contemporary work of Francesco Patrizi, or across the Channel to France and the slightly later writing of Michel de Montaigne. Patrizi, in his *Della retorica dieci dialoghi* (Ten dialogues on rhetoric) of 1562, associates rhetoric not only with fraud (31^r) but also with disorderly popular rule. The orator appeals only to plebeians, he says, who "have a wild beast in their hearts," and he tickles them and makes them bark as he pleases. Patrizi concludes: "He will be nothing if not the mover and disturber of the worst people" (42^r). Similarly, in his brief early essay "De la vanité des paroles" (On the Vanity of Words), Montaigne's arguments follow the same trajectory as Jewel's and Patrizi's. He begins by attacking rhetoric as a "lying . . . art" (*Oeuvres*, 292) which masks truth, deceives the eyes, and corrupts the essence of things. Then he asserts that well-regulated states never made much account of it: "It is a tool invented to manipulate and agitate a crowd and an unregulated populace, a tool which is employed only in sick states, like medicine; in those states where the common people, where the ignorant, where all have been able to do all things, as in Athens, Rhodes, and Rome, and where things have been in a perpetual tempest, there the orators flocked" (293). Montaigne concludes this opening portion of his essay by twice brilliantly inverting commonplace Renaissance judgments. First, he insists that eloquence flourished most at Rome when the state was at its worst, being shaken by civil war; thereby he denigrates the age of Cicero and the art of Cicero, which were admired throughout the period. Second, he alludes to the notion of the Hercules Gallicus leading people by their ears in such a way that he clearly condemns the rhetorical virtuosity involved while praising a state ruled by a single central authority. Monarchs need rhetoric less than others, he argues, "because stupidity and facility, which are found in the common people and which render it subject to be manipulated and led by the ears by the sweet sound of this harmony, without their coming to weigh and recognize the truth of things by the force of reason, this facility, I say, is not easily found in a single person; and it is easier to safeguard him from the effects of this poison by a good education and good counsel" (293). To be sure, Montaigne never says directly that rhetoric is seditious, but such a characterization is implicit in the constant connection he makes between rhetoric and civil disorder, a connection that cannot help but evoke the civil wars France experienced throughout his lifetime. The rhetor for Montaigne is thus not a Hercules who leads people to civilization but one who misleads them, turns them away from reason and truth, and produces anarchy and conflict. In light of what was said earlier about the presentation of the passions in the Renaissance discourse of rhetoric, it is especially noteworthy that Montaigne also defines the principal aim of the art to be the "moving of the affections" (293). Moreover, both he and Patrizi, when describing its effects on others, use three of the chief images employed by Renaissance rhetoricians for the passions: wild beasts, storms, and fires—although in every case their emphasis falls on the destructive nature of those phenomena. Clearly, as Montaigne puts it in his essay, rhetoric is poison.

All these writers echo arguments reviewed by their Latin predecessors, specifically by Quintilian in the second book of his *Institutio oratoria* and by Tacitus in his *Dialogus*. Quintilian, of course, wants to defend rhetoric, so he starts by acknowledging the charge that it leads to political subversion, a charge that prompted its banishment from both Athens and Sparta, but goes on to argue that to condemn rhetoric thus is to condemn a good thing because bad men misuse it (2.16.2–5). By contrast, Tacitus is much more critical, associating rhetoric with civil strife and proclaiming that it has become the equivalent of sedition and license since the peace of Augustus was established—although his suggestion that rhetoric is not needed at a time when the wisest men make all decisions allows for an ironic reading of his position, to say the least.[20] In any case, it is clear that the major political argument against rhetoric already exists in antiquity, and that Renaissance writers simply repeat it as they elaborate their views.

They do differ in at least one significant way from Quintilian and Tacitus, however, and that difference involves the specific historical context in which they are writing. For in the sixteenth and seventeenth centuries, at least, questions of political subversion are inextricably intertwined with questions of religious dissent. Renaissance writers on rhetoric often see their art as producing "faith" in the spectator, and such a tendency can only have reinforced associations between rhetoric and religion in the minds of Renaissance people, although the fact that preaching was considered a rhetorical genre should not be overlooked either.[21] Bacon, for instance, who recognizes the power of rhetoric but

[20] Tacitus, *Dialogus*, 36.2–4, 41.1–5.

[21] In the last book of his *Rhetoricorum*, George of Trebizond, for instance, declares: "Nothing carries off auditors to faith [*ad fidem*] more than if you move sharply the

also has grave doubts about it, directly associates the flowering of the discipline in the sixteenth century with the great religious upheaval of the age, the Reformation. Producing his own eccentric version of the history of the Renaissance revival of the classics, he says that Luther, in order to combat the Pope, "was enforced to awake all antiquity, and to call former times to his succors to make a party against the present time" (*Advancement of Learning* in *Selected Writings*, 180–81), with the result that ancient languages came to be studied more diligently and their style imitated, while that of the medieval schoolmen came to be despised.

> And again, because of the great labour then was with the people, . . . for the winning and persuading of them, there grew of necessity in chief price and request eloquence and variety of discourse, as the fittest and forciblest access into the capacity of the vulgar sort. So that these four causes concurring, the admiration of ancient authors, the hate of the schoolmen, the exact study of languages, and the efficacy of preaching, did bring in an affectionate study of eloquence and copie of speech, which then began to flourish. This speedily grew to an excess; for men began to hunt more after words than matter. (181)

Although Bacon does not associate this flowering of rhetoric directly with sedition and civil disturbance, his linking it to the Reformation could hardly fail to evoke such ideas for his contemporaries and encourage them to adopt the consciously antirhetorical program designed for "scientific" research which he spells out in his major writings.

The direct association of rhetoric with religion-based sedition does occur in one quite important text, Henry Cornelius Agrippa's *De Incertitudine et vanitate scientiarum* (On the uncertainty and vanity of knowledge). Like the other critics of rhetoric, Agrippa opens the chapter he devotes to it by denouncing it as a matter of flattery and lying, but he quickly shifts his attention to the more important danger it presents. To speak well is always useful, he admits, but it is also sometimes base, "most frequently dangerous, and always suspect" (29). There is consequently no place for rhetoric in a good commonwealth, "for equipped with it men often plot against states, and move seditions, while with

---

emotions you wish to move" (84'). Similarly, Agricola speaks of making *fidem* (*De Inventione*, 2), and de' Conti speaks of the rhetor's ability to *convertere* minds as he wishes (*Dialogus*, 152). The connection between rhetorical and religious belief goes back to antiquity, at least to the New Testament, whose notion of faith, *pistis* (Latin *fides*), has been shown to have been shaped by the rhetorical concept; see Kinneavy, *The Greek Rhetorical Origins of Christian Faith*.

this artful talkativeness they deceive some people, attack others, mock others, flatter others, and take possession of a certain tyranny over the innocent" (30). Reviewing the hostility to rhetoric in the ancient world, Agrippa notes that Plato wanted rhetoricians banished and that the most eloquent men—Demosthenes, the Gracchi, Cicero—were also *seditiosissimi* (30). Finally, he brings his denunciation into the present as he argues that since ancient times rhetoric has led to religious error, superstition, and suspicion of Holy Writ and has produced many heresies by means of its fallacious arguments, "which, injected into the ears of simple men, seduced them all from the word of truth" (32). Among those heretics Agrippa names Luther and concludes that many in Germany, praised for their eloquence, have become "the heads and leaders of heretics" (33), men he expects will soon stand before God's judgment.

Unlike Jewel and Patrizi, Montaigne and Agrippa, most writers on rhetoric in the Renaissance celebrate the art as the chief source of civilization, and supporting the status quo, they present the orator as its chief defender. In his oration on Quintilian and Statius's *Sylvae*, for instance, the Florentine humanist Angelo Poliziano stresses the positive role of the orator: "What can be so useful and productive as to be able to persuade with words all those things which you have found to be useful and advantageous to your state and to those people most dear to you, and to deter those same people from their wicked and useless courses?" (*Prosatori latini*, 882). George Puttenham argues similarly, although in his conception the orator's auditor becomes an unruly child who must be disciplined into rationality: "None other can so well beate [reason] into the ignorant head, as the well spoken and eloquent man" (*Arte*, 153). Most writers, however, identify the chief function of the orator in terms consistent with the myth of the orator-civilizer: he represses people's violent and destructive tendencies, thereby producing peace and order. In fact, they often celebrate the orator specifically for his ability to suppress sedition. Thus, Raphael Regius: "What can be more powerful and magnificent than to pacify the tumultuous sedition of the people by means of the speech of an eloquent man?" (*Panegyricus*, fvi^v). Similarly, Philip Melanchthon praises Cicero and Demosthenes for using eloquence as a sword to beat down "wicked and seditious citizens" (*Encomion*, 53), and Johann Heinrich Alsted declares there is no greater support for the state "than eloquence for the retaining of liberty and extinguishing the torches of sedition" (*Rhetorica*, 7^v).

Sedition is dangerous because it violates the supposedly "natural" order of things. Thus the English rhetorician Richard Sherry, writing in the mid-sixteenth century, argues for the usefulness of rhetors to the state by showing how they manage "the rude people" who "have commonly a preposterous judgement, and take the worst thynges for the beste, and the beste for the worst."[22] "Preposterous" in this sentence means getting things backward or upside down; the rhetor's eloquence functions to turn them right side up. Moreover, as the quotation from Regius suggests, the rhetor's words have a calming or pacifying effect, something Anto Maria de' Conti also stresses when he speaks of how, by means of eloquence, "the seditions and discords of the lower classes are calmed [*sedantur*]" (*Dialogus*, 152). Pierre Fabri sums up the positive function of rhetoric: "Eloquence is the queen of men, which, when joined to wisdom and knowledge, can inflame the lazy to all honorable perils, restrain mad spirits, pacify the wars of princes and popular seditions, and lead everything back to good peace and tranquillity" (*Le grand et vrai art*, 6; cf. Vives, *De Ratione*, 91, 94). This imagery of exciting and enflaming and of calming and pacifying fits an art that both works on the passions and takes as its aim the civilizing of beings whose natural state is imagined as barbaric, animallike, and destructive. No wonder M. Le Grand, after proclaiming rhetoric "the most important part of politics," goes on to reverse Plato's judgment in the *Gorgias*, which identified rhetoric with cookery and dialectic with health-giving medicine: "When the spirits of the people are disordered, and ills of the soul agitate the estates, eloquence has often brought health to sick provinces and dying states" (*Discours*, n.p.).

Although most rhetoricians celebrate their art as the source of civilization, some of them do admit, at least provisionally or in passing, the charge leveled by its critics that it can produce sedition or subversion. Guillaume Du Vair, for instance, in replying to those who say rhetoric is dangerous to civil government, confesses that "wicked men have been accustomed to use [it] to overturn laws, trouble the peace of the country, and bring to pass their evil designs" (*Traitté*, 397). Similarly, a Paduan professor of humanities, Antonio Riccobono, writing a defense of rhetoric at about the same time as Du Vair, identifies three general attacks on the art: by naturalists who see it as opposed to nature; by rationalists who despise it for being about words, not things; and by reformers "who contend that the art of rhetoric brings major ills to states and for that reason ought to be repudiated as most pernicious by all men."[23] Going beyond these writers, Henry Peacham creates a con-

---

[22] Richard Sherry, *A Treatise of Schemes and Tropes*, in *A Treatise of Schemes and Tropes (1550) and His Translation of "The Education of Children" by Desiderius Erasmus*, intro. Herbert W. Hildebrandt (Gainesville, Fla.: Scholars' Facsimiles & Reprints, 1961), 70.

[23] Antonio Riccobono, "De Studio artis Rhetoricae," in *Orationes* (Padua, 1592), vol. 1; cited in Giancarlo Mazzacurati, *La crisi della retorica umanistica nel cinque-*

stant awareness of rhetoric's destructive potential in his *Garden of Elo-quence* by placing a section called "The Caution" after his discussion of each figure of speech, thus reminding the reader continually that al-though figures may have many constructive uses, they may also be mis-used in a variety of ways, including ways that undermine social order and religion. The most vivid example his text offers involves the figure *protrope*, "a forme of speech, by which the Orator exhorteth and per-swadeth his hearers to do some thing" (77). Under "The Caution" he writes: "The greater power that this figure hath, the more mischiefe it may worke, if it be perverted and turned to abuse. . . . It is abused by moving and leading to unlawfull things, as by moving of sedition, tu-mults, or rebellion among the simple people, by leading ignorant per-sons into dangers and miserie, by seducing unstable mindes into false religion and vanities, and by many mo like effectes, which Sathan doth alwaies further to the uttermost of his power" (78).

Linking the power of eloquence with social turmoil and religious dis-sent, Peacham unites the major strands of criticism directed at rhetoric by its detractors in the Renaissance. Like all other celebrants of the art, however, Peacham admits these objections only in order to disarm his hypothetical opponents, to insist, with Du Vair and Riccobono, that a seditious rhetoric is simply a perversion of the true art. Luis de Granada agrees: he recognizes that eloquence misused can spread "fraud and the impiety of heretics" (*Ecclesiastica Rhetorica*, 13) but claims that it will defeat such evils if correctly employed. He goes on to argue, using an analogy pregnant with meaning for his contemporaries, that to refuse rhetoric because of its corruption by others would be the equivalent of refusing to use cannons and other firearms just because the Turks have been doing so. If one accepts these writers' intentions, then, one can say that their treatises raise the specter of a seditious rhetoric only in order to banish it (which is precisely what the critics of the discipline wished to do with rhetoric itself). Yet although Peacham, Granada, and the others strive mightily to free the rhetoric they advocate from contam-ination by its Satanic, seditious double, they fail. Their constant evoca-tion of that double defeats them, for its appearance in their works re-minds the reader repeatedly that the art they celebrate for its ability to civilize and control the seditious impulses of the mob is indistinguish-able from the art that incites sedition and threatens to turn the state topsy-turvy. J. Du Pré de la Porte sums up:

cento (*Antonio Riccobono*) (Naples: Libreria Scientifica Editrice, 1961), 120–21. For other examples of the identification of rhetoric with sedition within texts ostensibly concerned to praise the art, see Furetière, *Nouvelle allégorique*, 71; Speroni, *Dialogo*, 133–34; de' Conti, *Dialogus*, 154; and Puttenham, *Arte*, 166–67.

Eloquence has two handles, one of which, good, straight, and simple, corrects badly shaped spirits, and orders them to do their duty; and the other, perverse, always shifting, and malignant, strives only to disunite the wills of men and make them clash, furnishing them with matter for debates and civil contention, which throw them into a labyrinth of affairs from which they cannot get out unless God takes them by the hand. (*Pourtraict*, 26)

Unlike Du Vair, de' Conti, and the others just cited, most writers on rhetoric in the Renaissance prefer to respond to the challenges of their critics and the ambiguity of rhetoric simply by ignoring the issues of sedition and social upheaval. Nevertheless, virtually all writers on the subject may be seen to conjure up the specter of subversion and political resistance in a variety of ways, even if they never actively incite their readers to acts of rebellion. For all their orthodoxy, they cannot prevent their works—and rhetoric itself—from appearing, if only hypothetically at times, as a challenge to the status quo. First, consider what is implied by the fact that practically all their works were printed and hence read by some sort of general audience. Although a few writers, such as Jacques Amyot, may have aimed their treatises at actual rulers and never sought to have them published, the rest definitely wanted theirs to be. They thus provided knowledge of rhetoric, no matter what their conservative intentions, not merely to kings and members of the ruling class but to everyone who was able to read, a potentially vast audience that only increased in size as literacy spread and especially as more and more rhetorics were produced in the vernacular languages. Since printing made the art of rhetoric accessible to virtually all comers, and since it supposedly enabled its practitioners to become emperors of men's minds, rhetoric treatises had the capacity to create at least hypothetically an imbalance in power between their readers and legitimate rulers, putting a weapon in the hands of the former by means of which they could criticize, resist, and possibly even subvert the rule of the latter (see Parker, *Literary Fat Ladies*, 98).

Although rhetoricians never acknowledge the problem posed by an unrestricted readership, it nevertheless surfaces within their works in the unresolved ambiguity of the audiences they address. Usually, those works are dedicated to monarchs or noblemen or gentlemen—members of the ruling class—who are also occasionally addressed directly within the text. Yet those same works are almost invariably intended for a much broader audience of rhetoric students and teachers, and that audience is also addressed quite directly. In fact, some works follow the standard dedication to a particular noble patron with a preface addressed to a general audience. For the most part, this second audience lacks any specific social status; authors refer generally to "readers"—inevitably male—who may be defined not by their position in the social order but by their need for instruction, and whom the author courts by asking them to receive his work favorably. This potentially leveling effect of rhetoric, its implicit equation of kings with, if not clowns, at least all those who are literate, also surfaces repeatedly throughout the texts whenever sample speeches or other rhetorical performances are provided, for those samples by no means drop exclusively from the lips of actual rulers. George Puttenham, for example, prefers to illustrate rhetorical figures by citing the sayings of rulers, but they are not the only ones he credits with such wit and skill. Thus, after providing examples of sarcasm from the emperor Charles V and Henry VIII, he shows that a comparable figure of speech, *Asteismus*—which he defines as a kind of civil scoffing—has been practiced by the Roman Cato as well as by kings such as Edward VI and Charles V (*Arte*, 200). Even more strikingly, in defining the figure he calls "*Antiphrasis*, or the Broad floute," he speaks of a socially unpositioned "we" and an equally unpositioned "he": "When we deride by plaine and flat contradiction, as he that saw a dwarfe go in the streete said to his companion that walked with him: See yonder gyant: and to a Negro or woman blackemoore, in good sooth ye are a faire one, we may call it the broad floute" (201). These examples reveal what the fact of publication dramatizes as well: rhetoric is an art not restricted to legitimate rulers. One is thus prepared to greet with skepticism the claim made by Jacques Amyot that there are two distinct sorts of eloquence, one used by "public speakers who have striven entirely to flatter and please the people," and a superior sort used by "great persons . . . who have most occupied themselves with the ruling of states and empires" (*Projet*, 8). Indeed, as he unfolds his teaching, Amyot offers not two different rhetorics but a single one whose principal features fail to distinguish it in any way from the rhetoric that schoolboys from every social class were being taught throughout western Europe in the period. Consequently, if there are no truly discrete rhetorics for kings and commoners, and if rhetoric is indeed what Renaissance writers proclaimed it to be, an art of rule, then its subversive potential is at least as great as its potential to reinforce the status quo. In the hands of rulers it may serve to discipline those who manifest "preposterous judgement," but it may just as readily become a weapon in the hands of people much further down in the social hierarchy whose eloquence could, from the viewpoint of the ruler, turn the world upside down.

Rhetoric treatises and handbooks may be seen as unintended instruments of subversion for yet another reason, one again connected with the fact of their publication: as they detail the techniques by means of which orators control the responses of their audience and thus rule over it, those works can be seen as demystifying the activities of rulers and thus undermining their authority. When writers explain how rhetoric affects the passions, how structural devices, figures, and gestures all determine particular responses, they are revealing the secrets of their art not only to practitioners who may be, but are not necessarily, legitimate rulers but also to those on whom that art is supposed to work. In other words, rhetoric treatises offer prospective audiences a means of self-defense, even though they may never have been intended to serve such a purpose, any more than they consciously seek to demystify the behavior of kings and emperors. Occasionally, however, a writer will acknowledge the fact that rhetorical manipulation is in some sense deeply illegitimate, that it functions to create, rather than merely validate, the authority of the supposedly legitimate ruler.

Consider in this connection the *Arte of Rhetorique* of Thomas Wilson. His book is studded with statements reinforcing the status quo and acknowledging the innate superiority of those above him in the social hierarchy. The intrinsic merit of the noblemen Henry Duke of Suffolk and Lord Charles his brother is such, Wilson is convinced, that "the onely naming of them, will stirre honest hearts to speake well of them" (14). Later, as he is about to offer an exemplary speech of comfort to the Duchess of Suffolk, he recognizes the potential offensiveness of seeming "to take upon mee to teach my betters" (66) but excuses his presumption by identifying it as his duty. In general, Wilson affirms the principle that nature has taught humans to pay "Reverence to the superiour" (32). Nevertheless, at the very start of his treatise, as he unfolds his own version of the myth of the orator-civilizer, identifying the figure as Hercules and celebrating his ability to have brought men into cities and to have accepted their subjection to others, he produces a most remarkable series of rhetorical questions. They may aim at making the reader marvel at the power of oratory, but they simultaneously serve to demystify totally the activities of the ruling class.

> For what man I pray you, beeing better able to maintaine himself by valiaunt courage, then by living in base subjection, would not rather looke to rule like a Lord, then to live like an underling: if by reason he were not perswaded, that it behoveth every man to live in his owne vocation: and not to seeke any higher roume, then wherunto he was at the first appointed? Who would digge and delve from Morne till Evening? Who would travaile and toyle with ye sweat of his browes? Yea, who would for his Kings pleasure adventure and hassarde his life, if witte had not so won men, that they thought nothing more needfull in

this world, nor any thing whereunto they were more bounden: then
here to live in their duetie, and to traine their whole life according to
their calling. (vii^r–vii^v)

This passage can be read as an affirmation of the rightness of the social
hierarchy if one stresses that persuasion is a matter of reason, rather
than the arbitrary will and desire of the orator; in fact, Wilson insists
that what his orator argues for is "found out by reason" (vii^r) and even
identifies orators as God's elect. Still, if that is the perspective he
wishes to advance, the passage is remarkable for the way in which it
expresses not deference to legitimate authority but, rather, resistance to
it, even irritation at its infringement on personal liberty. Wilson seems,
for a moment at least, to speak like a Leveller *avant la lettre*, for he
appears to adopt a radical, antiauthoritarian tone and perspective as he
refers to "*base* subjection" and suggests that men are manipulated into
giving up their lives, as well as their liberty, merely for the "Kings *pleasure*." Most striking is the sentence, "Who would digge and delve from
Morne till Evening?" This question could simply refer back to the Fall
and to Adam's punishment, of course, but the problem is that it would
then have no relationship at all to the art of persuasion. For according to
the Bible, humans dig and delve not because they are persuaded to do so
but because they have no choice in the matter, thanks to their expulsion from the Garden. In the context of Wilson's passage, however, the
question seems to imply that they do have a choice, just as they can
choose to live like a lord or an underling, to serve the king's pleasure or
not. Digging and delving thus appear less matters of natural necessity
than the result of the orator's ability to persuade people to do things
they would not do of their own accord. Wilson's question could be read
as a protest, one that seems to echo the sentiments, and even some of
the words, of a popular antiauthoritarian couplet: "When Adam delved
and Eve span, / Who was then the Gentleman?" Wilson goes on after
this passage to exalt the orator as being "halfe a God" (vii^v) precisely for
his ability to persuade the naturally resistant, antiauthoritarian individual, whose sentiments have been captured here however fleetingly, to
accept his status as an obedient subject, someone who would "naturally" feel "Reverence to the superiour." No matter how much Wilson
argues for the status quo throughout his treatise and manifests the correct deference to authority, however, the damage has been done.[24]

Most Renaissance rhetoricians never come close to the revelations of

[24] For a fine analysis of these issues see Frank Whigham, *Ambition and Privilege:
The Social Tropes of Elizabethan Courtesy Theory* (Berkeley: University of California
Press, 1984), 1–31.

Wilson's passage, but they do something else that could be construed as potentially subversive and that certainly puts them at odds with the powers above them. Specifically, although Renaissance rhetoricians seldom imagine their orator practicing deliberative oratory before a republican assembly, they do see him practicing it in providing counsel to his superiors. They also see him offering counsel indirectly by means of the epideictic oratory he uses to celebrate rulers for their good qualities while denouncing others for their bad ones. This position as counselor, no matter how the orator hedges it about with expressions of deference, implicitly puts him in an intellectual and moral position above the person he advises. Even if his "counsel" amounts to praise for his master, praise is by its very nature coercive, as Bacon explains in his essay on the subject: "Some praises come of good wishes and respects, which is a form due in civility to kings and great persons, *laudando praecipere*, when by telling men what they are, they represent to them what they should be."[25] *Laudando praecipere*, "to teach by praising": as Bacon presents it here, praise is a matter not of sycophantic flattery but of educating and controlling the person one praises, even if one acts out of "good wishes and respects." The potential for opposition between the rhetor and the ruler is even clearer when one considers the way the former is repeatedly assigned the task of criticizing tyranny. For instance, Henry Peacham recounts his own version of the orator-civilizer myth by celebrating those "who by their singular wisdom and eloquence, made savage nations civil, wild people tame, and cruell tyrants not only to become meeke, but likewise merciful" (*Garden*, iii^v). Later he identifies the figure *philophronesis*, which involves using gentle speech with a stronger adversary, as being especially effective in civil affairs, for "it often appeaseth the malice of enemies, mollifieth the cruell hearts of tyrants, saveth the life of innocents, and preventeth the destruction of Cities and countries" (97). Similarly, Gracien Du Pont writes in the early sixteenth century that if nurses can quiet crying children, Arion can call dolphins to come to him, poets such as Sophocles can cure maniacs, and so on, then "with even more justice will . . . the eloquent tongue of a good orator appease the ire and anger of a tyrant."[26] Du Pont documents his case by noting how Cicero, by completely overwhelming Julius Caesar and putting him into an ecstasy, thereby forced him to change a sentence he had passed (ii^r). Sir Philip Sidney does not see his poet appeasing the tyrant so much as correcting him by means of repre-

---

[25] Francis Bacon, "Of Praise," in *The Essays*, ed. John Pitcher (Harmondsworth: Penguin, 1985), 215.

[26] Gracien Du Pont, *Art et science de rhethoricque metriffiée* (Toulouse, 1539; Geneva: Slatkine Reprints, 1972), i^v.

senting his actions in a tragedy, a work "that openeth the greatest wounds and showeth forth the ulcers that are covered with tissue; that maketh kings fear to be tyrants, and tyrants manifest their tyrannical humors" (*Apology*, 45). Sidney then recounts an anecdote from Plutarch about the tyrant Alexander Phereus, who, in murdering countless people, "was not ashamed to make matters for tragedies, yet could not resist the sweet violence of a tragedy" he witnessed (46).[27]

By presenting the rhetor explicitly as the critic of bad rulers, of tyrants, rather than of reigning princes, Renaissance writers on rhetoric attempt to protect themselves from charges of subversiveness. Nevertheless, the techniques they describe for mollifying the hard hearts of despots such as Alexander Phereus can just as easily be used on rulers never once associated with tyranny. More important, there are moments of slippage when the writer reveals—surely unwittingly—that the orator's manipulation is focused less on tyrants than on the powerful in general, including, of course, legitimate rulers. Thus, Henry Peacham may note that *philophronesis* "mollifieth the cruell hearts of tyrants," but his target is somewhat different when he speaks of *parrhesia*, a figure that involves craving pardon beforehand when the orator speaks to "those whom he feareth, or ought to reverence" (*Garden*, 113). Peacham says that this figure may be used "to insinuate, admonish, and reprehend" and is "the onely forme that boldly delivereth to great dignities and most high degrees of men, the message of justice and equitie, sparing neither magistrates that pervert lawes, nor Princes that do abuse their kingdomes" (114–15). Although one might argue that a prince who abuses his kingdom is actually a tyrant, Peacham's text makes no such restriction; he envisages his orator rebuking a legitimate monarch but doing so with tact and in safety. He then adds the caution that such a figure best befits a grave man who knows how to restrain the rude boldness involved and thus can avoid what may very well happen: "a contempt of his [i.e., the orator's] doctrine, and sometimes a punishment of his person, for now and then a rude *Vae vobis* [Woe to you], doth cause a *Coram nobis* [Appear before us]" (115).

Although Richard Rainolde fills his *Foundacion of Rhetorike* with assertions of loyalty to the reigning monarch and the status quo, he too allows the orator's role as the scourge of tyrants to become that of the

---

[27] Sidney notes that Alexander Phereus withdrew from the theater lest the work he was seeing should affect him too much—suggesting that for all the power Sidney attributes to poetry and rhetoric, human beings still retain the ability to resist and defeat it. For a helpful commentary on the way Sidney's text deconstructs its own argument, see Margaret Ferguson, *Trials of Desire: Renaissance Defenses of Poetry* (New Haven: Yale University Press, 1983), 153–62.

flagellum principum. He begins his work by showing how Demosthenes employed a fable to rouse the Athenians to resist Philip of Macedonia, who might easily be seen as a would-be tyrant. This example of an effective use of a fable is followed by another in which the Bishop of Ely, imprisoned by the Duke of Buckingham during the tyrannical reign of Richard III, defends himself from being induced to make potentially disloyal statements. Rainolde's third example comes even closer to his own day and is much more problematic, since it does not deal with someone who could be dismissed as a tyrant. It involves Henry VIII, identified as "a prince of famous memorie" (iiii^r), into whose control the Parliament gave over the "small houses of religion," and John Fisher, who protested by means of a fable from Aesop a decision he saw as preparatory to pulling down the great abbeys. It remains something of a mystery why Rainolde, an ambitious man, should recount an incident that celebrates the wit and skill of John Fisher, a cleric whom Henry had had executed and who was hardly a hero during the reign of Elizabeth when Rainolde produced his work.[28] The movement from Demosthenes to Ely to Fisher, however, does dramatically underscore the orator's role as the critic of rulers, whether those rulers may be dismissed as tyrants or not.

More revealingly, the independent-minded Furió Ceriol proclaims in the peroration to his *Institutionum Rhetoricarum Libri Tres* (Three books of instruction in rhetoric) of 1554 that the good orator is above kings, since he can bend them with his words.[29] And Johann Heinrich Alsted, after claiming that the orator's power gives him an empire (*imperium*) over men, goes on to conclude "that the power of orators is greater than that of the highest kings" (*Rhetorica*, Dedication, 8^r). What is clear from such examples, as from the slippage between tyrant and legitimate monarch in other works, is that rhetoricians see the orator not as the ruler's double but, at least potentially, as his most accomplished critic and opponent—sometimes, perhaps, even his superior. It is thus hardly surprising that rhetoricians would conclude that their art

[28] That Rainolde was self-willed, hard-driving, and ambitious can be deduced from the facts of his life. He went to Cambridge on a scholarship, never completed his medical degree, but practiced medicine without a license and was tried for doing so. He took holy orders and was granted a rectory by the queen in 1568 and an additional vicarage in 1578, but was tried for irregularity the next year. Most important, he dedicated his *Foundacion* to one of Elizabeth's favorites, Robert Dudley, the Earl of Leicester, and his *De statu nobilium virorum et principum*, a work still in manuscript, to the Duke of Norfolk. See the article on Rainolde in the *The Dictionary of National Biography*, ed. Leslie Stephen and Sidney Lee (Oxford: Oxford University Press, 1921–22).

[29] See Martí, *La preceptiva retórica española*, 60.

is capable of making its practitioner into a tyrant, as do both Juan Luis Vives, when he says that Roman rhetors exercised over others "a certain metaphorical tyranny [*quandam velut tyrannidem*]" (*De Causis*, 154), and Guillaume Du Vair, when he claims that orators' "commands are no less violent than those of tyrants surrounded by their guards and attendants" (*Traitté*, 410).

Perhaps the most subversive aspect of the orator as he is imagined by Renaissance rhetoricians involves his placement in the social and political hierarchy—or, rather, his non-placement, his uncertain placement, within it. Writings on rhetoric in the period implicitly raise the question of just who, and where, the rhetor is. Rhetoric, after all, is not exactly a profession; books that purport to teach it do not claim to be training specialists for some specific function in the social order in the way that medical, legal, and theological instruction aimed at producing doctors, lawyers, and theologians.[30] Indeed, most treatises include sections on all sorts of rhetoric, thus potentially serving the interests of future legislators, jurists and lawyers, courtiers, and preachers. Indeed, many writers extend the domain of rhetoric to include practically all social interactions, so that the questions of the orator's profession and particular place in the social hierarchy become moot. Hence, to call someone an "orator," except when that term is being employed as the equivalent of "ambassador," is to employ an honorific title more than to indicate a distinct profession. A training for generalists, rhetoric was a preparation for all careers and no career at the same time.[31]

Since the orator, by definition, exercises a nonprofession, it should hardly be surprising that he is socially unlocatable when he is represented in rhetorical treatises. To see what this means, let us return briefly to Bacon's allegory of the passions as the lower classes and the reason as king. In that allegory, eloquence is seen as serving king-reason by moving the commoner-passions or, alternatively, the imagination or the will, which may also be made to fit into the allegory because, as

[30] Note that the categories of lawyer and rhetorician overlapped in the Renaissance, so that they were sometimes identified with each other, as they are in Du Pré's *Pourtraict*.

[31] The two professions (in addition to teaching rhetoric) for which rhetorical training did in fact prepare people were service in secular or ecclesiastical bureaucracies and service as personal secretary. Such positions are seldom specified in the rhetorical treatises, however, perhaps because they were essentially dependent upon patronage rather than, say, acquiring a degree or passing an examination, for which formal training might indeed prepare an individual. Of course, one could acquire a patron using rhetoric to manipulate others, but unlike becoming a doctor or a lawyer, that was the means to a career, not a career itself. On the actual employment of those trained in rhetoric—and the rest of the liberal arts—see Grendler, *Schooling in Renaissance Italy*, 135–36.

mental faculties, they are necessarily part of the same body as the passions and the reason. But what does not "fit" is eloquence, which is
quite literally outside the body in question, and since the body includes
within it the entire state, eloquence and the orator who uses it have no
determined place in the state at all, even if they are imagined as playing
a role of the greatest importance in serving its ruler. Renaissance rhetoric is, as Joan de Guzman understood, the ultimate shape-shifter: "I say
that rhetoric is neither more nor less than another Proteus who converts
himself into everything he desires and takes everything as his material"
(*Primera Parte*, 15^v; cf. 9^v). Clearly, such a rhetoric makes its practitioner a version of Proteus, too. It identifies him as a version of the
Renaissance individual as self-fashioner, the protean figure described so
memorably in the myth with which Pico della Mirandola begins his
famous oration on the dignity of man. In Pico's work, God creates the
universe as an immense hierarchy of beings, plants, and things; then,
wanting someone to admire His handiwork, He creates man. Because
God has used up all his archetypes, however, and the entire universe is
filled, no position is left in the hierarchy in which to place this newly
created being. Nevertheless, God displays divine ingenuity and turns
seeming defeat into glorious victory, for He defines man as a being with
nothing proper to his nature and as sharing everything potentially with
all the other orders of the universe. He then addresses His creation:
"Neither a fixed seat, nor your own proper appearance, nor any function
peculiar to you, O Adam, do we give you, so that you may have and
possess, according to your desire and knowledge, whatever seat, appearance, or functions you yourself might desire."[32] Pico's protean man has
no fixed place; he is ontologically undetermined, unlocatable in the hierarchy of the universe, just as the Renaissance orator is in the social
hierarchy. Both figures can be, like God, simultaneously everywhere
and nowhere, everything and nothing; and both are, as a result, profoundly disturbing to an age that wanted to see the universe and the
social order reflecting it as fixed hierarchies in which everything had its
predetermined and appropriate place.

Although the Renaissance discourse of rhetoric rarely calls the orator

---

[32] Giovanni Pico della Mirandola, *Oratio de hominis dignitate*, in *De Hominis Dig-
nitate, Heptaplus, De Ente et Uno*, ed. Eugenio Garin (Florence: Vallechi Editore,
1942), 104–6. On the notions of self-fashioning and man as Proteus, see Thomas M.
Greene, "The Flexibility of the Self in Renaissance Literature," in *The Disciplines of
Criticism*, ed. Peter Demetz, Thomas M. Greene, and Lowry Nelson, Jr. (New Haven:
Yale University Press, 1968), 241–64; A. Bartlett Giamatti, "Proteus Unbound: Some
Versions of the Sea God in the Renaissance," in *The Disciplines of Criticism*, 437–
75; and Stephen Greenblatt, *Renaissance Self-Fashioning: From More to Shakespeare*
(Chicago: University of Chicago Press, 1980).

"another Proteus," it does speak with some frequency of his social mobility. As early as 1421 one finds the Sienese doctor Andrea Benzi praising the art because it has allowed so many individuals to attain "the greatest magistracies, the most resplendent glory, and the highest power" (Müllner, 111). Later in the century Andrea Brenta delivers a speech at Rome in which he recommends rhetoric to his audience as the means by which people of low stock can achieve the highest honors, a contention he supports by reference to what happened in ancient Rome: "It [rhetoric] flourished in this city, such that many were able to progress from the lowest orders to the highest dignities and even as far as the consulship" (Müllner, 76–77). Writing in the sixteenth century, Sperone Speroni has one of the characters in his *Dialogo della rettorica* demonstrate the value of epideictic rhetoric by telling a story in which it serves as a source of social advancement. The story begins in a hypothetical mood: if a man who possessed nothing (*nudo*) should come to Bologna and try to speak in the law courts, he would be dismissed as a base lawyer, nor would he be listened to if he offered political advice; however, through the exercise of epideictic rhetoric in the service of truth, "in a little time he will be feared and appreciated not only by his equals, but by lords and by kings" (111). Another of Speroni's characters recognizes this hypothesis as the actual story of the great Italian *littérateur* Pietro Aretino, who was widely celebrated in the period as the *flagellum principum*. The first speaker then responds by extolling such success, which, he says, is like ecclesiastical dignities in that it is won "by one's own industry, . . . and just as a particular gentleman once made Pope is adored by his lords, so the great ones of the world yield . . . to the good orator" (111). Finally, identifying rhetoric with the liberal arts in general, Joan de Guzman writes: "It is certain and established in all the world that not only have men of base fortune become famous by means of letters alone, such as a Socrates, son of a midwife, a Demosthenes whose father was not known, a Euripides who did not know who had been his mother, but even those who were considered illustrious through their ancestors were much more resplendent" (*Primera Parte*, 28^r–28^v). Although Guzman is careful to cite Alonso of Aragon and Alonso the Wise of Castille as examples of great men who raised themselves still higher by means of the liberal arts, the truly radical implications of his position emerge when he notes that even *women*, albeit very few of them, have been able to gain fame and social prominence through oratory.[33]

---

[33] Guzman's position is radical in the context of an age and a discourse that imagined rhetoric as an almost exclusively male art. That radicalism is somewhat qualified, however, by the fact that Guzman offers only one example of a woman orator,

Although rhetoric was a means for advancement in the Greek and Roman world, just as it was seen to be in the Renaissance, only Tacitus among ancient writers directly addresses this aspect of the art.[34] Tacitus contrasts the days of the Republic, when men rose by means of oratory (*Dialogus*, 8.2–4), with his own period—dominated by Caesar—in which servile flattery rather than public debate is the norm (13.4–6). He declares that the rule of Caesar is preferable to the civil strife of the preceding period, but he is clearly nostalgic for the days when eloquence made one a *patronus*, rather than just a member of a group of "insignificant clients [*clientulorum*]" (37.1). By contrast, Renaissance writers live in a time of real social mobility, and they look back to the ancient world, and particularly to the Roman Republic, for models of how one can rise by means of rhetoric. As noted in the preceding chapter, Julius Caesar is frequently celebrated in the same breath for his oratorical power and his achievement of political preeminence by means of arms. Andrea Benzi, writing around 1421, insists on the superiority of rhetoric to arms and claims that Peisistratos, Pericles, Philip, and Alexander, as well as Caesar, were able "to accomplish greater and more famous deeds by eloquence than by arms" (Müllner, 111). Andrea Brenta similarly declares that all the Romans strove for eloquence, even snatching time away from war to exercise it, just as Caesar did (Müllner, 76). Brenta's chief example of rising by means of oratory, however, is not Caesar but a man of low stock who came from the town of Arpino and who, thanks to his rhetorical skill, achieved "the highest . . . honors and magistracies" (76). Brenta is referring, of course, to Cicero, who is for obvious reasons the inevitable model for Renaissance writers. A passage from Richard Rainolde's *Foundacion of Rhetorike* exemplifies his culture's view of the great Roman orator. After discussing generally the kind of oration he labels a "comparison," which is defined as a form of epideictic oratory involving the praise of two good things or the condemnation of two bad ones, Rainolde unfolds a model speech in which he compares Cicero with his Greek counterpart Demosthenes. Both orators are celebrated for their personal virtues and their skill in speech, and they are then praised as self-made men: "Bothe Demosthenes and Tullie were borne, of verie meane parentes and auncestours: yet thei thorowe their learnyng and vertues, became famous, ascendyng to all nobilitee. Of their vertues and learnyng, not of their auncestours, nobilitee rose to

Aspasia of Milesia, and she lived in antiquity, not during the Renaissance. For other visions of the orator's social mobility, see Daniel Barbaro, *Della Eloquenza*, 367; and Puttenham, *Arte*, 304.

[34] According to Kerferd (*The Sophistic Movement*, 26, 131), the Sophists appeared in Greece at a time when social change and social mobility were possible.

them" (xlvii^v). Near the end of the speech, Rainolde reiterates this notion of self-raising while celebrating his heroes for another reason as
well, which has already been shown to call forth the specter of subversion: "You can not finde soche twoo Orators, who borne of meane &
poore parentes, that attained so great honour, who also did objecte
themselves to tyrantes a like" (xlviii^v). The fantasy of social mobility
that Rainolde articulates here is not meant to be subversive, of course.
Like all the other writers on rhetoric in the period, he has a deep invest-
ment in the supposed legitimacy of such advancement, which he presents simply as an appropriate reward for oratorical ability, wisdom, and
political skill. But in a world where rulers still derived their legitimacy
from their *blood*, from the supposedly fixed positions they inherited
from their ancestors, rather than from their handling of the word, it is
easy to see why such a vision of advancement might be construed as
subversion.

Chapter I argued that one of the orator's chief stylistic devices, metaphor or *translatio*, is by its nature a figure of conquest, invasion, and
domination: it involves the necessary crossing of boundaries in order to
appropriate terrain outside the self. Although such an act certainly fits
the notion of a rhetor-ruler, however, kings are not the only ones who
use metaphor. Indeed, it can be employed by those outside the social
order, by subversives and rebels, as easily as it can be by legitimate
monarchs. In other words, metaphor can be a powerful instrument of
social resistance and personal advancement, as well as a means for kings
and nobles to maintain their positions atop the hierarchy of society.
Revealingly, Johann Heinrich Alsted defines tropes in general with the
metaphor *usurpator* (*Rhetorica*, 12), thus underscoring their subversive
rather than socially conservative nature—and, by implication, saying
exactly the same thing about rhetoric itself. Tropes may be a means to
rule, but they are also a means for those at the bottom to rise to the top.
At the very least, as Michel de Certeau has argued, they provide a way
for ordinary people to secure a symbolic "place" for themselves through
language, a "place" they appropriate in order to unfold their identities
and to resist and critique the dominance of the privileged and the powerful.[35]

George Puttenham, unlike most Renaissance rhetoricians, actually
comes quite close to confronting the subversive implications of an art
which, he says, aims to lead its practitioner "from the carte . . . to the
Court" (*Arte*, 304). Sensing that the powers-that-be might feel threat-

---

[35] Michel de Certeau, *The Practice of Everyday Life*, trans. Steven Rendall (Berkeley: University of California Press, 1984), 1–42.

ened by such an advance, Puttenham attempts to deflect criticism by denigrating poetry, insisting that it is merely a matter of idleness and youthful folly. He claims that experience shows how "many times idlenesse is lesse harmefull than unprofitable occupation, dayly seeing how these great aspiring mynds and ambitious heads of the world seriously searching to deale in matters of state, be often times so busie and earnest that they were better be unoccupied" (314). This is not the only time in his treatise that Puttenham protects his art from the charge of subversion by asserting its essential triviality. A most important instance occurs when he deals with rhetorical figures, which he, like so many others in the Renaissance, defines as "in a sorte abuses or rather trespasses in speach," a characterization whose suggestion of subversiveness is confirmed when he immediately goes on to recollect that Athenian judges at one time forbade "all manner of figurative speaches to be used before them in their consistorie of Justice, as meere illusions to the minde, and wresters of upright judgement" (166). Puttenham's defense at this point is to claim that he is fashioning a poet who is not a judge but a "pleader, and that of pleasant and lovely causes and nothing perillous, . . . and before judges neither sower nor severe, but in the eare of princely dames, yong ladies, gentlewomen and courtiers, . . . and that all his abuses tende but to dispose the hearers to mirth and sollace by pleasant conveyance and efficacy of speach" (166–67). Since Puttenham is elsewhere so fervent in defense of the seriousness of his art, however, and since he insists that it is a means to bring the poet-orator to the court, his effort here to discount the social and political threat contained in the latter's activities rings hollow; it is a case of "the orator doth protest too much" and only serves to reconfirm the notion that poetry, as a source of personal mobility, may threaten the stability of the social hierarchy just as much as politically "aspiring mynds" do.

Puttenham's defense of the poet-orator is less than fully convincing because he, like virtually all writers on rhetoric in the Renaissance, is profoundly conflicted about society and his place in it. On the one hand, they all feel compelled to validate the social and political hierarchies of their world, in part because they cannot advance without the support of those above them, and in part because rising itself would be meaningless if the hierarchy within which it occurred lacked validity. On the other hand, social mobility denies the principle of fixity involved in hierarchy and, if it does not dissolve hierarchy, at the very least renders it fluid and unstable. This doubleness of response is played out in the writings of Renaissance rhetoricians as a series of tensions: between repeated, at times exaggerated expressions of deference, especially to the lords to whom treatises were normally dedicated, and celebrations of both the orator's social mobility and his political role as a critic of tyranny; between direct affirmations of the rightness of the existing social order and flashes of protest of various sorts against it; between the myth of the orator-civilizer and anecdotes about Hegesias and the Egyptians. In general, the writers are essentially outsiders who wish to get inside; they are learned men who lack the prerequisite of blood which would put them in positions of power and who have to rely on a substitute, the word, to get what they want.

A striking illustration of the conflicted response of Renaissance rhetoricians to the social position of the orator can be found in J. Du Pré de la Porte's *Pourtraict de l'Eloquence Françoise*. Consisting of a long introduction describing the nature and contemporary status of oratory and then ten of Du Pré's own orations, this rhetoric text, like so many others in the Renaissance, has a double dedication, first to Henri d'Orléans, Duc de Longueville, and then to the *orateurs* of Normandy: that is, to the lawyers who served in the provincial *parlement* and with whom Du Pré clearly identifies himself. In keeping with the fundamental conservatism of Renaissance rhetoricians, he insists upon the merely middling position of these *orateurs* in the social order, a position he defines by means of imagery derived from the body. Orators, he says, are the "spirits" (*esprits*) who link together magistrates or rulers as the "soul" (*ame*) of society to the people who are its "body" (*corps*) (3). As Du Pré continues his effort to define the social position of his orators, however, his images gradually confer on them an increasingly elevated social status: they are called the arms of Hercules, then metamorphose into the heart that vivifies the entire body, and finally become the sun in the fourth heaven (3–4). Thus, by the time he has finished, he is defining the group by means of images usually reserved for rulers and even for God (to whom he actually compares the orators for other reasons on the second page of his work). That Du Pré is not as radical as his imagery implies is revealed by his lament throughout his introduction that eloquence has been ignored by the true rulers of French society, the gentlemen and nobles, who have allowed unspecified inferiors to appropriate it for their own uses. His text most reveals his conflicted social position when he reviews the excuse some have offered for the situation he deplores: that the individuals who currently cultivate eloquence do so because those with a better title to it do not.

The social identity of those lower-class cultivators of eloquence becomes clear when Du Pré says they are like the "younger brother who at the refusal of the elder would seize the right to inherit [*preciput*], . . . the criminal who would run from the oar to the tiller which the pilot abandoned, and . . . the pawn who, having passed through the seven squares of the chessboard without being taken by the knights, is made a piece of honor" (18–19). He begins by identifying just that group of individuals, younger sons, who felt the greatest pressure toward social advancement in the Renaissance and who were, most memorably, in the vanguard of the invasion and conquest of the New World. Blaming the hereditary rulers of society for allowing such a situation to exist, Du Pré presents it initially as a violation of the right of inheritance, the *preciput*, and then, even more tendentiously, he identifies socially mobile orators with criminals confined to the galleys. In this passage, as in the earlier one defining the orator as the heart and the sun, his imagery gets away from him, and he ends with a figure that might not be read as negative at all. For by comparing the orator to the lowly pawn in chess, which can even become a queen if it manages to cross the board, Du Pré leaves behind the clear moral perspective of his first two comparisons for something that appears at least neutral. To be sure, he sets up a parallel with the two preceding comparisons not merely by noting that the pawn has advanced but by stressing that the knights have failed to stop it. But his imagery here turns society into a game whose rules specifically allow such an advancement to occur, as well as permitting inferior pieces to "take" superior ones. It is, moreover, a game which may have been the pastime of the upper classes but one in which victory belongs to the mentally agile, no matter what social stratum they come from. It is, finally, a game which, like Du Pré himself, seems to support the traditional order through its hierarchy of pieces but whose action involves elements of subversion, even including the killing of the king.

The deeply conflicted desire for social advancement felt by Renaissance rhetoricians, people who came, virtually without exception, from the lower classes of society, surely lies behind their fantasies about the power of oratory, their celebration of the orator as the *flagellum principum*, and their clear identification with ancient figures such as Demosthenes, Cicero, and, more revealingly, Caesar, all of whom supposedly came to prominence through their verbal skill. One of those fantasies is worth pausing over, for it not only reveals the mixture of dependence and hunger for power that characterizes the orator's condition but also shows the regressive nature of that hunger, which helps to explain why those fantasies had such an enormous hold on Renaissance rhetoricians and why they would obsessively repeat them in their works. The fantasy in question occurs in Puttenham's *Arte of English Poesie*. Writing of how poets had been generally esteemed by princes in the past but have now become contemptible, he urges his contemporaries to pursue the art "the rather for that worthy and honorable memoriall of that noble woman twise French Queene, Lade *Anne* of Britaine,

. . . who passing one day from her lodging toward the kinges side, saw in a gallerie *Maister Allaine Chartier* the kings Secretarie, an excellent maker or Poet leaning on a tables end a sleepe, and stooped downe to kisse him, saying thus in all their hearings, we may not of Princely courtesie passe by and not honor with our kisse the mouth from whence so many sweete ditties and golden poems have issued" (35). This anecdote has all the feel of a fairytale in which a benevolent mother figure descends on a sleeping child-hero and rewards him with a kiss, providing a kind of symbolic nourishment for the mouth out of which sweet poetry has come. Puttenham immediately distances himself from this exchange by conjuring up an imaginary chorus of unidentified speakers who attempt to specify the meaning of the anecdote, one suggesting facetiously that it means Puttenham wants the Prince to give him a helmet as a reward, another that it is simply a version of the Cynthia and Endymion story, and a third, speaking "shruggingly," that Puttenham slept with his poetry until a "Queene" ("quean"?) awoke him (35–36). All three explanations, however, serve only to direct attention toward Puttenham's own dependent relationship on *his* queen, Elizabeth, and his desire for nourishment in the form of "convenient countenaunce and . . . benefite as are due to an excellent artificer" (36). The fantasy element in the story involves not merely the evocation of a benevolent mother who stoops down to nourish her needy child but a suggestion of the child's magical control over the source of the food he needs, a control that is imaged in the queen's feeling compelled to act by what she calls her "Princely courtesie." In other words, thanks to his utter passivity in this scene, the poet projects an aura of pure, childlike innocence, a freedom from any charge that he or his works seek to coerce a reward from the queen, who is forced instead by her own feelings to give it to him. Puttenham's anecdote is perfectly paradoxical, a demonstration of the real dependence and need of the poet and a wish-fulfillment fantasy that transforms dependence into power.

Yet despite its attempt to register dependence as power, the anecdote reveals the real condition of relative helplessness, deprivation, and need with which many Renaissance rhetoricians had to cope, a condition they prefer to ignore in their works as they spin out, instead, their stories of orators advancing easily up the social ladder and rebuking kings and tyrants. Nevertheless, on occasion, the reality that many of them faced in their daily lives does find its way into their writings. Consider, for instance, the bitter complaints voiced by some writers about their failure to receive adequate rewards for their professional activities. Trying to analyze the reasons for the present low condition of English poetry, Sidney may refrain from attacking Elizabeth by name, but he does wonder out loud, using terms that cannot fail to evoke the queen, why "England (the mother of excellent minds) should be grown so hard a step-mother to poets" (*Apology*, 68). In a similar manner, Puttenham tells a story of a certain Diopithus of Egypt, who had retired from the court and was close to death when the king discovered his absence, was informed of Diopithus's feelings of inadequate treatment, and sent him a generous reward, which, unfortunately, arrived too late to help the dying man (*Arte*, 284–85). In comparison with Sidney and Puttenham, Raphael Regius is refreshingly straightforward in voicing his grievance. A teacher of rhetoric at Padua, he complains towards the end of his *Panegyricus* about the low salaries paid him and his colleagues, remarking ironically: "And we wonder if we find very few excellent professors of this faculty at this time." He concludes by telling his audience: "If, to support eloquence, you most irreproachable men will establish positions and honorable salaries as well for the teachers of this art, you will accomplish something most useful and fitting for the entire Academy of Padua" (fvi^v). Even more revealing is the passage at the start of Gerard Vossius's rhetoric in which he laments that oratory, buried in the time of his forefathers, has now been revived in only one or two countries. He praises the ancient world, by contrast, for honoring the art everywhere, and he recalls fondly that the Roman emperors cherished rhetors, that Domitian established a public stipend for them with tax monies, and that one orator actually earned 600,000 *nummi* (silver coins) a year. He ends with exclamations of indignation which significantly identify "esteem" with "price": "In what great esteem [*pretio*] were rhetors held then when they were obtained at such a great price [*pretio*]! And now, how has the dignity of the study of oratory practically collapsed!" (iiii^r). What Regius's and Vossius's complaints reveal is what must have been the case all over Europe: teachers of rhetoric were simply not paid very well and did not enjoy access to the corridors of power. Francesco Patrizi, constantly critical of the claims advanced by the rhetoricians, admits that the orator may sway the mob but asserts directly that he has little or no effect on kings (*Della retorica*, 42^r), a skeptical notion that completely explodes the rhetoricians' fantasies about the power of their art in the real world.

Perhaps the most dramatic revelation of the orator's ultimate powerlessness, is a simple historical fact which rhetoricians seem unable to keep out of their works and which must never have been very far from their consciousness. A striking instance of its intrusion into a rhetorical text can be found in the model speech from Richard Rainolde's *Foundacion of Rhetorike* referred to earlier, in which he celebrates the eloquence of Cicero and Demosthenes as enabling their social advancement and even allowing them to rebuke tyrants. Rainolde does not end his speech on this high note, however; instead, he adds one more section on how both "wer put to death" (xlviii^v) on the order of tyrannical rulers. Rainolde thus acknowledges what every rhetorician in the Renaissance knew: their hero Cicero may have been the king of Rome because of his eloquence, but that achievement did not prevent Mark Antony's thugs from murdering him and placing his severed head and hands on the *rostra* in the forum. As such anecdotes show, Renaissance rhetoricians knew full well that they were dependent on the great rather than the masters of their masters, and that the political, legal, and military power of their rulers, whether kings or tyrants, constituted an absolute limit for them. It is hardly surprising that, faced with such a reality, they would make exaggerated claims about the power of their art, even though their intermittent complaints about mistreatment and low salaries and their occasional references to Cicero's death all expose those claims as the product of a desperate compensatory fantasy.

Although Renaissance rhetoricians generally prefer to avoid facing the issue of their relative powerlessness, the same thing cannot be said about the writers who produce the literature of the period. In a variety of works they offer us wandering rogues and clever peasants, merchants and courtiers, counselors and aspiring noblemen, all of them needy, dependent, and aware of their relative powerlessness in different ways and all of them turning primarily to rhetoric, their skill with words, in order to overcome the social limits imposed on them. Literature, in other words, presents both the lack of social and political centrality which most people experienced in Renaissance culture and the fantasy of rhetorical power which animated their determined striving for advancement and their often desperate attempts to manage the authorities who controlled their lives. George Herbert, for instance, confronts these issues in one of his lyrics, "The Method," in which the relationship between the rhetor and the ruler is displaced into that between a human speaker and God.[36] The poem opens by stressing the speaker's neediness and dependence: he has failed to move God's "will" (4) through his prayers, and his desires thus remain unsatisfied. As he reviews various reasons for this failure, he employs images that directly evoke the discourse of rhetoric and, in particular, its fantasy of the orator's power

[36] George Herbert, "The Method," in *Works*, ed. F. E. Hutchinson (Oxford: Clarendon Press, 1941), 133–34; line references are provided in the text. My analysis is indebted to the discussions of Herbert's poetry in Michael C. Schoenfeldt, *Prayer and Power: George Herbert and Renaissance Courtship* (Chicago: University of Chicago Press, 1991); and Richard Strier, *Love Known: Theology and Experience in George Herbert's Poetry* (Chicago: University of Chicago Press, 1983).

over the auditor. Thus, after recollecting that on the previous day he prayed carelessly, he asks himself rhetorically: "And should Gods eare / To such indifferents chained be, / Who do not their own motions heare?" (17–19). The speaker then recalls that on another occasion he ignored a "motion" (23) from God and followed a contrary impulse instead, and again he asks himself: "And should Gods eare, / Which needs not man, be ty'd to those / Who heare not him, but quickly heare / His utter foes?" (25–28). These references to God's ear being chained or tied recall key metaphors from the discourse of rhetoric, metaphors of binding, tying, and dragging, which it uses to describe the effect of oratory on the auditor. More important, Herbert's images summon up the figure of the Hercules Gallicus, the ideal orator who leads his followers by means of chains or cords attached to their ears. Exemplifying the potentially subversive, antiauthoritarian side of Renaissance rhetoric, "The Method" identifies Hercules not with the ruler but, rather, with that ruler's lowly subject, the human speaker, who entertains the fantasy that he can control his master through the rhetoric of prayer. What Herbert's poem never lets us forget, however, is that the ruler in question is God, a being who is certainly no "lesse free" (20) than His human subjects, and that He, not the speaker, has the real *Power* (7) in the world. "The Method" thus forcefully reminds the reader of what rhetoricians knew throughout the Renaissance: subjects cannot really coerce rulers any more than Herbert's human speaker can coerce the ultimate ruler, God, into giving him what he wants. Ironically, of course, as the poem ends the speaker is filled with confidence that God will indeed acknowledge his prayers once he employs the right *method* in making them, but this confidence springs not from any conviction about the speaker's own power but from the fact that God is truly the exception to the rule about rulers: God will respond to him not because he has forced God to do so but because God "is *Love*" (8) and will, of His own accord, always answer the prayers of humble petitioners.

Earthly monarchs, by contrast, cannot be counted on to satisfy the needs of their subjects, no matter how persuasively the latter manipulate the rhetoric of prayer and courtship. Castiglione dramatically underscores this problem for the rhetor-courtier in the second book of his *Libro del cortegiano* when he has the principal speaker, Federico Fregoso, declare that even the most gracious courtier may, inexplicably, fail to find favor in his prince's eyes: "Although he is clever and prompt to reply and shows himself off well in his gestures, manners, words, and all else that is necessary, that lord will show that he holds him in little esteem, in fact, will be readier to treat him with disrespect."[37] As a re-

---

[37] Castiglione, *Il libro del cortegiano*, 240.

sult, Federico says, everyone at court will disdain this courtier, will mock him, and will even chase him away, just as they will embrace a total incompetent to whom their lord has taken a fancy. Even though Castiglione writes his entire book on the assumption that his ideal courtier can manage the rhetoric of his performance so as to succeed in the world, he is fully aware that earthly rulers are fundamentally unpredictable, may be whimsical as they bestow their "grace," and can be irrationally hostile even to the worthiest subjects and most skillful orators.

One of the most memorable representations in Renaissance literature of human dependence and need, coupled with a striking attempt to compensate for this situation by means of rhetoric, can be found in the anonymous picaresque novel *Lazarillo de Tormes*. Its protagonist is not only the lowest of the low, a powerless orphan and beggar driven to wander from town to town in a desperate attempt to feed and clothe himself, but he is also—rather, he also becomes eventually—a clever rhetor who uses his skill with language both to advance a rung or two up the social ladder and to manipulate his last and most powerful master, the man he addresses as *Vuestra Merced* ("Your Grace"). The depth of *Lazarillo*'s implication in the Renaissance discourse of rhetoric can be easily revealed by a brief consideration of its genre. Although credited by many critics as the originary picaresque novel, it owes important aspects of its generic form to the epistle—and the epistle was considered a rhetorical art throughout the period.[38] In fact, despite its length, *Lazarillo* resembles the familiar letter insofar as it is a first-person account of its narrator's life addressed to a particular person. Moreover, as Lazarillo explains the genesis of his "letter," it appears to be his response to one he has already received: "Since Your Grace writes that I should write to you and explain the situation at length, it seemed to me appropriate not to take it in the middle, but from the beginning" (7).[39] At the same time the novel is also deeply indebted to the confession, and particularly to Saint Augustine's *Confessions*, a work that presents itself as the antithesis of rhetoric. Immediately after his conversion, for instance, Augustine explicitly condemns rhetoric, the art he himself

---

[38] My discussion of *Lazarillo de Tormes* is indebted especially to Francisco Rico, *The Spanish Picaresque Novel and the Point of View*, trans. Charles Davis with Harry Sieber (Cambridge: Cambridge University Press, 1984); Alexander A. Parker, *Literature and the Delinquent: The Picaresque Novel in Spain and Europe, 1599–1753* (Edinburgh: Edinburgh University Press 1967); Claudio Guillén, *Literature as System* (Princeton: Princeton University Press, 1971); and Douglas M. Carey, "Lazarillo de Tormes and the Quest for Authority," *PMLA* 94 (1979): 36–46.

[39] Page numbers supplied in the text cite *Lazarillo de Tormes*, ed. Francisco Rico (Barcelona: Planeta, 1980).

practiced, as a matter of "lying madness and forensic wars."[40] The use of rhetoric is not only wicked in a confession but irrelevant: since God already knows everything one has done and everything one might wish to say, there is no place in a confession for art or artifice, let alone the art of rhetoric. *Lazarillo de Tormes*, however, is a confession with a difference. Its narrator is not speaking to God, or even to Your Grace as God's representative; he is attempting to explain his household situation and to justify himself to his social superior. The letter and the confession may both be forms implying candor, but there is room in this combination of them for the calculations of art, as Lazarillo suggests in his Prologue when he explains that he writes for the sake of praise and fame, and declares, citing Cicero, that "honor nourishes the arts" (6). His work is clearly not a sincere unfolding of a man's inner being but a carefully calculated rhetorical performance designed as self-defense. Thus, though we have no sure idea who wrote the novel, we do not have to construct an elaborate, hypothetical argument for that person's knowledge of rhetoric; the book *is* rhetoric from start to finish.

One can, moreover, be quite specific about the kind of rhetoric Lazarillo is practicing. As an account of its author's life in which he invites the reader to admire him for his success in achieving the lowly position of *pregonero* (77), or town crier, thanks only to his own "force and skill" (7), the novel is an example of epideictic rhetoric: it is self-praise as well as self-protection from "slanderous tongues" (78). It is also an act of deference or courtship to Vuestra Merced, its main aim being to control the hostile responses of this social superior so that Lazarillo may preserve his position and income. In its deference to Vuestra Merced, Lazarillo's work appears deeply conservative. At the same time, however, it may also be construed as subversive, a threat to the stable order of society from the viewpoint of those who hold fixed positions within it, for the novel not only defends Lazarillo's progress up the social ladder but mercilessly satirizes every authority figure with whom he comes into contact. Lazarillo's epistolary "confession" is more than self-defense; it is a power play. It shows that all the pain he has had to endure in the school of hard knocks that is his world has certainly taught him how to knock back.

To secure his position as town crier, Lazarillo must placate Vuestra Merced, to whom he elects to tell his life's story. That story could be read simply as an attempt to arouse pity—Lazarillo vividly presents his helpless, orphaned condition of suffering and deprivation—but his strat-

---

[40] Augustine, *Confessions*, trans. William Watts (Cambridge: Harvard University Press, 1960), 9.2.

egy is more complicated, for if there is one thing he has learned in his life, it is that language offers a kind of power to those who lack the power supplied by wealth and social position. From all his masters—the blind man working people by means of verbal rituals, the priest doing so by misusing religious language, the squire with his fictions about honor, the pardoner with the elaborate charade he stages with the constable—Lazarillo has learned that language, disconnected from both the world and the inner reality of those who employ it, can enable one to manipulate others and thereby obtain what is needed for survival. But he has gone one step beyond his masters, for he has learned how to use language not just to feed and protect himself but also to attack others, including the masters who have taught him what he knows, by revealing their viciousness and stupidity. In short, Lazarillo has learned what every Renaissance rhetorician knows: words are swords. By using them thus, by playing the satirist, he does more than get even with his masters, however; he also seeks to manipulate Vuestra Merced, to stimulate his fear by implicitly warning that he too could become Lazarillo's satirical target in some future, as yet unwritten, chapter of the novel. Observe in this connection what Lazarillo has said about the pardoner's staging of a phony miracle:

> In all this no one saw what he had done except me, because I went up to the altar to see if anything remained in the plates which could be turned into money as I used to do at other times. And when he saw me there, he put his finger to his lips, signaling me to be quiet. I did so because it suited me, although after I saw the miracle, I could hardly keep from blurting it out, except that the fear of my astute master did not allow me to communicate it with anyone, nor did it ever come out of me. Because I took an oath not to reveal the miracle, and I kept it until now. (75)[41]

Lazarillo has actually promised the pardoner something he promises no one else, that he will never reveal the wickedness he has seen his master perpetrate—and yet that is precisely what he is doing at this very moment. To be sure, his account gives us a Vuestra Merced who appears utterly innocent in comparison with all the other characters. But Lazarillo early in his story reveals that he has learned how to lie and deceive, so that we have no way of knowing whether anything he says is true. And that is precisely what Vuestra Merced has to fear. For even

[41] According to Francisco Rico, this incident occurs in the Alcalá edition of 1554; it is not in the contemporaneous one from Burgos. Rico bases his edition on that of Alcalá, but cites the passage from the Burgos edition in a footnote.

though Lazarillo's text says nothing to this master's discredit, what assurance can there be that Lazarillo will refrain from telling us the as yet undisclosed truth about Vuestra Merced, or making up a plausible lie, in order to blacken his master's reputation? In a sense, what the novel reveals to us—and is meant to reveal to Vuestra Merced as well—is that Lazarillo, forced to confess, has learned that "confession" can be turned into a rhetorical weapon of enormous power.

At the end of the novel Lazarillo has actually found a profession that valorizes his role as satirist: he has become a town crier, one of whose major functions is "to accompany those who are punished by justice and to declare aloud their crimes" (77). Lazarillo does not merely denounce criminals, however, but also hawks wines, and this second function is as important as the first for understanding the particular rhetorical strategy he is employing in his book. Just as he gives people pleasure by selling them wine, so he gives his audience pleasure through his writing; to be specific, he makes them laugh, both at others and at himself. He has learned from his many masters that no matter how painful and degrading his experiences may be, when they are narrated in the right way the audience listening to them will find them funny—and may well reward the person who is the source of their laughter. The blind beggar in the first chapter, for instance, after having been tricked with a turnip and then having beaten Lazarillo soundly, tells everyone about the episode, with the result that "the laughter was so great that all the people who were passing in the street entered to see the fiesta" (24). Again, in the next chapter, after the priest has beaten Lazarillo, who pretended that a mouse and a snake were stealing food from his master's chest, those who hear the story tell it over and over with pleasure: "Here they returned to tell my sufferings anew and to laugh at them, and I, sinner, to weep over them" (41). Such episodes teach Lazarillo that laughter is ingratiating; it brings people together in a festive community about him. As a result he constructs his novel as a series of funny, satirical stories about his masters, which are, like the one he offers about the pardoner, "very subtle and witty" (68). The chief butt of Lazarillo's humor, however, is himself. He lets us laugh at his simplicity and even more at his misfortunes, at his beatings and desperate hunger. He lets us laugh at his degradation, just as he is doing at the end by presenting himself as a complaisant cuckold, for by making a comic spectacle of himself, he entertains Vuestra Merced and thereby hopes to encourage his beneficence.

Lazarillo adopts this rhetorical strategy specifically because his "education" has taught him that by making a spectacle of himself he can bring the brutal fathers who rule his world to provide him with sustenance. Revealingly, he recounts that after the neighbors laughed at the story of the beating the priest dished out to him, "they gave me something to eat, since I was overcome with hunger" (41). It is precisely such an exchange that Lazarillo has made with the archpriest at the end: the archpriest gets the pleasure of sleeping with Lazarillo's wife—and of laughing at his expense—and in exchange Lazarillo not only gets to maintain his position as town crier but obtains additional food and other benefits as well: "Every year he [the archpriest] gives her [Lazarillo's wife] almost a load of wheat, her meat at Easter, and now and then a couple of votive loaves and his old, used stockings" (78). Of course, in order to get such things Lazarillo has to give something up, and that something, as the imagery of his story makes clear, is a part of himself. Recall his comment that the laughter provoked by the blind man's story "was so great that all the people who were passing in the street entered to see the fiesta" (24). The word "fiesta" here indicates that Lazarillo has become the center of a festival but also, metaphorically at least, the center of a feast. To gain nourishment, in other words, Lazarillo recognizes that he must first nourish others, even if that means he must become the main course at the banquet of his own degradation.

In concocting his epistolary confession, Lazarillo clearly uses rhetoric as a weapon to defend himself from others' attacks and to secure the fixed though humble position he has attained in the social hierarchy. By subtly, indirectly threatening to "expose" Vuestra Merced the way the blind man, the priest, and the others have been exposed, and by presenting his degradation as a comic spectacle for Vuestra Merced to enjoy, Lazarillo uses his skill with language in order to manage this last and most powerful of his masters. Yet he does so without any guarantee of success. In fact, his implicit, indirect threat to denounce his master by writing about him is a two-edged sword that could easily cut Lazarillo himself, for that threat could provoke Vuestra Merced to silence him by whatever means, legal or extralegal, are necessary. After all, throughout his life Lazarillo has been consistently mistreated by his masters and subjected to the hostilities of various civil authorities, so what reason is there to think that Vuestra Merced would not—or could not—do the same thing? One might, in fact, read Lazarillo's other rhetorical strategy of making a comic spectacle of himself as an attempt to forestall Vuestra Merced's retaliation: if Lazarillo appears merely a harmless clown, then Vuestra Merced may well laugh at him rather than angrily removing him from his relatively secure social position and sending him out to wander once again through a hostile world. Of course, all the novel provides is Lazarillo's story; the response of Vuestra Merced is literally outside the fiction. But since the possibility of Lazarillo's defeat is as real as that of his victory, his desperate deployment of the rhetoric of power only serves to emphasize what we must feel is his utter powerlessness in the end.

If rhetors' fantasies about the power of their art can be read as a response to their condition of dependence and powerlessness, one can also see those fantasies as exaggerated versions of what was equally true: namely, that rhetoric and rhetors—from preachers and lawyers through counselors and *parlementaires* to courtiers and even kings—did have an enormous impact on Renaissance culture. For proponents of rhetoric, however, the problem was that its impact often took the forms of sedition and rebellion, so that its critics, not surprisingly, were frequently determined to effect its complete banishment. John Jewel, for instance, toward the end of his *Oratio Contra Rhetoricam*, recalls with approval that the Spartans and the Romans under Cato expelled all the orators (1289). Henry Agrippa recommends something similar for his own age (*De Incertitudine*, 31–32), as does Montaigne in "De la vanité des paroles" (*Oeuvres*, 293). Responding to this pressure, rhetoricians often admit the various sins of their art but then argue, as noted above, that it is really a neutral instrument and can be used as easily for good as for ill. Such a reply does not go far enough, however, for in order to prevent the banishment of rhetoric—and hence of themselves—they must claim that it is not just a useful tool but an absolutely essential one. Hence, they adopt the strategy of representing their contemporary world hopelessly mired in conflict and disorder—as, in good measure, it certainly was—and then propose rhetoric as its savior. For instance, Giovanni Berardino Fuscano writes in 1531 that the decadence of Italy, which is due to the "barbarian" invasions of the French and Spanish, makes the eloquence of *soblimi ingegni* absolutely essential to the order of the state ("Della oratoria e poetica facoltà," 190); and an English Ramist, Dudley Fenner, says that his translation of Ramus's and Talon's works into English is necessitated by the existence of all the "strifes and subtilties" in the world.[42] A more memorable attempt to justify rhetoric can be found in the work of another English Ramist, John Hoskins, whose *Directions for Speech and Style* was probably written about 1599 or 1600. Although he admits that perfect moral qualities are desirable in people and are to be learned from Aristotle's *Ethics*, Hoskins claims that such teaching is unfit for the real world of the present because, "as Ma-

---

[42] Dudley Fenner, *The Artes of Logike and Rhethorike* (London, 1584), Aii[r]. See also Du Pré, *Pourtraict*, 24–25.

chiavel saith, perfect virtue or perfect vice is not seen in our time, which altogether is humorous and spurting, therefore the understanding of Aristotle's *Rhetoric* is the directest means of skill to describe, to move, to please, or to prevent any motion whatsoever."[43] In the Machiavellian world of the Renaissance—when traditional loyalties have been effaced, when faith is no longer something anyone can take for granted in any sphere of life, when propaganda is becoming an essential tool of the church, and monarchs recognize that their success as rulers depends in good measure on their ability to display power and magnificence in elaborate spectacles—the art of rhetoric, as Hoskins argues, has clearly become indispensable.

Ironically, as the critics of rhetoric insist, much of the disorder of the contemporary world is also due to rhetoric, so that what its defenders are proposing is to reestablish order not by banishing rhetoric altogether but by using more rhetoric—good rhetoric this time, to replace or drive out the bad. Johann Heinrich Alsted, for instance, sets up a contrast between bad eloquence, which he says is "dog-like and clearly diabolical" (*Rhetorica*, Dedication, 3ʳ) and should be banished (*proscribitur*), and good eloquence, which is sweet and useful and must be preserved as the weapon God gives people to fight against the monsters who obscure the sun of truth (6ᵛ). Thinking in religious terms, he recommends that perverse, lying rhetoric be cut off by fire and water (*Rhetorica*, 3: *igni & aqua interdicamus*) so that the purified rhetoric left behind can perform its essential function: curing "souls corrupted by the fall" (5). Rather than substituting a purified rhetoric for its diabolical twin, Guillaume Du Vair imagines good rhetoric simply expelling the bad when he argues that since Truth cannot enter into spirits possessed by passions—which he identifies as so many fires started by wicked eloquence—"one must of necessity act like those who soften iron in fire before tempering it in water, and pass the spirits of one's auditors through the heat and movement of eloquence before they take the temper of truth" (*Traitté*, 397).

Francis Bacon offers a more complex vision of good rhetoric counteracting and controlling bad rhetoric in his allegorical interpretation of the myth of Typhon in *The Wisdom of the Ancients*. In the myth Juno insists that she be allowed to create something without Jupiter's help, just as he gave birth to Athena without hers. She then produces out of the earth the monster Typhon, who grows up to make war on Jupiter, defeats him, and cuts the sinews out of his hands and feet. Mercury,

---

[43] John Hoskins, *Directions for Speech and Style*, ed. Hoyt H. Hudson (Princeton: Princeton University Press, 1935), 41.

however, steals them back and restores Jupiter, who attacks and finally destroys Typhon. Bacon proceeds to allegorize the myth in political terms: Jupiter is the king, Juno his kingdom, and Typhon the rebel. The king becomes a tyrant and administers the state without consulting anyone, relying only on his own wisdom (Athena), and this action prompts the people (Juno), because of their "innate depravity and malignant disposition," to produce the monster Typhon, or open rebellion, with its hundred heads, its flaming mouths, and its feathery body, which stands for "perpetual rumors, reports, trepidations, and the like." Mercury's recovery of the king's sinews means that "by affability and wise edicts and gracious speeches he reconciles the minds of his subjects" so that he is finally reunited with them and can destroy the monster of rebellion (*Selected Writings*, 409). Although not every detail of Bacon's allegory relates to rhetoric (and it is important to see that he blames the king himself as the ultimate source of the disorder in his realm), it is nevertheless clear that rhetoric is directly linked to rebellion and just as directly identified as the appropriate countermeasure. For Bacon as for Du Vair, the fire of civil disorder, which eloquence has helped to bring about among the people, is to be put out by the stronger fire of eloquence as it is used by the ruler.

To Jean Bodin, however, must be credited the most direct, albeit terribly tortured, expression of the notion that in the age of the Renaissance the only solution possible for the turmoil caused by rhetoric is more rhetoric. In the brief section devoted to rhetoric with which he ends the fourth book of *Les six Livres de la République*, Bodin discusses the evils of factionalism and civil strife, one cause of which he identifies as the liberty enjoyed by *harangueurs*, or "popular orators."[44] As he stresses the enormous power of rhetoric and invokes the figure of the Hercules Gallicus as an image of the orator, he declares: "I do not say [this] to praise eloquence, but because of its force which one more often employs for ill than for good" (660). Eloquence is bad because it misrepresents the truth, and because for every good person who uses it well there are fifty who abuse it. Orators "have moved the people to sedition, and many have changed laws, customs, religions, states; others have ruined them entirely" (660–61). Rather than supply examples from Athens and Rome, Bodin turns to his own age. He steers clear of France entirely, despite—or perhaps because of—the very troubled period it was going through during the second half of the sixteenth century when *Les six Livres* was written; instead, he talks about how eloquence caused the

---

[44] Jean Bodin, *Les six Livres de la République* (Paris, 1583; rpt. Scientia Aalen, 1961); page numbers cite this edition.

expulsion of the kings of Morocco and Persia. Coming closer to home, he invokes the example of John of Leiden, a famous Anabaptist preacher who seized the town of Münster in 1534, had himself proclaimed ruler, and was defeated and killed by the troops of Charles V the following year. Next, after mentioning Savonarola briefly, Bodin writes that a hundred thousand people have been inspired to take up arms against the nobility in Germany and that *harangueurs* there have inflamed princes to massacre and burn their heretical subjects. Like Bacon in the *Advancement of Learning*, Bodin blames rhetoric for the devastation produced by the wars of religion. He then rewrites a sentence from Cicero, although where the latter says only hypothetically that teaching eloquence without wisdom would be like giving weapons to a madman (see *De oratore*, 3.14.55), Bodin invokes the actual problems of his contemporary world: "Eloquence in the mouth of a mutinous *harangueur* is therefore a very dangerous knife in the hand of a madman" (661). At this point, one might expect him to reach the conclusion that the only reasonable option for a ruler would be to banish rhetoric altogether. Yet Bodin declares it indispensable, and as he does so, his sentence becomes ever more certain and definite, progressing from seeing eloquence as one possible means to create civilization to seeing it as the essential means to do so: "It is a means for those who would use it well to lead people from barbarism to humanity: it is the means to reform mores, correct laws, chastise tyrants, banish vice, maintain virtue" (661–62). Bodin continues by noting in passing that eloquence can charm men the way one charms snakes, and by the time he has finished, he has transformed it into the *best* means to counter sedition: "There is no means so great to pacify seditions and contain subjects in obedience to their princes than to have a wise and virtuous preacher, by means of whom one could gently move and bend the hearts of the most rebellious" (662). This conclusion is not Bodin's last word, however, for he reverts briefly to his critical posture—associating the power of eloquence with the success of *harangueurs* in the less than admired "popular state," then makes one last reversal to end with the more positive though qualified assertion that there is no need to fear tyranny when a *harangueur* has control of the people, provided, of course, that "he hates tyranny" (662).

Bodin's tergiversations in this passage reflect his ambivalence about rhetoric—as well as the ambiguity of rhetoric itself as it is imagined throughout the Renaissance. Countering the fantasy of an all-powerful Hercules Gallicus leading utterly passive and silent spectators by the ears is the opportunity that rhetoric treatises offer those spectators to become orators themselves, which one might well say was occurring in the religious uprisings and civil disturbances taking place all over Renaissance Europe. No wonder Bodin praises the power of rhetoric but fears it at the same time, seeing it as the supreme means to rule one's subjects but simultaneously linking it to the disorders, civil and religious, of his age. Like the rhetoricians, however, he does not recommend the banishment of rhetoric, not because banishing it would threaten his personal and professional identity but rather because he recognizes the sheer impossibility of doing so. Bodin shares Hoskins's view of the world; he assumes that he lives in the age not of Aristotle's *Ethics* but of his *Rhetoric* and of Machiavelli's *Prince*, an age in which the only way to deal with a state turned upside down by rhetoric is to apply yet more rhetoric. Rhetoric can restore order, of course, only if it is used correctly, and all Bodin's qualifications about the need for a *"wise* and *virtuous* preacher" and for a *harangueur* who *"hates tyranny"* suggest that he recognizes the truth of the situation: once the rhetor is empowered to act, there can be no guarantees about the outcome because control over him as well as over the responses of his audience can never be absolute. Ideally, from Bodin's viewpoint, the orator will serve the interests of the legitimate ruler, will be that ruler's "orator" or ambassador, but there is no assurance that he will not turn into the ruler's opponent, a subversive threat to the social order and a rebel. In the slippery, unstable world of Renaissance rhetoric—and of the Renaissance itself—there is simply no way to keep Hercules from metamorphosing into Hegesias.

In Bodin's conception, and in that of Renaissance rhetoricians generally, eloquence is absolutely ambiguous: it creates civil strife just as easily as it defends the state or imposes peace. To revert to a key image for it from Montaigne's "De la vanité des paroles," what some people would insist is health-giving medicine appears to him to be poison, even though he admits in the same breath that that poison can be used to cure the ills of disordered democratic and republican states. Imagining the rhetorically trained preacher as a physician whose task is to tear out vices by the roots from the souls of his auditors, Fray Luis de Granada also recognizes the very fine line between good and bad rhetoric, between medicine and poison: "I leave to the prudence of the preacher what caution is to be used in removing vices of this sort, lest we offer people poison or material of some grave offensiveness in place of health-giving medicine [*salutaribus pharmacis*]" (*Ecclesiastica Rhetorica*, 410). Ironically, the very term Granada uses here for "medicine," *pharmacis*, makes him so nervous that he feels compelled to qualify it with the adjective "health-giving," *salutaribus*. Granada's problem is that his word means both medicine and poison, precisely the two ideas he is trying to keep apart. In the Renaissance as in the modern world, however, medicine and poison are often simply indistinguishable. As a result, rhetoric, characterized in such terms, cannot help but unsettle, however much it may wish to reassure, not because the cure it offers may be worse than the disease it treats but because, more profoundly, it is both cure and disease at the very same time.

3 Circe's Garden, Mercury's Rod

In June 1485 the Florentine Neoplatonist Giovanni Pico della Mirandola sent what would become a famous letter to the Venetian humanist Ermolao Barbaro. The latter had written to Pico some two months earlier, praising him for his learning and eloquence, while attacking the Scholastics, the "Germans," for their lack of a "shining and elegant style." Pico, who had spent six years studying the writings of men Barbaro wittily dismisses as "barbaric," responds first by thanking him for his kind words and then by devoting most of the letter to a hypothetical speech that the maligned Germans might deliver in their own defense. In it Pico makes two complementary moves: he criticizes rhetoric, focusing on the issue of elegant style; and he exalts the philosophical writing of the Scholastics. There is a tongue-in-cheek quality about Pico's defense, for he not only writes in an extremely elegant Latin style, as Barbaro himself would later note, but declares at the conclusion that his speech is a mock encomium, and that his real aim has been to bring Barbaro to compose a praise of eloquence, just as Plato's Glaucon praised injustice in *The Republic* in order to goad Socrates to the praise of justice (*Epistola*, 358).[1] The question of its seriousness notwithstanding, Pico's letter does assemble some of the most telling arguments the Renaissance would make against rhetoric. He denounces it as deception and lies, as a trivial kind of theatricality, and as a vulgar display fit only

---

[1] For the translated phrase from Barbaro's letter and his comment on Pico's style, see Quirinus Breen, "Giovanni Pico della Mirandola on the Conflict of Philosophy and Rhetoric," *Journal of the History of Ideas* 13 (1952): 393, 403.

for fools or the mob (352, 354, 355). Most of all, however, he denounces rhetoric by means of an array of images and metaphors that identify it as morally and sexually degenerate; in Pico's vision it effeminizes the orator, turning him into a confusing, dangerous man-woman and thereby raising the specter of homosexuality.[2]

For Pico, the sensual appeal of rhetoric is a sign of degeneracy. It flatters the ear, for instance, in order to cover up its lack of substance: "We see, I say, in all these writers that the practice has come into use of seizing the reader from the start by means of a varied cadence and harmony, since there is nothing inside [them] that is not hollow and empty. If a philosopher had done this, Musonius would exclaim that it is not a philosopher who speaks, but a flute player who plays" (353). A little later Pico contrasts the "music" of philosophy, which is entirely free of any sensual element, with the debased music of rhetoric, as he has his spokesmen tell a hypothetical auditor to rise above the body and listen to "the celestial Apollo composing on his divine lyre a cosmic melody in ineffable modes. If with the ears of a philosopher you will have tasted these words, their honey-sweetness will seem to you the envy of Nestor" (354). In this last sentence, Pico shifts focus from the sense of hearing to that of taste to explain that philosophy, not rhetoric, offers real nourishment in the form of honey or, in a later passage, nectar (355). Responding to Lucretius's claim that philosophy needs the sugar-coating of eloquence, Pico concludes that such writing is fit only

---

[2] I recognize that there is a serious scholarly debate about this term. The word "homosexual" appeared only in the nineteenth century in Germany, where it was used to identify what was considered a pathological psychological condition. The Renaissance spoke instead of the sodomite (and a variety of synonymous terms, such as catamite, Ganymede, and hermaphrodite), and sodomy identified an activity rather than a character type. Complicating the matter still more, sodomy did not refer exclusively to male homosexual practices but included anal intercourse with women, intercourse with animals, and at times even nonsexual activities. Finally, as Jonathan Goldberg has observed, male homosexual activity is never described in its own terms; it becomes visible only within other discourses, such as those of sedition, demonism, and atheism. I am using "homosexuality" here as an equivalent for something like "sodomitical practices," and, as the argument of my chapter makes clear, I am restricting it to mean just those practices that Renaissance people thought men engaged in with other men or with boys. On its problematic nature for pre-nineteenth-century societies, see John Boswell, *Christianity, Social Tolerance, and Homosexuality* (Chicago: University of Chicago Press, 1980), 42–43; Jonathan Goldberg, "Sodomy and Society: The Case of Christopher Marlowe," *Southwest Review* 69 (1984): 371–78; Guido Ruggiero, *The Boundaries of Eros: Sex Crime and Sexuality in Renaissance Venice* (New York: Oxford University Press, 1985), 114–15; Alan Bray, *Homosexuality in Renaissance England* (London: Gay Men's Press, 1982), 55–57; and Bruce R. Smith, *Homosexual Desire in Shakespeare's England: A Cultural Poetics* (Chicago: University of Chicago Press, 1991), 1–12.

for children and the mob; beneath its false sweetness an author offers not medicine but poison (355).

Although Pico denounces the sensual appeal of rhetoric in fairly strong terms, he reserves his most vivid language to attack it as sexually degenerate. Thus, at one point he contrasts it with philosophy, which, he says, should be kept "clean and pure" (356: *sinceram & inpermixtam*), because to add anything to her (that is, rhetorical ornaments) would be to infect and adulterate her (*infeceris, adulteraveris*). Pico concludes that in such a serious matter "one should not play with tropes, or luxuriate in too many words, or play the wanton with metaphors (*nec ludendum tropis, nec verbis, aut nimis luxuriandum, aut translatis lasciviendum*)." Rhetoric here is a matter of play (*ludendum*) and pleasure (*luxuriandum*), but it also has a disturbingly sexual character (*lasciviendum*). That character appears even more dramatically in another passage: "Who would not approve the soft step, the clever hands, the playful eyes in an actor and a dancer, but in a citizen or a philosopher, who would not disapprove, censure, and abominate them? If we see a girl graceful in her manners and talkative, we will praise her, will kiss her. These things we would condemn and prosecute in a matron. Therefore, it is not we, but they [the rhetoricians], who perform Bacchanalias at the feet of a Vestal, who dishonor the gravity and chastity of philosophical matters as if with games and and curling irons" (353). In this passage, Pico contrasts the sober citizen with the lower-class actor and dancer, suggesting initially that his denunciation of rhetoric is based on class. As the passage continues, however, it shifts its focus to matters sexual. First, it refers to kissing, which seems harmless enough because prompted by the graceful behavior of a young girl, but that air of innocence is quickly dispelled as Pico creates the spectacle of orators behaving like bacchants at the feet of a Vestal Virgin. Orators, in other words, are condemned by their association with orgiastic sexuality: they perform Dionysiac rites that "dishonor the gravity and chastity of philosophical matters [*gravitatem philosophicarum rerum & castitatem . . . dehonestent*]."

Pico does not merely condemn rhetors as bacchants but stresses the sexual ambiguity, if not the homosexual character, of their behavior. Thus, as he rejects the use of rhetoric in philosophical writing, he asks: "For who would not condemn and detest curly hair [*cincinnos*] and rouge [*fucum*] in an honest virgin?" (352). In this sentence, once again, philosophy is a virgin, but rhetoric is not presented as violating her; rather, it corrupts her by means of curling irons and makeup. What is at stake here becomes clear when one recognizes that Pico is echoing a passage from the third book of Cicero's *De oratore* in which the same two words—and especially the unusual *cincinnus*—occur. One of Cicero's spokesmen, who has been praising the ornate style, pauses to qualify his recommendation, warning that human beings tire of such pleasures quickly and will feel disgust if there is no variety in them. He goes on: "And one is offended all the more quickly by the curls and rouge [*cincinnis ac fuco*] of the orator and the poet because . . . in writing and speech painted faults are detected not only by the judgment of the ears, but even more by that of the mind" (25.100). Cicero's "curls and rouge" are the sign not of an affected woman but of an effete and effeminized man, just as they are throughout Roman literature. A similar condemnation of rhetoric and the rhetor runs through Pico's letter, which plays a series of variations on the ideas of curly hair and makeup. For instance, the rhetors condemned for performing a Bacchanalia at the feet of a Vestal Virgin are said to dishonor philosophy "as if with games and curling irons" (353). In another passage, one finds a derivative of *fucus*, "rouge" or "makeup," that suggests a number of the word's negative metaphorical meanings, including "adulteration," "disguise," and "deceit": "If the auditor is not a fool, what does he hope for from painted speech [*fucato sermone*] other than treachery" (355). The notion of makeup as a kind of disease appears when Pico condemns the writer who is so preoccupied with surface decoration that he never penetrates to his real subject matter, "which we often see beneath a face colored [*infectum*: infected] by powder" (353). Although Pico frequently refers to a personified Rhetoric, as to a personified Philosophy, he is really talking about rhetors as well as the art they practice, and it must be remembered that rhetors, like philosophers, were exclusively males in Pico's day, just as they are in his text. That this condemnation may be taken as the equivalent of accusing rhetors of homosexual activity is not merely something one arrives at by the indirect route of teasing suggestions out of Pico's imagery; he actually makes that accusation directly: "What Synesius said about adolescence can be said fittingly about a speech: a long-haired speech is always sodomitical [*comatam orationem semper cinaedam*]" (353).

When Pico condemns the rhetor as a sodomite, as a man who looks and behaves like a woman, he is thinking about a particular female figure whose behavior the rhetor reproduces as he allures his auditors by means of sensual pleasure, orgiastic sexuality, curly hair, and rouge. Pico never says who that female figure is, but one possible name for her may be glimpsed in the following passage where his Scholastic philosophers declare "that no one would trust us if we affected verbal splendors and beauties [*veneres*], as if trusting too little in our subject matter, nor should we seek, supported thus, to drag men to our opinion by means of these allurements [*lenociniis*]" (352–53). Here the verbal adornments of rhetoric are called *lenocinia*, which could be translated not only as "allurements" but equally well as "excessive or meretricious ornaments," and which is derived from *leno*, meaning "bawd" or "pander." In other words, rhetoric looks like whoring. More significantly, however, its ornaments are also labeled *veneres*, a word that summons up the figure of Venus and suggests that that may well be the name for the particular female figure whose behavior the rhetor is aping. Nevertheless, although the image of the goddess of love certainly fits the argument of Pico's letter and has a particular role to play generally, as we shall see, in the Renaissance discourse of rhetoric, I would like to suggest an alternative candidate for the seductress whom Pico's rhetor becomes, a candidate who resembles Venus in crucial ways but whose behavior resonates powerfully with other aspects of rhetoric in Pico's letter and in the discourse of rhetoric generally. That candidate is Circe.

Like Venus, Circe is a figure of beauty who seduces men by holding out to them the lure of sensual pleasure. Originating in Homer's *Odyssey*, where she is doubled by the figures of the Sirens and Calypso, and serving as a model for Dido in Vergil's *Aeneid*, she has an extraordinary impact on the Renaissance. There her descendants populate literary works of all sorts and especially the lofty genre of the epic, where she appears in various guises from Ariosto's Alcina through Spenser's Acrasia down to Milton's Eve. In all these texts Circe is more than a seductress, however; she is also a witch or enchantress whose magic places her victims in her power and enables her to transform them into animals. As such, she is an especially appropriate candidate for the unnamed woman in Pico's letter, for it is precisely the magical ability of rhetoric to transform the auditor for which he denounces it. His Scholastics tell their opponents, the rhetors: "It is your affair, as you say, to be able to turn black into white and white into black as you will, to be able to raise up, cast down, amplify, and diminish whatever you want to, finally to transform [*transformare*] things themselves into whatever face and costume you might have wished by means of speech as if by the magical force of eloquence [*magicis . . . viribus eloquentiae*] you boast about" (352). Here Pico attacks rhetoric as deception and masquerade, which turn the world upside down, but mostly for its Circean ability to *transform* the appearances of the things, an ability directly identified with magic. Although Pico's rhetor does not rule over a magical island, as Circe and other temptresses frequently did, the letter nevertheless associates rhetoric with the pastoral and, by implication, its ideal landscape. Thus Pico says that the sort of speech practiced by the rhetor flows "out of the pleasant woods of the Muses" (355: *ex amoenis Musarum sylvis*), identifying rhetoric with pastoral by assigning it a location which doubly evokes that genre. First, rhetorical speech comes from the woods (*sylva*) of the Muses, a place that both suggests the country in which pastoral activities normally take place and invokes the lyric genre, *sylva* being a standard word for titles of lyric collections. But second, what is really indicative of pastoral is the adjective Pico employs to modify "woods": they are *amoenus*, a term translated as "pleasant" above but really a code word for the pastoral, since that genre is always conceived as being set in the *locus amoenus*, the "pleasant place."[3] Pico evokes this commonplace a second time, more obliquely, when he uses as a synonym for *eloquentia* "the amenity of speech" (355: *amoenitate dicendi*). Thus, he makes eloquence into a Circe figure in his letter not only by characterizing it as a magical seductress but also by conjuring up a vision of the pastoral realm in which ancient and Renaissance writers tend to place the temptresses who are Circe's kin and descendants.

The imagery of Pico's letter appears throughout the Renaissance discourse of rhetoric not just in works that attack the art but even in those that seek to celebrate it. For the latter take pains to distinguish between bad rhetoric and good, just as Pico does in his letter between rhetoric and philosophy, and their characterization of bad rhetoric is consistent with what Pico says in denouncing rhetoric generally. In response to this negative vision of rhetoric, when its defenders celebrate their art, they attempt to insist upon its exclusively male character both by identifying its practitioner as a man and by using a sexually charged, "masculine" imagery to define the relationship he establishes with his auditors. In essence, they model the rhetor on Mercury, who rules others with the aid of his potent rod. That they should want to present rhetoric this way should not be surprising; rhetors are supposed to be male because Renaissance culture, intensely patriarchal in character, allowed only men to exercise the public activities typically associated with the art.[4] The rhetoricians' characterization of the good rhetoric they advocate, however, is actually more complex than has been suggested so far. Despite their desire to dismiss bad rhetoric as feminine and effeminiz-

---

[3] On the *locus amoenus* and pastoral, see Ernst Robert Curtius, *European Literature and the Latin Middle Ages*, trans. Willard R. Trask (New York: Harper & Row, 1953), 195–200.

[4] On the notion that rhetoric was not a subject fit for women, see Constance Jordan, "Feminism and the Humanists: The Case of Sir Thomas Elyot's *Defence of Good Women*," in *Rewriting the Renaissance: The Discourse of Sexual Difference in Early Modern Europe*, ed. Margaret W. Ferguson, Maureen Quilligan, and Nancy Vickers (Chicago: University of Chicago Press, 1986), 253.

ing and to "save" its opposite by characterizing it in masculine terms, they wind up presenting the latter as a hybrid, as something both male and female. In other words, they define good rhetoric in terms that blur its supposed difference from the effeminized, homosexual rhetoric that writers such as Pico are attacking. That they should do so is related to the uncertain, changing nature of gender distinctions in their culture, in which an assertive patriarchalism and an exaltation of women existed side by side.[5] As we shall see, however, the sexually double nature that Renaissance rhetoric produces has even more to do with the particularly ambiguous, conflicted social position of Renaissance rhetoricians unfolded in Chapters 1 and 2, for it speaks directly to their simultaneous self-identification as both rulers (men) and subjects (women). In fact, one cannot help but connect the sexually ambiguous characterization they give rhetoric to the chief profession they practiced—teaching. That profession constantly exposed them to charges such as those made by Pico, charges they seem practically driven to provoke by the striking metaphoric language they employ. Finally, the sexually double nature of Renaissance rhetoric can be related to the ideals and aspirations of those men, for although it might be read as a confession of the degenerate, effeminate, homosexual nature of rhetoric, it might equally well be taken as the sign of the perfection of the art, implicitly validating its creators' social superiority and even, perhaps, affirming their right to rule.

Pico della Mirandola's condemnation of rhetoric is echoed throughout the Renaissance. The attacks on the art as magic, poisonous food, and wanton allurement, which appeared sporadically throughout the Middle Ages, really pick up their pace in the fifteenth, sixteenth, and seventeenth centuries.[6] Unlike Pico, most Renaissance critics primarily de-

---

[5] See Constance Jordan, *Renaissance Feminism: Literary Texts and Political Models* (Ithaca: Cornell University Press, 1990). My thinking about gender and rhetoric has been influenced by the unpublished essay of my colleague Dolora Wojciehowski, "Axiology at Face Value: Prosopopoeia and Gender in Plato, Hume, and Barthes," and especially by Patricia Parker's "On the Tongue: Cross Gendering, Effeminacy, and the Art of Words," *Style* 23 (1989): 445–65, and her *Literary Fat Ladies*.

[6] On the representations of rhetoric as a woman in the visual arts during the Middle Ages, see P. d'Ancona, "Le rappresentazioni allegoriche delle arti liberali," *L'Arte* 5 (1902): 137–55, 211–28, 269–89, 370–81; and Philippe Verdier, "L'iconographie des arts libéraux," in *Arts libéraux et philosophie au moyen âge*, Actes du Quatrième Congrès International de Philosophie Médiévale, 1967 (Montreal, 1969), 305–55. For written examples, some of which are critical, see Lactantius, *The Divine Institutes, Books I–VII*, trans. Sister Mary Francis McDonald, O.P. (Washington: Catholic University of America Press, 1964), 164; Geoffrey of Vinsauf, *Poetria nova*, trans. Jane Baltzell Kopp, in *Three Medieval Rhetorical Arts*, ed. James J. Murphy (Berkeley: University of California Press, 1971), 35, 60; Alan of the Isles, *Anticlaudianus*, in *Readings in Medieval Rhetoric*, ed. Joseph M. Miller, Michael H. Prosser, and

nounce rhetoric as subversion, but they also have recourse to the gendered imagery he employs, for they think of rhetoric as politically dangerous not just because it foments rebellion but because it is associated with enticement and magical allure, which are figured as feminine and thus implicitly threaten the male-dominated social order. For instance, in praising poetry John Rainolds contrasts it with rhetoric, which he denounces as being dressed up like a harlot, "singed with the curling irons of whores, . . . made effeminate with dripping pigments" (*Oratio*, 48). In his essay "De la vanité des paroles" (On the vanity of words), Montaigne identifies rhetoric as poisonous food and stresses that monarchs should be taught to guard against the "sweet sound of this harmony" (*Oeuvres*, 293). In fact, the association between food and rhetoric runs through this brief essay and recurs in "De l'institution des enfans" (On the education of children), where it is also joined to the idea of painting that Montaigne rejects: "He [i.e., the pupil] does not know rhetoric, nor how in a preface to capture the benevolence of the impartial reader, nor does he desire to know how. Truly, all beautiful painting is easily effaced by the luster of a simple natural truth. These niceties only serve to amuse the vulgar herd who are incapable of taking their meat in bigger pieces or tougher" (*Oeuvres*, 169). Like Montaigne, John Jewel denounces rhetoric in political terms, but also as an art of surface decoration which uses emotional appeals and figures of speech in order to seduce the listener. Rhetoric, he says, lays traps to capture the ears of the listeners and dresses up bad causes "with alien colors and allurements [*illecebris*]" (*Oratio*, 1286), here using a word, *illecebra*, also employed by Pico for the wiles of rhetoric (*Epistola*, 353). Finally, Henry Cornelius Agrippa attacks rhetoric as cosmetics (*De Incertitudine*, 28: *fuco orationis*), as a deceptive sweetness (hence, food), and as a seduction from truth (32). Informing and shaping all this imagery is the notion of rhetoric as an enticing, wanton, deceptive woman—in short, a harlot or prostitute—a conception which, according to Brian Vickers, animated the criticisms of rhetoric that abounded in England from about 1640 to 1680.[7] Nor should it be surprising that the equation could

Thomas W. Benson (Bloomington: University of Indiana Press, 1973), 223–24; Alberic of Monte Cassino, *Flores rhetorici*, in *Readings in Medieval Rhetoric*, 148; Martianus Capella, *The Marriage of Philology and Mercury*, bk. 5, *Rhetoric*, in *Martianus Capella and the Seven Liberal Arts*, trans. William H. Stahl and Richard Johnson with E. L. Burge (New York: Columbia University Press, 1977), 157–207; John Gower, *Confessio Amantis*, 7. 1564–69, in *The Complete Works*, vol. 3, ed. G. C. Macaulay (Oxford: Clarendon Press, 1901); and Hawes, *The Pastime of Pleasure*, chap. 7, in *The Works*, n.p.

[7] Vickers, *Classical Rhetoric in English Poetry*, 54. In *De l'esprit géométrique et l'art de persuader* (On the spirit of geometry and the art of persuasion), Blaise Pascal

be reversed in Renaissance thinking and that actual courtesans would occasionally be characterized as possessing significant rhetorical skills, especially since women were generally seen as being natural adepts at language, in keeping with the old adage "Women are words, men deeds."[8] The Elizabethan traveler Thomas Coryat thus warns the young Englishman: "Thou wilt find the Venetian Courtezan . . . a good Rhetorician, and a most elegant discourser, so that if she cannot move thee with all these aforesaid delights, she will assay thy constancy with a Rhetoricall tongue."[9]

One might expect that Renaissance works written to celebrate rhetoric—and that means the major portion of the discourse in the period—would seek to avoid even mentioning the idea of feminine allurement. As writers repeatedly strive to distinguish their discipline from its demonic feminine double, however, they ironically grant the latter a prominence in their works which it otherwise might not have. For instance, George of Trebizond says rhetorical speech should be beautiful and robust but then goes on to specify it should not be "rouged" (*Rhetoricorum*, 82^r), a sentiment reiterated by Philip Melanchthon (*Encomion*, 46) and by Johann Heinrich Alsted, who condemns bad rhetoric as "adulterous, rouged, flattering, and sophistic" (*Rhetorica*, 2). Similarly, M. Le Grand denounces the excessive eloquence of the Sophists, which, he says, was banished to Asia, "where it conducted a traffic in makeup [*fards*] and colors, and sold incense and perfumes" (*Discours*, n.p.). Other writers condemn bad rhetoric (and poetry) for being wanton and seductive. Thus, Henry Peacham warns against using proverbs that involve "wanton, unchast, and vile similitudes" (*Garden*, 31; cf. 47, 48), and he worries that figures such as *Protrope*, which exhorts and persuades the listener, may be abused and wind up "seducing unstable mindes into false religion and vanities" (78).[10] Alsted is even more tendentious as he labels excessive ornaments *lenocinia* (*Rhetorica*, 414):

---

also distinguishes two arts of persuasion, one of which appeals to the will and the senses, and the other to the reason. He denounces the former for appealing to our desire for pleasure, a technique that involves observing the "connections it [i.e., the matter] has . . . with delicious objects [*objets délicieux*] through the charms [*charmes*] which one has given it. As a result, the art of persuasion consists as much in that [method] of giving pleasure as in that of convincing [by rational proof], so much do men govern themselves more by caprice than by reason!" (*Oeuvres complètes*, ed. Jacques Chevalier [Paris: Gallimard, 1960], 594).

[8] See Parker, "On the Tongue," 452.

[9] Thomas Coryat, *Coryat's Crudities* (1611; rpt., Glasgow, 1905), 1:405, cited in Ann Rosalind Jones, "City Women and Their Audiences: Louise Labé and Veronica Franco," in *Rewriting the Renaissance*, 304.

[10] John Hoskins similarly urges the rhetor to avoid "superfluous and wanton conceits of figures" (*Directions for Speech and Style*, 6; cf. 13).

that is, the "allurements" associated with bawds. Finally, Sir Philip Sidney's *Apology*, written in part explicitly to counter the charge that poetry entices people to lust (58–59), includes a section condemning defective contemporary eloquence for being "apparelled, or rather disguised, in a courtesan-like painted affectation" (81).[11]

On three occasions, at least, the defenders of rhetoric represent the negative version of the art not merely as a seductive woman but as a witchlike mythical being—a Siren. Thus, in the late sixteenth century the Paduan professor Antonio Riccobono says that the enemies of rhetoric denounce its practitioners because they cling "to the allurements of words as to the rocks of the Sirens [*sirenios scopulos*]."[12] This same identification appears in Fulke Greville's *Treaty of Human Learning* to distinguish between true eloquence, in which words properly express thoughts, and its degraded opposite, which is called "rhetoric":

> Rhetoric, to this [i.e., logic] a sister and a twin,
> Is grown a siren in the forms of pleading,
> Captiving reason with the painted skin
> Of many words, with empty sounds misleading
>   Us to false ends by these false forms' abuse,
>   Brings never forth that truth whose name they use.[13]

The third example comes from the French Jesuit Nicholas Caussin, appearing near the start of his *De Eloquentia sacra et humana* when he discusses the history of rhetoric from the time of its initial triumph in ancient Greece. In that first age of rhetoric, he writes, orators were rulers and counselors, and the name of rhetor was considered such an honor that noble youths flocked to learn the art. This interest caused a new class of rhetors to appear who did not engage in civil affairs themselves but taught others; these rhetors Caussin clearly considers inferior to those who preceded them, and he underscores their inferiority by identifying them as "those who are learned in academic [*umbratilis*:

---

[11] Sidney's characterization of bad eloquence as a courtesan is shared by his French contemporaries Guillaume Du Vair and Jacques Amyot. Du Vair (*Traitté*, 409) declares that the rhetor who indulges in the niceties of style merely in order to tickle the ears of his auditors is acting "as an affected courtesan would do in a scene from a comedy." Amyot (*Projet*, 8) distinguishes what he considers royal eloquence fit for kings from its debased double which is "full of babbling and affectation just like a courtesan."

[12] Riccobono, *Oratio pro studiis humanitatis*, in Mazzacurati, *La crisi della retorica umanistica*, 171.

[13] Fulke Greville, *Treaty of Human Learning*, Stanza 107, in *The Later Renaissance in England: Nondramatic Verse and Prose, 1600–1660*, ed. Herschel Baker (Boston: Houghton Mifflin, 1975), 7.

shady] . . . eloquence" (8), an eloquence whose shade suggests the pastoral garden appropriate to Circe. From them in turn came the Sophists, defined as men who "began to affect the enticements of artful speech and certain allurements and, as it were, little Sirens [*sirenulas*] . . . of discourse" (8–9). As Caussin's history traces the decline of rhetoric, it shows just how ready he is to think of bad rhetoric as possessing feminine "allurements" and to equate it with Circean temptation.

Although Renaissance critics of rhetoric generally refrain from joining Pico in denouncing the negative version of the art as *cinaedus*, or *sodomitical*, their presentation of it as a Siren has much the same effect, since they wind up identifying male rhetors with women. What they are worried about comes across clearly when they attack the excessive use of tropes and figures of speech as "effeminate," or warn that certain gestures and facial expressions may be criticized with the same term (see Alsted, *Rhetorica*, 414, 449; and Granada, *Ecclesiastica Rhetorica*, 222, 340, 374). In other words, they are worried that the rhetor may be emasculated by the art he practices, turned into an effeminate man—a charge that evoked the specter of homosexuality in Renaissance culture just as it did in the Roman world.[14] Indeed, both Cicero and Quintilian are decidedly nervous about what they see as the effeminizing aspects of rhetoric, especially since Roman men normally defined themselves through action rather than talk. Cicero tries to solve this problem by displacing it onto the Greeks, condemning them for idleness and incessant loquacity and contrasting them with the Romans, who display the virtues of industry and decorum or tact. Although the latter must produce speeches in order to practice their profession, Cicero claims that they, unlike the chattering Greeks, speak only enough and at just the right moment (see *De oratore*, 2.4.17–18). Thus, he creates an aura of masculinity for his orators by contrasting them with the less than masculine *Graeculi*, or "Greeklings" (1.22.102). His diminutive suggests the lack of seriousness of Greek culture compared with the Roman, indicates the Greeks' inferiority in political power, and reminds the reader that many Romans owned Greek slaves. What is more, it identifies the Greeks as boys or boy-men, thereby evoking the vision of passive homosexual activity, which for the Romans—as for the Greeks themselves—completely demeaned *adult* males and rendered them effeminate. Quintilian is just as nervous about rhetoric as Cicero is, especially because by the late first century A.D., when Quintilian was writing, rhetoric had relatively little to do with the actual political life of the state, the management of which had traditionally been an important means for Roman

---

[14] See Smith, *Homosexual Desire*, 171.

men to define their identities. Revealingly, Quintilian directs harsh criticism at the rhetorical practices of his contemporaries because of their
predilection for extravagant and unnatural language, for words that are
sordida, lasciva, effeminata, and he goes on in the same passage to compare such a practice to using curling irons on one's hair and cosmetics
on one's face (*Institutio,* 2.5.10–12; cf. 8.Pr.19–20). Quintilian wants to
restore the virile eloquence of the age of Cicero, and as we saw in Chapter 1, both he and Cicero produce an image of rhetoric as an art of combat and competition fit for soldiers and gladiators. In short, they defend
their profession by creating a dramatic, masculine vision of the Roman
rhetor in order to counter that of an effeminized, Greekified chatterer
who, with his curly hair and rouge, plays the despised role of *cinaedus.*

When Renaissance writers denounce rhetoric as feminine, effeminizing, and sodomitical, they often repeat the notions, even the very words,
of their Roman forebears. This repetition is only apparent, however, for
the cultural context informing the meanings of those words changed
dramatically between the ages of Cicero and Pico. When the latter says
effoeminatus or *cinaedus,* he does not mean what the Romans meant by
those terms, because homosexuality did not have the same significance
in the Renaissance as in antiquity.[15] John Boswell and others have argued that homosexuality was not only widespread but generally tolerated throughout the urban culture of the ancient Mediterranean world;
the Romans were no different from the Greeks in accepting it as a normal practice; and even the early Christian Church did not condemn it
per se. According to Thomas Laqueur, ancient thinkers considered
men's sexual desire for other men to be as natural as their desire for
women, since the two sexes were not thought to be essentially differentiated from one another in biological terms.[16] It should be remembered
as well that the Greeks actually saw a grown man's homosexual relationship with a boy as a normal part of the educational process and as
reinforcing, rather than undermining, masculinity. There are, of course,
texts from both ancient cultures that criticize homosexual practices,
and the Roman satirists in particular attacked them as effeminizing and
linked them to what they saw as a decline in civilization. What the
Greek and Roman critics were objecting to, however, was the acceptance by the adult male of the passive role in the relationship, a role

[15] Actually, when Pico labels the rhetor *cinaedus,* he expicitly cites Synesius, a
Christian writer who flourished in the late fourth and early fifth centuries A.D. The
word was, however, widely used by Roman writers.
[16] Boswell, *Christianity, Social Tolerance, and Homosexuality,* 61–206; Smith,
Homosexual Desire, 33–42, 167–71; Thomas Laqueur, *Making Sex: Body and Gender from the Greeks to Freud* (Cambridge, Mass.: Harvard University Press, 1990), 46.

normally played by a child or a slave; such behavior was attacked not because it was homosexual per se but because it threatened to turn the social and political world topsy-turvy by having superiors and inferiors change places. Moreover, Roman satirists disliked any sort of excessive indulgence in erotic or sensual activity, so that when they condemned people for being *cinaedi* or *effoeminati*, they were more concerned with promiscuity than with sexual preference. Thus, both ancient cultures accepted homosexuality and criticized it only if it was excessive or involved an inversion of what was considered proper social hierarchy.

These attitudes towards homosexuality persisted well into the Middle Ages, changing substantially only toward the end of that period, when the tolerance of the ancient world eventually yielded to a complex and contradictory situation in which society fostered homosexual desire in a variety of ways but at the same time enshrined marriage as a norm and officially, legally, condemned sodomy as a horrendous crime against nature, the family, and the state. Bruce R. Smith observes that the "one salient fact about homosexuality in early modern England, as in early modern Europe generally, is the disparity that separates the extreme punishments prescribed by law and the apparent tolerance, even positive valuation, of homoerotic desire in the visual arts, in literature, and . . . in the political power structure."[17] On the one hand, according to Smith, the patriarchal nature of Renaissance culture actually fostered the homosocial and homosexual potential of male bonding. It placed boys and men together in a number of usually all-male settings and institutions, including schools and universities, confraternities and guilds, military organizations and the Church; it idealized male bonding in literary and artistic depictions of male friendship or love; and it largely ignored or laxly enforced its own laws against sodomy. Nevertheless, what distinguished the Renaissance from classical antiquity and even from the earlier Middle Ages was that those laws were in fact on the books. From the late medieval period on, Christian teaching categorized sodomy as a perversion and a sin against nature, and the Renaissance both continued this theological or religious evaluation and added the notion that sodomy was a political crime as well as a threat to the family. People accused of homosexual acts may have been brought to trial only infrequently, but when they were convicted, the punishments prescribed were severe; they included hanging if the offense was considered a political crime, and burning at the stake if religious. Boswell argues that the intolerance of late medieval and Renaissance culture was due partly to the tensions produced by increasing urbanization and

[17] Smith, *Homosexual Desire*, 13–14; see also 42–45, 171–84; and Boswell, *Christianity, Social Tolerance, and Homosexuality*, 269–332.

·partly to the anxieties Europeans felt because of their contact with the alien societies of Turks and Arabs on their fringes, anxieties they displaced onto minority groups within their borders—lepers, Jews, *moriscos*, homosexuals—whom they could control more effectively. This hostility toward homosexuality was also related to the increased status given marriage and the family in the period and to the growth of absolutism with its insistence on corporatism, uniformity, and conformity. Paradoxically, then, the same culture that idealized male friendship and was led by rulers who had "favorites," *mignons*, or *privados*, to whom they sometimes even said they were "married," simultaneously ridiculed, ostracized, incarcerated, and executed those condemned as sodomites.[18]

Although Cicero and Pico may both talk about rhetoric, the rhetor, or rhetorical style as being *effoeminatus* or *cinaedus*, they do not mean the same thing by those words, because they evaluate homosexuality in quite different ways. Pico may seem as hostile and satirical as his Roman forebears, but when he criticizes a speech as sodomitical, he is not merely implying that its creator is excessively emotional or is engaging in a practice that might invert the natural order of society. Rather, he is indicting that person for something his culture may have embraced in a variety of ways but condemned officially as sinful, unnatural, and politically subversive and found morally and religiously totally unacceptable. Thus we see once more how the Renaissance discourse of rhetoric, although clearly based on ancient writings, does not really represent a repetition, a "rebirth," of the classical past. Instead, Pico seems to manifest the bias of his increasingly absolutist culture, whose laws condemned sodomitical behavior as demonic and aimed to punish it with the utmost rigor. John Boswell sees an irony in situations of this sort: "Renaissance Italians who strove to be like their forebears in the smallest details of language and all the minutiae of art execrated feelings which classical Rome had immortalized in public sculpture, mythology, and literature of every sort."[19] Boswell misstates the case somewhat, however, for he ignores the fact that Renaissance artists in Italy and throughout Europe, while operating within the constraints and biases of

---

[18] Boswell, *Christianity, Social Tolerance, and Homosexuality*, 289–93; Ruggiero, *The Boundaries of Eros*, 109–11, 127–34; Goldberg, "Sodomy and Society," 371–78; Smith, *Homosexual Desire*, 42–45; and Jonathan Dollimore, *Sexual Dissidence: Augustine to Wilde, Freud to Foucault* (Oxford: Clarendon Press, 1991), 237–39. Smith (*Homosexual Desire*, 14) notes that England's James I could classify sodomy as a crime alongside witchcraft, murder, and incest and yet write earnest protestations of affection to his favorite, George Villiers, the Duke of Buckingham, and even speak of the "marriage" between them.

[19] Boswell, *Christianity, Social Tolerance, and Homosexuality*, 87.

their culture's laws and religion, did in fact manage to immortalize various forms of homosexual desire in works of art, including Shakespeare's sonnets, many of Michelangelo's finest sculptures, and courtly
romances and pastorals such as Sidney's *Arcadia*, with their prominent
episodes of cross-dressing. As we shall see, the Renaissance discourse of
rhetoric shares its culture's positive as well as its negative response to
homosexual desire. For if it could produce satirical attacks such as
Pico's on "sodomitical" speeches, it could also concoct an elaborate,
positive vision of the art as both feminine and masculine, both Circe's
garden and Mercury's rod, a hybrid creature that may be read simultaneously as a revelation of the homosexuality the culture condemned
and an expression of rhetoricians' yearning for perfection, a celebration
of their art, and a validation of their social importance.

In response to attacks on rhetoric as a Circean temptress and on the
rhetor as an effeminized man, Renaissance defenders of the discipline
use stereotypically masculine images for both rhetoric and the rhetor,
images completely consistent with the characterization of the latter as
the emperor of men's minds which was unfolded in Chapter 1. Their
desire that he should be perceived thus is hardly surprising in the context of an intensely patriarchal culture that saw men's superiority and
right to rule over women as God-given aspects of the nature of things.
On occasion, the rhetoricians themselves consciously affirm the rightness of this "natural" order, as George of Trebizond does when he declares that men are meant to rule, women to obey, and insists as a corol-
lary that women should generally be sparing in speech (*Rhetoricorum*,
46ᵛ). Thomas Wilson spells out the social vision involved when he condemns those who violate the proper arrangement of words in a sentence:

> Some will set the Cart before the horse, as thus. My mother and my
> father are both at home, as though the good man of the house did
> weare no breches, or that the graie Mare were the better Horse. And
> what though it often so happeneth (God wot the more pitty) yet in
> speaking at the least, let us keepe a naturall order, and set the man
> before the woman for maners sake. (*Arte*, 167)

Wilson's "naturall order," which places men above and ahead of
women, was also invoked by the Renaissance political theorists noted
in Chapter 1, who defined the ruler—especially the ruler of the absolutist state—as a patriarch. Hence, the rhetoricians' insistence on the masculinity of the orator and their definition of him as a ruler are perfectly

harmonious within the terms of their culture. Moreover, their attempt to distinguish the good rhetor-ruler from the bad by opposing a purely masculine to a feminine or effeminized figure follows the same cultural logic. As Rebecca Bushnell has shown, the Renaissance inherited from the ancient world, and particularly from the Greeks, the notion that the bad king or ruler—the tyrant—was effeminate. Ancient misogyny, which the Renaissance repeated in crucial ways, identified women as irrational beings who were governed by their appetites and excelled at deception; since these attributes were also assigned to the tyrant, it was inevitable that Western culture from the Greeks to the seventeenth century should conceive of him as an effeminate man.[20] It was also inevitable that in the Renaissance discourse of rhetoric the bad rhetor-ruler should be conceived in the same way.

To emphasize the masculinity of the ideal rhetor-ruler, Renaissance writers gravitate toward metaphors that suggest force and a will to dominate. Consider, for instance, how Nicholas Caussin praises eloquence for its ability to seize or capture (*capere*) the spirits of others, defining the process as a kind of airborne invasion that penetrates and takes possession of the auditor: "As if supported by its [i.e., Eloquence's] wings, the spirit of the orator flows into the very breasts of the auditors and possesses them in a form of servitude most pleasing to all" (*Eloquentia sacra*, 5). Cypriano Soarez is thinking in the same terms when he asks: "But [doesn't] speech, having been received by the air as by a vehicle, reach as many as possible with incredible rapidity in the briefest space of time, and finally enter the spirits of others . . . through the finest channels of their ears?" (*De Arte*, 7). For some writers, this invasion is pleasurable or "sweet." Bartolomeo Cavalcanti thus speaks of how naked speech alone, given the appropriate rhetorical ornaments, will be able to "penetrate the spirit of the auditor or reader with the force and sweetness that are desired" (*Retorica*, 249). Similarly, George Puttenham identifies the poet as "the most auncient Orator" who mastered the people by "insinuating unto them, under fictions with sweete and coloured speeches, many wholesome lessons and doctrines" (*Arte*, 206). Usually, however, writers stress the violence of the orator's penetration into the intimate interior of his listener's soul. For example, Angelo Poliziano asks rhetorically: "What is more admirable, when you are speaking to a great multitude of men, than to burst into their breasts and minds so that you impel their wills to go and come away as you wish, . . . and that finally you dominate their wills and desires?" ("Oratio super Fabio Quintiliano et Statii Sylvis," in *Prosatori latini*, 882).

---

[20] Rebecca Bushnell, *Tragedies of Tyrants: Political Thought and Theater in the English Renaissance* (Ithaca: Cornell University Press, 1990), esp. 20–25, 63–69.

Giorgio Valla, writing of the three levels of style, praises the highest—the most ample and ornate one—for its usefulness to the state and declares: "It is the function of this eloquence to manage [men's] spirits, to move them by all means, sometimes breaking through the senses, sometimes creeping into them."[21] Whether the orator operates in sweet or violent ways, whether he proceeds by overpowering the audience or insinuating himself into their senses by means of guile, all these rhetoricians consistently imagine his words as an invasion force, a kind of imperial, colonizing army which, entering people through their eyes and ears, plants its flag of conquest on the terrain of their souls. The seventeenth-century Englishman John Bulwer sums up the matter when, in writing on the use of the hand in oratory, he praises the ancients who by its means alone "extorted approbation from their auditors, and, . . . invading the mind through the eye, with easy accesses put themselves into the possession of the people" (*Chirologia*, 160).

If rhetoric is an invading army for Renaissance rhetoricians, it is also a kind of magic, a metamorphic art whose fundamental goal is the *transformation* of the auditor. For example, Rudolph Agricola tells his reader how speech (*oratio*) affects the listener: you can, he says, "transform him into whatever spiritual shape [*habitum*: dress] you wish, allure him, and hold him captive by the pleasure of listening" (*De Inventione*, 1). Similarly, in his dialogue on rhetoric, Daniel Barbaro has Nature tell the Soul how much she can accomplish with eloquent speech: "You will be able, of your free will, to soften those who are angry, urge on the lazy, restrain the ferocious, strengthen the weak, and transform each soul [*ogni anima tramutare*] from one contrary to the other by force." Barbaro's Soul immediately grasps the symbolic resonance in Nature's key phrase and responds: "That is a most excellent magic." Art then tells the Soul how to work on the emotions of the listener and concludes with a rhetorical question that links the magical control of the rhetor to the idea of rule: "By doing that with every emotion, won't you make yourself the lord [*signore*] of every person and the possessor of his soul?" (*Della Eloquenza*, 342, 356). In his *Ciceronianus*, Erasmus has his spokesman invoke a similar notion of the rhetor's magical power, crediting him in one passage with the ability to overpower

---

[21] Giorgio Valla, *Rhetorica* (Venice, 1514), II.i^v. René Bary declares the orator's genius to be a fire "which pierces and penetrates" (*Rhetorique*, 86), and Sidney's words suggest something similar when he places his poet above the philosopher, whose "wordish description . . . doth neither strike, pierce, nor possess the sight of the soul so much as that other doth" (*Apology*, 27). For other metaphors of invasion and possession, see Du Vair, *Traitté*, 403; Puttenham, *Arte*, 24; and Barbaro, *Della Eloquenza*, 356.

the hearer's soul (8), and claiming in another that he is capable of alter-
ing the shape of things just like a conjuror, infiltrating the hearer's mind
and arousing the emotions as by a "kind of spell [or witchcraft, or poi-
son]" (132: *veneficii genus*). The identification of orator or poet as a
magus also runs through Sidney's *Apology*: he insists on the "charming
sweetness" (6) of poetry; recalls that the Roman word for poet was
vates, which means "diviner, foreseer, or prophet" (10); notes that
"charms" comes from *carmina*, a word for both poems and incantations
(11); and speaks of how the poet commands "the well enchanting skill
of music" (38). In a wonderful move, Sidney ends his work with a kind
of mock peroration in which he adopts an ironic version of the poet-
orator's role as *magus* and says to his audience: "I conjure you all that
have had the evil luck to read this ink-wasting toy of mine, even in the
name of the nine Muses, no more to scorn the sacred mysteries of
poesy" (87). Sidney here is playing wittily with the vision of the exalted
poet-orator and his magical, conjuring power, which has been advanced
throughout his work with the utmost seriousness, just as it is by most
Renaissance writers on rhetoric.

The Renaissance magician-orator works his mysterious spells by appealing to the senses of his auditors and in particular by enchanting
their eyes and ears. Cypriano Soarez remarks—and his statement is typical—that an audience is affected by the gestures and voice of the orator, "of which the first moves the eyes, the other the ears, and through
these two senses all emotion penetrates the spirit" (*De Arte*, 327). Like
other Renaissance rhetoricians, Soarez is concerned here with the literal
physical appearance of the orator when he is performing; however, the
appeal to the sense of sight is often metaphorical, as the orator is told to
present his case through visual images, a requirement for vividness (*evidentia, enargeia*) which has deep roots in the classical past.[22] Thus, Sperone Speroni claims that the orator is a painter whose words should be
like "the colors of the vegetation" (*Dialogo*, 93; cf. 108), and Bartolomeo
Cavalcanti insists that the orator must bring the condition of those for
whom he pleads right before the eyes of his audience (*Retorica*, 209). In
Angel Day's manual on letter-writing, a passage on descriptive letters
stresses the value of vividness. It begins by comparing the writer to the
painter and providing a sample description of a landscape but finishes by
waxing ecstatic over contemporary cosmographers who have described
the "unknown delights" of countries unseen in so vivid a manner that
they "ravish us oftentimes, and bring in contempt the pleasures of our

---

[22] See, e.g., Aristotle, *Rhetoric*, 3.11.2; and Quintilian, *Institutio*, 6.2.32–34. On
Aristotle, see Shuger, *Sacred Rhetoric*, 193–210.

owne soyle: and manie times a huge wonder, of the unheard secrets never before reported of . . . such as the verie description and livelie delivery whereof, maketh us believe that our eies do almost witnes the same, and that our verie sences are partakers of everie delicacie in them contained."[23] In Day's conception, vivid writing not only brings the things described right before our eyes but provides us with such a powerful vicarious experience of the wonders of alien places that we are no longer satisfied with our native soil. Day thus produces an image of rhetoric as a powerful sort of magic indeed, one that utterly transforms the persons exposed to it and, as the word "ravish" suggests, takes possession of their spirits. We shall return to this idea of ravishment a little later.

If the eye, whether real or metaphorical, is essential for the magic of rhetoric to work, the ear is even more crucial. Here again there is ample classical precedent for such an emphasis; it goes back to Gorgias, who was famous in antiquity for his incantatory rhythmical speech. Isocrates likewise stresses the importance of rhythm, and Cicero in his *De oratore*, has his spokesmen tell the would-be orator to choose words on the basis of their appeal to the ear (3.37.150, 3.44.174). Most Renaissance rhetoricians share the view of the ancient world that "rhetoric is true music" (Guzman, *Primera Parte*, 243[r]) and that rhythm and harmony have a compelling effect on the listener. Thus, M. Le Grand claims that the rhythmic language of rhetoric pleases and does so because, as Saint Augustine says, the eye of the soul perceives in it a connection to the First Beauty, the supreme Reason which is God (*Discours*, n.p.). Other Renaissance rhetoricians focus on the notion of harmony and explain its appeal by invoking the idea of order, as the English Ramist Abraham Fraunce does when he recommends the "pleasant and delicate tuning of the voyce, which resembleth the consent and harmonie of some well ordered song."[24] Henry Peacham may be working with a similar notion when he praises the figure *Compar*, the use of balanced clauses and phrases, which, he says, must be measured "by a secret sence of the eare" (*Garden*, 58) and whose employment he justifies in the following manner: "This figure of all others is most straightly tied to number and proportion, and therfore is most harmonicall. The use wherof doth cheefly consist in causing delectation by the vertue of proportion and number" (59). Like most Renaissance rhetoricians, however, Peacham seems to prefer another sort of explanation for the appeal of words to the ear: sheer sensual delight. Indeed, he speaks of "delight" or "plea-

[23] Day, *The English Secretary*, 23–24. For other examples, see Wilson, *Arte*, 65, 131; and Puttenham, *Arte*, 155.

[24] Abraham Fraunce, *The Arcadian Rhetorike* (London, 1588), bk. 2, chap. 1.

sure" on many occasions (e.g., 41, 42, 44, 50, 54) and typically praises *Epanalepsis*, or the beginning and ending of a speech with the same word, for the "sweetnesse in the sound of the repetition" (46).[25] By focusing on the direct sensory appeal of oratorical language, all these writers not only make its effects appear irrational but heighten its mysteriousness at the same time. They thus enhance the identification of rhetoric with magic, for both arts appear mysterious, working at a distance without direct bodily contact as they control the responses of others. René Bary, in his *Rhetorique françoise* of 1659, sums it up succinctly: the orator "enchants the ear with his discourses" (93).

Renaissance rhetoricians clearly wish to appropriate magic, which can theoretically be practiced by either sex, for the male rhetor. Thus, as noted in Chapter 1, they identify the rhetor with Orpheus and Amphion, whose magically potent words could make stones build walls and cities, subdue others to their will, and even call the dead back to life. Henry Peacham, for instance, cites a passage from Horace's *Ars poetica* in order to praise Orpheus as a model of the eloquent orator who is "judged able, and esteemed fit to rule the world" (*Garden*, iii[v]), and Guillaume Du Vair celebrates eloquence as "the lyre of Amphion which drags forests, rocks, and rivers after it" (*Traitté*, 395).[26] This mythological identification of the orator makes him not only a male magician but a singer or musician, and it thus fits the emphasis on the ear in rhetorical theory. Moreover, it helps to explain the mysteriousness of the effect that oratory has on its audience by providing a visualizable image: it allows the orator's speech to be equated with the vibrating strings of Orpheus's or Amphion's lyre, and the reaction of the listeners, according to the contagion theory, can similarly be seen as a responsive vibrating of the strings of their passions.

The rhetorical transaction is sometimes imagined in other terms also

---

[25] The early Tudor rhetorician Leonard Coxe says the orator makes the logician's arguments "gay and delectable to the aere" (*The Arte or Craft of Rhethoryke* [London, 1524; rpt. Amsterdam, Walter J. Johnson, 1977], Aviii[v]); Sperone Speroni says the harmony of an oration "delights marvelously" (*Dialogo*, 100); and Marco Girolamo Vida, writing about poetry, asks: "Why need I go on further about how poets hold our ears captivated by sweetness when they repeat the same phrase" (*The "De Arte Poetica,"* trans. Ralph G. Williams [New York: Columbia University Press, 1976], 3. 143–45). Daniel Barbaro claims that the *numero*, or rhythm, of oratory generates "belief and delight" (*Della Eloquenza*, 386), and John Rainolds praises the *numeri*, or rhythms, that rhetoric shares with poetry and that "suffuse very pleasantly the senses of the auditors with the sweetness of their modes" (*Oratio*, 48).

[26] For other references to Orpheus and Amphion, see Sidney, *Apology*, 6; Rainolds, *Oratio*, 48; Fuscano, "Della oratoria e poetica facoltà," 193; Le Grand, *Discours*; Caussin, *Eloquentia sacra*, 2; Puttenham, *Arte*, 22; and Sturm, *De Universa ratione elocutionis rhetorica*, iv[v].

consistent with its characterization as an invasion and penetration or a magical possessing of the auditor's spirit. Jacques Amyot uses the notion of *imprinting* or *impressing* to identify the orator's effect on his auditor, arguing that although rational arguments are useful in persuasion, "it is fitting, in addition, to imprint [*imprimer*] certain passions on the spirits of the auditors, which have much more power than arguments and by which they let themselves be led and transported here and there" (*Projet*, 34; cf. 50–51). Implicitly, Amyot compares the spirit of the auditor to a wax tablet or, perhaps, a sheet of paper on which the orator imprints or impresses his words—a comparison that Henry Peacham spells out: metaphors, he says, "leave such a firme impression in the memory, as is not lightly forgotten. . . . In respect of their firme impression in the mind & remembrance of the hearer, they are as seales upon soft waxe, or as deep stamps in long lasting mettall" (*Garden*, 13–14). Guillaume Du Vair speaks in similar terms: eloquent men "not only paint their character [*moeurs*] on the tablets of our hearts but imprint in them, indeed with burning fire, the most lively and violent affections which can enter there" (*Traitté*, 400). George Puttenham declares that the figures of poetry enable it to carry people's judgments "this way and that, whither soever the heart by impression of the eare shalbe most affectionatly bent and directed" (*Arte*, 24). All this imagery is related to the domain of education: Erasmus is typical of Renaissance thinking on pedagogy in envisaging the child as a "smooth tablet," a *tabula complanata*, on which the teacher, functioning much like the rhetor, writes his lessons.[27] More important, the imagery also suggests the domain of sexual reproduction, for the woman's body, according to a tradition going back to the ancient world, is often imagined as a tablet on which the man makes an impression in an act analogized to that of generating a child through intercourse.[28] Thus, when the orator impresses or imprints himself on his auditor, his actions not only constitute an invasion and occupation of alien territory but possess a distinctly sexual aura as well. This aura is unmistakable when Johann Heinrich Alsted describes the effect that the orator's speech has on others, for he not only speaks of imprinting but imagines the result of

[27] Desiderius Erasmus, *Institutio matrimonii christiani*, in *Opera omnia*, ed. J. Clericus (Leiden, 1703–6), 5, col. 722C. The *tabula rasa* of which Locke would later speak is really a commonplace in Renaissance thought on education and goes back to the ancient world, in particular to Plato's comparison of the soul to a wax tablet in the *Theatetus*. See Leah S. Marcus, *Childhood and Cultural Despair: A Theme and Variations in Seventeenth-Century Literature* (Pittsburgh: University of Pittsburgh Press, 1978), 271 n. 43.

[28] See Page duBois, *Sowing the Body: Psychoanalysis and Ancient Representations of Women* (Chicago: University of Chicago Press, 1988), 130–66.

the process as a form of self-reproduction not unlike what is involved in the engendering of a child: the orator's speech "flows, as it were, into the spirits of others and . . . perfectly, . . . remarkably imprints in them its very own image" (*Rhetorica*, 5).

The notion that the rhetorical transaction is an aggressive, phallic assault may be teased out of many sets of images used by Renaissance writers. If one reviews the metaphors already investigated, for instance, metaphors of penetration, of entering into the other through the senses or through the slender orifice of the ear, a sexual interpretation seems almost inescapable.[29] The sexuality of the rhetor's actions is especially at issue throughout Guillaume Du Vair's *Traitté de l'Eloquence Françoise*. At one point, as he recollects the words of an unidentified ancient Roman, he constructs an elaborate comparison between eloquence and the earth, declaring that both produce very little when neglected or cultivated by servile hands. He goes on to insist, however, that the situation was very different at the height of Rome's glory: "The earth . . . rejoiced then under the victorious hands of those magnificent captains, and, glorying to feel [upon her] a cart crowned with laurels and a triumphant laborer, opened her bosom [*sein*] more liberally and shared her favors in a more prodigal manner" (399). Here Du Vair personifies eloquence as the female earth and identifies the orator as a conquering captain to whom she offers her body (literally her *sein*, or "bosom") and her obviously sexual "favors." Although in Du Vair's sentence the orator impregnates eloquence itself, not his auditors, the image still confirms both his power and his masculinity by stressing his sexual role as inseminator. It is precisely this role of which Giorgio Valla is thinking when, in the quotation given earlier, he talks of how the orator's eloquence first breaks into the senses of the auditor, in whom he then "implants [*inserit*] new opinions and tears up those already sown" (*Rhetorica*, II.i^v). Luis de Granada similarly thinks of correct delivery as a means to implant or graft (*inserere*) ideas in the spirits of one's auditors (*Ecclesiastica Rhetorica*, 357), and he even uses the same metaphor to describe the process of contagion: "As trees in trees, so emotions are grafted [*inseruntur*] in emotions: and thus some also take force and impetus from others" (366). J. Du Pré de la Porte's somewhat different set of images also give a distinctly erotic character to the orator's effect on the auditor. Recalling a story about how the infant Mercury stole

---

[29] On the sexual implications of aural penetration, we might recall both the long tradition of the Virgin's impregnation through the ear by the Word and Cleopatra's lusty response to Antony's messenger, "Ram thou thy fruitful tidings in mine ears, / That long time have been barren" (Shakespeare, *Antony and Cleopatra*, 2.5.24–25).

Apollo's arrows and quiver, Du Pré claims that eloquence will capture our hearts "so well that if we are angry at first to see our wills thus drawn away and we want to call them back to us, we no longer have our quivers, for the same eloquence stole them from us. That is to say, our resistance is vain and our hearts, so violently wounded, have no arrows left to shoot back. This makes us avow that there is no resistance at all which can fend off the blows delivered by an eloquent tongue" (*Pourtraict*, 22–23). Du Pré's images here of wounded hearts, vain resistance, and blows from the tongue all evoke the erotic love poetry of the Renaissance and make the rhetor's attack on his auditor a matter of aggressive, phallic sexuality indeed.

Equally suggestive of the sexual nature of the orator's eloquence are the frequent images of it as flowing liquid that fills up the auditor.[30] Although this imagery has many classical precedents, in the Renaissance it often acquires a particularly sexual charge.[31] Thus, John Rainolds praises the rhythms of rhetoric because they bring pleasure as they "suffuse [*perfundant*: flood] most pleasingly the senses of the auditors with the sweetness of its [rhetoric's] modes" (*Oratio*, 48). George Puttenham defines rhythm even more suggestively as "a certaine flowing utteraunce by slipper [i.e., easily pronounced] words and sillables, such as the toung easily utters, and the eare with pleasure receiveth, and which flowing of words with much volubilitie smoothly proceeding from the mouth is in some sort *harmonicall* and breedeth to th'eare a great compassion" (*Arte*, 91). Here the orator's performance is distinctly sexual: his words are associated with pleasure and the production of love ("compassion"), flow like liquid from his tongue, enter the auditor's ear, and there produce a reaction that is identified by the suggestive "breedeth." Nor are the English the only Renaissance writers who have recourse to this vision of the sexual flow of oratory. Luis de Granada writes that training in eloquence will enable a speaker to use words "so that whatever he may have conceived [*conceperit*] himself, he pours it forth [*transfundat*] into the spirits of the auditor by means of speech" (*Ecclesiastica Rhetorica*, Preface, n.p.). Granada's metaphors of conception and pouring forth suggest a notion going back to the ancient world, that in sexual intercourse the child, already conceived by the

---

[30] For examples, see Alsted, *Rhetorica*, Dedication, 8ᵛ, and *Rhetorica*, 3; Du Pré, *Pourtraict*, 72; Peacham, *Garden*, 3ʳ, 121; Caussin, *Eloquentia sacra*, 5, 462; Granada, *Ecclesiastica Rhetorica*, 7; Soarez, *De Arte*, 179; and George of Trebizond, *Rhetoricorum*, 33ᵛ.

[31] For the classical precedents, see Plett, *Rhetorik der Affekte*, 27. Terence Cave (*The Cornucopian Text*, 13) discusses this imagery briefly in relation to the Renaissance emphasis on copiousness.

man and contained in his semen, is merely being transplanted into the woman's womb. Finally, there is a revealing example of this sexualized imagery in a passage from the *Logique* (1662) of Antoine Arnauld and Pierre Nicole who, as they denounce the pompous oratorical high style for the errors it leads people into, are virtually the only Renaissance writers to attack rhetoric in terms that suggest masculine rather than feminine sexuality. "It is strange," they write, "how often a false reasoning flows [*coule*] sweetly in the train of a [rhetorical] period which fills up the ear."[32] In a common alternative to the image of a sweetly flowing stream, some Renaissance rhetoricians represent the orator's words, especially when he employs the high style, as a fierce river or flood that rushes violently into the auditor and sweeps him away. Thus, Jacques Amyot recommends that the orator use a vehement language which appeals to the passions and which, "rushing fiercely like a torrent, bears away the auditor with it" (*Projet*, 42). In the same vein, the English rhetorician Thomas Farnaby writes of the sublime style: "It does not creep into the senses, but rushes in: like a rapid torrent swollen by winter rains or mountain storms, it overwhelms the fields, tumbles down rocks, makes a way where it does not find one. It carries the auditor with it even if he is struggling against it, and it forces him to go in the direction it carries him."[33] Cypriano Soarez also insists on this image; of rhetoric in general he says: "Let it flow not as tiny fountains are compressed in pipes, but as the broadest rivers [flow] through entire valleys, and let it make a way for itself even if it did not find one" (*De Arte*, 178).

If the imagery of rivers and flowing water makes the oratorical transaction seem sexual in nature, the imagery of ravishment does so even more dramatically. Thomas Wilson, in the dedicatory epistle to his *Arte of Rhetorique*, celebrates the worthiness of eloquence by asking: "If pleasure maie provoke us, what greater delite doe wee knowe, then to see a whole multitude, with the onely talke of man, ravished and drawne which way he liketh best to have them?" (ii^v). Here not only does the ravishment of the auditor provide "pleasure" and "delight" for the speaker, but the latter is imagined as "having" the former, a notion carrying a distinctly sexual charge in this context. Sir Philip Sidney thinks of poetry in similar terms when he defines it as "heart-ravishing knowledge" (*Apology*, 10), while across the Channel Jacques Amyot argues that the peroration of a speech especially ought to "ravish [*ravir*] and transport" the listener (*Projet*, 40). Writing somewhat earlier in the

---

[32] Antoine Arnauld and Pierre Nicole, *La logique, ou L'art de penser*, ed. Pierre Clair and François Girbal (Paris: Presses Universitaires de France, 1965), 277.

[33] Thomas Farnaby, *Index Rhetoricus* (London, 1625), 30.

sixteenth century, Gracien Du Pont praises Cicero for having been able, by means of his sweet speech, to control the mighty Julius Caesar and put him in a state of ravishment (*ravy*) so that the strength of his hands was totally annihilated and he behaved "as if he were in an ecstasy."[34] Latin rhetorics in the Renaissance are more insistent on the idea of ravishment than vernacular ones, simply because, as they stress the power of eloquence, they have recourse to forms of the verb *rapere*, which means to seize and carry off, to snatch, and to drive, as well as to ravish. Thus, Rudolph Agricola writes of what the orator must accomplish by means of style: "One must use force, and the mind must be ravished [*rapienda*], and the spirit must be carried off from itself and placed, as it were, beyond itself" (*De Inventione*, 160–61). Similarly, Anto Maria de' Conti declares that eloquence "ravishes [*rapit*] and transforms the minds of men" (*Dialogus*, 157; cf. 160), and Erasmus writes in his *Ecclesiastae* of how speech "ravishes [*rapit*] the emotions of the auditors."[35] Finally, George Puttenham recommends using rhetorical figures "because the eare is no lesse ravished with their currant tune, than the mind is with their sententiousnes." As Puttenham unfolds the experience involved, he specifies what is implied by the rhetoricians' concept of ravishment: the use of figures will "breede no little alteration in man. For to say truely, what els is man but his minde? which, whosoever have skil to compasse, and make yeelding and flexible, what may not he commaund the body to perfourme?" (*Arte*, 207). As Puttenham unpacks it, the metaphor of ravishment implies two things: first, that the person affected is not only having a pleasurable sexual experience but is indeed being inseminated, bred in and made yielding and flexible; and second, that he has been placed in a kind of trance or ecstasy, made the powerless subject of his ravisher.

If all this highly charged imagery of penetration, magical possession, imprinting, flowing, and ravishing creates a distinctly masculine aura for the Renaissance rhetor, so do the iconographic and mythographic traditions in which he is identified with Orpheus, Amphion, and the Hercules Gallicus. In this last case, note that whereas representations of Lady Rhetoric tend to make her a static figure who simply stands in place, representations of Hercules stress his activity, his leading or dragging his followers by means of chains. Hercules may not be represented as invading his audience sexually, but his chains do penetrate their

---

[34] Du Pont, *Art et science de rhethoricque metriffiée*, ii[r].

[35] Desiderius Erasmus, *Ecclesiastae sive de ratione concionandi libri quatuor* (Basel, 1535), 2:126, cited in Rainolds, *Oxford Lectures*, 409 n. 77. For other examples of *rapere*, see Rainolds, *Oxford Lectures*, 150; and George of Trebizond, *Rhetoricorum*, 51[v], 81[r], and 84[r].

bodies and do allow him to possess them. Renaissance rhetoricians knew that Hercules was a version of Hermes or Mercury, a god who also appears frequently as an emblem of the art, typically carrying a symbolically charged, potent, phallic rod—his caduceus. One of its defining characteristics is underscored by Guillaume Du Vair, who claims that through it Mercury is able "to command the powers of heaven, earth, and hell" (*Traitté*, 395). More directly suggestive of the sexual nature of that rod is the brief passage from the section of Nicholas Caussin's *De Eloquentia sacra et humana* dealing with the force (*vis*) of eloquence, in which, after describing how it sails through the air, flows into the auditor's breast, and takes possession of him, he concludes that the Roman emperor Julian "compares it not unwisely to Mercury's rod [*Mercurii virga*]" (5). A lengthy tradition stretching back through the Middle Ages, on which both Du Vair and Caussin are drawing, stresses the magical powers of the caduceus, but in the context of the erotically charged language we find in their works—and in the Renaissance discourse of rhetoric generally—that implement also invites a sexual reading that points to the masculine nature of oratory and its practitioner.[36]

The sexual language used by Renaissance rhetoricians also makes rhetoric, at least potentially, a most sinister and troubling affair, for if the orator's performance constitutes a violent, irresistible sexual penetration of the auditor, then that performance looks uncomfortably like rape. Indeed, the discourse resonates with the word itself, which appears in barely disguised form every time a vernacular writer speaks of *ravishment*, and more directly in Latin texts whenever one encounters the verb *rapere*. That rhetoric should evoke rape should not be surprising, since rape is a crime of violence, an assault on a victim who is penetrated and possessed sexually by the attacker. Rape also has overtones of abduction, the binding and carrying off of the victim, as the Latin word itself and the complex legal history of rape both suggest.[37] Strikingly, Renaissance rhetoricians often speak of the male rhetor-ruler binding or tying the auditor. Nicholas Caussin, for example, praises eloquence as

[36] On Mercury's rod, see Giovanni Boccaccio, *Genealogie deorum gentilium libri*, ed. Vincenzo Romano (Bari: Laterza, 1951), 2.7, 12.62; Isidore of Seville, *Etymologiarum libri*, ed. W. M. Lindsay (Oxford: Clarendon Press, 1911), 8.11; and Pierre Bersuire, *Reductorium morale*, ed. J. Engels (Utrecht: Instituut voor Laat Latijn der Rijksuniversiteit, 1962, 1966), 15. 1, *De formis figurisque deorum*. Mercury's caduceus contains two sinewy serpents as well, but it is striking how often it is referred to simply as a rod.

[37] On rape as a crime of violence and abduction as a component of its definition, see Kathryn Gravdal, *Ravishing Maidens: Writing Rape in Medieval French Literature and Law* (Philadelphia: University of Pennsylvania Press, 1991), esp. 2–18; and the essays in Nazife Bashar, ed., *The Sexual Dynamics of History: Men's Power, Women's Resistance* (London: Pluto Press, 1983).

"efficacious in seizing and binding [*illigandis*] spirits" (*Eloquentia sacra*, 5) and talks of how speech "allures [*allicit*] minds" (459). And in his *De Ratione dicendi*, Juan Luis Vives declares: "Speech both allures [*allicit*] minds to itself and rules in the emotions" (89).[38] The terms used by these and other authors—*allicere* and *illigare*, as well as the related *illecebra* ("allurements")—all come from the verb *lacio*, whose noun equivalent *laqueus* means "snare" or "noose"; in effect, when rhetoricians use such words, they represent the rhetor as ensnaring and binding his auditor with a "rope" of words. In a related image Daniel Barbaro writes that the orator manages his auditors through their emotions "because these . . . seem the true and powerful cords [*funi*] with which others are drawn by our wills" (349). This imagery too conjures up the figure of the Gallic Hercules, whose chains often look like ropes in the illustrations; though they provide an image of ruling, they also suggest abduction and thus point unmistakably in the direction of rape.

In rape the will is a central issue. Crucial in legal definitions is the question of consent; rape involves taking or possessing a person *against his or her will*. In England, for instance, a parliamentary act of 1576 condemned the rape of a woman, putting it in the same class with theft and murder. But there were very few prosecutions, in part because some women became pregnant as a result of their ravishment, thus allowing defendants, says Nazife Bashar, to invoke "the widely held legal dictum that conception proved consent: 'Rape is the forcible ravishment of a woman, but if she conceive it is not rape, for she cannot conceive unless she consent.'"[39] This dictum gives priority to the issue of will and makes bodily penetration to some extent secondary. Thus, in a rape trial involving a woman named Margery Evans (which may have shaped Milton's *Comus*), the chief question turned "not upon th'external Act whether it was done or not but whether it was in the patient voluntary or compulsory."[40] Renaissance rhetoric, as noted in Chapter 2, also displays an intense focus on the will. Although it does grant the auditor free will, that will is imagined as being overpowered and directed, sometimes even obliterated and replaced, by the omnipotent will of the orator. Rhetoric thus resembles rape not just because it is a verbal act of violence, an invasion of others involving the forcible penetration, pos-

---

[38] For other examples, see Agricola, *De Inventione*, 1, 154; and Soarez, *De Arte*, 135.

[39] Nazife Bashar, "Rape in England between 1500 and 1700," in *The Sexual Dynamics of History*, 36, quoting Nicholas Brady, *The Lawes Resolution of Women's Rights or the Lawes Provision for Woemen* (1632), 396.

[40] See Leah S. Marcus, "The Milieu of Milton's *Comus*: Judicial Reform at Ludlow and the Problem of Sexual Assault," *Criticism* 25 (1983): 318, which cites a manuscript record of the trial, EL 7399:1, at the Henry E. Huntington Library.

session, and binding of their spirits, but also because it is the orator's assertion of his triumphant will whereby he co-opts the less powerful wills of those he addresses.

Ironically, Renaissance writers produce this disturbing vision of rhetoric as rape in their effort to "save" it for its male practitioners, to defend its moral respectability and deny that the rhetor is a version of Circe. Perhaps responding to the generic association of Circe and her sisters with the epic, a few rhetoricians not only identify the orator with Mercury and his rod—Mercury is, after all, the chief intermediary between gods and heroes in the epic—but also on occasion identify the orator with Circe's great heroic opponent, Odysseus or Ulysses. Thus, M. Le Grand, arguing that letters—and hence, rhetoric—are better than arms, declares the "tongue" or *langue* of Ulysses to be superior to the "arm" or *bras* of Ajax (*Discours*, n.p.). Guillaume Du Vair likewise presents Ulysses as a model orator whose voice, he says—citing a French translation of Homer and using imagery we have seen—"was like the flood from a wavy ravine, which dragged along with it whatever it encountered" (*Traitté*, 398). Joan de Guzman repeatedly identifies the orator with Ulysses, presenting the latter as the model defender of ambiguous cases at one point (*Primera Parte*, 19ᵛ) and as the originator of eloquence at another (32ᵛ). To buttress his claim that the study of rhetoric will enable us to command the wills of our auditors, Guzman cites a passage from Ovid's *Ars Amatoria* (2.123–24) praising Ulysses' eloquence: "Ulysses was not handsome, but he was eloquent, and still he twisted [*torsit*: tormented] the watery goddesses with love" (*Primera Parte*, 29ᵛ). Guzman also allegorizes as eloquence the magical herb *moly*, which Mercury gave the Greek hero (22ᵛ). This allegory was fairly widespread in Renaissance culture, thanks to its being the subject of Alciati's emblem *Facundia difficilis*, or "Eloquence is difficult," which depicts Mercury flying down to give the herb to a seated Ulysses. The accompanying epigram describes the flower and compares it to eloquence: "They call it *moly*. With difficulty it is torn up, though just barely, by its dark root, but its flower is gleaming [*purpureus*] and just like milk. Brilliance of speech and eloquence attract all, but such a great achievement is a work requiring great labor."[41] *Moly* enables Ulysses to counteract the enchantments of Circe, who has only a slender magic wand and whose defeat is completed when he forces her to submit by brandishing his sword. Circe's wand may well appear a variant of the staffs and scepters, symbolic and regal power, with which figures of Lady Rhetoric or Queen Eloquence were often equipped in the Renais-

---

[41] Alciati, *Emblemata* (Venice, 1546).

sance. The Italian mythographer Giovanni Pietro Valeriano makes the connection explicit, identifying the wand as a bad or inferior version of eloquence as opposed to the good eloquence symbolized by Mercury's caduceus. The latter, says Valeriano, combines in itself the rod (*virga*) of rule with the serpents of prudence and symbolizes the general notion that "speech rules men's spirits." In contrasting Circe's wand with Mercury's caduceus, Valeriano uses the same word, *virga*, for both in order to dramatize the difference between them: "The companions of Ulysses are transformed into the shape of brutes by the tip of one rod [*uno virgae capite*], that is, by false persuasion and folly; they are restored to their human appearance by the tip of another rod [*altero virgae capite*], that is, by true discipline and knowledge of things."[42] No wonder Ulysses appealed so strongly to Renaissance rhetoricians as an image for the orator: he is a heroic figure of force and a master of persuasion, but, more important, he is *male*. His victory over Circe is the victory of *masculine* rhetoric, of Mercury's phallic rod and Ulysses' equally phallic sword, over the inferior *feminine* rhetoric of Circe with her diminutive wand and her alluring garden of delights. It is also, finally, a victory which, as Ulysses brandishes his sword in order to compel Circe to yield her bed to him, resembles nothing else but rape.

The notion that rhetoric is rape also surfaces in Renaissance literature. Thomas Carew's "An Elegy upon the Death of the Dean of Paul's, Dr. John Donne" uses it to laud Donne's achievements in the two rhetorical arts of poetry and preaching.[43] The elegy is built on a contrast between Donne's eloquent works and the inferior, largely mythological poetry based on Ovid which preceded him and which, Carew fears, will now return, reducing the art that he and Donne have practiced to the level of mere "ballad-rhyme" (67). Carew composes this poem, he says, because an ordinary funeral sermon would be insufficiently eloquent, would be "unkneaded, dough-bak'd prose" taken "from the flower / Of fading rhetoric, short-liv'd as his hour" (4–6). Rhetoric is fading because, Carew implies, its master Donne is dead, although his coffin continues to stimulate others by means of its "dumb eloquence" (73). Reinforcing this identification of Donne with rhetoric, Carew praises him in terms that evoke many of the salient features of the art as it was conceived by Renaissance rhetoricians. Most important, he presents Donne as a ruler, the possessor of an "imperious wit" (47) who made the English language *bend* to serve his fancy and established a "just reign" (62) over poetry

---

[42] Valeriano, *Hieroglyphica*, 116.
[43] I cite Carew's "Elegy" from *The Later Renaissance in England*, 230–31; line numbers are provided in the text.

during his life. Carew ends his poem with the now famous epitaph that makes Donne both king and priest: "Here lies a king that rul'd as he thought fit / The universal monarchy of wit; / Here lie two flamens, and both those the best: / Apollo's first, at last the true God's priest" (93–96). Moreover, the elegy insists upon the images of the "flame" (14; cf. 21) burning in Donne's soul and the "melting heart" (18) that exits through his eyes and moves all those who read or heard him, just as the discourse of rhetoric speaks over and over again of the fire of passion in the orator's heart which kindles a similar blaze in his auditors. Most striking, Carew praises Donne for having "committed holy rapes upon our will" (17), rape and the will coming together in this line just as they do in legal discussions of rape in the period—and in the Renaissance discourse of rhetoric.

It might be objected that Carew's "rape" primarily means "seizure"— just as *rapere*, the verb from which it comes, means "to seize" or "to snatch"—and that to give the word a sexual meaning is to force it in a direction Carew would not wish it to go. Nevertheless, in the context of the entire poem a sexual meaning seems inescapable. Before the line in question, for instance, Carew speaks of how Donne's flame *shoots* heat and light, and afterward he refers to Donne's "*melting* heart." His other metaphors for Donne's activities also generate a sexual meaning. Thus, he recounts how Donne, having cleared out the "Muses' garden" and thrown away other poets' seeds of "servile imitation," "fresh invention planted" (25–28): in other words, Donne, like the rhetor, here becomes the *planter* of the seeds of poetry. He is later praised for having "open'd us a mine / Of rich and pregnant fancy" (37–38), a phrase which suggests either insemination or giving birth: Donne is imagined as either forcing an entry into the womb or assisting at a birth as a kind of doctor. The poem insists upon Donne's *masculinity* as it praises him for having "drawn a line / Of masculine expression" (38–39). This image, like those of planting and inseminating, is (as noted in works on rhetoric) a very old metaphor for a man's sexual intercourse with a woman. Moreover, Donne is imagined as forcing the English language itself to serve him in a way that is quite suggestive of sexual intercourse: the language becomes a woman who is made to bend and "With her tough thick-ribb'd hoops to gird about / Thy giant fancy" (49–50). Donne's phallic potency as a poet is underscored here by his implied penetration of the language and his size ("giant"), just as it is by the contrast Carew sets up between him and other poets who could not subdue the language and who possess only "soft melting phrases" (51).

Although Carew modestly confesses that he himself is incapable of matching Donne's accomplishments, the elegy is nevertheless remarkable for its duplication of Donne's complexity of syntax and metaphorical inventiveness. Even more, Carew strikingly duplicates what one might call the gendered politics he sees in Donne: just as the latter's reign over both poetry and his auditors is imaged through sexual metaphors suggesting rape, so Carew begins his poem with a rhetorical question in which he identifies poetry as a woman and presents himself as *forcing* her: "Can we not force from widowed poetry, / Now thou art dead, great Donne, one elegy / To crown thy hearse?" (1–3). Moreover, as he ends his poem, Carew has recourse one final time to a potentially sexual image, for his promise to "incise" (92) his epitaph on Donne's tomb repeats the notion of writing as sexual intercourse which was earlier suggested by the reference to Donne's "line / Of masculine expression" (38–39). Thus, like the Donne he admires, he is a masculine figure of power for whom writing resembles intercourse, who would force a reluctant female poetry to do his will, and whose completed poem offers eloquent testimony that he has indeed succeeded in having his way with her.

Rape is, of course, "merely" a metaphor for Carew, as it is throughout the Renaissance discourse of rhetoric, but its sexual meaning is sufficiently disturbing in the elegy that he feels impelled to build in qualifications as soon as he has uttered the word, first by specifying that the "rapes" involved are made merely "upon our will," and second by identifying them as "holy." Ironically, such gestures betray the author's nervousness and direct attention to the fact that rapes may be made upon the body and may be most unholy affairs indeed. Unholy rapes are precisely the subject of another literary text from the Renaissance, one text that links rhetoric to masculine aggression and conquest and dramatically identifies the rhetor as a literal rapist. That text is Tirso de Molina's drama *El burlador de Sevilla* (The trickster of Seville). Whereas Carew's poem essentially continues the discourse of rhetoric by emphasizing its key equation of rhetoric with power and rule, Tirso's play, as it literalizes the idea of rape, offers an implicit—and severe—critique of that discourse, undermines the myth of the orator-civilizer, and mocks the claim that the orator is a hero like Hercules or Ulysses.

That Tirso's Don Juan is a rhetor almost goes without saying: although he does not speak before public assemblies or law courts, he spends much of his life praising women and persuading them to sleep with him. He practices, in other words, a species of epideictic oratory, comparing Tisbea to the sun (629–32), for instance, and admiring Aminta's beautiful feet and "alabaster throat" (2088).[44] Even more, Don Juan is a master of persuasive discourse, adept at making ethical appeals

---

[44] Tirso de Molina, *El burlador de Sevilla y convidado de piedra*, ed. Joaquín Casalduero, 6th ed. (Madrid: Cátedra, 1982); references are to line numbers in the play.

designed to move his victims. He elicits pity from Tisbea and admiration from Aminta, although in both instances his main strategy is to hold out the lure of social advancement through marriage, while presenting himself as a man of honor who is willing to violate social rules for the sake of love. Thus he tells Aminta, using the rhetorical device of *anaphora* to give his speech a sense of emotional intensity and an air of heroic conviction: "And though the kingdom murmurs against it, and though the king contradicts it, and though my angry father resists it with menaces, I must be your husband" (2046–50). Don Juan is not the only character in the play who practices such epideictic rhetoric or shows himself adept at courtly compliment and compelling self-presentation. Most notably, Don Gonzalo de Ulloa, the king's counselor, displays these skills in a lengthy scene in the first act, most of which is taken up with his formal speech of praise for the city of Lisbon. The king responds to this set piece enthusiastically: "Don Gonzalo, I esteem more hearing from your tongue this succinct account than to have seen its [the city's] greatness. Do you have children?" (858–62). The king's question leads to his offer to unite Don Juan, the son of his favorite and chief minister, with Don Gonzalo's daughter. Strikingly, Don Gonzalo's speech occurs between the two halves of Don Juan's affair with Tisbea, thus setting up an implicit comparison between the two speakers, the first of whom increases his family honor by his eloquence, while the second increases his conquests as a rake. In both cases, rhetoric is a means for personal advancement, although advancement, to be sure, of a very special sort in the case of Don Juan.

For Don Juan, as for Renaissance orators generally, rhetoric means power over others and thus serves to confirm his characterization as a powerful man, a *poderoso* (1780), as Aminta's hapless betrothed Batricio calls him, using the term as a synonym for "nobleman." To produce power, rhetoric manipulates belief, and belief is, if anything, the central issue in Tirso's play: Don Juan, his father Don Pedro, the Marqués de la Mota—in fact, virtually all the men—repeatedly pledge their honor and ask others to trust their words, almost all of which are lies. Tisbea worries that Don Juan cannot be trusted, repeating to him over and over the refrain "May it please God that you do not lie!" (612). Aminta, directly identifying rhetoric as the issue, admits her bafflement in response to his advances: "I don't know what to say; your truths are covered with lying rhetoric [*retóricas mentiras*]" (2051–53). In fact, throughout the play a consistent counterpoint is set up between verbs such as *creer* (to believe) and their contraries, *engañar* (to deceive) and *fingir* (to feign). The most famous line in the work, Don Juan's repeated, mocking, insouciant "¡Qué largo me lo fiáis!" focuses directly on the issue of trust: though it is normally taken to mean something like "How much time you give me (to pay back my moral debt)," or "How much time you grant me (to repent)," and though its economic connotations should not be ignored in the context of a bankrupt Spain whose aristocracy was also overwhelmingly in debt, nevertheless the crucial verb *fiar* means "to guarantee," "to confide in," "to trust." Don Juan's phrase thus underscores the fact that he is given trust—and violates it as often as he gets it.

It might be claimed that Don Juan's use of "lying rhetoric" on the lower-class Tisbea and Aminta would seem to make him a seducer rather than a rapist, since he appears to persuade rather than force them to do his will. However, *El burlador de Sevilla* actively works to deconstruct the opposition between seduction and rape which was a staple of legal discourse. The play opens by presenting Don Juan as a rapist rather than a seducer: he tricks his first victim, Isabela, not by convincing her to love him but by assuming a disguise as her lover Don Octavio in order to enjoy her favors. Taken by deception, she is clearly a victim of rape, a fact which the play later underscores by having her compared to Europa, whom Jupiter raped, disguised as a bull (2167–68). Don Juan similarly attempts to rape Doña Ana, although she discovers his identity and prevents him from reaching his goal. By contrast, although Aminta is indeed persuaded to go to bed with Don Juan on the basis of his promise of marriage and thus seems a victim of seduction, she identifies herself with the Roman matron Lucretia (2009) when she initially resists his advances, an identification that invites us to use rape as a label for her ultimate fall. More important, all the women with whom Don Juan has slept, or attempted to sleep, in the play are identified at one point by Catalinón as *forzadas* (2312). The word *forzada* means "raped" or "ravished," not "seduced," and its root meaning of "forced" indicates what is involved: there is no question of free choice for women whom Don Juan has *forced* to do his will. Since Catalinón is referring indiscriminately to both Doña Isabela and Doña Ana, his master's rape victims, as well as to Tisbea and Aminta, whom Don Juan might be thought to have seduced, Catalinón obviously sees rape and seduction simply as versions of each other. This blurring of distinctions is reinforced by the fact that all four of the women are condemned equally by various men for having lost their honor; such condemnations may rightly be attacked as the product of the men's misogynism, but they nevertheless have the effect of establishing yet another equivalence among Don Juan's victims. The play thus suggests that whether Don Juan pretends to be a noble woman's lover or uses promises of marriage to lure a lower-class woman into bed, the similarities in the situations are more important than the differences: all the women are deceived, *engañadas*; all are, to use Catalinón's word, *forzadas*. As a result, not only does the play deconstruct the opposition between rape and seduction, but it points to the way that that opposition is actually undermined in the discourse of rhetoric insofar as it presents persuasion as a matter of compulsion. Despite its insistence on the free will of the auditor, it just as insistently stresses the power of the rhetor whom the auditor cannot resist; the rhetor's will co-opts that of the auditor, whose freedom thus ironically becomes slavery. Tirso has Aminta invoke this irony when she succumbs to Don Juan: "To your will [*voluntad*], husband, mine inclines itself from this day on; I am yours" (2092–94). The moment she is persuaded to give herself freely to Don Juan, his will reigns supreme over hers. Seduction and rape are indistinguishable.

Don Juan does not refer to his actions as either rape or seduction; he calls them *burlas*. *Burla* might seem to be simply a synonym for *engaño* (see 889 and 891), since both words mean "trick" or "deception." *Burla*, however, can also be translated as "prank" or "escapade" or "practical joke," and this last term is especially appropriate, for a *burla* is a sadistic display of cunning and power meant to humiliate the person the joke is played on. Indeed, in its participial form, *burlado*, the word means not only "tricked" but "mocked" or "scorned," as when Tisbea, abandoned by Don Juan, sees his treatment of her as a just kind of mockery, since she made a career of mocking men before he came along: "I am she who always used to mock men so greatly [*hacía . . . burla tanta*]; those who mock [*burla*] others always wind up being mocked [*burladas*] themselves" (1013–16). *Burlas* are the particular province in Tirso's work of young men who play them on women as well as on one another. In fact, Spanish offers as a possible synonym for *burla* the word *mocedad*, which means "youthful prank" as well as "youth" (it is derived from *mozo*, "young man"), and although the play does not make much use of this alternative, Don Juan's initial escapade with Isabela is identified by his uncle as a result of the young man's having been deceived by his own *mocedad* (117). Playing *mocedades* or *burlas* is a way for young men to define themselves: when Don Juan and the Marqués de la Mota meet in Seville, they first wittily mock various courtesans and prostitutes in a kind of ritual review of women they have known and deceived, and then the former asks his comrade about his most recent *perros muertos* (1250; literally, "dead dogs"), a slang expression for *burlas*. As soon as Mota speaks of his real love for Doña Ana, however, Don Juan shows himself quite eager to deceive his supposed friend; in a comic aside Catalinón warns that the Marqués should not talk about Ana lest "the great trickster of Spain deceive you" (1279–80). The fact that Don Juan (and Catalinón) speaks of *burlas* rather than crimes or sins fits a character who resolutely refuses to worry about either human or divine retribution for his acts: he will not face the moral seriousness of his deeds, which he prefers to think of as merely jokes or pranks. By contrast, the king of Spain does take Don Juan's actions seriously, and although he initially allows him to escape punishment by marrying him to the Isabela whose honor he violated, the king's attitude is clear when he refers to Don Juan as a *rapaz* (1058), a word which, like *mozo*, may be translated simply as *youth* but which means something more like "lackey," "servant," or "little squire." The king's word belittles Don Juan by lowering him on the social scale, but it also condemns him for being "greedy" or "rapacious"—meanings of *rapaz* when it is used as an adjective. Moreover, the king's word is related etymologically to *rapere*, evoking the idea of sexual assault and abduction and reminding us again that Don Juan's *burlas* are rapes.[45]

Don Juan's fundamental stance toward the world is combative and rivalrous. Although his principal activity is to *burlar* women, it might be argued that he is just as competitive with men, or even that he sleeps with women because he can defeat members of his own sex by possessing the women they desire. Revealingly, Don Juan comes to Isabela disguised as Octavio, steals Aminta away from the man to whom she is about to be married, and becomes interested in Ana only when Mota says he is in love with her. Don Juan's relationship with Tisbea is something of an exception, for she is not attached to any other man, but since she has had a career of scorning men, Don Juan's triumph over her can be read as a symbolic triumph over all those she has rejected. Moreover, the other men in the play share Don Juan's attitude: when he rapes or seduces their women, they see *themselves* as having been lessened—*burlado* (337), as Octavio puts it—by the women, who thus serve as Don Juan's representatives. Whether he is seen as defeating men or women, however, Don Juan acts in order to acquire fame. Although he protects himself by telling the ravished Isabela that he is "a man without a name" (15), his primary motivation in the play is to make a name for himself, something he sees himself accomplishing by means of such feats as sleeping with Mota's beloved Ana, a deed he revealingly tells Catalinón, is "a trick worthy of fame" (1476: *burla de fama*). Through such feats he has won his "name": "Seville calls me *the Trickster* [*el Burlador*], and the greatest pleasure I can have is to deceive a woman

---

[45] The etymology of *rapaz* as a noun is uncertain; most likely it derives from the adjective with the same spelling, which comes from Latin *rapax*, which in turn derives from *rapere*. See *Diccionario crítico etimológico castellano e hispánico*, ed. Joan Corominas and José A. Pascual (Madrid: Editorial Gredos, 1981).

and leave her without honor" (1313–17). Don Juan is the figure identified by Tirso's title, *El burlador de Sevilla*, and that phrase is a pun: it
means both that Don Juan is the trickster who comes from Seville and
that he is the person who has tricked all of Seville—that is, all the
inhabitants of the city. The phrase also sounds like an honorific title or,
rather, like a parody of such titles, so that to call Don Juan *el burlador
de Sevilla* makes his actions pure parodies of the sort of epic deeds such
titles usually designate. His father, Don Diego, wants to claim that Don
Juan is a genuine hero and boasts to the king of Spain that Don Juan is,
"although a youth, gallant and valorous, and the young men of his time
call him the Hector of Seville, since he has accomplished so many and
such surprising youthful exploits [*mocedades*]" (1084–87). Considering
what we have learned about Don Juan before this point in the play,
however, and considering as well that there is no other evidence to support an identification of him with someone like Hector, we can read
Don Diego's words only as unintended irony. Don Juan's *mocedades*,
his "youthful exploits," are not admirable deeds but *burlas* that put him
at the antipodes from Hector, the model defender of both city-state and
family. Don Juan's *mocedades* may give him the right to call himself *el
burlador de Sevilla*, or even *el gran burlador de España* (1280), but they
do not make him a hero.

Tirso's play devotes much of its energy to satirizing Don Juan by contrasting him with one of the great heroes of the ancient world, Aeneas.
The episode with Tisbea, in particular, directly recalls that of Aeneas
and Dido: like Aeneas, Don Juan is shipwrecked on the shore of the
woman's home; like Dido, Tisbea falls in love with her guest; and like
Aeneas, Don Juan loves and leaves her. Lest the reader miss the comparison, when Catalinón rebukes his master for repaying Tisbea's hospi-
tality by abandoning her, Tirso has Don Juan reply: "Fool, Aeneas did
the same with the queen of Carthage" (899–900). Moreover, Tirso follows Vergil's lead in this episode by describing love through the metaphor of fire, a metaphor which is eventually literalized as the holocaust
that consumes Tisbea's hut, just as a similar fire consumed the body of
the dead Dido. Despite all the parallels, however, Don Juan is no
Aeneas. For instance, when he arrives at Tisbea's shore after the ship-
wreck, he must be carried out of the water on the shoulders of Catalinón, whereas Aeneas carried his father Anchises out of the burning
city of Troy. More important, although Tisbea resembles Dido, she is
identified not with Rome's enemy Carthage but with Troy (2137–42),
and at one point she denounces Don Juan as the Trojan horse (613–16).
Thus, although Tirso may base his episode on the *Aeneid*, he reverses
the moral poles: Tisbea is assigned the sympathetic position of the vic-

timized Trojans; Don Juan, failing to match the heroic accomplishments of Aeneas, is equated with the Greeks whom Vergil represents as
cunning, predatory, and destructive. A similar negative judgment of
Don Juan's actions, once again seen through the lens of Vergil's epic,
surfaces at the crucial moment just after Don Juan, accused of being a
"traitor" and a "coward" (1588), has brutally slain Doña Ana's father.
Don Juan flees, leaving his friend the Marqués de la Mota behind, and
the latter comments, seeing the light from the torches of the approach-
ing guard: "What can it be at this hour? A cold seizes my heart. From
here it all seems a Troy which is burning" (1617–20). In the context of
the slaying that has just occurred, Mota's reference to Troy suggests
that Don Juan resembles not Aeneas, who defended the city, but its
attacker Pyrrhus, the son of Achilles, who pitilessly slew its aged king.
The inverse of Aeneas, Don Juan is the destroyer of cities, not their
founder, and he is thus also the inverse of the orator imagined by the
Renaissance as the heroic source of civilization.

Don Juan is deficient as well when judged according to a second set of
heroic accomplishments: namely, Spain's triumphs in the *Reconquista*,
which culminated in the final expulsion of the Moors in 1492 and then
led to the gradual expansion of Spanish power around the world. Although the *Reconquista* is never mentioned directly, it is implied when
Don Juan declares: "I am a noble knight, head of the Tenorio family, the
ancient conquerors [*ganadores*] of Seville" (2030–33). The irony of this
remark should be apparent: whereas his ancestors once took Seville
back from the Moors, Don Juan is reduced to "conquering" helpless
women, whose "honor" is significantly equated with castles and towers
(208, 1570). Nor is he a heroic *conquistador* like Diaz or Pizarro. The
play specifically invokes the history of Spanish expansion into Africa,
Asia, and the New World when Don Gonzalo delivers his lengthy set
speech describing the glories of Lisbon, whose ruler was the vassal of
the Spanish king in 1625 when Tirso's play was first performed in Naples. Celebrated as the eighth wonder of the world, graced with riches
from around the globe, Lisbon is emphatically a city crowded with
splendid palaces and churches and teeming with abundance; even the
fleet in its harbor "appears a great city where Neptune rules" (735–37).
This fleet brings home the wealth of Spain's far-flung empire, an empire
that it also serves to extend. Significantly, we learn that Lisbon's arsenal
contains countless ships, among which are "the ships of the conquest"
(828), and that the Portuguese king, the Spanish king's cousin, is prepar-
ing an armada of thirty ships for an *empresa* ("undertaking," "enterprise") to Goa, Ceuta, or Tangiers (700–704). As noted earlier, Don
Gonzalo's praise of Lisbon is placed structurally right in the middle of

Don Juan's affair with Tisbea, so that like the reference to the conquest of Seville it sets up an ironic contrast between the heroic enterprises of Spain's *conquistadores* and Don Juan's predatory behavior with women. Tirso's Don Juan is clearly not Molière's fearless libertine or Mozart and Da Ponte's erotic juggernaut. Rather, he is a failed hero, a moral bankrupt, whose rapes are no more than a pathetically diminished, ultimately self-destructive version of the grand exploits of his countrymen.

Don Gonzalo's speech in praise of Lisbon returns to the ancient epic from yet another direction when it explains the origins of the city's name: "The royal palace, whose hands the Tagus kisses, is the edifice of Ulysses, . . . from whom the city takes its name in the Latin language, calling itself Ulisibona" (814–16, 817–20). Ulysses is celebrated here not merely as a heroic adventurer but as a founder of cities, whereas his negative counterpart, Don Juan, destroys them. In this context, the Tisbea episode can be read as a rewriting of Ulysses' encounter with Circe or Calypso (as well as a version of the Dido episode from the *Aeneid*), for she, like Circe, "enchants" (431) her victims but is finally tamed by the superior power of Don Juan/Ulysses. If Tisbea is Circe, however, she is a Circe turned mortal and devastated by Don Juan's betrayal and flight; and if he is Ulysses, then he is not the heroic man of many turns who is celebrated in the *Odyssey* but the cunning, predatory, almost demonic Ulysses of Vergil's poem. In the Renaissance discourse of rhetoric, as we have noted, Ulysses is presented as a model of eloquence, his encounter with Circe a contest between good and bad versions of the art. By contrast, while the Tisbea episode indicates that Don Juan possesses a tongue every bit as potent as Ulysses's, it also shows that the eloquence he commands has very little to do with heroism. It identifies the rhetor as a rapist, not the founder of civilization but one of its deadliest enemies.

Ironically, the Renaissance identification of rhetoric as rape is self-defeating. For if it may be construed as an attempt to create a rhetor who is unambiguously masculine and immune to criticisms of sexual degeneracy, it actually does no such thing, since the rhetor's audience, the people he is imagined as entering and possessing, are unequivocally *male*. Virtually without exception, rhetoric treatises and handbooks are addressed to men: to students and lawyers, preachers and political leaders. More important, the imagined auditors who actually appear in rhetoric texts are almost always men. Consider, in this regard, Guillaume Du Vair's *Traitté de l'Eloquence Françoise*, a text heavily invested in sexual imagery for the orator. In a passage concerned with the pleasure eloquence brings its practitioner, Du Vair actually seems close to identifying the orator's audience as female.

From it [eloquence] he will derive a perpetual course of pleasures which will accompany all his actions and which will make him enjoy a happiness [*resjoüissance*] truly divine, which is an enjoyment whose cause and principle is in those who possess it. One could not estimate, let alone express, unless one has experienced it in oneself, what contentment he receives when, in the middle of a great and celebrated assembly, he sees the old love [*aymer*] him, the young admire him, and all put aside their own affections in order to embrace his [*tous deposer leurs propres affections pour espouser les siennes*]. (396)

Du Vair not only links eloquence to pleasure here but implies the sexual nature of that pleasure by identifying it as *resjoüissance*, which means "enjoyment" but also suggests sexual pleasure (*jouissance*).[46] In keeping with this suggestion, he presents the orator as being loved (*aymer*) by his auditors and ends by stressing how they strip themselves of their self-love (*deposer leurs propres affections*) and do not merely "embrace," but "marry" (*espouser*) his affections. Those auditors, however—*les vieillards, les jeunes*, and *tous*—are identified by means of either masculine or gender-neutral nouns, despite the fact that Du Vair's imagery may seem to imply a feminine identity for them. The passage thus confirms the rule that when the Renaissance orator speaks, his words invade and possess, impregnate and inseminate—indeed, rape—an audience composed primarily of *men and boys*. Nor should it be forgotten in this connection that Orpheus, one of the chief male mythological figures associated with rhetoric, is said to have given his love to young boys after his unsuccessful attempt to bring Eurydice back from Hell.[47] Since this information is contained in what was arguably the most widely read Latin classic in the Renaissance, Ovid's *Metamorphoses*, the specter of homosexuality cannot help but appear every time Orpheus is offered as the model for the orator.

If the identification of the rhetor as rapist or as Orpheus reinforces the notion of a potentially homosexual rhetoric, Renaissance writers produce that same result in another way: they insistently use feminine images for rhetoric—for *good* rhetoric—which coexist in the discourse with the masculine images we have already reviewed. Those feminine images crop up in discussions of the rhetor's creative activity: that is,

[46] The verb from which *jouissance* derives, *jouir*, means "to enjoy," but from the medieval period onward it is frequently used to mean "to enjoy the sexual favors" of a woman; see *Grand Larousse de la langue française* (Paris: Librairie Larousse, 1975), and Edmond Huguet, *Dictionnaire de la langue française du seizième siècle* (Paris: Didier, 1946).

[47] Ovid, *Metamorphoses*, trans. Frank J. Miller (London: William Heinemann, 1932), 10.84. I owe this reference to my colleague John Rumrich.

whenever rhetoricians define that part of the discipline known as invention, and whenever they discuss the orator's discovery of the most effective style. Patricia Parker has argued that both invention and style are
widely identified as feminine in Renaissance rhetoric because, like
women, they are associated with disorder and danger to the status quo
(*Literary Fat Ladies*, 97–125); however, they are represented as feminine
also because, like mental processes in general, they are thought of as a
matter of creation or generation and are, as a result, sometimes actually
imaged in terms of giving birth. For instance, Giorgio Valla calls the
beginning of an oration its *caput*, or "head," and as he defines what that
is, his terms invoke the idea of birth: "The head of the oration, which
we call the beginning, is to be drawn out of the viscera [*visceribus*] of
the case itself" (*Rhetorica*, II.iiii^r).[48] George of Trebizond similarly imagines the orator as conceiving (*concipere*) things in his mind (*Rhetoricorum*, 59^v), speaks of each word as being born [*nata*] at almost the
same instant as the thing to which it refers (60^v), and, when he considers various techniques for amplifying speech, talks about how a
proper oration should be "full," *plena*, an adjective, that might well suggest pregnancy—as does his saying that the oration should possess plen-
itude (*plenitudo*) and fecundity (*faecunda oratio*) (74^r-74^v). Cypriano
Soarez also imagines the production of eloquence as a process of conception and giving birth, a notion that he reinforces when he speaks of
eloquence as a sword that must be drawn from its *vagina*, a word that
means "sheath" but also directly evokes the relevant female anatomy:
"Eloquence, moreover, is the bringing forth of all things which you have
conceived in your mind and proferring them to the audience. Without
doing so, those prior things are superfluous and like a hidden sword
which remains in its sheath" (*De Arte*, 185).[49] Bartholomew Keckermann, writing about the importance of delivery, constructs an elaborate
analogy between producing an oration and generating a child: "Just as it
would make no difference to have formed an infant in the mother's
womb unless it was brought forth happily into the light, so the formation of a speech is entirely in vain unless it is pronounced and recited

[48] On the same page, Valla speaks of the beginning and end of the oration as the
best places for generating—literally, giving birth to—emotion (*ad motum animi gig-
nendum*), although the generation he is talking about occurs in the auditor rather
than the author of the speech.

[49] Elsewhere, Soarez says that an abundance of things will give birth to an abundance of words and that human need gave birth to metaphor (*De Arte*, 189, 197). In
his *Chirologia*, John Bulwer claims that the hand is a more effective "midwife" (17)
than the tongue in bringing to light the conceptions in the speaker's mind. See also
Erasmus, *Ciceronianus*, 34; Sidney, *Apology*, 16, 72; and Granada, *Ecclesiastica Rhetorica*, 120–21.

rightly and properly" (*Systema*, 468). In all these cases the rhetorical theorists are attempting to appropriate for the male orator the generative powers of women, tapping into a male fantasy of power in which men produce children without having recourse to the other sex. But their language also does something quite different: it reinforces the notion that their art is fundamentally feminine, and hence effeminizing for its male practitioner.

If the creative dimension of rhetoric leads Renaissance thinkers to represent their art as effeminizing, so does their recurrent conception of style as bodily adornment and cosmetics. Theoretically, adornment might be gender-neutral, since men wear clothing just as women do, but when rhetoricians think about the dress of style, they see it as feminine. Thus, when Gerard Bucoldianus speaks of how the "body" (*corpus*) of a speech needs to be dressed, that body is a woman's, as his word for its beauty, *veneres*, indicates: "The entire body of a speech . . . should be dressed and made luminous with figures, as though with certain colors, so that the speech may have grace and beauty."[50] Bartholomew Keckermann is equally typical when he cautions the would-be orator about overdoing the use of *ornatus*, which means both "stylistic decoration" and "apparel": "Stylistic decoration ought to be modest and matronly, not whorish. Women who are too sumptuously and splendidly adorned give cause for suspicion that they are insufficiently careful guardians of their chastity" (*Systema*, 178). George Puttenham similarly defines rhetorical ornamentation as "disguising" and goes on to identify poets with "great Madames of honour," who, he says, do not like to go naked but must be clad in "kindly clothes and coulours" (*Arte*, 149–50). And George of Trebizond, writing about the need for ornamentation, declares that "the emotions are excited by the kind [*genere*] of speech more than by invention itself, for invention, either naked [*nuda*] or having been brought forth in an inappropriate style, is too frigid [*frigida*]" (*Rhetoricorum*, 84^r). George here personifies invention as a naked woman who does not need merely stylistic clothing, but stylistic clothing of the appropriate sort, lest she prove "frigid." Implying that if clothed in the proper style this Lady Rhetoric would be warm, George suggests the idea of her sexual seductiveness without ever stating it directly. Seduction can, of course, be practiced by members of either sex, but George's metaphors here identify it—and rhetoric itself—as feminine.

Although the notion that rhetoric "allures" the auditor has already been read as part of the complex of ideas identifying the rhetor as a

[50] Gerard Bucoldianus, *De Inventione & Amplificatione oratoria* (Leiden, 1534), 123.

masculine rapist, that notion can just as easily fit an image of him as Circe, especially since the aspect of eloquence involved is often identified as its "beauty," its *venustas* or *veneres* (see Granada, *Ecclesiastica Rhetorica*, 39; Bucoldianus, *De Inventione*, 123; and Alsted, *Rhetorica*, Dedication, 6ʳ). Employing distinctly erotic imagery, J. Du Pré de la Porte identifies this allure as an enchantment, a love potion that an unambiguously female Eloquence gives to the auditor: "Truly it is the property of Eloquence to enchant spirits by the lure of her uncommon graces, her sweetness being a magical potion which, sucked in by the hearing, descends insensibly to the heart, with a marvelous power to make us embrace everything she desires, so strongly that we are ravished and drawn by the invisible lodestone of her exquisite beauties" (*Pourtraict*, 5–6). As the Renaissance discourse of rhetoric conceives them, allurement and ravishment are hardly the exclusive province of men.

Nor does the equation of eloquence with flowing liquid make it necessarily masculine. In the quotation from Du Pré, the liquid that penetrates and satisfies the auditor come from a female figure, reminding us that the water imagery running through the discourse of rhetoric may actually be linked to *either* sex, insofar as both men and women may be said to flow in some sense during the act of conception. In fact, the flowing forth of the rhetor can be read not just as an image of insemination but as one of birth, so that the water imagery, which earlier seemed to "save" rhetoric as a masculine activity, actually allows for a reading that makes it, if not exclusively feminine, at least sexually indeterminate. Moreover, the quotation above from Du Pré also reminds us that the magic the rhetor practices can be that of a witch as readily as that of a *magus*. Instructively, alongside the attacks on bad rhetoric as the art of the Sirens, the discourse of rhetoric on several occasions also praises the good version of the art in those terms. For instance, in the dedication to his *Rhetorica*, Johann Heinrich Alsted recalls that Cato the grammarian was called the "Attic Siren" (3ᵛ). A more interesting example occurs in a late seventeenth-century text, Emanuele Tesauro's *Il cannochiale aristotelico* (The Aristotelian eyeglass), a work that identifies wit, *argutezza*, as the most important freature of speech. Wit, claims Tesauro, is the light of oratory and poetry, the seasoning of civil conversation, and the means to separate the elite from the plebeian. It is also essential to rhetoric: without it, the art will seem "blunted and fainthearted; nor is there any people so wild and inhuman that at the appearance of these flattering Sirens [*lusinghevoli Sirene*] their rough face does not brighten with a pleasing smile."[51] Here Tesauro assigns to

---

[51] Emmanuele Tesauro, *Il cannochiale aristotelico*, ed. August Buck (Turin, 1670; rpt. Bad Homburg: Gehlen, 1968), 1.

the Sirens the mission Renaissance rhetoricians normally gave to Orpheus and Amphion or to the mythical orator-civilizer. This positive view of the Sirens of rhetoric also lies behind their appearance on the frontispiece to Nicholas Caussin's *Eloquentia sacra et humana* as part of a complex allegory celebrating eloquence, and the same view shapes the passage in which Joan de Guzman has one speaker compliment the other for what he says about the value of writing: "Ulysses did not marvel so much at the singing of the Sirens as I do considering what you think about the exercise of writing" (*Primera Parte*, 30ᵛ).

The positive evaluation of the Sirens by Renaissance rhetoricians may appear surprising, since their ultimate source, the *Odyssey*, treats them as a danger, just as it does Circe and Calypso. But a tradition of allegorical interpretation going back at least to Cicero's *De finibus* informs these examples. In the fifth book of that work, Cicero argues that the Sirens' episode in Homer supports his contention that learning is inherently attractive: the Sirens do not "call back those who are sailing on by means of the sweetness of their voices or the newness and variety of their singing, but, because they have claimed that they know many things, men cling to their rocks out of a desire to learn."[52] This passage attracted the attention of Renaissance writers such as Claude Mignault, who cites it in his commentary on Alciati's emblems in order to oppose all the other authorities who identify the Sirens as dangers. Mignault is skeptical of Cicero's reading of Homer but concludes by noting that the ancients praised writers by calling them Sirens, as when Sophocles was dubbed a "new Siren." The most striking development in the Renaissance, however, is that Cicero's praise of the Sirens as figures of *wisdom* is transformed into a praise of them as figures of *eloquence*, which actually contradicts Cicero's assertion that they do *not* attract men by the sweetness of their singing. This move demonstrates once again how different the Renaissance can be from the classical world it models itself on. Thus, Filippo Picinelli, writing near the end of the period, admits that the Sirens may be whores but argues, citing Cicero, that they are also figures of virtue, a virtue he then identifies not with wisdom but with eloquence: "The Siren, equipped with her musical organ, refers to the epigraph 'I take you by means of sweetness.' It is the natural character of virtue which drags the human mind by its most sweet allurements into loving it. Eloquence is able to break the most obdurate spirits and soften them by its marvelous sweetness." Similarly, the Italian mythographer Giovanni Pietro Valeriano writes that although the hieroglyph of the Sirens symbolizes for some the dangerous allurements

---

[52] Cicero, *De finibus bonorum et malorum*, trans. H. Rackham (Cambridge, Mass.: Harvard University Press, 1914), 5.18.49.

of Venus, "wiser men have asserted that it is a hieroglyph of eloquence and of the most felicitous force of persuasion, whence we have that dictum about Cato Grammaticus: Cato Grammaticus, the Latin Siren."[5]
[3]

Two aspects of rhetoric as it is conceived in the Renaissance enhance its identification as a magical, feminine art of allurement. First, it is frequently associated with the sense of taste. Sperone Speroni, for instance, develops an elaborate contrast between food for the body, whose importance he dismisses, and food for the mind or the intellect. The latter, he says, is permitted to depart from "the truth which nourishes it, sometimes so as to be able to taste that which is pleasant, in order to enjoy itself." Food that is merely pleasant, according to Speroni, is what is provided by rhetoric and poetry, which are like "fruit at the tables of lords who, after dinner, when they are full, sometimes to please the palate eat some out of gentility." The normal diet of wise men, Speroni implies, will involve something more substantial than this fruit, whereas for the common people, who do not care for knowledge but yet form part of the state, "speeches and rhymes are their entire food and all the fruit of their lives" (*Dialogo*, 135). In Speroni's conception, rhetoric and poetry may be inferior to philosophy, but they are clearly still forms of nourishment.

Nor is Speroni the only Renaissance rhetorician to think this way. Despite the Platonic attack on the art as mere cookery, Thomas Wilson celebrates the rhetor by comparing him to a cook who is able to "mingle sweete among the sower," whose speech has "juice," and whose audience is drawn by his "sweetnesse of utteraunce" (*Arte*, 4, 169, vii[r]). Speaking of the orator's need to vary his style, Wilson instructs him occasionally to tell a merry tale or narrate a strange wonder: "For, like as when a mans stomack is full, and can brooke no more meate, hee may stirre his appetite, either by some Tart sawce, or els quicken it somewhat by some sweete dish: Even so when the audience is wearied with weightie affaires, some strange wonders may call up their spirites, or els some merie tale may cheare their heavie lookes" (105). Wilson's emphatic identification of oratorical speech with food is not really matched elsewhere in the Renaissance discourse of rhetoric, but there is a widespread tendency to refer to some notion of the *sweetness* of the art: Philip Melanchthon declares that sweet (*suavis*) speech is the finest adornment of man (*Elementorum*, 460), and both Bartolomeo Cavalcanti and Daniel Barbaro praise the *suavità* of eloquence (*Retorica*, 249;

[53] Claude Mignault, in Alciati, *Emblemata*, (Leiden, 1591), 423; Picinelli, *Mundus Symbolicus*, 171; Valeriano, *Hieroglyphica*, 150.

Della Eloquenza, 385).[54] That rhetoricians should think of their art as food and, in particular, as sweetness is almost inevitable, since the root of the Latin verb for persuasion, *suadeo* (hence, *persuadeo*), is the same as the root of the adjective *suavis*. All these references to rhetoric as sweetness and food reinforce the connection between that art and Circe, for although Circe may be a temptress, sex constitutes only part of her appeal; in the *Odyssey* she lures Odysseus and his men less by sex than by the offer of food, a comfortable house, and a chance for rest and relaxation. In other words, Circe's appeal is at least in part *maternal*; to enter her abode is to regress, to escape the adult, masculine world of strife and reenter the feminine realm of nurture and comfort. Nor is this realm restricted to the *Odyssey*; versions of it appear throughout the Renaissance as epic writers from Ariosto to Tasso to Milton associate the lure of the temptress with food as well as sex. Given this context, one could easily come to the conclusion that for the Renaissance, rhetoric—that is, good rhetoric—is really Circe's spell.

This identification is reinforced by one further aspect of the Renaissance discourse of rhetoric: its tendency to represent rhetoric, and especially style, as a garden. According to Michael Cahn, classical rhetoric considered itself an *ars* or *techne* and titled itself accordingly—as Aristotle's *Art of Rhetoric* does—although some writers, such as Cicero, personalized their works by providing an individual's name for them (e.g., *Brutus*). While these practices clearly continue in the Renaissance, a new set of nonstandard titles appears which make rhetoric a garden or forest, a treasure house or chest, or even, in keeping with what we have just been discussing, a kind of food. Cahn writes: "To give a sample of such nonstandard rhetorical titles I quote the following: *Synonymorum Sylva, The Forest of Fancy, Garden of Eloquence, Treasure-house, Mel Homileticum, The Rich Cabinet, The Pearls of Eloquence, Treasurie of Similies*. Whereas the traditional titles of *Methodus, Tabulae, De ratione . . .* and *Ars* suggest a systematic organization of rhetorical knowledge, these colorful and metaphoric titles stress the copious wealth of their material (words) and its practical value rather than its methodical presentation."[55] Cahn stresses that these titles reflect an antimethodical bias in Renaissance treatises and suggest a model of instruction in

---

[54] For other examples, see Alsted, *Rhetorica*, Dedication, 3ʳ, and *Rhetorica*, 9; Granada, *Ecclesiastica Rhetorica*, 46, 352; Rainolds, *Oratio*, 48; Fraunce, *The Arcadian Rhetoric*, Aviᵛ, bk. 2, chap. 1, and bk. 1, chap. 15; Hoskins, *Directions for Speech and Style*, 8; and Sidney, *Apology*, 6, 10, 19, 30.

[55] Michael Cahn, "The Eloquent Names of Rhetoric: The Gardens of Eloquence," in *Anglistentag 1990 Marburg: Proceedings*, ed. Claus Uhlig and Rüdiger Zimmermann (Tübingen: Max Niemeyer Verlag, 1991), 133.

which copiousness, imaged through metaphors of spatial extension and culinary richness, has become the main concern of rhetoric. This model draws on the very old idea of rhetorical ornaments or rhetoric itself as *flores*, or "flowers," and it tends to organize itself by the alphabet rather than by the parts or offices of rhetoric. To find examples one need only consider the stylistic rhetorics that were being produced in the Renaissance even before the Ramist reorganization led the discipline to be largely restricted to style. These texts, such as Henry Peacham's aptly named *Garden of Eloquence*, list tropes and figures in alphabetical order. Moreover, even if many of them are not titled "Gardens" or "Treasuries," they do think of style in such terms. For instance, Richard Sherry, writing in the mid-sixteenth century, calls his *Treatise of Schemes and Tropes* a "garden" and refers to rhetorical figures as "flowers," which he says he has extracted from all the best orators so that the student, in addition to having "the corporall eie pleasure," will know "of everi one the name & propertye" and never lack "fruite and delectacyon."[56] In Sherry's concept, the "garden" of rhetoric is not merely a place adorned by beautiful flowers but a source of nourishment and pleasure as well.

Conceiving rhetoric as a garden of delights directly evokes the figure of Circe and her Renaissance descendants. Ariosto and Tasso, for instance, place the chief temptresses of their epics on islands that are also pastoral gardens, offering both nourishment and sex to lure the writers' heroes to a life of repose and idleness. Spenser puts Acrasia in the Bower of Bliss, and Milton takes this tendency to its extreme by situating his temptress, Eve, in *the* Garden, which he characterizes throughout *Paradise Lost* in terms of pleasure, fruitful abundance, sexual satisfaction, and freedom from strife. Milton also explicitly identifies Eve with Circe, just before the Fall, when he remarks that all the animals of Eden were "more duteous at her call, / Than at *Circean* call the Herd disguis'd" (9.521–22), and it is, of course, Eve's persuasive words and personal "charm" (9.999) that ultimately prompt Adam's decision to eat the fruit and thus to transform himself from man to beast.[57] It should hardly be surprising, then, that Renaissance rhetoricians, identifying rhetoric as a temptress and sharing many of the assumptions and attitudes of Ariosto and Tasso, Spenser and Milton, should think of it as a Circean garden.

Sir Philip Sidney provides a good example of the unintentional way in which Renaissance thinkers, on occasion, turn the art they cherish into

---

[56] Sherry, *A Treatise of Schemes and Tropes*, 15–16. Luis de Granada (*Ecclesiastica Rhetorica*, 414) uses the related trope of the forest (*sylva*) for the material out of which an oration is made.

[57] Milton, *Paradise Lost*, in *Complete Poems and Major Prose*.

the Circean magic they abhor. Although, as we noted earlier, Sidney sometimes identifies poetry with magic and enchantment—"charms"— and characterizes it directly as female, in other places he clearly wants to insist on its masculinity, claiming that it guides us through life, befits the profession of arms, and stimulates true courage, and that the poet should share the laurels of victory with warriors (*Apology*, 64, 61–62, 68). Yet consider how this heroic poet acts: "He doth not only show the way [to knowledge], but giveth so sweet a prospect into the way, as will entice any man to enter into it. Nay, he doth as if your journey should lie through a fair vineyard, at the first give you a cluster of grapes, that full of that taste, you may long to pass further" (38). One cannot help but see Sidney reproducing the genre of romance epic (as well as the Bible) in this passage, and that genre has him represent poetry as a garden offering the reader sweet food and seducing, *enticing*, him into its beautiful, protected interior. To be sure, Sidney's Neoplatonic conception of his art leads him to declare that this garden should be considered only a way station on the quest for knowledge, but it is nevertheless an integral aspect of poetry for him. Here Sidney does what so many Renaissance rhetoricians do: he starts out with a "masculine" image of the rhetor-poet as guide to life but slips into a characterization of that figure's behavior which evokes visions of Circe and her garden of delights.

For a final and extremely ironic example of this problem, let us return briefly to the letter by Pico della Mirandola with which this chapter began. Although most of it is devoted to an attack on rhetoric as a Circean art, Pico also spends time defending its contrary, philosophy. On closer inspection, however, the latter turns out to be a superior form of rhetoric, for it is defined as a "kind of speech" (*genus dicendi*) which, although dealing with the truth, aims at persuasion just as rhetoric does. Referring to the philosopher's discourse, Pico declares that the auditor "will be especially persuaded by three things, the life of the speaker, the truth of the case, and the sobriety of the speech" (*Epistola*, 355). These "three things" to be found in philosophical discourse are, of course, the *ethos*, *logos*, and *pathos* defined by Aristotle as parts of rhetoric. Moreover, such philosophical discourse is especially exemplified by Holy Scripture, as Pico sees it (probably following the lead of Longinus), and it is characterized as affecting the reader in much same way that Renaissance rhetoricians see the "masculine" version of the art affecting the auditor. Consider how Pico has his Scholastics argue for the power, the *rhetorical* power, of Scripture: "Tell me, I ask you, what moves and persuades more strongly than the reading of the Sacred Scriptures. No, they do not move, do not persuade, but compel, agitate, convey force. You read crude and rustic words, but they are animated, flaming, sharp, penetrating into the depths of the spirit, transforming the entire man by means of miraculous power" (355). This passage recalls the words of praise Pico uses near the start of his letter for the eloquence of Barbaro's rhetorical style: "It is marvelous how persuasive you are, and how you impell the spirit of the reader to go wherever you wish" (351). Pico completes the philosopher's identification as a superior, very masculine orator, when he has his Scholastics tell their hypothetical opponent that if he actually studies them, he will find that they "have had Mercury not on their tongue, but in their breast" (352).

Despite Pico's insistence that philosophy and rhetoric are opposites and that the first is a superior, masculine art of truth and power while the second is a debased, deceiving, feminine and effeminizing one, he fails to maintain this opposition, for his characterization of philosophy often turns it into a version of the Circean rhetoric he denounces. Influenced by the fact that in Latin "philosophy," like "rhetoric," is feminine in gender, Pico personifies it as a woman throughout his letter. To give one striking example: after denouncing as disfiguring (*devenustari*) the decoration and painting associated with rhetoric, he proclaims that by contrast "philosophy displays herself naked, in view everywhere" (356). Elsewhere, implicitly developing the contrast between superficial rhetoric and deep philosophy, Pico associates the latter with interior spaces suggestive of the female body. Thus he tells the student of philosophy to seek "the deep hidden places [*penetralia*] of the spirit" (354), and he identifies philosophy as one of the discourses that "flow from the horrendous cave in which Heraclitus said truth lay hidden" (355). In both passages the interior, implicitly feminine space associated with philosophical speculation also has overtones of the sacred: in the first one, *penetralia* means "the sanctuary of a temple," while in the second, the "truth" referred to cannot help but recall the "truth" of scripture mentioned a few lines earlier. Moreover, the interior space within the metaphorically female body of philosophy is presented as being *full*: its interior, he says, is "full [*plena*] of gems and rare and precious furnishings"; further, not only philosophy but the ideas or views it contains are "full" (354: *sententias plenas*). *Plena* in both passages may be rendered as "full," but it is also a standard locution for "pregnant" from antiquity through the Renaissance. Since this representation of philosophy as female is complemented by images for it involving feasts and honey as well as divine music (354, 355), it seems very close indeed to the magical, alluring Circean rhetoric Pico is determined to attack.

Pico's letter epitomizes the gender confusion one encounters in Renaissance rhetoric generally, duplicating the failure of that discourse to "save" the art for its male practitioners. As an image of the lofty rhetoric he prefers, Pico would offer us Mercury with his potent, phallic rod, but this image fails to displace that of Lady Rhetoric, who in her turn overlaps and blends with her despised double, Circe. Her presence makes Pico's philosopher, like his rhetor, *effoeminatus*, turning him into a disturbingly ambiguous character who is both male and female and who may appear homosexual as a result. Ironically but revealingly, that possibility surfaces just when Pico is trying to affirm the supremely masculine power of philosophy, its ability to invade and possess the auditor. He recalls Alcibiades' claim that he was never affected by the mere rhetoric of Pericles' polished speeches but that by the "naked and simple words [*verbis nudis & simplicibus*]" of the philosopher Socrates "he was ravished [*rapi in furorem*], placed beyond himself, and willy-nilly had to do that which Socrates commanded" (355). Here, just when Pico is trying hardest to establish the value of philosophy as a masculine art of persuasion, he identifies it with the sexually ambiguous, homosexual art of rhetoric he disparages.

Perhaps the most dramatic evidence of the sexual doubleness of Renaissance rhetoric can be found in its mythography and iconography. That the Renaissance thought of good rhetoric as masculine is underscored, as we have noted, by its identification of the art with such male figures as Orpheus and Amphion, Hercules and Mercury. This identification is matched, however, by characterizations of it as a woman. Actually, the rhetoricians themselves frequently pronounce the discipline a queen or lady: Sidney sees poetry as a matron (when she is not being a courtesan); Gabriel Harvey identifies eloquence with both Helen and Venus.[58] And in the visual arts, illustrations of rhetoric as one of the liberal arts continue the medieval tradition of representing it as a woman. Usually she is presented as a queen or matron, sometimes even placed in a niche much as a saint might be on the facade of a church; in a few cases there are touches of ambiguity, as in an English printer's colophon that depicts Rhetoric with smoke or mist coming out of her mouth, suggesting that the art confuses the truth.[59] The frontispiece to

[58] See Vives, *De Ratione*, 93; Regius, *Panegyricus*, fvii[v]; Speroni, *Dialogo*, 99; Fuscano, "Della oratoria e poetica facoltà," 190; Erasmus, *Ciceronianus*, 6; Du Vair, *Traitté*, 396; Sturm, *De Elocutione*, iv[r]; George of Trebizond, *Oratio*, 366; Sidney, *Apology*, 8; and Harvey, *Rhetor*, n.p. In his *Il riposo*, a literary work of 1584, the Italian poet Raffaello Borghini, associating each of the liberal arts with a particular planet and a part of the body, identifies rhetoric with Venus and *le parti vergognose*, "the shameful parts," once again evoking the possibility of seduction in connection with the art (cited in Chew, *The Pilgrimage of Life*, 348 n. 13).

[59] See Dominic A. LaRusso, "Rhetoric in the Italian Renaissance," in Murphy, *Renaissance Eloquence*, 53; Chew, *Pilgrimage*, 113.

Nicholas Caussin's *Eloquentia sacra et humana* brings both sexes together in what is clearly intended to be read as an allegory celebrating eloquence. It features the bust of a woman representing the goddess of eloquence situated atop an altar, with a cornucopia in one hand and a caduceus in the other, and surmounting a shield containing the coat of arms of Louis XIII, to whom the work is dedicated. On the side with the cornucopia there is a male figure bearing an offering; on the side with the caduceus, a female figure. Under the altar and flanking the title of the work are two figures: on the left a male statue with a device beneath his feet defining him as the force of speech; on the right a female statue identified by the Greek word for persuasion with a device featuring a picture of the Sirens. Thus, in Caussin's allegory, eloquence appears as an idealized goddess of force and persuasiveness who contains both sexes within her. Similarly—to return to a written text briefly—one of the dedicatory poems prefacing J. Du Pré de la Porte's *Pourtraict de l'Eloquence Françoise* begins by praising eloquence as a queen but then shifts gender in midsentence and identifies it with Nestor and the "Gallic Orpheus": "Thus the Queen of well speaking, animating herelf in this beautiful portrait, ravishes our senses, and attracts them with an insensible lodestone; for by the charms of your book, you make one see in France the revival of the glory of old Nestor and that of the Gallic Orpheus who led hearts as trophies attached to chains of gold" (Dedication, 36). In general, then, the iconographic tradition duplicates what one finds throughout the discourse of rhetoric: eloquence and its practitioner are imagined as both a king or a hero and a queen or a matron, as both Mercury and Circe.

Perhaps the most dramatic example of Renaissance writers' inability to think of rhetoric strictly in masculine terms appears in a passage from the *Hieroglyphica* of Giovanni Pietro Valeriano in which he discusses a strikingly sexual representation of Mercury. In it the god is depicted as being old but exceedingly virile, "with his nature obscenely excited and most robust particularly in that part" (246). Valeriano does not say where he saw this image—indeed, he may simply be making it up—but it captures perfectly the notion that rhetoric is a distinctly masculine art whose force and potential for aggression, for *rape*, are dramatized by its erect phallus. Yet as he explains how this image represents the force (*vis*) of rhetoric, his language subtly shifts the gender of the figure from male to female; the god's erection metamorphoses first into a stuffed garment, then into a lap or bosom (*sinus*) containing fruit, and finally into the sign of offspring: "The dress in this picture was stuffed, and its lap held fruit, the sign of offspring, surely because speech, whose symbol is Mercury, has a certain ability to generate and bring things to pass" (246–47). Like the images of generation scattered throughout rhetoric treatises, Valeriano's Mercury with his lap full of fruit not only exemplifies the widely shared fantasy in which men reproduce themselves without having recourse to women but also serves as a tacit admission that rhetoric is female as well as male. Wherever Mercury's rod appears in the discourse of rhetoric, it would seem, Circe and her garden are never far behind.

Erasmus's *Moriae Encomium (The Praise of Folly)* is arguably the contemporary literary text most fully involved in the gender politics characteristic of Renaissance rhetoric. As its title indicates, the work is an example of epideictic oratory, a brilliantly ironic speech of praise, whose celebration of its subject is both a criticism of it—if Folly praises it, can it be good?—and a subtle reevaluation of it in positive terms: what Folly praises turns out to have, on balance, decidedly attractive features. More important, this ironic speech is delivered not by a man, as virtually all formal orations would have been in the period, but by a woman—a fact that Folly underscores in a variety of ways from the start of her performance. This deliberate gender displacement is central to Erasmus's ironic vision, for it allows him to satirize women as talkative and frivolous and at the same time to affirm their ability to practice an art that rhetoric treatises wanted to imagine almost exclusively as man's work. Continually engaged in a dialogue with Renaissance works on rhetoric, the *Praise* is both an extension and a critique of what one finds there. In particular, as its female speaker characterizes herself, she not only attacks the masculine exponents of the art but also embraces many of its essentially feminine aspects, producing an image for herself which oscillates between negative and positive poles. Moreover, although Erasmus has Folly set herself up in opposition to male rhetors, he also has her appropriate a number of the "masculine" aspects of the art. This move can be seen as serving to liberate Folly from gender altogether, placing her, like the rhetoric she is identified with, in an ideal position beyond masculinity and femininity. At the same time, it confirms her status as a sexual hybrid, making her not an effeminized man —as rhetoric and the rhetor have been—but a masculinized woman.

Folly initiates her claim to be a real orator by distinguishing herself from the "Sophists," teachers of rhetoric who "inculcate certain disquieting trifles into boys and display a more than womanish obstinacy in quarreling" (10).[60] She then attacks "the vulgar herd of orators" be-

[60] Desiderius Erasmus, *Moriae Encomion*, in *Ausgewählte Schriften*, vol. 2, ed. Werner Welzig (Darmstadt: Wissenschaftliche Buchgesellschaft, 1975); page numbers in the text cite this edition.

cause they spend thirty years producing one single speech and try to impress their audiences by sprinkling their Latin orations with Greek tags (12–14). This attack returns periodically throughout the *Praise*, as when Folly rehearses the condemnation made by critics of rhetoric in the Renaissance who saw it as subversive of the social order: "The Catoes give proof of this matter sufficiently, I think, since one of them troubled the tranquillity of the state with insane accusations, and the other entirely subverted the liberty of the Roman people, while he defended it only too wisely. Add to these the Brutuses, the Cassiuses, the Gracchi, and even Cicero himself, who was no less a plague to the Roman state than Demosthenes to the Athenian" (52). Finally, in the long catalogue of her followers which occupies the middle of the work, Folly returns to those she calls Sophists, deriding them, together with lawyers and logicians, for quarreling over trivialities, being more garrulous than twenty women, and losing the truth through too much altercation (126–28).

Folly claims that by contrast she is a real Sophist (10), an especially apt identification, since the Sophists were famed from antiquity on for their ability to make language turn black into white and white into black. She insists that her speech, since it is extemporaneous, is true, and that unlike bad rhetoric it is free of "cosmetics," or *fucus*; in fact, her speech is, she says—using a familiar notion from the discourse of rhetoric—the mirror, the *speculum*, of her mind (12). As she goes on, she presents herself through a series of identifications with such things as emotion and pleasure and even prudential wisdom, all of which are key concerns of rhetoric; they also make her the prime defender of human sociability, of what she calls the "play of life" (64: *vitae fabulam*). As she describes this play, she insists that humans should perform their parts with a ready will. Praising her follower Philautia, or Self-love, she asks: "Finally, how are you going to act with decorum [*cum decoro*] in every office of life, either with yourself in private or among others—for that is the principal thing not only of art but of all action, to act in a decorous fashion whatever you do [*decere quod agas*]—unless this Philautia is present at your right hand, who rightly takes the place of sister to me?" (46–48). As she spells out her chief rule for social behavior— "to act in a decorous fashion"—Folly reveals her deep involvement with rhetoric, for the principle of decorum she argues for in the social sphere is nothing less than one of the basic principles espoused by every Renaissance, as well as ancient, writer on the art of rhetoric. Folly may envision life as a well performed play, but it is equally true that she sees it as a well-shaped and -delivered speech.

Much of Folly's self-presentation focuses on traits linking her to the female vision of rhetoric in Renaissance treatises and handbooks. From the start she identifies herself with creativity, generation, and birth. Her father, she says, was Plutus, whom she dissociates from money and celebrates as the ruler of gods and men, who engendered her when he was young and heated with nectar, and who is responsible for all of life itself, for all "war, peace, empires, plans, judgments, meetings, marriages, agreements, treaties, laws, arts, sports, serious matters" (16). Indeed, Folly claims that humans produce offspring only because of her intervention, and she even identifies herself with the members of generation, which she calls (using an image that has great play in the discourse of rhetoric) "that sacred fountain from which all things imbibe life" (22). In rhetorical terms, Folly associates herself with invention and the stylistic principle of amplification or *copia*. She also extends her identification with life and creativity by portraying herself as a nurturer, a maternal figure whose ministrations ensure the happiness of her foolish children. Food and drink, bodily pleasure and festivity are her province: her fools are "plump . . . and sleek," like hogs (28); through her agency people "load their stomach," and "their entire spirit is fed with laughter, joking, and witticisms" (40); and her psychic effect on her followers is like that of wine, a "perpetual inebriation" (108). Indeed, Folly envisages the good society as a banquet and offers everyone a clear choice: "Either drink or get out" (64). Her favorite metaphors seem to be the same gustatory ones that rhetoricians use for their art: alchemists are deceived by a "honeyed hope" (90); those who identify others' accomplishments as their own enjoy "the sweetest kind of madness" (100); and the flattery she recommends is "the honey and seasoning of all human intercourse" (104). Finally, Folly takes the idea of nurturing one final step and claims that she can both restore youth and prolong it indefinitely: "Mine are the herbs, if they exist, mine the spells, mine that fountain which not only calls back lost adolescence, but, what is more desirable, makes it perpetual" (30). A divine mother, Folly offers herself as the savior of the world.

Like the feminine figure of rhetoric, however, Folly is profoundly ambiguous. Consider, for instance, the particular effect she claims to have on her followers, an effect dramatized in the opening paragraph of the *Praise* when the mood of her audience is apparently transformed instantaneously from sadness and gloom to happiness. The power Folly possesses is the power of metamorphosis, of which she boasts: "Let him come who will and compare my benefit with the metamorphoses of the rest of the gods" (28). Of course, the metamorphoses recorded in Ovid's famous work were anything but an unmixed blessing. Moreover, although Folly claims that her speech is free from cosmetics, she contradicts herself later on when she celebrates her ideal play of life as a matter of "fiction and cosmetics" (62: *figmentum et fucus*) and praises the human spirit because it is formed "so that it is taken much sooner by cosmetics [*fucis*] than by truth" (104). Note that Folly speaks of her relationship to her followers as the "allurement of folly" (24: *stultitiae lenocinium*), *lenocinium* here being the same word used for the illicit sexuality and seductiveness of bad rhetoric. When one considers these details and adds to them Folly's boasting that her morons are as fat and sleek as the hogs of Acarnania (28–30), her notion that people are happiest when closest to the level of the animals (72–74), and her taking the part of the pig Gryllus against Ulysses (78), then one cannot help but identify her with the female deity central to Renaissance rhetoric—Circe. In fact, Folly makes this connection herself, claiming that all the "Medeas, Circes, Veneres, Auroras" (30) are only inferior versions of herself. In addition, although Folly seems to inhabit the entire universe rather than live in a magical garden like Circe's, she does boast that she was born in the gardenlike Fortunate Isles, where all good things are given without labor (18). Thus, if Folly is linked to the positive, generative, feminine pole of rhetoric, which its defenders celebrated, she is also identified with its opposite, with Circe, and this identification makes her a most sinister figure indeed.

Erasmus characterizes Folly as Circe in the *Praise*—or at least in its first three quarters—because, as she speaks for worldly wisdom, he wants his readers both to experience the lure of that wisdom and to acquire a deep distrust of it. In particular, he wants them to feel the attractions of Folly's vision of the good society but to realize that she is deceiving them when she claims that it can really be built on the basis she offers. Ironically, Folly herself tells the truth about human existence at the very moment when she is arguing for the beneficial effects of illusion and self-deception. Like the professional fool or jester who is licensed to speak the truth, she may tell her followers that life is to be embraced as a matter of "fiction and cosmetics," but her every utterance exposes the fictions and the cosmetics for what they are. A concrete example: at one point she claims that the good life comes about "partly through ignorance, partly through not thinking, sometimes through forgetfulness of evil, sometimes through hope of good." Yet when she notes that old men continue to delight in living only because of her gift of ignorance and forgetfulness, she argues her case *by directly exposing the wretchedness of their condition*: "You see these old men of Nestor's age, in whom not even the appearance of man remains, stammering, doting, toothless, white-haired, bald" (68–70). By listening to the *form* of Folly's arguments, one might be persuaded to live a life of ignorance, but if one attends to their *content*, one cannot ignore the unpleasant truths of the human condition Folly herself reveals.

The universe Folly inhabits is the universe as it is imagined in the discourse of rhetoric—a shadowy place where there are no absolute truths and certainties, where custom and convention rule, where everything seems contingent and open to discussion. In such a universe, what one aims for in order to create a happy society is consensus, a shared set of beliefs, even if that means a mutual participation in ignorance. Consensus is precisely what rhetoric strives to bring about (although rhetoric is also the means to undo consensus), but the very fact that such a consensus is rhetorical will always make it at best contingent. Rhetoric, like Folly, works to create faith, asking the listener not just to believe arguments but to believe in the orator himself, as though—like Folly—he were a kind of god. Yet the very fact that those arguments are rhetorical exposes them to doubt, undermines faith, makes the orator seem —again like Folly—a deceiver. It should hardly be surprising that Erasmus, writing at the dawn of the Reformation, focuses on these issues or that, finally, he juxtaposes the inadequate, rhetorical faith Folly stands for throughout the first three quarters of the *Praise* to an altogether different sort of faith at the end. There he has his spokeswoman, still functioning as a rhetor, define Christian folly, the true faith that will eventually lead one out of the cave of this world into the light of God's absolute truth, to total transcendence of insecure, contingent human experience (202, 208). Folly argues that even in this life Christian fools can have a foretaste of the final bliss that can redeem their lives. This Christian folly is vastly different from the willful ignorance and deceiving hopes that characterize the folly celebrated earlier in the work, and it solves the problem created by the rhetorical nature of that earlier folly simply by transcending both the world and rhetoric too. At the last gasp, in other words, Erasmus's spokeswoman uses her art of persuasion to arrive at the point where persuasion itself becomes totally irrelevant and rhetoric disappears. Folly thereby subtly critiques that art and the faith it aims to produce as fruitless except insofar as they bring the listener to the point of seeing their fundamental inadequacy and then moving beyond them to the true faith of Christianity.[61]

Although Erasmus's Folly possesses many of the feminine traits associated with rhetoric, she also has characteristics linking her to the masculine vision of the art. Specifically, she not only presents herself as the

[61] For a fuller statement of this interpretation, see Wayne A. Rebhorn, "The Metamorphoses of Moria: Structure and Meaning in *The Praise of Folly*," *PMLA* 89 (1974): 463–76. My argument is also indebted to Kahn, *Rhetoric, Prudence, and Skepticism in the Renaissance*, 89–114.

true ruler of the world, able to command even kings and emperors, but describes her effect on her followers as a madness by which they are *seized* or *held* (88: *tenentur*). More important, Folly appropriates the myth of the orator-civilizer for herself or, rather, for her follower—and attribute—Flattery.

> What force compelled stony, oaken, and wild men to enter into civilization, except flattery? For the famous lyre of Amphion and Orpheus signifies nothing else. What thing recalled the Roman people back to the concord of civilization when they were going to extremes? Was it a philosophical oration? Not at all. It was the ridiculous, childish story made up about the belly and the other members of the body. (54–56)

But there is another way in which Folly acquires a male as well as a female identity in the *Praise*: she is Erasmus's mouthpiece. In the prefatory letter to Thomas More, Erasmus tells his readers that *he* has feigned her character and that *he* has praised Folly, "though in a way not entirely foolish" (6). Indeed, as critics have remarked, we seem to hear the voice of Erasmus the satirist especially in the long middle section of the work in which Folly catalogues her followers.[62] Moreover, Donald G. Watson has suggested that in creating the fiction of performance in his work, Erasmus is replicating what went on in the *sociétés joyeuses*, which existed in communities throughout western Europe during the fifteenth and sixteenth centuries.[63] The *sociétés* consisted of informally organized groups of young, unmarried men, often studying at universities or pursuing training in the law, who periodically put on parodic, festive entertainments, *sotties* (fool plays) and farces, much in the spirit of the traditional Feast of Fools. The main character in those plays, Mère Sotte or Mère Folle, ruled over a world composed of fools and was arguably the model for Erasmus's Folly, so that insofar as the *Praise* can be equated with Mère Folle's performance in a *sottie*, one can say it invites us to see that a young man, hidden beneath her skirts and ass's ears, has been playing her part. Thus, Erasmus's spokeswoman turns out to be male as well as female, just like the Renaissance rhetor and his art, although in this case we have a woman hiding a man under her gown rather than the reverse. Such an inversion and confusion of

[62] Critics making this claim include Johan Huizinga, *Erasmus and the Age of Reformation* (New York: Harper & Row, 1957), 74; and Hoyt H. Hudson, "The Folly of Erasmus," introduction to his translation of Desiderius Erasmus, *The Praise of Folly* (New York: Random House, 1941), xxvi.

[63] Donald G. Watson, "Erasmus's *Praise of Folly* and the Spirit of Carnival," *Renaissance Quarterly* 32 (1979): 333–53.

things is perfectly in keeping with a work that revels in the notion of a universe turned topsy-turvy. As Folly herself puts it: if, on this great stage of fools, one were to strip off the disguises of all the actors, including hers, "there would suddenly arise a new appearance to things," and one would discover the marvelous fact that this person, "who was just recently a woman, would now be a man" (62).

In its own way, Erasmus's *Praise of Folly*, like the Renaissance discourse of rhetoric generally, produces a figure for the art that crosses and confuses categories most people wanted to keep distinct. It is both male and female, king and queen, rapist and seducer, *magus* and witch. For this special hybrid creature the Renaissance had available a special name, a name wonderfully appropriate when one considers the various mythological figures associated with rhetoric. Recall that the art is identified both with its patron Mercury or Hermes and with a being whom we have been calling Circe. But recall also that behind Circe there is the figure of an even more elevated temptress, a female deity with whom the Greek goddess Peitho, "Persuasion," was sometimes identified and whose image is summoned up every time a Latin text refers to the "beauty," the *venustas* or *veneres*, of eloquence.[64] That figure is, of course, Venus or Aphrodite, and if we substitute her name for Circe's and combine it with the name of her male counterpart, then it is clear what the special name for the hybrid figure of rhetoric must be—Hermaphrodite.

Although we have arrived at this name by a rather circuitous route, on at least two occasions Renaissance rhetoricians get there more directly. When Joan de Guzman praises the infinitely changeable nature of rhetoric, he claims that Homer presents this notion allegorically through the character of Proteus in the *Odyssey*, and that Ovid does so likewise "in the fable of the Hermaphrodite" (*Primera Parte*, 15ᵛ). J. Du Pré de la Porte, focusing on the moral ambiguity of rhetoric, also has recourse to this mythological figure: "Those who doubtless considered this [moral ambiguity] have feigned Mercury as the Hermaphrodite for us, since the orators, who are his children, do not take any more trouble to have themselves recognized [as one or the other] than the Hermaphrodite does to have one judge which of his two sexes is predominant" (*Pourtraict*, 26–27). This doubleness, which Guzman celebrates, disturbs Du Pré, who shares his culture's general discomfort with actual hermaphrodites and insists that the rhetor must be one sex or the other

[64] On Peitho and Aphrodite, see Kinneavy, *Greek Rhetorical Origins of Christian Faith*, 34–35.

—that is, either a contemptible sophist or an admirable orator-philosopher: "But since it is not permitted that he can be both natures indifferently, and since he must be fixed in one or the other without being able to change from it, it would be desirable to constrain these chameleons to take the part of the sophists or of the true orators to whom one can give no better name than philosophers" (27).[65] Significantly, although Du Pré prefers that the rhetor should be a "true orator" rather than a sophist, it is not at all clear which of the two figures is Hermes and which Aphrodite. Thus, both Du Pré and Guzman, quite independently, reach the same conclusion we have arrived at by examining the gendered imagery of treatises and handbooks: namely, that rhetoric is hermaphroditical. To speak of it as such is not a simple matter, however, for the Hermaphrodite had a number of quite different associations in Renaissance culture. By pausing over them, we should be able to see why rhetoricians in the period were drawn to the figure, for as the Hermaphrodite symbolizes both their loftiest aspirations and their gravest fears, it captures the real ambiguity they felt about themselves and their art.

The Hermaphrodite had quite positive connotations in at least two Renaissance discourses outside of rhetoric: Neoplatonic philosophy and alchemy. In the first, writers such as Marsilio Ficino and Giovanni Pico della Mirandola seized on a variety of hybrid deities from antiquity, including Hermaphrodite, Hermathena, and Hermeros, to serve as allegorical symbols for the workings of the world. Those figures were seen as representing an esoteric, higher truth and wisdom greater than the sum of their parts, and as they were "unfolded"—that is, separated and analyzed into their components—they not only revealed the nature of the universe but epitomized the way the universe moved from unity to multiplicity and back again. Moreover, the Neoplatonists interpreted Genesis 1.27 ("So God created man in his own image, in the image of God created he him; male and female created he them") to mean that the original, perfect human being created by God was androgynous or hermaphroditical and that the separation of man and woman represented a later, inferior state in human evolution. Finally, the figure acquired a political function, according to Edgar Wind: "Among French humanists of the sixteenth century *l'androgyne de Platon* became so acceptable an image for the universal man that a painter could apply it without impropriety to an allegorical portrait of Francis I."[66] The Her-

---

[65] On the Renaissance insistence that hermaphrodites had to be classified according to a dominant sex as either male or female, see Laqueur, *Making Sex*, 135–36. Du Pré goes on to offer an alternative figure for rhetoric, one combining artful speech with prudence—the Hermathena (*Pourtraict*, 34–35).

[66] My discussion of Neoplatonic philosophy and the Hermaphrodite is indebted to

maphrodite may have appeared a hybrid monster, but as such it symbolized a greater-than-human perfection; containing both sexes, it had a completeness ordinary mortals lacked, and it was thus available to be used as an allegorical representation celebrating earthly rulers. All these symbolic meanings were reinforced by the alchemists, who identified the Hermaphrodite with the Rebis, the substance that appears in the ultimate stage of the process of transmuting base metals into gold and is presented as the union of the "king" (equated with sulphur, the sun, and gold) and the "queen" (equated with mercury, the moon, and silver). In one alchemical book, for instance, there is a striking illustration of the creation of the Hermaphrodite-Rebis in which the naked, two-headed figure stands above the embracing Hermes and Aphrodite; in the accompanying Latin emblem the author tells the reader: "Do not scorn this double sex, for the same male and female will give you, in one and the same thing, a king."[67] The discourse of alchemy thus not only reinforces the idealization of the Hermaphrodite in Neoplatonism—the figure is the ultimate form of perfection and represents human and spiritual completeness—but gives it an even more pronounced political significance as well. It should consequently be easy to see why Renaissance rhetoricians would be attracted to such a creature, for it does much more than capture their sense of the sexual doubleness of rhetoric; it also suits their exaltation of the art as one fit for the highest beings, for kings and emperors and even gods.

At the same time, when Renaissance rhetoricians imagine rhetoric and the rhetor as the Hermaphrodite, they produce a very different impression. That word and the concept of man-woman it entailed also meant sodomite, and it thus possessed troubling implications for its creators, most of whom made their living as teachers.[68] Although sodomy was associated during the period with a variety of locales, ranging from the court to taverns and barbershops, it had long had an especially close connection in people's minds with schools and universities. First, there was the general awareness of what was called "Greek love," that intense and distinctly erotic bonding between master and pupil characteristic of Greek education, which Renaissance teachers admired for

Edgar Wind, *Pagan Mysteries in the Renaissance*, rev. ed. (New York: Norton, 1958), 200–214; for the quotation, see 213–14.

[67] Michael Meier (Majerus), *Secretioris naturae secretorum scrutinium chymicum* (Frankfurt, 1687), 112, cited in Wayne Shumaker, *The Occult Sciences in the Renaissance: A Study in Intellectual Patterns* (Berkeley: University of California Press, 1972), 183. Sources to which my discussion of alchemy is indebted include Wind, *Pagan Mysteries*, 214; Shumaker, *Occult Sciences*, 172–96; and E. J. Holmyard, *Alchemy* (Harmondsworth: Penguin, 1957).

[68] James M. Saslow, *Ganymede in the Renaissance: Homosexuality in Art and Society* (New Haven: Yale University Press, 1986), 77–79.

other reasons and could not help but evoke when they styled their schools academies and gave the writings of Plato an elevated position in the curriculum. More important, Renaissance society typically thought of sodomy in a way that linked it to the master-student relationship, for they saw it as involving an older man who had intercourse with a younger man or a boy. So deeply ingrained was this model that in Venice, according to Guido Ruggiero, no matter what their age, the "partners described as passive were usually labeled boys or adolescents."[69] The association between homosexuality and teaching goes back at least to Dante, who peoples the portion of his hell reserved for the sodomites with "clerks and great litterati of great fame," including the Latin grammarian Priscian, the thirteenth-century jurist and law professor Francesco d'Accorso, and Dante's own "teacher," the notary—and rhetorician—Brunetto Latini.[70] Boccaccio later comments on this canto from Dante's work by stating the conventional wisdom about pedagogues: the majority are sodomites, "because most have young pupils who are fearful and obedient because of their age, and are thus at the dishonest as at the honest commands of their teachers."[71] This association and the fears it prompted continued unabated throughout the Renaissance, so that in Venice during the sixteenth century, for instance, the Ten (the chief civil authority) finally "ordered that no school could have any private or secret rooms for instruction; all teaching had to be done with groups in public halls. The Ten clearly felt that homosexual activity with young boys was often initiated in these settings and that these schools were dangerous headquarters for sodomy." Ironically, as Ruggiero suggests, the paranoia of the authorities reached the point that any association whatsoever between older and younger men was suspect, even though social conventions dictated that the old were responsible for the instruction of the young.[72]

The schools to which Ruggiero refers were schools of fencing and abacus, but there is no reason to think that grammar schools, which were responsible for the teaching of Latin grammar and rhetoric, failed to cause a similar anxiety. Nor is there any reason to think that what Ruggiero has documented so well for Venice was not typical of all the states of western Europe. Indeed, writing about England, Bruce R. Smith

[69] Ruggiero, *The Boundaries of Eros*, 118. Much of the information in this paragraph is derived from Ruggiero's book.

[70] Dante Alighieri, *Inferno*, trans. Charles S. Singleton, 2 vols. (Princeton: Princeton University Press, 1970), 15.106–7. Note that Latini was not literally Dante's teacher; rather, the poet studied and was influenced by Latini's works.

[71] Cited in Dante, *Inferno*, 2, *Commentary*: 269.

[72] Ruggiero, *The Boundaries of Eros*, 138–39.

remarks that there was probably widespread homosexual activity, although all we have to base such statements on is court cases: "Schoolmasters being arraigned for abuse of their pupils, masters for abuse of their apprentices, householders for abuse of their servants constitute all the record we have about ordinary people." Smith notes that among the most famous cases was that of the playwright Nicholas Udall, who "was fired as headmaster of Eton in the 1540's because he 'did commit buggery . . . sundry times' with one or more of his scholars."[73] In fact, throughout the European Renaissance, sodomy and education were so firmly connected that Ariosto can hardly be thought atypical when he worries about the matter in his sixth satire. Ariosto wants a tutor for his son and asks his friend Pietro Bembo to find someone in Padua or Venice who has good "morals" (14: *costumi*), since in this age, he says, "there are few humanists without that vice which did not so much persuade as force God to make Gomorrah and its neighbors sad" (25–27).[74] Significantly, Ariosto seeks a tutor to teach his son *Greek* as well as to make him a good poet, and when he contemplates what good poets are capable of doing, he recounts the myth of the poet-civilizer. Identifying the original poets with Orpheus and Amphion, he characterizes them as men who, "with good style, and even more with good works, persuaded people that they should come together . . . and forced the most robust . . . to let themselves be placed under the laws" (72–73, 76, 79). Thus, like Renaissance rhetoricians, Ariosto, juxtaposes the sexually ambiguous humanist rhetorician and schoolmaster to the ideal orator and poet who is the mythical civilizer of humanity.

Ariosto's satire, like most of the historical evidence from the period about sodomy and education, has a strongly negative cast, and it is likely that the vision of a hermaphroditical rhetor and rhetoric in Renaissance rhetorical writings would have elicited a similar reaction from many readers. The presence of that double-sexed image in those works can thus be read as a kind of indirect admission by the writers that members of their profession actually did engage in behavior their culture condemned as perverse, as a crime or a sin. In other words, the presence of that image in their works can be seen as a staging or acting out of deeply felt anxieties, a bringing up to consciousness and a confronting of fears and guilt and desire. In the course of most educational interactions, such things doubtless were—had to be—profoundly repressed. What the discourse of rhetoric presents, when looked at from this perspective, is a return of the repressed; it constitutes a reckoning

---

[73] Smith, *Homosexual Desire*, 194, 84.

[74] Ludovico Ariosto, *Satire e lettere*, ed. Cesare Segre, intro. Lanfranco Caretti (Milan: Riccardo Ricciardi, 1954); references are to lines.

with that which rhetoricians could not allow themselves to show but, for a variety of reasons, secretly needed to see.

To evoke the specter of hermaphroditism or sodomy was not just a matter of eliciting and confronting negative judgments, however; the strong male bonding that was characteristic of Renaissance culture also meant that there were positive evaluations of and responses to homosexual desire in a variety of social and political contexts, as well as in art and literature. Consequently, although the rhetoricians' production of a hermaphroditical vision of the art they defend seems to invite criticism and hostility, it might also be read as aiming to produce the contrary effect. It can be interpreted as an affirmation of the highly charged, erotic bond—the *love*—that connected rhetoricians to their students. Because of the official condemnation of sodomy in Renaissance society, they were inhibited from speaking such feelings openly, but one text comes very close to doing so: Joan de Guzman's *Primera Parte de la Rhetorica*, which is fashioned as a dialogue between his friend the Licenciado Fernando de Boan, who assumes the role of teacher, and Guzman's own noble pupil, Don Luis de Gaytan. The author frequently relies on literature and myth, not only to find appropriate symbolic figures or tales for the art he is defining but also to celebrate the close relationship between the two interlocutors. Significantly, at one point he has the Licenciado compare the two of them to Achilles and Patroclus, and then has Don Luis respond in kind: "All this [discussion] fills me with a particular desire, and I believe that Hercules did not seek Hylas with such solicitude as I will have to seek you from hence forward" (11^r). Both sets of identifications are surely meant to enhance the status of the speakers by equating them with heroes, but it noteworthy that both involve male characters who are attached to each other by bonds of love. What is more, the statement by Don Luis directly focuses on his *desire* for his teacher. Although homosexual love or sodomy is never mentioned in this passage, it can hardly remain invisible to a reader who knows the stories of Achilles and Patroclus, Hercules and Hylas. The same thing might be said generally about the image of the Hermaphrodite in the Renaissance discourse of rhetoric: the attentive reader cannot help but feel that it points to—perhaps celebrates—the forbidden topic of male love.

The Hermaphrodite allows Renaissance writers to express the ambivalence they felt not merely about their art but about their own position in Renaissance society, for the figure symbolizes both their intense aspirations to rule, to be kings, and their fearful recognition that such aspirations on the part of those who were subjects would only be judged by their culture as perverse, illegitimate, and illicit. Usually, rhetoricians in the Renaissance were men striving to rise above the social stations they inherited at birth, an advancement that their talents and training and especially their ability with language were supposed to make possible. The acquisition of rhetorical—and other—skills in the process of education did, in fact, enable many of them to gain positions not just as schoolmasters but as bureaucrats and legislators, notaries and lawyers, secretaries and courtiers. In other words, a training in rhetoric and the other liberal arts enabled people from the lower and middling classes to move up the social ladder and, in some cases, even to hobnob with the elite. What that training normally could *not* do, except in the rarest of instances, was to allow them actually to become part of the elite; Sir Thomas More's rise to the rank of Lord Chancellor is the glorious exception that proves the rule. The result was that Renaissance rhetoricians, like the vast majority of those they trained, remained in the middle, well above the bulk of the population, consisting of peasants and craftsmen, but distinctly below the nobles and merchant-magnates who ruled states and city-states throughout Europe. This middle condition meant that Renaissance rhetoricians could identify themselves both with and as rulers, as we saw in Chapter 1, and with and as subjects, as we saw in Chapter 2. In the patriarchal culture of Renaissance Europe, where rulers were figured as males, subjects, in a complementary move, were equated with women.[75] Consequently, it should now be easy to see one final reason why Renaissance rhetoricians would have been led to characterize the rhetor as a Hermaphrodite, as both man and woman: his double nature reflects their own doubleness, their sense that they were, or could be, both rulers and subjects, both men and women, in terms of the culture within which they lived. In fact, the Hermaphrodite was a fantasy figure who extended that double nature in both positive and negative directions. On the one hand, it represented the fond dream rhetoricians had that some day even the least of them might rise up to become ideal, complete human beings, worthy to rule as emperors of men's minds. On the other, it constituted their nightmare, the fearful vision in which they stood condemned for their ambitions, stigmatized and punishable as guilty sodomites, forever condemned to an inferior position as irredeemable Outsider or Other. Renaissance rhetoricians were drawn to the figure of the Hermaphrodite, in other words, because

---

[75] See Jordan, "Feminism and the Humanists" (in *Rewriting the Renaissance*), 245. Jordan notes that the equation of woman with subject was by no means a simple one in Renaissance Europe, especially in the light of contemporary redefinitions of ruler-subject relationships and the presence of female rulers such as Isabella of Aragon and Elizabeth of England. Nevertheless, some version of the equation *was* made throughout the culture.

through him they could express the unresolved, and unresolvable, ambiguity of their condition. Through him they could imagine themselves residing at the very center of the universe and simultaneously, paradoxically, enduring the fate of a total and permanent marginalization. Through him, in short, they could think their lives.

4 Banish the Monsters

In 1658, near what is traditionally considered the end of the Renaissance, the French lawyer, abbé, and *littérateur* Antoine Furetière published a remarkable little book, the *Nouvelle allégorique ou Histoire des derniers troubles arrivez au royaume d'Eloquence* (Allegorical novella, or The history of the late troubles that occurred in the Kingdom of Eloquence). Although best known today for his novel the *Roman bourgeois*, Furetière also composed satires and spent years compiling a dictionary of the French language. Of all his works, however, the *Nouvelle allégorique* was the most famous during his life, and because of its flattering treatment of the Académie Française, it is credited with having paved the way for his entry into that institution. Both a literary work and a rhetoric text, the *Nouvelle* is a telling illustration of the political nature of rhetoric: in it Eloquence is a kingdom, Rhétorique its queen, and her sister Poésie the monarch of an adjacent realm. Rhétorique rules with the aid of her prime minister, Bon Sens, relying—as rhetoric is said to do throughout the Renaissance—on *adresse*, or "skill" (7), more than physical "force," to ensure obedience. Nevertheless, a sentence that alludes to the Hercules Gallicus dramatizes the power, indeed the violence, involved: "She never used any other violence against her subjects except to send them her great provost named Persuasion, with a company of beautiful words, his archers, who dragged them chained by the ears with chains of gold and silk" (7). Moreover, although Queen Rhétorique is presented as anything other than a world conqueror—indeed, her *enemies* are characterized thus—her state nevertheless has an imperialistic dimension: her troops include the famous Abbé de Maroles (a contemporary translator of the Latin classics), "who pushed his conquests as far as the lands of Tibullus, Catullus, Propertius, Statius, Plautus, and Martial, lands formerly unknown to all those of his nation" (33). The "lands" Maroles conquers are ancient, but Furetière makes him seem like one of the explorers who extended French and other European control into the Americas. Moreover, when Furetière recounts how Rhétorique is supported by the forty barons of her council who reside in the Académie, situated on a "high eminence" (94), he is obviously alluding to the Académie Française with its forty members and to its founder and protector, His Eminence, Cardinal Richelieu. All these details make the Kingdom of Eloquence a flattering allegory of the absolutist state of Louis XIV, who was one of Furetière's most important patrons. The *Nouvelle* also identifies the French language, which the Académie was established to codify, as an important reflection, extension, and instrument of the monarch's political program. Furetière's book thus documents once again the way in which the Renaissance discourse of rhetoric conceives its subject not merely in political terms, but in terms of the particular politics, the absolutism and imperialism, of the period.[1]

Such plot as the *Nouvelle allégorique* has involves a war fought to protect the realm of Eloquence from the invading army of Captain Galimatias; for Furetière, rhetoric means combat. Little attention is actually devoted to the war itself, however, most of the text being taken up with descriptions of the opposing forces. This emphasis betrays Furetière's real concern: to generate a clear set of distinctions between the proper rhetoric of the queen and the improper one of Galimatias, whose name means "gallimaufry" or "farrago." Furetière contrasts the two leaders and their followers throughout his text, and he marks the end of their war, which threatened fundamental conceptual confusion, by having them sign a peace treaty reestablishing more firmly than ever the boundaries that have been violated. Those boundaries separate good and bad rhetoric, which Furetière distinguishes in terms of interrelated conceptual categories, including morality, social class, and oppositions between cleanliness and dirt, civilization and barbarism. Ultimately, he locates the differences in two opposed visions of the body, both human and political. He juxtaposes what Mikhail Bakhtin has called the classical and grotesque bodies: the first is completed, limited, and self-contained and can be read as an expression of the "official," upper-class

[1] The details of Furetière's life are taken from the introduction to the *Nouvelle allégorique.*

culture of the Renaissance; the second is unfinished, transgresses its own boundaries, constantly interacts with the world around it, and is tied to folk and popular culture and to rituals of inversion such as carnival.[2] Thus, Furetière's text reveals what we have seen in so many Renaissance rhetorical works: the discourse is concerned not just with persuasion but with issues and problems absolutely central to the culture which produces it and which it helps to define and produce in its turn.

The ethical opposition that Furetière writes into the distinction between good and bad rhetoric is revealed by the initial gesture precipitating the war. Bon Sens provokes it when, in order to purify the queen's army, he expels the *équivoques*, the puns or quibbles or equivocations, who then are said to transfer themselves to their proper realm, that of Galimatias. Bon Sens has two important reasons for his decision: these troops are "very licentious," and they have "a certain double spirit which one had to distrust, for they said one thing and did another" (10). The *équivoques*, in other words, are morally suspect because they violate the law and are duplicitous characters who hide away their motives in order to deceive others. A similar judgment occurs in a later episode in which the queen's chief opponent is identified as Chicane ("chicanery" or "pettifogging") and dismissed as "a mistress of intrigue" (72). By contrast with bad rhetoric, which is associated with deception and intrigue, its good counterpart must be implicitly identified with clarity, directness, and rational moral choice. Moreover, the denunciation of the *équivoques* as "licentious" points toward another positive ethical principle, that of restraint. Revealingly, although most of the *allégories* are assigned to Galimatias—since they, like the *équivoques*, employ a double sense—Furetière declares that those reformed by Sappho (Madeleine de Scudéry) in her novels may now serve the queen: "These troops had made themselves acceptable because they marched with great restraint and no longer lived in the ordinary license of warriors" (29). Restraint here identifies a principle of personal self-control and adherence to one's proper role and position; in rhetorical terms, it looks very much like decorum.

The opposition between good and bad rhetoric in the *Nouvelle* also involves the issue of class and amounts to a distinction between the nobility and gentry on one side and the people on the other. Thus, Rhé-

---

[2] Bakhtin, *Rabelais and His World*. Problems with Bakhtin's approach include its tendency toward ahistorical categories and its uncritical nostalgia for folk culture, but the notion of the two bodies as symbolic focal points in literary texts, representing opposed systems of behavior and belief, is quite defensible. See Peter Stallybrass and Allon White, introduction to *The Politics and Poetics of Transgression* (Ithaca: Cornell University Press, 1986).

torique is a *Princesse* (7), the chief members of her council are *Barons* (8), and the Greeks and Latins who join themselves to her as *authorités* are restricted to "the noble, proper [*propre*], and polished among them" (15). By contrast, the Greek and Latin *authorités* who follow Galimatias are lower class (15), while he himself is merely a captain, an "obscure man born from the dregs of the people" (11). In Furetière's conception, the "people" is a broad and somewhat amorphous concept, stretching down to those at the bottom of the social order, as the reference to "dregs" suggests, and reaching high enough to include academics: the realm that Galimatias rules is called *Pédanterie*; its capital, *Gymnasie*. The "people" also includes merchants: when Rhétorique abandons the realm of Justice to her enemy at the end, it is taken over by "the merchants from the coast of Barbary and Bragging" (72); and the ironies and sarcasms who follow Galimatias fetch their arms from the marketplace, from *la Halle* (14). The class opposition in Furetière's text is overdetermined, for not only does he label the upper classes *honnestes gens*, "honest people" (37), but he also associates them with the leading lights of the contemporary world, such as Mlle. de Scudéry, while linking the people to *older* authors as well as literary and rhetorical forms (13, 16, 21). Ironically, at one point Rhétorique's province of Romanie ("Novel Land") is described in terms usually associated with popular rather than aristocratic and upper-class fantasy; it is, says Furetière, "a true land of cockaigne" (25: *un vray païs de caucagne*). In countless medieval and Renaissance texts the Land of Cockaigne is a peasant's dreamland, a topsy-turvy realm in which there are mountains of food and rivers of wine free for all to enjoy.[3] Furetière's Land of Cockaigne is, by contrast, a distinctly aristocratic paradise: "There one found the most beautiful temples, palaces, and gardens imaginable. There one saw only festivals, promenades, balls, and rejoicings. It was peopled solely by galants and the illustrious; never did one see there an ugly woman or an ill-made man" (25–26). The opposition of classes in the *Nouvelle allégorique* shades into one between the court and the country. While Rhétorique presides over a court and lives in the castle of the Académie, some of the followers of Galimatias are "rough and quite vulgar people" (57: *gens rudes et fort grossiers*), and his province of Gymnasie is controlled by professors of Scholastic philosophy dubbed "base [*vilains*] and ridicu-

---

[3] On the Land of Cockaigne, see F. Graus, "Social Utopias in the Middle Ages," *Past and Present* 38 (1967): 3–19; Antoinette Huon, "'Le Roy Sainct Panigon' dans l'imagerie populaire du XVIe siècle," *Travaux d'Humanisme et Renaissance* 7 (1953): 210–25; and Carlo Ginzburg, *The Cheese and the Worms: The Cosmos of a Sixteenth-Century Miller*, trans. John and Anne Tedeschi (Baltimore: Johns Hopkins University Press, 1980), 82–86.

lous greybeards" (78). Significantly, the greybeards are not only *vilains*, "base" or "rustic," but also "ridiculous." Furetière's work is a satire and never lets the reader forget that Galimatias and his followers are comic spectacles.

Even more insistent than the distinction of classes in the *Nouvelle* is an opposition involving linguistic and national identity that ultimately becomes one between inside and outside, civilization and barbarism. Thus, Galimatias's troops are said to come from all nations; they include Arabs, Hebrews, Greeks, Latins, and Italians (15, 19, 102). Indeed, his capital city is said to have flourished at one time, but "because it has served as a retreat for all sorts of nations and has wanted to speak all sorts of languages, [it] has suffered the desolation of Babel, so much so that one finds only confusion there" (10–11). By contrast, Rhétorique's party is almost exclusively French, except for those Greeks and Latins, noted above, who meet the standards of nobility, propriety, and good manners. In Furetière's work France, the French, and the French language stand at the center; everything else is foreign, strange, eccentric. In a witty play on the idea of "far-fetched," the comparisons who troop after Galimatias are said to limp (*clocher*) "because they came from very far away, having been purchased from Pliny, Solinus, Strabo, and other foreign [*forains*: itinerant] merchants" (17). The foreign in Furetière's conception is virtually identical with the barbarous; variants on *barbare* recur repeatedly in descriptions of Galimatias and his followers (37, 72, 79). Ironically, when haranguing his troops he praises them, and the popular rhetoric they represent, by identifying them with the barbarian hordes who sacked Rome and Greece (59). Even more striking, when one considers the contemporaneous activities of absolutist, imperialist France in North America, Furetière states that the *plaideurs*, the "litigants," who follow Galimatias are "extremely coleric and more vengeful than the Iroquois" (71).

For Furetière, good rhetoric is associated with French civilization, bad rhetoric with wild and savage nature. Thus, Galimatias's follower Invective heads a faction labeled a "wild [*farouche*] and barbarous nation" (71), and once peace has been established, the inhabitants of Pédanterie are forbidden entry into the realm of Poésie, where they would be condemned as "wild beasts, like rats" (102). The wildness, animality, and barbarism that Furetière attributes to the party of Galimatias, just as the French attributed those qualities to the tribal cultures of North America, conveniently justify their conquest, turning what could be read as an imperialistic power grab into a supposedly admirable moral triumph. In keeping with the myth of the orator-civilizer reviewed in Chapter 1, Furetière thus presents the activities of Queen Rhétorique and her followers as a matter of domesticating the savage. Only those figures of speech, for instance, are allowed into her realm which have been tamed: the *antithèses* who serve her are not the "libertines" who follow Galimatias but those who are "dextrous and docile" (27: *adroites et dociles*); and the Abbé de Maroles's translating of the Latin classics is identified as a domesticating of them: "He tamed them and placed them beneath the yoke of his severe versions" (33). Ironically, although Furetière, like the rest of the Renaissance, defers to the ancients, his commitment to the superiority of French civilization allows him to intimate here that Greece and Rome seem barbaric by comparison.

Summing up all the contrasts in Furetière's work is the Bakhtinian opposition between the well-formed, clean, beautiful body of good rhetoric and the misshapen, dirty, diseased, monstrous body of its contrary. Although Rhétorique herself is never labeled "beautiful," her territories and followers sometimes are (27, 47); and not only do her followers avoid contagious disease (101), but those Greeks and Latins who are allowed to join them must be *propre* (15), a word which, earlier translated as "proper," also means "clean." Perhaps the most important descriptive term associated with Rhétorique herself is *adresse*, which occurs on the very first page of the story where we learn that the queen rules by its means (7). This crucial word appears again at the climax of the tale when she and her prime minister decide to renounce force and to use *ruse* and *adresse* to defeat their enemy. Paired with *ruse*, *adresse* here could be translated as "skill" or "cunning" or "ingenuity," but the primary sense of the word is not the mental ability that "ingenuity" implies but, rather, physical agility. *Adresse* is the noun form of the adjective *adroit* ("adroit" or "dexterous" in English). Both words come from the Latin *dexter*, which means "right" or "right hand," then, by extension, someone who is skillful with his or her right hand, and finally, by several further extensions, someone who possesses physical agility, mental skill, and ingenuity. Thus, although *adresse* indicates the queen's mental ability, it also conjures up a bodily image of her not only as beautiful and healthy—as other details from the text imply— but as well-proportioned and balanced, agile, quick, and self-contained.

The adjectival form *adroit*, occurs in a passage that dramatically underscores the different bodily configurations Furetière assigns to good and bad rhetoric, the passage in which he distinguishes the *antithèses* who follow the queen from those who follow Galimatias: hers are not those libertine antitheses "who always wanted to march in a mob and on one another's tails, but . . . those who were adroit and docile" (27). Here Rhétorique's followers share her bodily dexterity while those of her enemy form a confused heap, their bodies extending illegitimately beyond their limits and mingling confusedly with those of others. Significantly, Galimatias begins the war by overflowing (creating *un grand débordement*) his political limits and invading the realm of Eloquence (23). The unwieldy bodies of Galimatias and his followers appear bloated, always threatening to burst their seams, and many of them are enormous: the cavalry includes "hyperboles" whose heads seem to threaten the skies and who are "colossal and gigantic" (18); Lady Chicane aids the *authorités* to cause writings to swell (72: *enfler*); and the syllogisms of the false Aristotle are "powerful and dangerous *colossuses*, horrible and hideous to see" (76). Bad rhetoric, in other words, has a grotesque body, ill made (*mal fait*) like the bodies of the men who are forbidden access to Romanie, and disfigured like the "comparisons," most of whom "limped" and were "extremely deformed, all of them being skinned because they had been pulled in too much by the hair" (17).

The grotesque body of bad rhetoric is also dirty, being associated from the start with "the dregs" (11: *la lie*) of the people. In a nasty dig at academics, Furetière makes dirt the badge of all the inhabitants of Pédanterie: after the war has ended, he says that whenever they wish to come to the court of Rhétorique, they must appear in their appropriate costume—that is, "in filthy robes, flat shoes, dirty linen and other marks of their profession" (100). Finally, the body of bad rhetoric is identified with disease: to gain access to the court of Rhétorique, the followers of Galimatias must appear in such a way "that one would recognize them as stricken with plague by their white wands" (100). Using a pun on *figure* (as "rhetorical figure," "bodily shape," and "face"), a pun that runs throughout the entire work and underscores insistently the connection rhetoric has with the body, Furetière proclaims at the end that Galimatias will always be easily spotted when he trespasses on Rhétorique's realm, for he will inevitably be betrayed by "a barbarous word or a bad figure" (103). In another passage this pun reminds us of the way Renaissance people imagined the state itself as a person, as a body politic. In a digression devoted to a war fought in the realm of Poésie between reason and rhymes, Furetière aligns the latter with bad rhetoric and notes that they destroyed the cadence and harmony of Poésie by introducing hiatuses and cacophonies, and thereby "disfigured [*défiguroient*] entirely the face [*la face*] of the State" (39). If the monstrous body of bad rhetoric—Galimatias—may also be read as a symbol of the monstrous political body he rules, then the well-proportioned body of good rhetoric, which is the queen, may be taken to represent her equally well-proportioned state.

Just as Furetière divides his allegorical characters into two opposing groups, so he constructs the rudimentary plot of his little work in terms of an initial violation and then a reestablishment and redefinition of the boundaries between them. The initial decision of Bon Sens to chase the licentious, deceptive *équivoques* into the land of Pédanterie is intended to reinforce the boundary between the two realms, since it involves the placement of opposed sorts of *équivoques* in the two distinct regions where they belong. By contrast, Galimatias's reaction to this decision is to cross the border between his realm and Rhétorique's, thereby confusing the two states and the distinctions they entail. Galimatias's nature as a boundary crosser is linked to—perhaps it would be better to say that it is expressed in—his association with dirt, for dirt, according to Mary Douglas, is matter out of place which is both polluting and extremely powerful as a result.[4] Galimatias and his followers pollute by creating confusion: like the "descriptions" who follow him, he is linked to obscurity (11, 18); his acrostics are disorderly, and his antitheses fight among themselves (21, 63); and his double, Lady Chicane, is said to have confused (*embrouiller*) things in the country of Dicae (Justice) for more than a century (72). Furetière sums up this characterization when he declares that Galimatias could not respond adequately to the dissension in his own army because "he was naturally muddle-headed [*brouillon*]" (64). In keeping with Douglas's analysis of dirt, however, Galimatias is also presented as powerful, ironically more powerful than Rhétorique. His followers vastly outnumber hers (27, 62), and he is actually winning the war until, at the eleventh hour, Rhétorique and Bon Sens persuade Aristotle to switch sides. Although Galimatias is then forced to make peace, he is still granted control of the two portions of Rhétorique's realm he has conquered: Dicae or Justice (forensic rhetoric) and Homiliaire or Homilyland (preaching). Thus, the story ends with Galimatias seeming to enjoy more of a victory than Rhétorique does. The triumph is hers, however, insofar as the purpose of the peace treaty is to clarify and confirm boundaries: it assigns Gymnasie to Galimatias, Rhétorique not being allowed to enter it; similarly, Galimatias is denied access to the Queen's court, though he is permitted to make what conquests he will outside the realm of Eloquence in the provinces, especially in those "beyond the Loire" (99). Finally, the treaty specifies elaborate rules for the few occasions when the inhabitants of one country travel to the other. With the peace, the dangerous, powerful, polluting confusion that Galimatias represents is expelled from the land of Eloquence, leaving a purified, orderly, unified realm behind. The structure

---

[4] Mary Douglas, *Purity and Danger: An Analysis of the Concepts of Pollution and Taboo* (London: Routledge & Kegan Paul, 1966), esp. chap. 1.

of the *Nouvelle* parallels that of rituals of inversion, such as carnival, in which the temporary topsy-turviness of the carnivalesque disrupts the social order but finally results in the production of a clearer, firmer set of distinctions or boundaries separating the licit from the illicit—in this case, good rhetoric from bad.

The realm of Queen Rhétorique, in which rhetoric means proper rule—as well as rules and regulations—is an idealized version of the absolutist French state of Louis XIV, Richelieu, and the Académie Française. Furetière identifies her realm's political character when he explains how its forty barons issued rights of citizenship to all proper inhabitants (that is, words) and "excluded pitilessly all the barbarians and foreigners" (8–9). Galimatias's realm, though it seems to be identified with the "foreign" land of Pédanterie, is really associated with France as well but with the France of all who are excluded or marginalized by those at the political center: that is, those who live at the court and in the capital city of Paris. The realm of the marginalized is indeed larger than the other one, since it includes the vast mass of the population as well as the "foreign" lands in which Galimatias is permitted to operate freely: namely, the provinces of France situated "beyond the Loire." Ironically, although these provinces had been part of France for centuries, Furetière's text suggests they were still regarded by the center as less than French. After all, these were the provinces in which the langue d'oc and Provençal were still spoken and whose Cathars and Protestants had been and were still only the most prominent examples of regional resistance to Paris. Furetière's opposition between good and bad rhetoric thus translates into a social and political division of France in which the boundaries are both the fairly amorphous ones of social class and taste and the firmer geographical one separating Paris and central France from the denigrated and dominated south.[5]

Insofar as the opposition between Rhétorique and Galimatias equates with one between two portions of France itself, it invites the reader to interpret the war they fight as a re-vision of the civil wars that plagued France throughout the Renaissance and included, most recently, the rebellion of the Fronde against Louis XIV (1648–53). Furetière stresses the internecine nature of the war when he recounts as its parallel a secret conspiracy *within* the queen's province of Dicae, a conspiracy led by Invective, who is identified as a haranguer and accused of having already "excited several popular seditions" (71). Similarly, Furetière recounts that *within* the realm of Poésie a previous war, paralleling that between

[5] One of the projects of the Académie Française was to produce a language free from the "soil" of regional dialects; see Fumaroli, *L'âge de l'éloquence*, 647–48.

Rhétorique and Galimatias, was fought between reason and rhyme. This war, initiated by the rhymes, is labeled a "revolt and sedition," and when reason wins it, the rhymes are banished quite literally from the center—imagined as a city—and forced into the periphery: "They would inhabit from then on the suburbs and were forbidden to go lodge among the hemistiches and the other good citizens dwelling in the heart of the city" (41). Such passages show how deeply political Furetière's work is, how it enters into the ongoing attempt by the absolutist French state to define itself symbolically in terms of a valued center and a despised periphery. Furetière contributes to this process by revising history, for although the struggles of the recent civil wars pitted Catholics against Protestants, Catholics against other Catholics, and various factions of the aristocracy and the bourgeoisie both against one another and against the monarchy, the *Nouvelle* reduces this complex set of oppositions into a simple, binary one that reproduces precisely the vision of France that Louis XIV and Richelieu wished to impose.

Furetière is not the only Renaissance writer who attacks bad rhetoric as he does. Critics of rhetoric typically denounce it as ethically, socially, and aesthetically repugnant, as a grotesque figure, a monster. By contrast, its defenders, while acknowledging such criticisms, duplicate Furetière's strategic maneuvers, although their attempts to separate good and bad rhetoric are less complete, less successful, less "pure," than his appear to be. If we compare their works with Furetière's, we will see that the discourse of rhetoric does undergo a certain limited development during the course of the Renaissance, in the sense that a number of its basic concerns reach something like their logical conclusions by the end of the period. We will also see that an even more striking version of that development is made by literary texts. Those texts, like Furetière's, appear increasingly determined to banish the monsters of bad rhetoric, if not to do away with the art altogether. They are all, however, doomed to fail in the attempt.

Throughout the Renaissance the discourse of rhetoric, like Furetière's *Nouvelle*, is bedeviled by problems of ethics, social class, and the body. For starters, rhetoric's defenders are constantly forced to confront the charge that to play the orator is to lie.[6] In response, they almost invariably adopt the strategy of Bartolomeo Cavalcanti, who, after admitting that rhetoric can be employed for both good and ill, insists that only the man who uses it for morally praiseworthy ends is a true rhetor (*Re-*

---

[6] For examples, see Jewel, *Oratio*, 1286; Pico della Mirandola, *Epistola*, 352; Patrizi, *Della Retorica*, 40ʳ; Agrippa, *De Incertitudine*, 27; Montaigne, "De la vanité des paroles," in *Oeuvres*, 292; and Ramus, *Dialectique*, 128–29.

torica, 5–6).[7] This strategy is not original with the Renaissance; it derives from Cicero's *De inventione* (1.2.3) and, more directly, from Quintilian's *Institutio oratoria* (1.Pr.9–20; 12.1.1–32), both of which respond to Plato's criticisms of rhetoric in the *Phaedrus* and the *Gorgias*. In essence, Renaissance defenders of rhetoric "solve" the ethical problem their art produces simply by defining it out of existence, by proclaiming that the orator is what Quintilian, following Cato, calls him, "a good man skilled in speaking" (12.1.1: *vir bonus dicendi peritus*), and that his fraudulent double is not an orator at all. Although Renaissance writers repeat Cicero's and Quintilian's defense of rhetoric, sometimes citing their very words, their conception of bad rhetoric often has a decidedly nonclassical coloring. When Francesco Patrizi, for instance, condemns oratory as lying, he sees this tendency as a consequence of humanity's loss of its original, Edenic language, a loss that has produced "deceptions, injuries, litigation, judges, lawyers, laws, tribunals, and orators" (*Della retorica*, 31ʳ).[8] In keeping with this Christian vision, and drawing on the widespread notion that rhetoric works on people's beliefs, Sperone Speroni remarks—with stern disapproval—that the rhetor can easily deceive his audience because he creates a mere imitation of truth, which the ignorant people all too willingly "makes its God and worships" (*Dialogo*, 94). In a world where Protestants and Catholics were competing savagely for the allegiance of the populace, it should hardly be surprising that the rhetoric used by each group to firm up its faith would be simultaneously feared as supporting a bogus religion. The Counter-Reformation rhetorician Cypriano Soarez is typical in wanting Christian precepts to purge rhetoric of its errors: cut off its "license to lie," he urges, as well as its "repulsive vice of wounding others," and we can restore the beauty of the Christian eloquence practiced by the saints (*De Arte*, 9–10). Ironically, the move Soarez recommends may save rhetoric from moral attack, but it keeps alive what the critics of the discipline say throughout the Renaissance: "orator" is just another word for "liar."

As we saw in Chapter 2, the critics of rhetoric also denounce it in class terms as a rabble-rousing performance that lowers the orator to the level of the mob. As a result, the Renaissance discourse of rhetoric is

---

[7] For other examples, see Alsted, *Rhetorica*, 2; Keckermann, *Systema*, 504; Peacham, *Garden*, 35, 52, 68–69, 75, 79, 167; Ermolao Barbaro's letter to Giovanni Pico della Mirandola, in *Prosatori latini*, 854; de' Conti, *Dialogus*, 154–55; and Soarez, *De Arte*, 9.

[8] For similar views that rhetoric is a product of the divorce between words and things, see Mazzacurati's remarks on Carlo Sigonia and Jacopo Sadoleto in *La crisi della retorica umanistica*, 70, 94.

shot through with a fear of social degradation, the reciprocal of the exaltation of the rhetor as the emperor of men's minds. That fear surfaces whenever writers strive to distinguish the orator from the socially despised actor, whom he so closely resembles—another maneuver with important antecedents in antiquity. Cicero, for instance, while admiring the skill of the actor Roscius and wanting the ideal orator to take him as a model, declares that actors can offer pleasure only to the ear, whereas the orator's cause should hold his audience by appealing to its intellect (*De oratore* 1.59.251, 259). What Cicero fears is social debasement, a fear he reveals when he says the orator should use the mimicry of the actor only in passing, for that technique is insufficiently *liberale* (2.62.252). *Liberale* here indicates the upper-class status of the free man (*liber*) as opposed to the status of the slave. Quintilian shares Cicero's vision, acknowledging the similarities between the orator and the actor, especially where delivery is concerned, but stressing the need for the former to maintain his distance from the latter. He urges the orator to keep the use of theatrical gestures under control "lest, when we would capture the elegance of the actor, we lose the authority of a good and dignified man [*viri boni et gravis auctoritatem*]" (*Institutio* 11.3.184). Quintilian's reference to "a good and dignified man" here echoes his general definition of the good orator as a *vir bonus dicendi peritus* and serves to underscore not merely the moral excellence of the orator but his upper-class status as one of the *viri boni*, the "best people" or optimates.

The Roman rejection of bad rhetoric as theater continues in the Middle Ages. Alain de Lille (Alanus de Insulis), for instance, dismisses sermons involving buffoonery and rhythmic melodies as fit only for the theater or the pantomime, and Martianus Capella insists that the rhetor must avoid the gestures of actors.[9] In the Renaissance such statements proliferate, just as the theater undergoes an enormous development. Thus, Giovanni Pico della Mirandola wants philosophical writing, which he styles a higher form of rhetoric, to have nothing "theatrical, applause-inciting, or popular" about it (*Epistola*, 354), and Juan Luis Vives relates that Roman oratory declined in the Empire when people started going to hear speeches "as if to an entertainment in the theater"

[9] Alain de Lille, *Summa de arte praedicatoria*, in *Readings in Medieval Rhetoric*, 231; and Capella, *Martianus Capella and the Seven Liberal Arts*, 205. See also Thomas Waleys, *De Modo Componendi Sermones Cum Documentis*, in *Artes Praedicandi: Contribution à l'histoire de la rhétorique au moyen âge*, ed. Th.-M. Charland, O.P. (Paris: Vrin, 1936), 373. On the medieval recognition of the close relationship between oratory and theater, see Jody Enders, *Rhetoric and the Origins of Medieval Drama* (Ithaca: Cornell University Press, 1992).

(*De Causis*, 168). Erasmus joins this chorus as he distinguishes between the art of the orator and that of the actor (*Ciceronianus*, 88); Francis Bacon does likewise when he praises the Jesuits for using drama as a means to teach boys various skills but declares that the theater in general is "disreputable."[10] Worries about the orator's theatricality surface especially when rhetoricians consider *actio*, or delivery. In the early fifteenth century George of Trebizond insists that the orator's gestures should not be those of "actors" (*Rhetoricorum*, 59ʳ), and more than a century later Luis de Granada is saying the same thing: that one should not imitate theatrical manners for fear of "degenerating to the gesticulating and frivolity of actors" (*Ecclesiastica Rhetorica*, 369). Writing of the orator's gestures, John Bulwer warns that striking the breast with one's hand is too "scenical" and that applauding oneself is "a gesture too plebeian and theatrically light" (*Chironomia*, 219, 221).[11]

Renaissance rhetoricians' fears of social degradation do not focus exclusively on the theater. When J. Du Pré de la Porte, for instance, complains about the low status of contemporary rhetoric, he does so because it is associated with "men who are obscure, ignorant, pedantic, and mercenary" (*Pourtraict*, 17). Thomas Wilson similarly instructs the orator to "avoyd all grosse bourding [joking], and alehouse jesting, . . . all foolish talke, and Ruffine maners" (*Arte*, 137–38); George of Trebizond warns him to control his body "lest . . . we seem to be common workmen" (*Rhetoricorum*, 59ᵛ); and John Bulwer condemns such things as thrusting out the elbows, which makes one look like a man "of some sewing occupation," and moving the hands slowly and ponderously, which is "rustical" (*Chironomia*, 226, 228).[12] As Bulwer's reference to "rustical" hand movements suggests, the opposition between upper and lower classes, which informs the writing of Renaissance rhetoricians, is doubled, as it is in Furetière's *Nouvelle*, by one between the city or court and the country.

As Renaissance rhetoricians make the ideal orator the source of civilization, so their worry about social degradation is turned into—mystified as—a fear of barbarism. Thus, Richard Sherry defines the stylistic fault revealingly called *Barbarie* as that "whych turneth the speche from his purenes, and maketh it foule and rude," and he then provides examples

[10] Bacon, *Advancement of Learning and Novum Organon*, 208.

[11] See also Peacham, *Arte*, 138–39; Keckermann, *Systema*, 507–8; Alsted, *Rhetorica*, 444–45; Sidney, *Apology*, 78; Puttenham, *Arte*, 42, 140, 271; and Fraunce, *The Arcadian Rhetorike*, bk. 2, chap. 3.

[12] See also Granada, *Ecclesiastica Rhetorica*, 348; Peacham, *Garden*, 36; Keckermann, *Systema*, 504, 511, 516; Hoskins, *Directions for Speech and Style*, 9; and Day, *The English Secretary*, 4.

of it which, he says, have been produced by barbarous men.[13] Just as typically, the Italian Raphael Regius denounces the bad rhetoricians of the late fifteenth century for having scared away students "by the filthy barbarism" of their words (*Panegyricus*, fvii^r). "Barbarism" here is a historical category, the set of rhetorical and linguistic practices of the previous age which rhetoricians proclaim they have transcended as they rehearse their belief in the "myth of the Renaissance," the notion that their culture has displaced that of the Middle Ages and witnessed a rebirth of the classical world. Philip Melanchthon, for instance, argues that only eloquent speech is true speech and complains that people in the previous age, living "in eternal darkness," lacked the eloquence that the Romans fittingly classified as part of *humanitas* because it could bring one out of barbarism (*Encomion*, 48, 50). M. Le Grand similarly structures the history of France, noting that although his countrymen possessed native sources of eloquence going back to the ancient Druids, the barbarian invasions of the Middle Ages impeded the development of rhetoric until such Renaissance writers as Ronsard and Du Bellay found ways to "pronounce their thoughts more clearly" (*Discours*, n.p.). It is to this "myth of the Renaissance," with its dismissal of late medieval writing in the name of a reborn classical rhetoric, that Ermolao Barbaro refers in his letter attacking the Scholastics, the letter that prompted Pico della Mirandola's famous ironic reply in defense of the "barbarous Germans."[14]

The fear of barbarism, which surfaces repeatedly in the discourse of rhetoric, also possesses a geographical or spatial dimension in some texts, just as it does in Furetière's. For instance, Puttenham endorses only that language "spoken in the kings Court, or in the good townes and Cities within the land," not what one hears "in the marches and frontiers, or in port townes, where straungers haunt for traffike sake, or yet in Universities where Schollers use much peevish affectation of words out of the primative languages, or finally, in any uplandish village or corner of a Realme, where is no resort but of poore rusticall or uncivill people" (*Arte*, 156–57). This distinction between a civilized center and a rustic, barbarous periphery also appears in Thomas Wilson's condemnation of those "Barbarous Clarkes" who "thinke *Rhetorique* to

---

[13] Sherry, *A Treatise of Schemes and Tropes*, 35–36. See also Puttenham, *Arte*, 257–58; and Latomus, *Summa*, K6^v.

[14] See the opening of Chapter 3. Note that Puttenham faults the "licentious maker" for employing French words as though they were English, just as "all your old rimers and specially *Gower*" used to do, a practice "utterly to be banished from our schoole, and better it might have bene borne with in old riming writers, bycause they lived in a barbarous age" (*Arte*, 95).

stande wholie upon darke wordes" (that is, inkhorn terms) and "seeke so far for outlandish English, that they forget altogether their mothers language" (*Arte*, 161, 162). Sir Philip Sidney uses the same opposition when he complains about the faulty diction of contemporary poets that has turned "eloquence" into "affectation": "They cast sugar and spice upon every dish that is served to the table, like those Indians, not content to wear earrings at the fit and natural place of the ears, but they will thrust jewels through their nose and lips because they will be sure to be fine" (*Apology*, 81–82). Like Furetière, Sidney concocts an imperialistic vision in which good rhetoric implicitly occupies the symbolic space of the civilized center and is defended with sarcasm from its "barbarous" counterpart, from "Indians" who, like Furetière's "vengeful . . . Iroquois," live outside the pale of Europe and whose domination and domestication the passage makes appear inherently justified lest they and their "unnatural" customs contaminate and corrupt the center.

To defend the orator's upper-class status, rhetoricians reach back to Plato and conceive him in the terms of the *Phaedrus* as an educator, or invert the attack on him in the *Gorgias* as a cook who harms the body by presenting him instead as a noble physician who cures it. Thus, Thomas Wilson presents him as a teacher and preacher (*Arte*, 29, 86), and George of Trebizond compares rhetoric directly to medicine: "Naturally that [medicine] cures the diseases of individuals, this [rhetoric], the diseases of both individuals and the state" (*Rhetoricorum*, 80^v). Similarly, Johann Heinrich Alsted proclaims the century in which he lives to be sick (*Rhetorica*, Dedication, 7^r) and makes the orator the doctor to cure it (*Rhetorica*, 5), and J. Du Pré de la Porte declares that good eloquence "sets badly made spirits upright again and orders them for their duty (*Pourtraict*, 26).

One of the most interesting treatments of the orator is that of Henry Peacham, who not only sees him as a teacher and physician (*Garden*, 24, 38, 176) but turns him into a noble knight straight out of Renaissance romance. In Peacham's imagination the orator's figures of speech become weapons "wherewith we may defend our selves, invade our enemies, revenge our wrongs, ayd the weake, deliver the simple from dangers, conserve true religion, & confute idolatry" (iv^r). Peacham then imagines the orator's world in terms of the landscape of romance, although a landscape also colored by Christianity: it is a "wildernesse," a place of "darkenesse" (92), and a "vale of misery, where mens harts are often fainting, and their mindes falling into despaire," where they lie "still opprest under their heavy burthen, never able to rise againe, without the strength of comfort and consolation" (100–101). Peacham celebrates the orator as a knight in shining armor who serves as the people's guide through the wilderness and brings them the saving illumination they so desperately need (92, 120, 123, 148, 181).

If the good rhetor is a chivalric hero, then bad rhetoric is a monster, a grotesque body, to be driven away or slain. Sometimes, that body is merely hinted at, as when excess is being denounced. Luis de Granada, for instance, rejects the "confused piling up of words signifying the same thing" (*Ecclesiastica Rhetorica*, 39), while Bartholomew Keckermann more directly recalls Furetière's Galimatias (Farrago) when he censures copiousness taken to extremes for being a "farrago of synonyms and phrases" (*Systema*, 437). More frequently, the grotesque body is suggested through the idea of category confusion, as when Joan de Guzman declares that a speaker does not deserve the name of orator who gets things topsy-turvy (*Primera Parte*, 16^v: *preposterando las cosas*), and J. Du Pré de la Porte condemns the orator who, lacking in art, mingles his own material indiscriminately with that of others and, as a result, "makes monsters of it" (*Pourtraict*, 73). In particular, as they attempt to define decorum, rhetoricians summon up images of the grotesque body. When George Puttenham defines the quality that makes a speech pleasing as "decencie"—which, like "decorum," comes from the Latin verb *decet* ("it is fitting")—he contrasts this notion with its contrary, "deformitie." People will be repelled by a speech, he proclaims,

> if they discover any illfavorednesse or disproportion to the partes apprehensive, as for example, when a sound is either too loude or too low or otherwise confuse, the eare is ill affected: so is th'eye if the coulour be sad or not liminous and recreative, or the shape of a membred body without his due measures and simmetry, and the like of every other sence in his proper function. These excesses or defectes or confusions and disorders in the sensible objectes are deformities and unseemely to the sence. (268)

Puttenham's governing metaphor here is "illfavorednesse," which specifically invokes the idea of the appearance of the body (or the face, the "favor," to be more precise). This metaphor is reinforced and elaborated when he reviews the response of the eye, insisting that the object it sees must be "liminous" (that is, "luminous") and pleasurable, and then directly identifies that object as a body with all its members in place and possessing an appropriate, symmetrical shape. By contrast, a defective speech is imagined as a disproportionate body marked by hyperbolic excess as well as "confusions and disorders." In his mind's eye, Puttenham clearly sees that body as monstrous.

Puttenham is not alone in conceiving defective rhetoric this way. Following the lead of Quintilian (*Institutio*, 7.Pr.2–3), J. Du Pré de la Porte warns the rhetor not to make the exordium of a speech too long, lest the head should be "too large for the body, which would be monstrous" (*Pourtraict*, 83), and Bartholomew Keckermann declares that a speech "which has distorted members is no less ugly [*deformis*] than that which is crippled in some part" (*Systema*, 128). Puttenham is also thinking of the monstrous when he denounces "foul speech," one form of which involves rhymes made on the same sound: "There is also another sort of ilfavoured speech subject to this vice, but resting more in the manner of the ilshapen sound and accent, than in the matter it selfe" (*Arte*, 261). Speech here is, implicitly, an ugly body: it is "ilfavoured"; its sounds are "ilshapen." Perhaps the most dramatic use of body metaphors is to be found in the *Primera Parte de la Rhetorica* of Joan de Guzman, who, like Du Pré, insists that one's beginnings should fit "with the rest of the body of one's speech, since otherwise they would appear monsters." Guzman uses a striking simile to elucidate what he means, comparing such a speech to "a dwarf . . . who, no matter how well shaped his face and how fine his features, produces great ugliness, since his face is that of a man and his body that of a creature" (85ᵛ). Later, he compares poorly arranged speeches to "crazy figures which have their feet where they should have their arms, and their chest where they should have their shoulders, and therewith they have all the rest switched about" (97ʳ). Guzman's imagination could properly be termed Mannerist as he transforms poorly arranged speeches into the grotesques of an Arcimboldo.[15]

If a badly organized speech can be monstrous, so can the speaker's body, a danger stressed whenever rhetoricians consider delivery. They warn against inflating the cheeks, sticking out the nose and lips, twisting the body about absurdly in all directions.[16] Contemplation of such faults provokes vicious satire in Thomas Wilson: "Some pores upon the ground as though they sought for pinnes. *Tullie* telles of one *Theophrastus Tauriscus*, who is saied to declaime arsee versee. Some swelles in the face, and filles their cheekes full of winde, as though they would blowe out their wordes. Some sets forth their lippes, two inches good beyond their teeth. Some talkes as though their tongue went of pattines. Some shewes all their teeth" (*Arte*, 220). Even more striking is a passage in which the German Lutheran Bartholomew Keckermann ridicules Catholic friars. An excessive use of the body, he says,

---

[15] See also Alsted, *Rhetorica*, 414; Granada, *Ecclesiastica Rhetorica*, 177; and Du Pré, *Pourtraict*, 92.

[16] For examples, see Du Pré, *Pourtraict*, 80; Granada, *Ecclesiastica Rhetorica*, 349; Bulwer, *Chirologia*, 5; and Vossius, *Oratoriarum Institutionum Libri Sex*, 386.

is practiced by some histrionic little friars (although once upon a time actors were expelled from the Church and even denied the sacred sacrament of communion) to the extent that today we see some of them deliver popular sermons to the people from the stage with a remarkable straining of their voices. Their faces have fickle, wandering, and impudent eyes. They throw their arms about, dance with their feet, move their loins lasciviously, turn about with varied motions, use inversions, circumlocutions, and regurgitations, and finally gesticulate like mimes with their entire bodies and turn themselves all about because of the mobility of their spirits. (*Systema*, 529)

Here Keckermann moves from the friars' absurd physical gestures to the contorted style of their preaching ("inversions, circumlocutions, and regurgitations") and back to the wild gesticulations of both body and spirit. He attacks them for a lack of control and stability, for turning everything topsy-turvy, and for their sexuality (the wandering eyes and lascivious loins), all of which degrade the sacred, making it the performance of a lower-class mime. That these little friars deliberately mock religion Keckermann suggests with his next sentence, which contains an ironic reference to Demosthenes: "You remember perhaps the opinion of Demosthenes who, when asked . . . what was most effective in speaking, replied, Delivery." Keckermann's irony gets lost in translation, for he does not have Demosthenes use the usual Latin word for delivery, *actio*, but rather its latinized Greek equivalent *hypocrisis*. *Hypocrisis*, like *actio*, does mean delivery (as well as acting), of course, but from the New Testament on it also had the meaning it suggests to an English reader—hypocrisy.

The topsy-turviness, confusion, and disorder characterizing the "body" of bad rhetoric are all produced by boundary violations: either the body has grown beyond its proper limits, or pieces of it protrude into the space around it, or its members are rearranged, or it is missing some crucial part. As a result, we find that in the Renaissance discourse of rhetoric generally, as was the case with Furetière's work, the body in question—whether of oratory, the oration, or the orator—is also identified as being dirty and diseased. We have already noted that Raphael Regius identifies the bad rhetoric of his day with "filthy barbarism" (*Panegyricus*, fvii[r]). Johann Heinrich Alsted similarly condemns it as "a plague to the state" (*Rhetorica*, 2), and J. Du Pré de la Porte warns contemporary orators about "the spots which deform" their art (*Pourtraict*, Dedication, 22). Thomas Wilson mocks certain orators as "slovens" for failing to wear the clothing of style in a "clenly" manner (*Arte*, 161), and John Bulwer, writing about delivery, also complains of "slovenly orators . . . who wallow in the dirt" in that they lack knowledge of the proper use of gestures, without which the mouth becomes "a running sore and hollow fistula of the mind" (*Chirologia*, 153; *Chironomia*, 157). Not only does Bulwer's language here identify the failed rhetor with disease and dirt, but it links that dirt to excrement ("fistula"). Significantly, he later warns: "No gesture that respects the rule of art directs itself to the hinder parts" (*Chironomia*, 242). One final example: J. Du Pré de la Porte lumps the monstrous together with dirt and disease when he instructs the orator to remove "those excesses and swellings of words, those monstrous points, those pedantic phrases, those indirections and circumlocutions, and those blistered notions which are the abysses and the abscesses of speech" (*Pourtraict*, 106).[17]

Although Bakhtin identifies the grotesque body with folk culture, rhetoricians usually connect the two only indirectly, as when they link that body to rusticity. George Puttenham, however, provides an interesting exception to this rule. Throughout his *Arte of English Poesie* he contrasts the decorous and the deformed, denouncing "foule and intollerable" figures (180), the "mingle mangle" of languages in a speech (259), and imaginations that create "very monstruous and illfavored" images (35). He also denigrates "ordinarie rimers" whose verse goes "ill favouredly and like a minstrels musicke" (85), language implying his opposition to the folk culture those minstrels purveyed. His most dramatic rejection of that culture occurs when he discusses the high style of epic and tragedy, which is "disgraced and made foolish and ridiculous by all the wordes affected, counterfait, and puffed up, as it were a windball carrying more countenance than matter, and can not be better resembled then to these midsommer pageants in London, where to make the people wonder are set forth great and uglie Gyants marching as if they were alive, and armed at all points, but within they are stuffed full of browne paper and tow, which the shrewd boyes underpeering, do guilefully discover and turne to a great derision" (165). Attacking the hyperbolic tendency built into the high style, Puttenham compares this rhetorical activity to one associated with popular festivity, the celebration occurring on Midsummer's Eve (the eve of St. John's Day, June 24), which featured a parade of giants.[18] Although those giants might seem to

---

[17] For other examples, see Puttenham, *Arte*, 180; Wilson, *Arte*, 49–51, 69, 135–36, 181; and Valla, *Rhetorica*, II.iii[v]. The distinction between the dirty and the clean is also used by rhetoricians to underline the historical opposition they envision between the late Middle Ages and their own age; see George of Trebizond, *Rhetoricorum*, 65[r]; Pico della Mirandola, *Epistola*, 354, 356; and Regius, *Panegyricus*, fvii[r].

[18] On this festival, see François Laroque, *Shakespeare et la fête: Essai d'archéologie du spectacle dans l'Angleterre élisabéthaine* (Paris: Presses Universitaires de France, 1988), 82, 84, 153.

be versions of Bakhtin's grotesque body, Puttenham's attitude to them is hardly Bakhtin's. He does not embrace them as ambiguous figures whose excessive size is an affirmation of life and growth at the same time that it makes them the object of ridicule; rather, like most giants in traditional folklore, as Walter Stephens has argued, they represent a threatening Other, and the parade and the mockery signify their defeat and domestication by the triumphant dominant culture.[19] In fact, Puttenham repeats this pattern of defeat and domestication as he mocks the hyperbolic high style for being a mere "windball carrying more countenance than matter." Thus he not only identifies bad rhetoric with the grotesque giants of traditional folklore but emphatically rejects both of them.

If bad rhetoric possesses a monstrous body, good rhetoric must have a beautiful one. Writing about *dispositio*, or arrangement, George of Trebizond compares the members of an oration to the parts of the body and says all should be in their proper places, as they are in Cicero's works (*Rhetoricorum*, 54ᵛ). Similarly, Bartholomew Keckermann declares that "an oration . . . ought to be similar to a beautiful body, in which we marvel not so much at the members themselves as at their mutual joining together" (*Systema*, 128).[20] Moreover, the beautiful body of a speech should be properly adorned with the dress of a beautiful style, a style which, for Thomas Wilson, is regal or imperial: "Elocution getteth words to set forth invention, and with such beautie commendeth the matter, that reason semeth to be clad in Purple, walking afore both bare and naked" (*Arte*, 160).[21] The concept of decorum also implies a beautiful body: "Our owne Saxon English terme is [*seemelynesse*] that is to say, for his good shape and utter appearance well pleasing the eye, we call it also [*comelynesse*] for the delight it bringeth comming towardes us, and to that purpose may be called [*pleasant approche*]" (268–69). Here decorum is not primarily a matter of right timing, which may well be what the original Greek concept meant, but the visual concept implied by "good shape" and "comeliness."[22]

---

[19] Walter Stephens, introduction to *Giants in Those Days: Folklore, Ancient History, and Nationalism* (Lincoln: University of Nebraska Press, 1989).

[20] For additional examples, see Soarez, *De Arte*, 125; Caussin, *Eloquentia sacra*, 303; Du Pré, *Pourtraict*, 92; Granada, *Ecclesiastica Rhetorica*, 177; and Guzman, *Primera Parte*, 62ʳ.

[21] For other examples of style as dress, see Granada, *Ecclesiastica Rhetorica*, 44; Alsted, *Rhetorica*, 197; Keckermann, *Systema*, 179; and Bucoldianus, *De Inventione & Amplificatione oratoria*, 123. Whenever rhetoricians speak of the *ornamenta* of style, they necessarily imply that a speech has a body.

[22] Angel Day (*The English Secretary*, 4) likewise identifies decorum with comeliness and opposes it to "base, filthie, or scurrile matter."

Comeliness should also characterize the actual body of the ideal orator, and Thomas Wilson summarizes what that means:

> The head to bee holden upright, the forehead without frowning, the
> browes without bending, the nose without blowing, the eyes quicke
> and pleasant, the lippes not laied out, the teeth without grenning, the
> armes not much cast abroade, but comely set out, as time and cause
> shall best require: the handes sometimes opened, and sometimes
> holden together, the fingers pointing, the breast laied out, and the
> whole bodie stirring altogether, with a seemely moderation. By the
> which behaviour of our bodie after such a sorte, we shall not onely
> delite men with the sight, but perswade them the rather the trueth of
> our cause. (*Arte*, 221)

The body Wilson imagines is chiefly defined by its opposition to the
grotesque. The speaker is told to avoid actions and gestures that appear
ridiculous particularly because they transect the proper boundaries of
the body. Thus, he is instructed not to blow his nose or "lay out" his
lips or cast his arms about; instead, when he moves his body, it should
stir "altogether, with a seemely moderation." The comeliness of the
body here results from its being contained within its proper bounds and
creating through its movements an impression of unity and compact-
ness. This body will be dignified, controlled, and self-possessed, thus
testifing to the existence of comparable moral, intellectual, and social
qualities in the orator himself. No wonder Wilson concludes his paragraph with the claim that such a body will not only delight the audience
but persuade them in and of itself to believe in the truth of the orator's
cause.[23]

The beautiful body of good rhetoric is represented graphically by illustrations of the Hercules Gallicus, who, though old and gray, possesses a
body of heroic proportions. This Hercules is not completely distinct
from the Hercules of the twelve labors, whose triumphs are presented in
Alciati's *Emblemata* as the triumphs of true goodness and eloquence
over immorality and bad rhetoric. In the Paduan edition of 1621, for
example, a heroic Hercules is depicted standing at ease, surrounded by
little scenes representing his labors (Emblem 138). The poem under-
neath the picture begins by identifying his eloquence, rather than his
physical prowess, as his defining feature: "His eloquence goes beyond
the praise of unconquered strength." The poem continues with an allegory of his labors, which include untangling the deceitful words of the

---

[23] For other prescriptions concerning the body, see Soarez, *De Arte*, 330; Bulwer,
Chironomia; and Fraunce, *The Arcadian Rhetorike*, bk. 2, chap. 3.

Sophists; triumphing over "feminine . . . wiles"; cleaning away filth and bringing culture to men; and punishing barbarism and savagery. In other words, the poem embodies in Hercules and his opponents the main traits which, throughout this book, we have seen separating good and bad rhetoric from one another. More important, it identifies Hercules' heroic labors as a matter of defeating monsters, a point Claude Mignault underscores in his commentary on this emblem in the Leiden edition of 1591 (see 507). Fittingly, in Joan de Guzman's dialogue on rhetoric, Don Luis Gaytan, who acts the part of pupil, praises his teacher Fernando de Boan as just such a Hercules figure: "In removing certain opinions of things which some of our orators hold, you have seemed to me like a Hercules, tamer of monsters, and pacifier of the universe" (*Primera Parte*, 275[r]).[24] For Renaissance rhetoricians, in short, Hercules embodies not just the ideal orator who, as ruler and conqueror, leads his subjects by means of chains of gold and amber but the hero who ensures the purity of good rhetoric by eliminating its opposite—which is just what the rhetoricians strove to do through their denunciations and satire. Hercules' labors are theirs, as is his fundamental aim: to banish the monsters.

Although rhetoric books characterize the bad orator and his art in terms of the grotesque, they seldom directly correlate bad rhetoric and *literally* monstrous bodies. Literary texts do. Thus, as he contrasts good and bad education in his *Gargantua*, Rabelais sets up a confrontation between two kinds of characters as well as two kinds of rhetoric. On the one side there is the young giant Gargantua, given a time-wasting "medieval" training by a foolish pedagogue who is labelled a *sophiste* and thus associated with defective rhetoric (47).[25] On the other there is the young page Eudémon ("the good or beautiful spirit"), who demonstrates the benefits of proper instruction before the court of Gargantua's father by delivering an elegant formal oration. A eulogy for Gargantua, that oration is "produced with such proper gestures, such clear pronunciation, such an eloquent voice, and such ornamented and proper Latin,

[24] Du Pré tells a fable in which the heroic orator, identified as a lawyer, forces "the monster of legal quibbling to come to light who was hidden in the recesses of some filthy trial" (*Pourtraict*, 80), so that the judge can destroy it. Although for Du Pré it takes a judge as well as an orator to expel the monster, what is important is that the task parallels Hercules' labors and that this monster, like the monstrous body of bad rhetoric, is associated with filth.

[25] Page numbers cite Rabelais, *Oeuvres*. According to the editors, in earlier editions of Rabelais's novel, Gargantua's first master was called a *théologien*, a designation changed to prevent persecution by the Church. Significantly, to replace his original satirical term, Rabelais chose one that implies both defective philosopher and defective rhetorician.

that he [i.e., Eudémon] resembled a Gracchus, a Cicero, or an Emilius of the past more than a youth of this century" (50). Not only is Eudémon's superiority demonstrated by his mastery of *proper* rhetoric, but it is also evident in his body, for he appears "so well curled, so well attired, so well brushed, so honorable in his behavior that he seemed far more like some little angel than a man" (50). By contrast, Gargantua's bad education under the *sophiste* was focused more on his body than his mind, specifically on a carnivalesque body that is anything but orderly, clean, and neat (see 62–63). That body urinates and spits, coughs and yawns, wallows in bed, plays endless games, eats and drinks to excess. As a result of his disorganized, overly indulgent, excessive education, not only does Gargantua become foolish, but his body betrays his mental condition; when he hears Eudémon's oration, he responds by crying out "like a cow" and hiding his face in his hat, nor is it "possible to get a word out of him any more than a fart out of a dead donkey" (50). In short, Gargantua's bad education has made him a grotesque man-animal. Significantly, the first step taken by his new master, Ponocrates ("the strong one"), who also trained Eudémon, is literally to purge his pupil and then to subject him to a thorough disciplining of both mind and body. As a result, Gargantua comes to speak like Eudémon, continually citing classical authorities and finally, near the end of the novel, delivering a masterly oration in Ciceronian style to the defeated army of his enemy Picrochole.

Rabelais is not the only writer of literature who establishes a correlation between physical grotesqueness and defective rhetoric. Shakespeare's Falstaff provides a fine example of it, as does Molière's Tartuffe, both of whom, in admittedly quite different ways, indulge in verbal excesses that match their physical bulk. Perhaps the most grotesque figure of all appears in Thomas Nashe's satirical novel *The Unfortunate Traveler*. At one point its protagonist, Jack Wilton, listens to a ridiculous oration—supposedly delivered in honor of the Duke of Saxony—which is stuffed with foolish redundancies, absurd puns, pedantic jokes, and obscure inkhorn terms. Not only is the speech grotesque, but the orator makes rhetoric itself into a monster: "Welcome, said I? Oh, orificial rhetoric, wipe thy everlasting mouth and afford me a more Indian metaphor than that for the brave princely blood of a Saxon. Oratory, uncask the barred hutch of thy compliments, and with the triumphantest trope in thy treasury do trewage unto him" (480).[26] Rhetoric here acquires a mouth that salivates and slobbers and then metamorphoses into a trea-

---

[26] Page numbers cite Thomas Nashe, *The Unfortunate Traveler*, in *Elizabethan Prose Fiction*, ed. Merritt Lawlis (New York: Odyssey Press, 1967).

sure chest ("barred hutch"), thus becoming gigantic—and monstrous. But the grotesque oration Jack hears has nothing on the person who delivers it: "A bursten-belly inkhorn orator called Vanderhulk they picked out to present him [the Duke] with an oration, one that had a sulphurous, big, swollen, large face like a Saracen, eyes like two Kentish oysters, a mouth that opened as wide every time he spake as one of those old knit trap doors, a beard as though it had been made of a bird's nest plucked in pieces which consisteth of straw, hair, and dirt mixed together" (480). This striking passage not only stresses the monstrous size of the appropriately named Vanderhulk, whose body threatens to burst out of all limits, but underlines his grotesqueness in other ways as well. It makes him appear half-human and half-animal, associates him with disease and evil (his "sulphurous" face), links him to the barbarous ("Saracen"), and mocks him as disorderly and dirty. In short, practically all the negative features symbolized by the deformed body of bad rhetoric are present in this portrait.

If Renaissance literature assigns bad rhetoric a grotesque body, it also supplies rhetoricians with a set of special names to designate the figure they are rejecting. Those names mark another difference from the classical past, for although a few may come from the ancient world, none of them served as labels for bad rhetors there. Anto Maria de' Conti, for example, has one of the speakers in his dialogue attack the orator by saying he is nothing more than a ropedancer (*schenobates*), a juggler (*praestigiator*), or a mountebank (*circulator*) (*Dialogus*, 153).[27] Significantly, these terms were not used in antiquity to attack orators; they come from literary texts and were employed by satirists such as Juvenal and Petronius to catalogue the hucksters, small-time entertainers, and other riffraff one could find on the streets of Rome.[28] Such characters still thronged the streets of de' Conti's Europe, and, more important, they abound in the literature of the period. Not surprisingly, comparable names for them appear in vernacular rhetorics. Thus, Daniel Barbaro identifies bad rhetors as *ciurmatori*, "con-men" or "deceivers" (*Della Eloquenza*, 341), and his compatriot Francesco Patrizi speaks of a *truffatore*, or "deceiver," and a *bugiardo*, or "liar" (*Della Retorica*, 40ʳ). *Ciurmatori* and *truffatori* often performed as mountebanks, selling the

[27] Indulging in anti-Catholic satire, the Protestant Johann Heinrich Alsted also focuses on the body as he mocks overly histrionic delivery: "Monks and Jesuits are troubled by that vice nowadays, and they seem to be actors or boxers or ropedancers rather than orators, and especially ecclesiastical ones" (*Rhetorica*, 445).

[28] *Schenobates* is found only in Juvenal; *praestigiator* is anteclassical (Plautus) and post-Augustan (Seneca); and only *circulator* occurs throughout the period during which Cicero and Quintilian lived; see *A Latin Dictionary*, ed. Charlton T. Lewis and Charles Short (Oxford: Clarendon Press, 1962). Note that Giovanni Pico della Mirandola also attacks rhetoric using the verb *praestigiari* (*Epistola*, 352).

equivalent of "snake oil" in order to "gull" (*uccellare*) their hapless prey, and that is precisely what Bernardino Tomitano denounces rhetoric for in his work on the Tuscan language: "Rhetoric . . . is full of deceptions [*inganni*] to gull [*uccellare*] persuasion."[29] French rhetoricians have their own terms, although some of them derive from Italian, to identify the bad rhetor; they call him *charlatan, fourbe* ("rogue"), *imposteur,* and mock him for mounting a *banque* and producing empty *babil,* or "babble."[30] Similarly, the Englishmen Sir Philip Sidney and George Puttenham, defining the counterimage to their idealized poet-rhetor, compare him to "mountebanks" (*Apology,* 70) and "*Cantabanqui, . . .* blind harpers or such like taverne minstrels" (*Arte,* 96–97). Finally, John Bulwer warns the orator against making overly subtle movement with his fingers lest he look like a juggler or a thief (*Chironomia,* 229).

Although all these names differ from language to language and text to text, the repetitions and continuities among them make it apparent that we are dealing with a family of related characters, all kith and kin of the folkloric figure known as "Trickster."[31] Like him, they are duplicitous, morally ambiguous beings opposed to the laws and rules of civilization. Like him, they are degraded and marginal people dwelling near or at the bottom of the social order or outside its boundaries. Like his, their bodies are grotesque as they continually contort and transform themselves. Appropriately, Thomas Wilson identifies his negative version of the orator, the lawyer, with the animal figure that has epitomized the trickster for Europeans since the late Middle Ages: he denounces the lawyer as a fox (*Arte,* 37).

As Peter Stallybrass and Allon White have argued, "the body cannot be thought separately from the social formation. . . . [It] is neither a purely natural given nor . . . merely a textual metaphor, it is a privileged

---

[29] Bernardino Tomitano, *Quattro libri della Lingua Toscana* (Padua, 1570), 3.109, cited in Mazzacurati, *La crisi della retorica umanistica,* 102.

[30] Le Grand uses all these terms (*Discours*); Du Vair disagrees with those who attribute eloquence to "chatterers and charlatans who entertain and numb auditors with a vain babble" (*Traitté,* 401); and Du Pré complains of "Charlatans" and "double spirits" and, alluding to mountebanks, says there are too many talkers "who make of the bar a bench where they display only babble instead of drugs" (*Pourtraict,* 54, 71).

[31] The literature on the trickster is voluminous. A basic bibliography would include Barbara Babcock-Abrahams, "'A Tolerated Margin of Mess': The Trickster and His Tales Reconsidered," *Journal of the Folklore Institute* 11 (1975): 147–86; Robert D. Pelton, *The Trickster in West Africa: A Study of Mythic Irony and Sacred Delight* (Berkeley: University of California Press, 1980); Paul Radin, *The Trickster: A Study in American Indian Mythology* (1956; rpt. New York: Schocken, 1972); and Laura Makarius, "Le Mythe du 'Trickster,'" *Revue de l'Histoire des Religions* 175 (1969): 17–46. See also Rebhorn, *Foxes and Lions,* chap. 1.

operator for the transcoding of these other areas. Thinking the body is thinking social topography and vice versa."[32] In terms specific to the Renaissance, to the analogical mind-set of the period, the human body and the body politic are mirror images of each other.[33] That they are so in the discourse of rhetoric should be evident from the oppositions we have reviewed between barbarism and civilization, the wild lower and refined upper classes, the margins and the center, for all these oppositions are repeatedly paralleled by juxtaposed images of the body as monstrous or beautiful, contorted or shapely, grotesque or decorous. In fact, the discourse of rhetoric thematizes the equivalence of body and body politic by means of an exemplary oration that it rehearses repeatedly, sometimes alluding to it briefly, sometimes paraphrasing it, sometimes unfolding it at length. That oration is the fable of the belly, supposedly recounted by Menenius Agrippa at a crucial moment in Roman history in order to manage the unruly *plebs*. It occurs, by my count, in no fewer than nine texts from the period, including rhetoric manuals, poetics, and two "literary" works: namely, the *Remaines of a Greater Worke Concerning Britaine* (1605) by the English historian William Camden, and Shakespeare's *Coriolanus*. By looking at these versions of the fable, we will be able not only to grasp more fully the central role of the body in Renaissance rhetoric but to see once again how that discourse is reproduced and complicated in the domain of literature.

Although the fable goes back at least to Aesop, the most important source for its Renaissance retellings is a passage in the second book of Livy's history which recounts how the common people of Rome, enraged by the high price of food and the refusal of the Senate to control usury rates, left the city and encamped on Mount Sacer three miles away. Authorities in Rome, concerned about threats of foreign wars, sent Menenius Agrippa, a member of the *plebs* himself, to speak to the rebels. Agrippa told them the fable of the belly, according to which, at a time when the various parts (*membra*) of the body (*in homine*) were independent and could speak, they complained that all things obtained

---

[32] Stallybrass and White, *The Politics and Poetics of Transgression*, 192. These authors actually argue for the existence of homologies in *four* areas—psychic forms, the body, geography, and the social order—and claim that cultures use the symbolisms of all four, often substituting from one area to another, in order to think themselves. What I have said about the Renaissance discourse of rhetoric certainly fits their analysis, and although I emphasize two of the four domains, the body and the social order, the other two do appear occasionally in the course of my analysis.

[33] Leonard Barkan has documented a tradition stretching back into antiquity which saw the human body as an analogue to the state; see his *Nature's Work of Art: The Human Body as Image of the World* (New Haven: Yale University Press, 1975), 61–115.

by their labor went to the stomach, which did nothing to deserve them. Hence, they rebelled: the hand would not bring food to the mouth, the mouth take it, or the teeth chew it. "While in this anger, they wanted to tame the stomach by hunger, the members themselves and the entire body all at the same time came to a complete wasting away" (2.32.10).[34] In this way it became apparent (*apparuisse*) that the stomach was important, enabling all the parts of the body to live by supplying blood for them from the food it digested. Livy describes the effect of Agrippa's story: "By comparing from this how the intestine sedition of the body was similar to the anger of the *plebs* at the senators [*patres*], he prevailed upon [*flexisse*: bent] the minds of the men" (2.32.12). Finally, Livy reports, the people entered into negotiations with the Senate, which led to the creation of their own political representatives, the Tribunes, as a check on the power of the patrician class. Writing as a historian, not a rhetorician, Livy focuses on the internecine strife of the Roman people; for him, Agrippa's oration is important because it resolves an internal crisis and leads to the creation of a new political institution.

When the fable of the belly appears in the Renaissance discourse of rhetoric, it is changed in significant ways from its source, primarily because its framework is so very different. It is offered not as part of a historical narrative but as an example of the power of oratory, a theme present in Livy but really of secondary importance to him. Thus, at the dawn of the Renaissance, in the fourteenth book of his *Genealogy of the Pagan Gods*, Boccaccio defends the usefulness of poetical fictions and cites Agrippa's recitation of the story as an example of the power of art to turn rage into gentleness.[35] Much later in the Renaissance, Sidney does something similar, arguing that such fables enable the poet to "draw the mind more effectually than any other art doth" (*Apology*, 41). The fable is also used to document claims about the power of oratory by such writers as Raphael Regius (*Panegyricus*, fv[r]), Anto Maria de' Conti (*Dialogus*, 157), and Thomas Wilson (*Arte*, 197).[36] Nicholas Caussin's version of it is particularly revealing, compared with Livy's. It occupies a small chapter in the first book of his *Eloquentia sacra et humana*, in which he is reviewing the major orators of antiquity. The chapter con-

[34] Livy, *Books I and II* (of *Ab urbe condita*), trans. B. O. Foster (London: William Heinemann, 1967).
[35] Giovanni Boccaccio, *On Poetry*, trans. Charles G. Osgood (Indianapolis: Bobbs-Merrill, 1956), 50.
[36] Although he does not reprise the fable from Livy, Du Pré sets up a long comparison between the stomach, which makes blood and feeds it to the rest of the body, and the orator who digests food and then gives it to the judge, who converts it into blood and spreads it throughout the kingdom (*Pourtraict*, 6–7). A little later Du Pré compares the orator to the lungs.

sists of an introduction declaring that Agrippa's eloquence (*facundia*) ought to be venerated and that the fable shows how the great orator "healed discord by means of speaking" (29). The frame of the fable thus stresses both the power of rhetoric and its value as medicine for the body politic. The remainder of the chapter consists of a transcription of Livy's text but with a number of minor changes, at least one of which dramatically underscores the special vision the Renaissance has of the art of rhetoric. The last sentence reads: "By comparing from this how the intestine sedition of the body was similar to the anger of the *plebs*, he [Agrippa] bent the wills of the men to the Senators" ("Comparando hinc quam intestina corporis seditio similis esset irae plebis, in Patres flexit hominum voluntates"). The sentence in Livy's text is identical up to the phrase *irae plebis,* "the anger of the *plebs,*" but whereas Caussin inserts a comma at that point, most modern editors of Livy delay the comma until after "in Patres." Thus, modern editions make the senators the *object* of the plebeians' anger: *irae plebis in Patres,* "the anger of the *plebs* at the Senators." By contrast, Caussin makes them the object of the plebeians' deference: "in Patres flexit hominum voluntates" ("he bent the wills of the men to the Senators"). Caussin also writes *voluntates* in place of Livy's *mentes,* thus concluding with the idea that the plebeians' "wills" were bent, rather than their "minds." Both these alterations of Livy's text are consistent with the particular political emphases of Renaissance rhetoric. Caussin's stress on the plebeians' *deference* to the *Patres*—a word which, significantly, also receives capitalization in his version—fits the Renaissance insistence that rhetoric means rule from on high, just as his focus on the *will* suits a conception of rhetoric in which the subject's will is dominated by that of his superior.

Renaissance retellings of the fable reveal the characteristic politics of the period in another way as well. In Livy one encounters a narrative of the struggle between senators and plebeians, the struggle that Machiavelli in the *Discorsi* recognized as the central facet of Roman history. Renaissance rhetoricians, by contrast, stress the unruliness of the lower classes—"a beast, or rather a monster that hath many heddes," says Thomas Wilson (*Arte,* 198)—and the need to impose order on them from above. Indeed, the Renaissance versions of the story eliminate the fact that Agrippa comes from the people himself, although Livy clearly states that he was "dear to the *plebs* because he took his origin from among them" (2.32.8). By omitting this detail, most Renaissance versions allow the reader to infer that since Agrippa speaks on behalf of the Senators, he must be one of *them.* More important, they also omit any reference to the complex negotiations between the patricians and the commoners which led to the creation of the office of tribune and which

Livy says occurred *after* the conclusion of the fable. Most strikingly, in Shakespeare's *Coriolanus* (1.1.254) the office of tribune is presented as being in existence even *before* Agrippa pronounces his fable.[37] In effect, the Renaissance versions reveal their writers to be committed to a strictly hierarchical *polis* in which the lower classes appear naturally prone to violence and sedition, and order is just as naturally imposed from on high by an eloquent orator-civilizer who is identified with the ruling class. As Raphael Regius puts it, changing the basic metaphor of the fable most revealingly: Agrippa deserves praise because, by his efforts, the *plebs* were controlled and "subjected to the Senate from which, as from its head, it seemed to have been torn" (*Panegyricus*, fv^r).

Regius's image of the Senate as the "head" of the people leads to a third important difference between Renaissance versions of the fable and Livy's: in the latter the notion that the human body is a microcosm of the state is implicit; in the former it is made explicit and detailed. In *Coriolanus*, for instance, the figure of the body receives a direct interpretation, an "application," as Agrippa tells the citizens: "The senators of Rome are this good belly, / And you the mutinous members" (1.1.147–48). But Agrippa's view is challenged by the First Citizen, who attempts a very different allegorical reading: "The kingly-crowned head, the vigilant eye, / The counselor heart, the arm our soldier, / Our steed the leg, the tongue our trumpeter," and the belly, "the sink [cesspool] o' th' body" (1.1.114–16, 121). This reading denigrates the senatorial belly while assigning elevated functions to the plebeian members—although it also, somewhat confusingly, implies a monarchical view of the body in question (the "kingly-crowned head"). Strikingly, neither the First Citizen's allegory nor Agrippa's persuades anyone of its validity, a failure that suggests the general inadequacy of rhetoric in the Rome of Shakespeare's play. Equally interesting is a rather different use of the figure by the English rhetorician Richard Rainolde, who declares that the human body was created by God as a "Microcosmos, a little worlde" (*Foundacion*, vi^v), and who interprets the fable as saying that just as all the body's parts, even the meanest, are valuable, so "in a kyngdome, or common wealth, the moste meane and basest state of man taken awaie, the more principall [i.e., the upper classes] thereby ceaseth: So God to a mutuall concorde, frendship, and perpetuall societie of life, hath framed his creatures" (vi^v–vii^r). Thomas Wilson prefaces his presentation of the fable with a lengthy discussion of the usefulness of fables in managing the responses of popular audiences which are composed primarily of fools who "can not brooke sage causes" and whom he denominates, as

---

[37] Shakespeare's plays are cited by act, scene, and line from *The Complete Works*.

noted above, "a beast, or rather a monster that hath many heddes." For Wilson the people are a monstrous version of the body politic, one naturally suffering from disunity and fractiousness, so that his retelling of Agrippa's fable, which contains a repetition of their rebellion, also offers a cure for it: "Undoubtedly fables well set forth, have done much good at divers times, and in divers Commonweales. The Romaine *Menenius Agrippa*, alledging upon a time, a Fable of the conflict made betwixt the parts of a mans bodie, and his bellie: quieted a marveilous stirre that was like to ensue, and pacified the uprore of sedicious Rebelles, which els thought for ever to destroy their Countrey." (*Arte*, 198). Like Shakespeare and Rainolde, Wilson makes an explicit connection between the body in the fable and the body politic, and he also suggests, in emphasizing the orderliness of the orator's speech ("fables well set foorth"), that there is a profound identity between the "body" of eloquent discourse and the ideal "body" of the state.

If the fable of the belly dramatizes Renaissance notions of the power of eloquence, the necessity of rule by those at the top of the social hierarchy, and the ideal state as a beautiful and harmonious body, it also performs an important function for the orator himself: it makes him the source of the language by means of which the political order is defined, thus assigning him an indispensable place within it. In fact, his inclusion in the state is enacted within the fable itself, for insofar as readers are led to infer that Menenius Agrippa is a member of the senatorial class, he is implicitly identified with the aristocratic belly for which he is the spokesman. Thus, the nourishment the belly dispenses to the other "members" of the body politic can be equated not just with the food supplied by generous patricians but also with the orator's words, which are credited with healing that body and which help create and sustain it as well. Of course, not all versions of the fable permit the reader to link the orator with the belly. In the work of William Camden, for instance, Pope Adrian equates the Church with the belly and uses the fable to argue that all the tribute given to it is justified. In Adrian's account Agrippa disappears, his place being taken by the heart and the reason: the members of the body, wasting away, called a meeting and "with one accord desired the advise of the Heart. Then Reason layd open before them that hee against whome they had proclaimed warres, was the cause of all this their misery."[38] Nevertheless, even though a literal orator does not appear here, the fable still grants him a place in

---

[38] William Camden, *Remaines of a Greater Worke Concerning Britaine*, cited in Geoffrey Bullough, ed., *Narrative and Dramatic Sources of Shakespeare* (London: Routledge & Kegan Paul, 1964), 5:552.

the body politic since his function is performed by either the heart or the reason, who serve as advisers to the other afflicted parts.

Perhaps the most emphatic identification of the orator with the belly occurs in Shakespeare's *Coriolanus*, which clarifies what at best remains implicit in most other accounts. Those accounts take their cue from Livy, who never allows the belly to speak and who has recourse to an impersonal construction at the crucial moment of realization, a construction that utterly fails to identify who the responsible party is: "From this [wasting away] it became clear [*apparuisse*] that the belly, too, had no small function" (2.32.11). Livy may imply that the members of the body grasped how essential the belly was, but he avoids attributing this realization to anyone. By contrast, Shakespeare follows Plutarch's version of the fable (in his life of Coriolanus) rather than Livy's, although he greatly amplifies his source, elaborating the opposition of members and belly into an oratorical contest in which both get to speak, the members first accusing the belly of uselessness and the latter then taking up its own defense. Before coming to that defense, however, Agrippa interrupts his narrative in order to create suspense, and as he does so, he begins to impersonate and thereby identify himself with the belly. Thus, after having used indirect discourse to summarize the objections voiced by the members, Agrippa pauses with the incomplete phrase "The belly answer'd—" (1.1.103). When he is asked by the impatient First Citizen, "Well, sir, what answer made the belly?" (104), Agrippa's response is yet another delaying tactic:

> Sir, I shall tell you. With a kind of smile,
> Which ne'er came from the lungs, but even thus—
> For, look you, I may make the belly smile
> As well as speak—it tauntingly replied
> To th' discontented members, the mutinous parts
> That envied his receipt; even so most fitly
> As you malign our senators for that
> They are not such as you.
>
> (1.1.105–12)

When Agrippa refers to the belly's smile and says "even thus," one may well imagine that he himself smiles at his audience, just as his subsequent reference to the belly's taunting reply indicates the tone of his own speech. His delay also allows him to compare the mutinous citizens to the body's members. When Agrippa finally produces the belly's reply some twenty lines later, he drops the indirect discourse and begins mouthing the very words that organ speaks:

"True is it, my incorporate friends," quoth he [i. e., the belly],
"That I receive the general food at first
Which you do live upon; and fit it is,
Because I am the store-house and the shop
Of the whole body."

(1.1.129–33)

Agrippa continues this speech for another dozen lines, although he interrupts it once again for an exchange with his audience. In making the
belly speak, he employs the rhetorical figure of *prosopopeia*, which, in
Henry Peacham's definition, a speaker uses "when to a thing sencelesse
and dumbe we faine a fit person," the orator doing so "to no other end
then to further his purpose and to confirme and make his cause evident" (*Arte*, 136). Shakespeare's text makes it clear, however, that more
is involved than merely making one's case ("cause") more visually striking ("evident"), for *prosopopeia* also allows the orator momentarily to
become the thing he personifies, to imbue it with the life and force of
his bodily presence. Since Shakespeare's play prevents us from deciding
whether Agrippa is actually a member of the senatorial class (he refers
to "our senators" at 1.1.111), his move may even be read as a version of
the fantasy of social mobility that Renaissance rhetoricians expressed in
their works. In other words, Shakespeare's Agrippa does considerably
more than support the patricians' cause as he tells his story. Within the
allegory of the body politic he has constructed, by speaking the very
words of the belly he identifies himself with and thereby becomes, at
least in his imagination, the ruling class. Thus, *Coriolanus* shows how
the orator can use the fable of the belly to articulate his social and political indispensability, how he can inscribe himself in—and as—the very
bowels of the body politic.

In the Renaissance discourse of rhetoric the fable of the belly is an
ideological move, a piece of political theorizing that mystifies power
relationships in two ways: first, it asserts the putative naturalness of the
conventional hierarchical organization of the state; second, it justifies
the privileges of the ruling class, the senatorial belly, by presenting it
not as the beneficiary of the labor of others but—falsely—as the source
of nourishment for the entire body politic. One would thus expect the
fable to serve a conservative agenda of validating the status quo, something we have seen rhetoricians otherwise frequently engaged in doing.
As *Coriolanus* suggests in its own way, however, it is entirely possible
for a specific version of the fable to complicate or even undercut its
ostensible ideological function. In this regard, consider what Thomas
Wilson does. Although he invokes the story to illustrate how useful

fables can be in persuasion, he restricts his summary of it to just one short sentence. This move may be explained as a matter of aesthetic tact, an unwillingness to repeat a story already extremely well known, but it might also be read as a political gesture anything but conservative in character. For Wilson follows that single sentence by rehearsing at length a quite different fable used by Themistocles to persuade the Athenians not to change their governing officials. This fable concerns a "scabbed Foxe" whose body is fed upon by numerous flies. The fox is persuaded to have them shooed away, "whereupon there ensued such hungrie flies afterwards, that the sorie Foxe being all alone, was eaten up almost to the hard bone." Themistocles explains to the Athenians that they are the fox and their officials the flies, and that the fox is better off keeping his usual flies about him "because thei are filled and have enough, that heretofore suckt so much of your bloud" (*Arte*, 198). Like the fable of the belly, Themistocles' fable appears to justify the status quo—the continuing rule of the officials in question—but it can actually be read as simultaneously undermining it. Whereas Agrippa's story presents the ruling class/belly as the source of nutrition for the state, the story of the fox identifies the ruling class/flies as predators, sucking the blood of the people rather than supplying them with its nutrients, as the belly does in Livy. The tale of the fox thus not only criticizes the ruling class, whose continuing dominance it "justifies" only as the lesser of two evils, but also implicitly critiques the fable of the belly, which mystifies privilege as natural and essential to the state. Wilson's embrace of such a critical position in this passage is compatible with the frequency of satirical passages in his work and his tendency to lionize such skeptics as Socrates (147), Erasmus (39), and Diogenes (200). Indeed, in the conclusion to his section on fables he briefly considers feigned narrations, praising Lucian and "Thomas More for his *Eutopia*" (199), a pair of writers who, like the others cited, were social critics and masters of Menippean satire, just as Wilson himself may be said to be.

Like Wilson, the English rhetorician Richard Rainolde is also a defender of the status quo whose presentation of the fable of the belly actually undermines its seemingly conservative purpose. Rainolde begins the section of his book devoted to fables by retelling Aesop's story of the shepherds who were persuaded by an offer of peace from the wolves to give up their dogs, with the result that the dogs were killed and the sheep harmed. Rainolde then shows the student of rhetoric how to expand this fable: one should praise its author, summarize its moral—the "cloked and fained frendship, of the wicked and ungodlie" (*Foundacion*, v^v)—and dilate upon the nature of wolves, dogs, sheep, and shepherds. Considering the last, he declares that "thoughe meane," the shepherd "is a right profitable and necessarie member, to serve all states in the commonwealthe" (vi^v). The identification of the shepherd as a *member* of the commonwealth prompts Rainolde to imagine the latter as a body analogous to the human one, which brings him to the fable of the belly. Menenius Agrippa used it, he says, in order to lead the people and Senate of Rome "to a concorde, and unitee," and it shows that the "vilest parte of the bodie, and baseste is so necessarie, that the whole bodie faileth and perisheth, the same wantyng, although nature removeth them from our sight, and shame fastnes also hideth theim" (vi^v). Rainolde reinforces this interpretation as he returns to the original fable: "The Prince and chief peres doe decaie, and al the whole multitude dooe perishe: the baseste kinde of menne wantyng. Remove the Shepeherdes state, what good followeth, yea, what lacke and famine increaseth not: to all states the belie ill fedde, our backes worse clad" (vii^r). In essence, Rainolde has reversed the fable the Renaissance inherited from Livy. Whereas for everyone else the belly is equated with the aristocracy, here it has become the lower classes, whose low status— and hence implicit association with dirt—may be responsible for the slippage in the passage from the belly to those parts of the body, the genitals, which "nature removeth . . . from our sight, and shame fastnes also hideth." Rainolde makes the fable of the belly speak for those base parts, thereby transforming it from a justification of upper-class privilege into a defense of the essential value of even the lowliest members of the body politic. Perhaps he does so because, like Wilson, indeed like most rhetoricians, he is not in fact a member of the ruling class and thus feels a need to justify himself in this way. At the same time, he seeks social advancement by a more conservative route, conspicuously dedicating his work to Elizabeth's favorite, Robert Dudley, the Earl of Leicester. Thus, like his fellow rhetoricians, Rainolde registers a fundamental ambivalence about the social order: he is willing to endorse the privileged position and prerogatives of the ruling class, but he is also anxiously driven to defend his own value as essential to the well-being of the state, since that value is the basis of his claim for advancement. In fact, his revision of the fable of the belly actually bespeaks the powerful drive for advancement animating him, for it effectively puts him— and other commoners, "shepherds"—in the place normally assigned the ruling class: that is, the belly, in Livy's fable. Through his revision Rainolde achieves a vicarious social elevation while dramatizing the vital role he plays in the commonwealth, and he thereby gives his work a subversive character that belies his deference to the status quo. What is more, he undermines the interpretations of the fable of the belly which one generally encounters in Renaissance rhetoric, revealing as a self-serving illusion the vision of a harmonious body and body politic promoted by the aristocracy, while destroying as groundless fantasy the rhetorician's own unproblematic incorporation into the state.

Ironically, the repeated rehearsals of the fable of the belly within the Renaissance discourse of rhetoric testify not to rhetoricians' confidence in their social centrality, but to their keen sense of exposure and insufficiency. Moreover, as they seek to incorporate their art and its practitioners into the vision of a well-arranged, self-contained, decorous, and dignified body, one that does not violate boundaries and is free from any taint of moral duplicity, the very defensiveness of their maneuver calls attention to the contrary image of rhetoric, which they want to occlude. It reminds the reader that certain fundamental aspects of the art leave it open to attack as immoral, low, grotesque. What is most devastating to their celebration of rhetoric, however, is that they endow their good version of the art with features that make it seem as morally and socially compromised and in some ways as grotesque as its rejected double.

In the first place, despite the rhetoricians' insistence on the orator's probity, ethics remains a problem for him precisely because *ethos* always is. On the one hand, *ethos* is seen as something *expressed* by the speaker, welling up from within him and revealing his character. This notion appears in such assertions as Luis de Granada's that the orator must feel the emotions he would implant in his auditors: "Our first care should be that affects and emotions are in us, for then they will burst forth by their own natural force, and as they are true emotions, they will truly affect our auditors" (*Ecclesiastica Rhetorica*, 359).[39] Bartolomeo Cavalcanti is even more insistent: "Speech reveals our interior and hidden sentiments, and is almost a mirror in which our spirit can be perceived" (*Retorica*, 216). Henry Peacham styles the orator's mouth "a plentifull fountaine, both to powre forth the inward passions of his heart, and also . . . a heavenly planet to shew forth, (by the shining beames of speech) the privie thoughts and secret conceites of his mind" (*Garden*, iii[r]; cf. 47, 64, 105).[40] On the other hand, *ethos* is also seen as

---

[39] Shuger writes that certain aspects of Granada's *Ecclesiastica Rhetorica* "indicate a movement away from the Ciceronian emphasis on aural rhythm and periodicity toward a greater stress on emotional expressiveness—a movement found throughout Renaissance rhetoric" (*Sacred Rhetoric*, 77).

[40] For other examples, see Vives, *De Ratione*, 130; Alsted, *Rhetorica*, 5; Puttenham, *Arte*, 160–61; Giovanni Pontano, *Ad Alfonsum Calabriae ducem de principe liber*, in *Prosatori latini*, 1060; and Gerbiers, *The Art of Well Speaking*, 23. John Bulwer, writing about the use of gestures, says they reveal the mind of the speaker (*Chironomia*, 157).

something one constructs—by means of rhetoric, of course. It is, in other words, a matter of art rather than nature. Thus, although Cavalcanti may present speech as the mirror of the spirit, he almost immediately counters this assertion: "We should not doubt that it can be so formed that our nature appears in it and that certain customs almost shine through it, customs which, expressed thus, can acquire authority and belief for us" (*Retorica*, 216). As Cavalcanti details the particular qualities our speech should manifest as our nature so that we are accounted good men, *ethos* is clearly a construct and just as clearly thrusts the rhetor into the realm of seeming—and, potentially, deceiving. Although Cavalcanti warns that in trying to project a religious character orators should take pains not to appear *simulatori* (217), his conception of *ethos* actually makes such a charge more, rather than less, likely. Since gestures and looks also play a role in the manufacture of *ethos*, Luis de Granada, who insists (as noted above) that the orator must feel the emotions he wishes to instill in his audience, says that he should "put on in delivery, as it were, his very own looks and facial appearance which he impresses on and represents [*affigit & repraesentet*] to the minds of his auditors" (*Ecclesiastica Rhetorica*, Praefatio, n.p.). For Granada, even the orator's body is a representation, a fiction. Renaissance rhetoricians in general want to have it both ways, to see *ethos* as an expression of a determined, individual identity and, at the same time, as the result of the rhetor's verbal artifice. They create confusion by desiring the impossible, that *ethos* should be at once nature and art, reality and appearance, authentic and inauthentic.[41]

Renaissance rhetoricians are most ambiguous about the ethical status of their art precisely when one might expect just the opposite: that is, when they unfold the contagion theory and insist that the orator can move others only if he is first moved himself. The display of feeling would seem to be the authentic act par excellence, yet it is hardly a matter of wearing one's heart on one's sleeve. Vives, for instance, claims that the orator "will move the emotions [of others] by a certain connection of nature, if he is truly moved or simulates well that he has been moved [*probe simulet se motum*]" (*De Ratione*, 166). Similarly, Guillaume Du Vair speaks of "passions which the orator seizes or

---

[41] For other examples see Puttenham, *Arte*, 152; Du Vair, *Traitté*, 410; George of Trebizond, *Rhetoricorum*, 65ᵛ; Peacham, *Garden*, 68–69; and Guzman, *Primera Parte*, 160ʳ. To some extent, Renaissance rhetoricians take their cue from the ancient world. Aristotle states that to be persuasive the orator should either have a good character or *appear to have one* (*Rhetoric*, 2.1.7); Quintilian attempts to hierarchize that ambiguity: "Aristotle thinks that the strongest argument derives from the speaker's character if he is a good man, which, as it is best, so it transcends merely seeming to be good, although that seeming is acceptable too" (*Institutio*, 5.12.9).

feigns" (*Traitté*, 410). Rudolph Agricola not only accepts the notion that the orator may feign his emotions but provides a kind of justification for his doing so: "It makes no difference to the emotions [of the auditor] whether something is thus or only appears to be so" (*De Inventione*, 330). And Sir Philip Sidney takes a step beyond Agricola, insisting that feigned examples actually move people better than real or historical ones (*Apology*, 33).[42]

Although the key terms we have been reviewing here—"feign," "simulate," "seem"—do not inevitably suggest moral turpitude, that is often what Renaissance rhetoric texts imply. The notions of feigning and the fictional are still, to some degree, unstable concepts in the period. Sidney's careful defensive arguments that the poet merely offers us fictions of what should or should not be, and that since he "nothing affirms," he "therefore never lieth" (*Apology*, 57), actually show just how close feigning and lying were in the minds of Renaissance thinkers.[43] A revealing comparison may be made between Sidney and Rainolde, who wrote just a few short years earlier. Both writers consider fables valuable teaching devices, but whereas Sidney sees them as fictions, not lies, Rainolde says that a "fable is a forged tale, containing in it by the colour of a lie, a matter of truthe" (*Foundacion*, ii^v). Rainolde identifies that "truthe" as the moral kernel of the fable which the orator extracts from beneath its lying exterior. Indeed, the confusion between feigning (or "forging") and lying is revealed in a casual comment made by yet another sixteenth-century English rhetorician, Leonard Coxe, who uses the two terms in a doublet: "It is the nature of poetes to fayne and lye."[44] And when George of Trebizond argues that feigned arguments will be effective only if mixed with true ones, he opposes the truth (*verum*) indiscriminately to both the false (*falsum*) and the feigned (*finguntur*) (*Rhetoricorum*, 5^v–6^r), so that these last two concepts blur in his work, just as they do throughout the Renaissance discourse of rhetoric. Consequently, when rhetoricians tell the orator to simulate emotions or virtues, his creating of fictions would have inevitably raised the specter of fraud in the period and made him morally suspect.

Despite efforts to present the orator as a *vir bonus*, Renaissance rhetoricians undermine his moral authority by using terms that make him a trickster and deceiver. For instance, Thomas Wilson wants the orator to vary the arguments at the conclusion of an oration, "for if the repetition

---

[42] For other examples, see Valla, *Rhetorica*, II.i^v; Soarez, *De Arte*, 328; Hoskins, *Directions for Speech and Style*, 25; and Latomus, *Summa*, D7^r.

[43] Note that a very similar argument is offered by Boccaccio more than two centuries earlier; see *On Poetry*, 62–63.

[44] Coxe, *The Arte or Crafte of Rhethoryke*, Bv^r.

should be naked, and only set forth in plaine words without any chaunge of speech, or shift of *Rhetorique,* neither should the hearers take pleasure, nor yet the matter take effect" (*Arte,* 114). Note how Wilson doubles the word "chaunge" here by calling it a "shift," a word that may simply mean "garment"—the garment of style—but can also mean "trick" or "stratagem" or "deceit," thus evoking the idea of fraud. George of Trebizond makes a similar misstep when he discusses *ductus,* the conducting or managing of an oration. *Ductus,* he says, can be either *simplex,* if one simply says directly what is the case, or *figuratus,* "when, although the very nature of the case requires us to do something different than what we want, and it does seem to be done in that way, nevertheless our auditors are forced, in a most secret manner [*occultius*], to take the direction we want" (*Rhetoricorum,* 49ʳ). Sometimes the idea of deception is suggested by a rhetorician's discussion of style, as when Puttenham defines tropes and figures as being "in a sorte abuses or rather trespasses in speach, because they passe the ordinary limits of common utterance, and be occupied of purpose to deceive the eare and also the minde" (*Arte,* 166). Consider as well Guillaume Du Vair's explanation of why modern orators should study the works of Aeschines and Demosthenes: they "will recognize there the ruses and sleights-of-hand [*les ruses & tours de souplesse*] of the orators of that time who by means of great artifice managed one of the most subtle and ingenious peoples who ever lived" (*Traitté,* 410). In Du Vair's conception rhetoric is a battle of wits, and the orator who wins does so because of his *ruses & tours de souplesse,* which make him look like a mountebank or charlatan.

If Renaissance rhetoricians fail to insulate good rhetoric from charges of immorality, they also fail to ensure its upper-class status when they make the art of kings look like the show of a lower-class swindler. This slippage may be inevitable, since good rhetoric, like bad, is intended for all audiences; the danger of contamination by contact with the "low" is thus inevitable. More important, the fact that the orator's *ethos* is constructed, that it changes both from speech to speech and even within the same speech, exposes him to social degradation by making him look like an actor. This possibility remains merely a potentiality in most rhetoric books, as when George of Trebizond notes that Cicero's identity shifts from speech to speech (*Rhetoricorum,* 80ᵛ), or when Angel Day's samples in his letter-writing manual involve his becoming a host of different people. Even the orator's use of figures implicitly entails his acting of a variety of parts, as George Puttenham suggests when he fancifully "Englishes" Greek rhetorical terms, personifying tropes and figures: the figure of disorder called *hyperbaton* becomes "the Trespasser";

hypallage, which puts a wrong word in place of a right, is "the Change-ling"; and *paradiastole,* which turns the worst sense to the best, is iden-tified with flattery and dubbed "the Curry favell" (*Arte,* 180, 182, 195).[45] As Puttenham's poet uses these figures, he implicitly assumes the char-acters they represent. Rudolph Agricola explicitly connects such self-representation to the idea of acting when he speaks of how the orator's language must have "color" (*De Inventione,* 332), a word with two dis-tinct but related meanings. First, Agricola follows medieval rhetoricians who identify figures of speech as *colores;* second, he returns to the an-cients, for whom "color" meant the particular emotional tonality or shading an orator gives an entire speech.[46] Thus, Agricola uses one word to link style with the "expression" of emotion and character. He then observes that "although many people say exactly the same thing whether they are expounding or arguing, nevertheless, one of them ex-hibits the color of a person who advises, another that of one who is angry, another that of one complaining, another that of one grieving" (332). Revealingly, when Agricola illustrates his point by speaking of the *colores* or different characters adopted by satirists, he switches his met-aphor and refers to *personae* instead. *Persona* can be translated as "char-acter," but its root meaning is "mask," specifically the mask worn by an actor. Thus, not only does Agricola's discussion dramatize the fact that the orator's character is a construct, but by making him an actor it confirms his lower-class status and renders him indistinguishable on this score from his negative counterpart.

He is also indistinguishable at times on another score, for although rhetoricians emphasize the beauty and decorousness of the body associ-ated with good rhetoric, some of its aspects actually evoke the grotesque body of its contrary. Chapter 3 has already demonstrated that good rhet-oric is hermaphroditic, both male and female, a figuration making it unmistakably grotesque. But good rhetoric is also grotesque because of its emphasis on *copia* and *amplificatio,* the means by which the rhetor expands his text. This expansion betrays an anxiety about the inability of words, no matter how many are used, ever to bring us into real con-tact with the world, and it simultaneously generates a complementary anxiety that the process of dilation itself will get completely out of hand.[47] The emphasis on *copia,* or plenty, is responsible for the naming

---

[45] On the psychologizing of figures in Puttenham, see Plett, *Rhetorik der Affekte,* 81.

[46] On the difference between medieval and classical notions of "color," see Murphy, *Rhetoric in the Middle Ages,* 39.

[47] The first anxiety is analyzed in Cave, *The Cornucopian Text,* esp. 3–34; the sec-ond in Parker, *Literary Fat Ladies,* chap. 2.

of rhetoric texts as storehouses or gardens or treasuries, and it also helps to account for the tendency among Renaissance rhetoricians to produce huge treatises, a tendency that reaches a climax of sorts in the seventeenth century with the immense volumes of writers such as Caussin, Keckermann, and Vossius.[48] Excessive size is, of course, one of the indicators of the monstrous. Although rhetoricians typically deny that they are recommending anything excessive, consider Thomas Wilson's discussion of amplification. Initially he says it will make the orator's work "vehement," "pleasant," and "well stored with copie" (*Arte*, 116), but later his terms shift: the orator who "can praise, or dispraise any thing plentifully, is able most copiously to exaggerate any matter" (117). The key verb "exaggerate" leaves him exposed to the charge that amplification is just another word for verbosity or excess, a charge that Wilson directly provokes with his next statement: "Againe, sentences gathered or heaped together, commende much the matter" (117–18). Despite his intention to praise amplification, when "copie" becomes "exaggeration" and then turns into a *"heap"* of sentences, the decorous body of oratory begins to take on a distressingly messy appearance.[49] Heaps are also a problem for Luis de Granada, who defines "Congeries," or "Heaping Up," as one of the prime techniques to achieve *amplificatio* (*Ecclesiastica Rhetorica*, 130), even though he earlier rejected the achievement of eloquence through "a tumultuous heaping up [*congeriem*] of words signifying the same thing" (39). Since "congeries," meaning a confused mass or pile, is a standard word used to define *copia* or *amplificatio*, the result is that whenever rhetoricians treat this topic, they inevitably make their art look too excessive, too disorganized, too grotesque for comfort.

Perhaps rhetoricians keep evoking grotesque bodies simply because rhetoric is inescapably grotesque by its nature. The grotesque is produced by boundary violations, and rhetoric is celebrated throughout the Renaissance for its ability to cross borders and infiltrate utterly disparate disciplines. Recall the passage in which Vives argues that rhetoric,

---

[48] On *copia* and the titles of Renaissance rhetorics, see Cahn, "The Eloquent Names of Rhetoric," 129–38. On the size of works by Caussin, Keckermann, and Vossius, see Conley, *Rhetoric in the European Tradition*, 157–62. Ramus and his followers often produced very short rhetorics, since they limited the art to *elocutio*, *actio*, and *memoria* and provided merely brief definitions and limited examples. In a sense, however, the Ramists were antirhetorical rhetoricians. Writers who attempted to teach all the parts of rhetoric felt a need to be comprehensive, as the thousand pages of Caussin's *Eloquentia sacra* testify.

[49] Cf. Hoskins, whose enumerated techniques for achieving amplification include "accumulation," the heaping up of terms of praise or abuse (*Directions for Speech and Style*, 24).

"like a kind of universal tool, has been diffused through all things of which we speak" (*De Causis*, 159); to be "diffused through all things" means to violate the boundaries that keep those things apart. According to Alsted, this capacity of rhetoric is an attribute of its noble nature: "This lady does not have any fixed region within whose boundaries she is fenced in, but she has equipment which all teachers of all subjects can use to adorn letters, dialogues, orations, sermons, consultations, and the like" (*Rhetorica*, 5–6). Du Pré de la Porte praises rhetoric in similar terms: "It seems that rhetoric is nowhere a stranger and that everything which the mind is capable of handling derives from her domain" (*Pourtraict*, 62). And Guzman labels rhetoric a god because of its boundary-crossing metamorphic ability: "I say that rhetoric is neither more nor less than another Proteus who turns himself into everything he desires and takes everything as his material" (*Primera Parte*, 15ᵛ).

Guzman's reference to Proteus makes his—and others'—celebrations of rhetoric most problematic, for Proteus is hardly a heroic figure, nor is his ability to shift his shape entirely attractive. Generally, although the boundary crossing that Proteus represents may spell freedom and creativity for many thinkers in the Renaissance, it is simultaneously threatening, since it seems to unsettle the stable structure of the universe.[50] Although Guzman responds positively to Proteus, just as other rhetoricians do to the boundary-crossing capacity of their art, their readers may well have been disturbed by such matters. Revealingly, rhetoricians themselves sometimes betray a nervousness about the protean nature of their art. For instance, since they often regard tropes as *violations* of proper signification—remember that the chief trope, metaphor, bears in its very name the idea of boundary crossing—they then feel compelled to legitimate them by distinguishing proper from improper forms. Thus, Luis de Granada defines a trope as "the changing of a word or a locution in a correct manner [*cum virtute*] from its proper signification into another" (*Ecclesiastica Rhetorica*, 231). Even more striking, when Nicholas Caussin says metaphor is "the transfer of a certain word usurped [*usurpata*] from its proper referent to an improper one" (*Eloquentia sacra*, 401), the strong sense of impropriety in *usurpata* leads him immediately to distinguish proper from improper metaphor on the basis of the similarity (*similitudo*) between the two words or notions involved: "One should not always exchange metaphors; it was fitting for the poet to call the foot of the mountain its root, but not to call the foot of a man his root" (414). Caussin's attempt here to insist on decorum, on what is fitting, is doomed, for it is not clear

[50] On Proteus in the Renaissance, see Giamatti, "Proteus Unbound," 437–75.

what supposedly transparent, unimpeachable standard makes one metaphor decorous and another not—especially since just a few sentences
later he declares that the best metaphors are those that impart sense to
inanimate objects, "as [when one says] of a weapon: it desires to fly into
the opposing army" (414). Nor can one help but note that all Caussin's
metaphors mix and confuse categories as they violate boundaries. In essence, metaphors create monsters, whether one imagines people and
mountains with roots or weapons with desires.

One of the best examples of Renaissance nervousness about the protean nature of rhetoric is contained in a passage near the end of Antonio
Riccobono's *Oratio pro studiis humanitatis* (Speech on behalf of the
humanities). After alluding to Aristotle's claim that oratory has all subjects for its province, he declares:

> Although the special function of the orator is to treat of civil matters,
> nevertheless eloquence has not been circumscribed with railings, has
> no fixed borders and established limits for itself. It wanders and sallies
> forth wherever it pleases, and disputes of all things even pertaining to
> other disciplines so that it makes them its own. Nor should one think
> [*censenda est*] it has gone outside its limits and seized [*occupare*]
> those things which belong to others, since by means of its industry it
> cultivates the enormous field of all things which is open to all.[51]

Over and over this passage repeats the notion that rhetoric is a dynamic
activity free to cross boundaries as it wishes and to take possession of
(*occupare*) what it encounters. Riccobono celebrates rhetoric for its mal-
leability and power; for him as for so many others in the Renaissance, it
is the supremely imperial art. Nevertheless, despite his enthusiasm, he
allows a certain misgiving about rhetoric's capacity for boundary violation to surface when he insists that because it cultivates the territory it
invades, its violation of proper limits should not be seen as such. This
attempt at rationalization actually underscores the potential immorality
involved in violating boundaries and reveals that an imperialistic power
grab cannot be mystified as just a matter of farming.

By crossing boundaries, rhetoric, like Furetière's Galimatias, has the
potential to create intellectual, social, and political confusion—a problem rhetoricians normally prefer to ignore, although in his brief panegyric on eloquence Walter Haddon gets carried away and actually
praises the art for turning things topsy-turvy: "Pericles, the ruler of
Athens, since he was so very effective in speaking, was said to have

---

[51] Riccobono, *Oratio*, cited in Mazzacurati, *La crisi della retorica umanistica*, 176.

mixed up [*permiscere*] all of Greece with his lightning and thunder."[52]
As we saw in Chapter 2, the critics of rhetoric lambasted it for precisely
this capacity, which they associated with sedition and rebellion, and
their attacks prompted its defenders to insist that their art was a source
of order, a cure for ills which, ironically, rhetoric itself helped to produce. Still, many of them recognized that the doctor himself was sick
and sought, in consequence, to reform the art they practiced. This effort
explains not merely the endless production of rhetoric books in the period, all promising to correct the defects of their predecessors, but the
radical redefinition of the discipline undertaken by Peter Ramus and his
followers. Ramus himself was building on the pioneering work undertaken by Rudolph Agricola, and we can grasp the energy directing their
reforming efforts by noting the latter's dismay at the great confusion,
the filthiness (*colluvies*), which he saw afflicting the realm of learning.
Agricola laments: "All things, as though they had sprung out of a cave,
have burst through the rightful bounds [*ius & fines*] of their neighbors,
nor do we learn almost anything at this time in its proper place" (*De
Inventione*, 142–43). Agricola's view of boundary violation here is
purely negative: it is filth and confusion and an assault against what is
right (*ius*).[53] But as we have seen, rhetoric is by its very nature a boundary violator, and that means that although it may be liberating in some
constructions, it will always be threatening, despite the best efforts of
rhetoricians to make it appear otherwise. Whether good or bad, it will
always be a monster, so that to banish the monster means nothing less
than to banish rhetoric itself. Such a move is impossible, of course, for
as Vives and Riccobono and countless others knew, rhetoric is infused
in all things, present wherever language is in use. To paraphrase that
master of rhetoric Falstaff: to banish the monster of rhetoric is to banish
communication, banish human society, banish all the world.

Despite its obsession with drawing firm boundaries between good and
bad rhetoric, Furetière's *Nouvelle allégorique* also demonstrates that
the two are, finally, inseparable and that real banishment is impossible.
Note that when Queen Rhétorique finally defeats Galimatias, her victory results from her decision to "make use of ruse and adroitness
[*adresse*]" (96) rather than to meet her enemy in battle. Her reliance on
"ruse," on trickery, here makes her look like the *équivoques*, Lady Chicane, and all her other enemies, thus undoing the moral distinction
Furetière sets up between the two versions of rhetoric. What is more,

---

[52] Haddon, *De laudibus eloquentiae*, 5.

[53] Ramus is likewise obsessed with the idea of maintaining sharp boundaries between discrete subjects, an obsession that helps drive his program of reform; see his
Attack on Cicero, 22, 42.

the pairing of *ruse* with *adresse* actually undermines the positive conception of the human body which, we claimed earlier, informs Furetière's vision of good rhetoric. Because of that pairing, the adroitness displayed by the crafty rhetorician suggests a cunning physical maneuvering, a contorted twisting and squirming out of tight places which make the rhetor resemble his demonic twin, the déclassé acrobat, magician, or ropedancer. Ironically, Furetière's use of language actually convicts the art he would defend. In fact, his attempt to keep good and bad rhetoric separate is doomed from the start, if only because the two share many of the same properties and attributes: that is, the same followers. Though most of the *équivoques* are banished to Galimatias's realm, for instance, a number of them do stay behind with Rhétorique; both rulers make use of *authorités* and of Greek and Latin authors; and harangues serve in both armies. Furetière generalizes: the troops composing the queen's army are "for the most part of the same nature as those who served in the enemy camp," the only difference being that her followers are "better disciplined and seasoned" (27). Moreover, when the war is over and peace arranged, the treaty ironically completes the blurring of distinctions between the two realms: it cedes Dicae and Homilaire to Galimatias but insists on the queen's right to appoint the individuals who manage those regions; it allows Galimatias's follower Captain Hableur (Bragging) to live at Rhétorique's court; and it permits his other followers to enter her realm on occasion, provided they identify themselves by wearing dirty clothing. Moreover, Rhétorique lets some of her opponent's subjects—the well-behaved ones—purchase goods in her kingdom, implicitly on the basis of the principle of "free trade" (104: *la liberté du commerce*). In fact, the constant trade permitted by the treaty means that the boundaries between the two realms will be transgressed repeatedly, thus undoing the effects of a war that originated with an invasion and was fought ostensibly to reestablish the violated boundaries. This treaty provision reminds us that absolutist France was also a mercantilist power and recognized that the health of those at the center depended on commerce with those on the periphery and beyond, just as the military maintenance of its empire made it dependent on the common people and on the French who lived "beyond the Loire." The treaty that denies the monstrous Galimatias entry through the front door of Rhétorique's kingdom lets him in at once through the back. And from the viewpoint of rhetoric, this procedure is absolutely right. Furetière's final insistence on *la liberté du commerce* not only reconfirms the essential identity—the exchangeability—of Rhétorique and Galimatias but reminds us that the principle of free movement and the violation of proper boundaries it entails are, after all, the defining features of the art.

Furetière's text can be construed as a rite of purification, which would banish the monster of bad rhetoric in order to preserve the good version of the art left behind. As such, it speaks to an important historical development in Renaissance culture which Peter Burke has documented in his *Popular Culture in Early Modern Europe.*[54] According to Burke, the beginning and end of the period are marked by strikingly different responses to folk and popular culture on the part of the upper classes. At the start, the members of those classes share the culture of the common people while possessing a second one based on literacy and formal training; by the end, those classes have withdrawn from that first culture entirely, rejecting its literature and art and ceasing to participate in popular festivities. They have also internalized an *ethos* based on self-control and reason according to which popular activities appear crude, superstitions are to be mocked, and figures such as mountebanks and quacks ridiculed. They define themselves, in other words, both positively in terms of values such as rationality and restraint, and negatively against the lower classes and the typical activities those classes indulged in. Although Burke never speaks of opposed visions of the body, one can easily see a similarity between what he argues about developments in Renaissance culture between 1500 and 1650 and the position of Mikhail Bakhtin, who, associating the classical body with the upper classes and the grotesque one with the people, claims that the two bodies and cultures existed side by side in the Middle Ages, merged briefly in the early Renaissance, and then were driven apart definitively by the triumph of absolutism. Furetière's *Nouvelle*, appearing at the moment of that triumph, represents an end-point for the historical process Burke and Bakhtin describe.

Hints of that process can be found in the discourse of rhetoric, since beginning with George of Trebizond's *Rhetoricorum Libri V* of the 1430s, rhetoricians shape their works around the oppositions analyzed in this chapter and through them strive to distance the rhetor from the popular culture about him. That we are dealing with a *process* in the case of rhetoric can be seen if we compare Furetière's work with that of his predecessor Thomas Wilson, whose *Arte of Rhetorique* appeared in 1553. Like all the other Renaissance rhetoricians, Wilson sets up an op-

---

[54] Burke, *Popular Culture in Early Modern Europe.* See also Stalleybrass and White, *The Politics and Poetics of Transgression*, esp. chap. 1.

position between good and bad rhetoric in terms of ethics, class, and the body. Accordingly, as we have seen, he warns the orator "to avoyd all grosse bourding [joking], and alehouse jesting, but also to eschue all foolish talke, and Ruffine maners, such as no honest eares can once abide, nor yet any wittie man can like well or allowe" (137–38). This quotation implies that the orator is—or aspires to be—a member of the upper classes whose behavior must separate him from those below him. Wilson's position is more complicated, however, for despite his warnings against language and gestures that could lower the orator socially, he declares that the use of merry tales and witty quips is essential to the art, for they are so powerful that they permit even a "varlet or common jesture . . . to abashe a right worthie man" (135). Thus, for the orator to succeed, Wilson believes he must from time to time be a clown: "Even these auncient Preachers, must now and then play the fooles in the pulpit, to serve the tickle eares of their fleting audience, or els they are like sometimes to preach to the bare walles" (3–4; cf. 101). Wilson does seem grudging in commending the role of fool, but he offers a much more positive evaluation when he catalogues his "heroes," who include Erasmus (39), Socrates and More (147), Lucian and Diogenes (199–200). All these figures are master satirists and ironists who not only mock the monstrous world around them but often play the fool and even include themselves among the mocked. In other words, they engage in precisely the kind of self-reflexive satire that Bakhtin insists is typical of the carnivalesque and of popular culture. Wilson's clearest embracing of this culture occurs when he is attacking the common practice he sees among contemporary rhetors of using "darke wordes" and inkhorn terms (162). To illustrate what he means, instead of denouncing things from a superior, detached position, he interrupts the flow of his text with a letter, supposedly written by a Lincolnshire man, which is almost incomprehensible—and very funny—because of its verbosity and Latinate diction. Wilson wants us to laugh at the letter and its writer, and just before he cites it, he declares it "such a letter as William Sommer himsefe, could not make a better for that purpose" (163). The reference to Will Summers, Henry VIII's famous jester, not only identifies the letter as a stylized clown act but lets us see that Wilson himself is taking on Summers's role. By supplying the letter, in other words, Wilson temporarily abandons his usual dignified posture of teacher and speaks with the voice of the self-parodying fool. He becomes the clown-satirist, both the mocker and the mocked, a person not only witty in himself, as Falstaff would say, "but the cause that wit is in other men."

By contrast, the satire in Furetière's much later work is quite straightforward. The author never plays the clown, as Wilson recommends and sometimes does himself. Furetière instead maintains a detached position well above the fray, mocking the grotesque bodies and behavior of Galimatias and his followers from the viewpoint of reason and restraint, never stooping to grimaces or gesticulations that would make him resemble those he satirizes. Anything but a buffoon or clown or trickster, Furetière is at one with the noble, polite, and *propre* people who are admitted to Rhétorique's court—just as, in real life, he would eventually become one of the forty "barons" in the Académie Française. Whereas Wilson still embraces the popular figure of the fool and identifies with other writers—such as Erasmus, More, and Socrates—who could be seen as doing likewise, Furetière looks down on the tradition of folk humor that focused on the grotesque body and seeks to expel it with ridicule from his world.

Far more insistently and dramatically than rhetoric manuals, literary works in the Renaissance characterize bad rhetoric as ethically suspect and socially ambiguous, while presenting the bad orator as a grotesque clown and trickster. What is more, those works mark a clearer progression than rhetoric texts do between the beginning of the period and the end, a progression going from a qualified tolerance of the orator-trickster to a fierce desire to banish him. Thus, in the *novelle* imitating Boccaccio's which were written in Italy during the fifteenth century, the fast-talking characters who figure as their protagonists are rarely defeated or expelled; on the contrary, they triumph in their duplicity and even seem at times to speak for the community as they deride and stigmatize the fools who are taken in by their rhetoric. Something similar might be said about the rhetor-princes who dominate the stage of society in Machiavelli's works, and it is notable that Erasmus, combining classical and folk traditions in his *Moriae Encomium*, makes its speaker an orator-trickster who may be the object of satire but who also mocks others tellingly and serves as the ironic mouthpiece for her creator's views. We noted earlier that Rabelais distinguishes good and bad rhetoric as two different versions of the human body, but although he clearly embraces something like the classical norm for his heroes, it is significant that Gargantua, even after the educational transformation that enables him to deliver elegant Ciceronian orations, remains a giant and engages in comic escapades. Moreover, the trickster Panurge, who produces the marvelous mock encomium on debts in the *Tiers Livre* as well as other rhetorical displays, remains a central figure in their world. By contrast, toward the end of the sixteenth century a lesser degree of tolerance for orator-tricksters appears in important literary texts. Here one thinks of such characters as the literally grotesque hunchback Richard III and the immense Falstaff; the host of scoundrels who people "city comedy" in England, including Ben Jonson's Volpone, Mosca, Face, Subtle, and Dol; the disfigured picaresque hero of Francisco de Quevedo's *La vida del buscón* (The life of the swindler); the treacherous Don Juans of Tirso and Molière; the fat, red-faced Tartuffe; and the literally diabolical, hideously ugly Satan of *Paradise Lost*. Even in this group there is a slight progression: Shakespeare and Jonson are rather more ambivalent about their orator-tricksters than later writers tend to be. Shakespeare, for instance, may have Falstaff banished at the end of *Henry IV, Part 2*, but throughout the *Henriad* he catalogues the triumphs of Henry V, who is also a master of rhetoric. And Jonson may have Volpone and Mosca imprisoned, and Subtle and Dol chased off in *The Alchemist*, but Face remains behind at the end, and the sharpers in *Epicoene* and *Bartholomew Fair* triumph in their plots. By the end of the Renaissance, however, in such texts as *Tartuffe*, the Don Juan plays, and *Paradise Lost*, there is no room for the orator-trickster at all.

To understand the reasons, in particular the political reasons, why the Renaissance became increasingly less tolerant of the orator-trickster, let us look briefly at three texts that span the period: Machiavelli's *La mandragola* of around 1519, Ben Jonson's *The Alchemist* of 1610, and Molière's *Tartuffe* of 1664. All three not only center on rhetorically adept tricksters but involve them in a specific kind of boundary violation: namely, they feature outsiders who intrude into, and in some sense usurp, someone else's house. *La mandragola*, for instance, has two protagonists: Callimaco, a gentleman who, having lived in France for many years, has no particular social attachments in Florence, where the play unfolds; and his "assistant," the utterly *déraciné* parasite Ligurio. By the end of the play, both Callimaco and Ligurio are firmly ensconced in the home of their dupe Nicia. Like Ligurio, the three tricksters in Jonson's comedy also have no "place" in society, although Face has achieved a position as a servant in the house which he and his two cronies take over to operate their swindle, a position he manages to preserve at the end of the play even though his master, Lovewit, has every good reason to chase him away. The title character in *Tartuffe* is a total outsider: he is lower class, lacks property and a place of abode, and is a provincial in a play full of Parisians comfortably installed in their own homes. Nevertheless, Tartuffe does not merely enter the house of his dupe Orgon, but actually gains legal possession of it, at least until, in the very last scene of the play, he is exposed and arrested by the agent of the king. With one exception, all these characters descend from the clever parasites and tricky slaves of Roman comedy, but they appear much less rooted in the social order than any of their ancestors and much more in need of all their skill with words if they are to survive in a world that has assigned no place to them. The one exception, Callimaco, in fact fits this pattern too, for although he is modeled on the youthful protagonists of Plautus and Terence, he differs from them in one significant way: whereas they have homes which are literally represented on the stage, he comes from outside Florence and has no definite position, no house, in the city. All these characters are driven by their appetites for food, money, and sex, but the deepest hunger motivating them is really an ontological one, a hunger for being, which derives from their totally mobile, unattached condition and which they attempt to satisfy both by exercising power over their prey and by taking possession of that prey's house.

It should be clear that all three plays deal generally with the social mobility marking Renaissance culture, a mobility that held out the promise of fortune and status to some while propelling many into poverty and subjecting others to a condition of dispossession and seemingly endless wandering. Social mobility is, as we saw in Chapter 2, a subject that obsesses rhetoricians throughout the period; it produces their deepest fear of social degradation and animates their keenest fantasy about social advancement: their notion that orators are or can become the emperors of men's minds. Profoundly expressive of both the fear and the fantasy, the orator-tricksters who appear in the plays of Machiavelli, Jonson, and Molière—like the orators who are imagined in handbooks and treatises—and like the rhetoricians who create them—are all rootless creatures who appear to come out of nowhere and are always just a short step away from descending back into the nameless, indeed "place"-less, places from which they have come. Driven by desperation, they all strive to raise themselves up through their mastery of language, using it to conquer and subdue to their own the wills of others. That they should seek to invade and possess the houses of their prey is consistent with their urge to rise, for it allows them to enter the social order and acquire a literal as well as symbolic place within it. The importance of the house as a place is indicated by the settings of the three plays, for in different ways they all represent it literally on the stage, thereby giving it a presence, a reality, for the audience as well as the characters. Those characters may come and go, but the house remains before our eyes; unchanging, secure, and stable, it is the locus of need and desire. Even Callimaco, who has money and status, is drawn to the house of his dupe, and by the end of the play he has gained entry into it as a permanent guest, with the promise from his dupe's wife that after her husband's death she will marry him, thus giving him absolute possession. The house serves as a trope for the political order; it is a microcosmic kingdom whose centrality harmonizes with the particular politics of the Renaissance, which, we have seen, is reflected in the discourse of rhetoric. Throughout the period, rule is conceived as the prerogative of hereditary princes whose houses—architectural, familial, political—stand at the symbolic centers of the states they control. In other words, just as Renaissance rhetoric texts conceive the rhetor's rule over his auditor in a way that adumbrates the centralizing politics of absolutism, so the orator-tricksters of Machiavelli, Jonson, and Molière seek to enter and possess a house that symbolizes the absolutist state. The authors thus allow their plays to be read as commentaries on the politics of absolutism in which all meaningful social movement can only involve an assault that aims to capture the center—or is defeated and expelled out toward the margins.

Reading the three plays in sequence, one notes that the orator-tricksters go from success to failure—and become increasingly less attractive in the process. In Machiavelli's comedy the entirety of the action is focused on Callimaco's and Ligurio's gaining access to the house of the archdupe Nicia and, in Callimaco's case, to Nicia's wife, Lucrezia. Their activities may be regarded as part of Machiavelli's satire, his denunciation of a society in disarray in which religion has ceased to have any meaningful function and whose members are driven by nothing more than their appetites for money, sex, and food. At the same time, Machiavelli's satire is double-edged, for he embraces those appetites and admires the energy driving his orator-tricksters as they carry out their complicated deception. Machiavelli's acceptance of these characters is revealed by his plot, which winds up satisfying not only those who perpetrate it but those who are its victims as well. Since Nicia and his wife are unable to have a child, Callimaco's success in getting into bed with her and the likelihood of her pregnancy, which Nicia thinks *he* has caused, guarantees his happiness as well as that of the adulterous couple. Moreover, the play emphasizes that this comic "solution" to Nicia's problem, this "cure" for the "disease" of sterility and unhappiness, is a restoration of health and a rebirth that Callimaco brings about both by playing his role as "doctor" and by undergoing a symbolic death and resurrection in Lucrezia's arms. Machiavelli's play, which was in fact written to be acted during the season of carnival, thus perfectly captures the ambiguity of the carnivalesque: if it satirizes its characters and the Florence they represent while mocking professions and institutions such as medicine, religion, and law, it simultaneously celebrates the protean energy associated with that satire and mockery as the source of social revitalization.

The happy outcome of *La mandragola* depends in part on Callimaco's sexual vitality, but mostly on his and (especially) Ligurio's ingenuity, mastery of language, and ability to play roles—in short, their command of rhetoric. Ligurio concocts the central fiction of the mandrake root, which, appropriately enough, is based on a set of folk superstitions, and with it he gains Nicia's faith far more easily than traditional religion ever seems to have done. The fiction is actually an elaborate scenario that calls for Callimaco to pass himself off as a doctor and then to play the role of the *garzonaccio* (2.6.76), the "youth," whose sleeping with Lucrezia after she has taken the mandrake root potion supposedly removes its poison while making her fertile.[55] More important, the fiction not only allows Callimaco a single night in bed with her but gains him a permanent place in Nicia's house as her doctor. In an ironic Freudian slip, Nicia pronounces Callimaco a *bastone* (5.6.111), a "rod," who will support his old age, and though the image has wonderfully comic phallic associations, it also suggests the traditional scepter of rulers in Renaissance society—perhaps even the largely symbolic club in the hand of the Hercules Gallicus. It suggests, in other words, that Callimaco's ability with words and his skill at acting have made him the emperor, if not of all men's minds, at least of Nicia's. In Ligurio's brilliant fiction, Nicia thinks he still rules his house, just as he believes he is the father of his child. As members of the audience we are in on the secret, however, and like the tricksters in the play we look down on the dupe from a perspective of superior knowledge and intelligence. Machiavelli constructs the action so that we cannot sympathize with Nicia but instead share Ligurio's and Callimaco's contempt for his stupidity, despise his venality and immorality, and see his being tricked as a just reward for one who revels in his own presumed cleverness but is too witless to see how he is being manipulated. Although *La mandragola* celebrates the success of its orator-tricksters, it does leave one wondering just how secure that triumph is at the end, less because Nicia might discover the truth than because of the potential for rivalry between his deceivers. In order for Callimaco to have achieved his aims, he has had to depend upon Ligurio's plot, and since the servant here is demonstrably cleverer than his master, the imbalance between them creates the potential for future competition, for a struggle that the tricky servant may conceivably win, just as the Renaissance *condottieri* whom Machiavelli discusses in his political writings often proved shrewder foxes than the princes they served.

The rhetoric that lets Callimaco and Ligurio rule Nicia's house does as much for Ben Jonson's three tricksters in *The Alchemist*. In fact, al-

---

[55] Machiavelli, *La mandragola* (in *Il teatro e tutti gli scritti letterari*), cited by act, scene, and page in this edition.

chemy, which in this play constitutes a powerful language that commands the belief of its victims, is, among other things, an equivalent for rhetoric, and Subtle, Face, and Dol use it brilliantly to lure their gulls into Lovewit's house and persuade them foolishly to part with their wealth in the vain hope of gaining even more. The tricksters also subject their prey to a variety of degrading experiences—including lodging one of them in the privy—which may be necessitated by the complicated plotting but which also reinforce the tricksters' sense of power. Fittingly, in the comic argument that opens the play, Subtle and Face are identified by Dol as "Sovereign" and "General" (1.1.5), and she herself later plays the "Queen of Faery" (see 3.5), appropriating a well-known allegorical identity of Elizabeth I.[56] All these titles are ironic, since the three sharpers come from the lowest reaches of the social order and never change their status, no matter what costumes they wear. In fact, whereas Callimaco and Ligurio create a fiction which, in a sense, becomes the reality of their world at least for Nicia, the fictions manufactured by Subtle, Face, and Dol are all exploded by the end of the play, just as surely as the alchemical experiment itself, albeit by design, goes up *in fumo* (4.5.66), so that tricksters as well as dupes are finally defrauded of their hopes. As *La mandragola* draws to its close, Callimaco and Ligurio use their rhetorical skills to preserve their position in Nicia's house, whereas *The Alchemist*'s Subtle and Dol are expelled from Lovewit's house, forced to escape from capture by climbing "over the wall, o' the back-side" (5.4.133). Although Face remains behind, he is deprived of his role as "General" and has to assume his former position as Lovewit's butler. His defeat, however, as we shall see, is more apparent than real.

Like Machiavelli, Jonson creates a world in which everyone competes with everyone else, in which all are tricksters or would-be tricksters, and in which some become gulls simply because they let their desires overpower them or allow themselves to be moved by impulses of morality or generosity. Jonson's satire is harsher than Machiavelli's, however, and his trickster protagonists not nearly so attractive, even though the audience is put in the position of colluding with them, allowed to share in their plotting, and encouraged to look down on virtually all the other characters in the play as moral and intellectual inferiors. There is no carnivalesque embracing here of the energy and inventiveness of the tricksters, however, despite their resemblance, as playwrights and actors, to their creator. Although Subtle, Face, and Dol do possess an en-

---

[56] Ben Jonson, *The Alchemist*, ed. Alvin B. Kernan (New Haven: Yale University Press, 1974), cited by act, scene, and line.

gaging energy and inventiveness, their activities are almost purely negative: they prey upon others and rejoice in sadistic thoughts of hooking and snaring and milking them; they are balder, more threatening versions of what Ligurio represents—parasites. Repeatedly, Jonson characterizes their dupes as hungry children who mistakenly turn to the three tricksters in order to be fed, and if this comparison serves to lessen our esteem for the dupes, it simultaneously undercuts the tricksters, since it emphasizes the cruelty and betrayal of innocence involved in their deceptions. Most damning to the tricksters—and the rhetoric they employ—in *The Alchemist* is Jonson's insistent identification of them with filth and excrement and stench, from the opening exchanges of Subtle and Face about flatulence and dunghills, through their placement of one of the dupes in a privy, down to the great explosion of the experiment, about which Face reports, "All [is] flown, or stinks" (4.5.97). Whereas in *La mandragola* only the dupe Nicia is associated with excrement, in *The Alchemist* all the characters are. More important, there is still an ambiguity about the excremental in Machiavelli's play, Nicia being, as it were, a kind of fertilizer essential for the growth of a renewed social order in the end. In Jonson's play, people are dung who must be swept out the door, just as the rhetoric they use, equated with foul air, is insubstantial and unreal and must be allowed to dissipate in the atmosphere.

Nor does *The Alchemist* hold out the possibility of renewal that Machiavelli's play implies. Like Florence, London is sick, literally in the grip of the plague, which is responsible for Lovewit's having abandoned his house and enabled Subtle, Face, and Dol to set up shop there. Those characters and, indeed, all the characters in the play are bearers of the plague, the plague of immorality, all of them linked to the bad air—in the forms of flatulence and fumes, privy vapors and tobacco smoke—considered the cause or carrier of the disease. Their occupation of Lovewit's house is thus more disturbing than the tricksters' entry into Nicia's house in *La mandragola*, for Machiavelli's characters bring a cure for sterility, whereas Jonson's bring disease, the plague of unrestrained appetite, amoral competitiveness, and rhetoric that is fundamentally subversive as it replaces the proper owner of the house with parody rulers, with completely illegitimate clown-kings. As a result of Jonson's harsh condemnation of his orator-tricksters, there is an incredible pressure in the play to banish these monsters, these creatures who are half man, half dog (see the opening scene), and repeatedly identified with filth. And banished they are in the last act, when Lovewit returns and drives out dupes and tricksters alike. The play thus ends, or seems to end, as a kind of rite of purification that separates the true ruler from all the demonic parodies of him, thereby ensuring the triumph of law and order and health. Yet Face (albeit reduced to Jeremy the Butler) does remain behind, and—even more unsettling—Lovewit turns out to be yet another trickster himself, cheerfully pocketing the loot that Subtle, Face, and Dol have acquired and marrying the woman whom Subtle and Face have marked off for themselves. Lovewit is directly linked to the bad air of the plague when, in order to confirm his marriage, he asks for a pipeful of tobacco (see 5.5.141). Instead of a cleansing ritual, then, the end of the play offers a continuation of disease and disorder, a disorder all the more apparent because Lovewit has been putting on costumes and playing roles at Face's behest throughout the last act, thus turning the social order topsy-turvy as the servant manipulates and controls his master. The play finally offers no viable figure of a ruler; the wicked orator-tricksters may have been banished, but the good orator-trickster who remains behind is almost as unsavory as the monsters he has chased away.

Even more than *The Alchemist*, *Tartuffe*, written at the end of the Renaissance and at the height of absolutist rule in France, is hostile to the orator-trickster, as hostile as the almost contemporaneous *Nouvelle allégorique*. Molière spares no pains to make his title character unattractive, identifying him from the start as a religious hypocrite driven by base appetites for food, sex, and money, appetites which he cannot control and which degrade him, making him appear farcical as he acts them out. All these characteristics are symbolized by his name, which combines *truffer* (from the Italian *truffare*, "to deceive") and *tarte*, a word for "cake" or "pie," which stresses his gluttony, just as his obesity does. Other characters number him among the "charlatans" (1.5.361), call him a *gueux*, or "beggar" (1.1.63; 2.2.484), and ridicule his obscure, provincial background.[57] Dorine, the companion of Orgon's wife, Elmire, stresses not only Tartuffe's low social status and provinciality but his association with aspects of popular culture. He is not a man, she remarks ironically, "who wipes his nose with his foot" (2.3.643), a gesture that is not only socially indecorous but identifies Tartuffe as a kind of acrobat or clown. Dorine continues her "praise": "He is noble in his own country, well put together in his person; / He has a red ear and his complexion is florid" (2.3.646–47). Tartuffe is anything but noble, of course, and his florid coloring is meant to suggest his sexual and other appetites, his Judas-like capacity to betray those who trust him, perhaps even his quasi-diabolical status. Moreover, consider the compound im-

---

[57] Molière, *Le Tartuffe*, in *Théâtre complet*, vol. 1, ed. Robert Jouanny (Paris: Garnier, 1962), cited by act, scene, and line.

age that results when these traits are combined with the earlier allusion to acrobatics and with later suggestions that Tartuffe is an "ape" (2.3.655) and that he comes from a "little town" (2.3.657) where, "during carnival" one can enjoy "The ball and the king's orchestra, to wit, two bagpipes, / And sometimes Fagotin [a famous ape] and marionettes" (2.3.664–66). Taken together, these details make Tartuffe a carnival clown; he bespeaks the carnivalesque, but a carnivalesque with no trace of the ambiguity for which Bakhtin praises it and which it has in Machiavelli and, to a much lesser degree, in Jonson. Although Tartuffe possesses a remarkable flair for the rhetorical and the histrionic, these traits are devalued in the play: he is mocked for his grimaces (1.5.321, 362) and his ridiculous faking of a "transport of zeal" (3.3.910), both of which reinforce the negative image of him as a clown, since they render the body monstrous through distortion. Moreover, his tricks are so glaringly obvious that the audience cannot possibly want to identify with him and are invited instead to share the judgment of virtually all the other characters. In fact, Molière deliberately delays Tartuffe's entry until the third act in order to have Dorine, Elmire, and the others establish a clear, condemnatory viewpoint of him before he appears on stage. That viewpoint will also be shared, apparently, by Orgon's neighbors (see 5.5.1823–26). Thus, whereas Machiavelli and Jonson allow the audience to see the world through the eyes of the orator-tricksters, Molière makes us share the perspective of those who plot *against* him, bringing us to align ourselves with them and the neighbors, with sophisticated Parisians who possess tact, reason, and civility and who live in the center rather than coming from the ridiculous, carnivalesque provinces.

To advance socially, Tartuffe relies on his rhetorical skill. A master of equivocation (see 4.5.1485–1506), he is capable of turning things inside out with words, as when he reinforces his *ethos* as an innocent by simply appearing to accept the accusations made against him by Orgon's son Damis (see 3.6). Tartuffe is a stand-in for Molière's chief satirical target, the members of the Compagnie du Saint-Sacrament, who were well known both for their zealous piety and the rhetorical skill with which they combatted what they saw as worldliness and tepid religiosity. This group, which counted the brilliant young preacher Bossuet as one of its protégés, not only provoked the worldly Molière's scorn for what he felt was its hypocrisy but aroused his wrath when it seduced away his patron, the Prince de Conti, and later conducted a temporarily successful campaign to have *Tartuffe* banned in France. Just as rhetoric in the Renaissance made—or seemed to make—its practitioners, such as the Brethren of the Blessed Sacrament, kings even over the legitimate monarch, so Tartuffe's abilities allow him to rule everyone through his control over the head of the family, Orgon, and eventually to dispense with him and become the real *maître*, the "master" (4.7.1557) of the house. Like the Renaissance rhetor, Tartuffe sees himself as a kind of hero, referring to his anticipated seduction of Elmire as his *gloire* or "glory" (4.5.1461), and using this same word to characterize his success in leading Orgon around by the nose (4.5.1525). According to the other characters in the play, Orgon was sane and level-headed before he met Tartuffe, and as they explain his transformation, they have recourse to terms that yet again serve to identify Tartuffe with the Renaissance orator, this time the orator as temptress, witch, or *magus*. Thus, Dorine says that Orgon takes Tartuffe "for a mistress" (1.2.189), and Cléante grumbles to Orgon: "Can it be that a man has the charm today to make you forget everything for him?" (1.5.263–64). Orgon himself actually praises the way Tartuffe *charms* and *ravishes* others (1.5.270–71). Damis, flabbergasted at Orgon's behavior, blurts out his indignation: "What! His discourses seduce you to the point . . ." (3.6.1108)—an exclamation he never gets to finish. The effect of these references to mistresses, charms, ravishment, and seduction is to characterize the relationship between Tartuffe and Orgon in the same magical and sexual terms which, in Chapter 3, we saw rhetoricians use for the orator and his auditor—and with the same unsettling results. Although all the images stress the power of Tartuffe over his prey, they also identify both characters as sexually unstable, as both male and female and hence hermaphroditic, just as the rhetor is. The images thus reinforce the sense that the boundary-crossing Tartuffe is indeed a monster, and certainly more of one than the orator-tricksters with whom we have been comparing him. There is little that is grotesque about Callimaco and Ligurio, and though the trio of sharpers in *The Alchemist* may be associated with dogs and dirt and excrement, they are not fat, grimacing, sexually ambiguous, and grotesque—like Tartuffe.

The increased monstrousness of Tartuffe may be correlated with the increased threat he poses to society, the symbolic focus for which is the house he invades. Note that at the end of *La mandragola* Nicia is still the nominal master of his own house, and that Subtle, Face, and Dol take over Lovewit's house only for a brief period in *The Alchemist*. By contrast, Tartuffe not only invades Orgon's house but tricks Orgon into signing it over to him and then plans to drive Orgon and his family out into the street. Moreover, although the house may represent society in all three plays, it does so in different ways. The action of *La mandragola* takes place on the street in front of Nicia's house and other buildings; it is located in a *public* space where competition, such as that between the orator-tricksters and their dupe, is an accepted norm. It is a liminal space in which the order of society can be reworked as the disease and unhappiness associated with Nicia are defeated by the health and joyful sexuality of Callimaco and Ligurio, who then take it off stage into Nicia's house in order to transform it as well. Although the house may be the symbol of society and hence of us as the audience, we always remain outside, detached enough to see its problems and to appreciate Callimaco's and Ligurio's cure for them. Like that pair, we are free to come and go, move in and out, as we choose. By contrast, *The Alchemist* moves us *inside* the house itself for most of the action. To be sure, when Lovewit returns, we do go outside temporarily to meet him on the street and to encounter his neighbors there for the first time. One might say that this stepping out into the fresh air fits the symbolic character of Lovewit at this point, since he seems to represent a fresh new perspective, a desire for release, a hope that the dirt and disease associated with the tricksters may be swept away. Lovewit is like us, a witty character who sees through frauds and laughs at the superstition and credulity of others. Significantly, however, as Face draws him into the plot, Lovewit enters the house, and we find ourselves once again inside. There we remain until the end of the play, when Face asks *us* to accept some of the loot, too, and to show our approval by our applause. By keeping us inside Lovewit's house and reinforcing in various ways our identification with him—including the fact that the house is located in exactly the same district of London, Blackfriars, in which *The Alchemist* is being put on—Jonson denies us any real escape from a world dominated by rhetoric, deception, and tricksters. The effect of the play is to induce a kind of moral and social claustrophobia, which stimulates our desire for the banishment of Subtle, Face, and Dol but then returns with a vengeance when Lovewit reenters the house at the end.

If anything, this claustrophobia is even greater in *Tartuffe*, for although we hear about neighbors and the larger world outside of Orgon's house, we never leave it during the play. Moreover, inside the house there is no escape from Tartuffe who, using his rhetoric to manipulate Orgon, controls the lives of all the characters until he gets Orgon to hand over the very deed to his property. But even if there were an outside, would we wish to go there, any more than Orgon and his family do at the end? This play, like Furetière's *Nouvelle*, limits the universe to just two symbolic realms: the house, which is the world of the upper classes, including the audience that has been brought to identify with them; and the outside, the world of common people, beggars, and provincials, the world of the streets, which is simultaneously the world beyond the Loire—in short, the no-place from which Tartuffe has come.

In the symbolic geography of Molière's play, there is a civilized center which we have constantly before our eyes, and a region of *terrae incognitae* we never see but which is signposted, as it were, with the warning, "Here be monsters." Since one of those monsters has invaded and taken over the civilized center, the pressure to eliminate him is almost unbearable.

As one goes from Machiavelli to Jonson to Molière, the movement of the house into a position of complete centrality on the stage can be correlated with the increasing absolutism of Renaissance culture in which one house, the house of the ruler, has theoretically displaced all others. That the house and the actions focused on it have political significance the plays themselves demonstrate. Machiavelli, for instance, invites us to engage in political allegory when he has Lucrezia dub Callimaco her *signore, padrone, guida* (5.4.109). Jonson does much the same thing by identifying Subtle and Face as "Sovereign" and "General." Molière is even more suggestive: he has Mariane refer to her father as a *père absolu* (2.3.589), thus encouraging us to read Orgon as a version of the *roi absolu*, Louis XIV. In all three plays, what we witness is the usurpation of the ruling house and the symbolic dethroning of the ruler by people from the margins of society who achieve their ends by means of rhetoric. In other words, the plays are concerned with political subversion, addressing in particular the fantasy that rhetoricians entertain in their works about orators who use their art to fend off, rebuke, and even rule over kings. As we go from play to play, not only do the symbolic importance and centrality of the house become ever greater, but so does the legitimacy of its owner, so that the subversion involved becomes increasingly less tolerable until the only thinkable solution to the threat it poses to social and political stability is banishment of the subversive element. In the political allegory of *La mandragola* the "legitimate" authority, Nicia, is not really all that legitimate; his stupidity, greed, and incompetence deprive him of any right to rule, while Callimaco's and Ligurio's intelligence and energy serve to justify the power they come to wield behind the throne. By contrast, Subtle, Face, and Dol may possess intelligence and energy, just as Tartuffe does, but they are morally corrupt. More important, Lovewit allows himself to be morally compromised and manipulated at the end, thus undermining his right to rule in his own house, whereas Orgon's admiration for Tartuffe's supposed piety, though it may be misplaced and cause hardship for his family, hardly makes him guilty of moral turpitude. In fact, Orgon is credited with a variety of virtues, and except for his blind spot with Tartuffe, he seems well qualified to rule. As a result, his dethroning becomes quite problematic and brings the play closer to tragedy than comedy. *Tartuffe* could be read as an implicit warning about the dangers of absolutist rule: a single, powerful adviser such as Richelieu is seen as being able, thanks to his rhetorical skill, to control the monarch, thus turning the entire state topsy-turvy—which is precisely what happens in Molière's play when a beggar, a *gueux*, displaces the legitimate owner of the house.

Tartuffe not only attacks the dangerous, subversive power of rhetoric but, until the last moment, seems utterly pessimistic about the ability of legitimate authority to withstand that power. Various responses to Tartuffe are tried and invariably found wanting. Mariane, for instance, seems willing at one point to accommodate herself to her father's will and accept marriage with Tartuffe, but the fundamentally intolerable nature of such a course is made clear to her by Dorine's ridicule of her future spouse as a carnival clown. For Mariane to marry Tartuffe would be to let herself be "tartuffified" (2.4.674: *tartuffiée*): that is, made into a creature like him and thus degraded socially and morally. By contrast, Mariane's brother Damis prefers violence, intending to challenge Tartuffe to a duel at one point and, at another, to cut off his ears. But Damis's adolescent heroics are not countenanced by Molière's spokesman, the civilized and refined Cléante, who tells him to moderate "these brilliant [*éclatants*] transports: we live under a reign and in a time when one handles one's affairs badly by means of violence" (5.2.1639–41). Not only do Damis's outbursts sort ill with the culture of Louis XIV's France, but they make him resemble Tartuffe, who, as the master of feigning "brilliant transports," beats Damis handily when the young man literally bursts out of his hiding place and accuses Tartuffe of trying to seduce Elmire. In a civilized world where violence has no place and where words have more power than swords, Damis's solution to the problem of Tartuffe is no solution at all.

Unfortunately, neither is that of Cléante, Elmire, and Dorine. They stand for an alternative rhetoric to the one employed by their opponent, a rhetoric characterized by restraint and understatement, by the maintenance of the "proprieties" (2.2.505: *bienséances*) and an affirmation of the golden mean (see 5.1.1609–28). For them, excess in any form is unacceptable: it makes prudes *sauvages* (4.3.1330), turns zealots like Tartuffe into grimacing clowns, and creates scandals by making mountains out of molehills. Elmire, confronted with Orgon's charge that she was not sufficiently shocked by Tartuffe's advances, replies that one need not respond to every affront with "fire in one's eyes and injuries on one's lips" (4.3.1326). Her rhetoric here denies the fire of passion that is so central in Renaissance thinking on the subject. Instead, she says: "I simply laugh at such propositions, and I do not like making a stir [*l'éclat*] about them; I prefer that we show ourselves wise with gentleness [*douceur*]" (4.3.1327–29). Here she rejects what she calls *l'éclat*, which means not only a "stir," but also "brilliance," "blaze," and "burst" or "outburst" and is associated throughout the play with both the violence of Damis and the theatrical rhetoric of Tartuffe. But when Elmire embraces as an alternative the notion of showing oneself wise with *douceur*, which means "sweetness" as well as "gentleness," she is obviously still deeply involved with rhetoric which, throughout the Renaissance (as we have seen in Chapter 3), repeatedly stresses that notion as well. This is precisely the same rhetoric Elmire's brother Cléante endorses as he juxtaposes it in the following quotation to the extremism of Orgon (and implicitly, of Tartuffe as well): "Well! None of your transports! You never maintain a sweet [*doux*] moderation" (5.2.1607–8). The good rhetoric defined by Cléante, Elmire, and Dorine is the twin of the one defended by Furetière in his *Nouvelle allégorique*, just as the rhetoric of hyperbole and grimaces which they reject resembles the one associated with Galimatias. Yet just as Queen Rhétorique can defeat her enemy only if she adopts his techniques and fights him by means of *ruse et . . . adresse*, so Molière's protagonists can hope to expose Tartuffe's hypocrisy only by resorting to the sort of trickery, both verbal and physical, he excels at. Whereas Furetière ends his tale with the triumph of the queen, however, Molière does not allow his protagonists to succeed. Perhaps he wants us to feel that their adoption of Tartuffe's rhetoric compromises them too much—it "tartuffifies" them just as it would Mariane—or perhaps he simply wishes to affirm a kind of Gresham's law of rhetoric: in a world where rhetoric rules, bad rhetoric will always drive out good.

And that is almost what happens in *Tartuffe*. At the very end, however, Louis XIV rides to the rescue, exposing Tartuffe, arresting him, and carting him off to prison. Actually, Louis never appears on stage, being represented there by L'Exempt, the Gentleman or Officer of the King's Guard. Louis is described by his emissary in such a way that he clearly approximates the God on whom Molière's protagonists have been calling for aid: seeming infinitely distant yet benevolently concerned, he has been watching over his subjects' affairs all along and only waited to intervene until Tartuffe betrayed his villainy for all to see (5.7.1904–44). Unlike mere mortals, Louis cannot be deceived by "all the art of imposters" (1908), and his "sovereign power" (1935) enables him to dispense justice to the deserving and to rectify wrongs in a way that the violence of Damis and the trickery of Cléante, Elmire, and Dorine never could. Standing outside the house that constitutes the world of the play, Louis speaks no lines, engages in no debates, crosses no boundaries; as he wields his seemingly irresistible power, which has worked in mysterious ways to eliminate Tartuffe, he appears well beyond the taint of rhetoric. As a result, he seems to solve the ultimate problem posed by that art, the problem that bad rhetoric and good rhetoric are, finally, indistinguishable, for not only does he banish Tartuffe (and with him the monster of bad rhetoric), but his transcendence of human limitations—his seeming existence beyond discussion, persuasion, even language itself—appears to free the world, including Orgon's house, from any dependence on the art. Molière's solution is radical: do away with rhetoric altogether.

Nevertheless, Louis is not really above rhetoric at all. The last scene of the play shows that he fully embraces precisely the rhetoric of power and rule that was advocated throughout the Renaissance. Consider: his deliberate delay in exposing Tartuffe, although explained as a device to allow the latter to incriminate himself, can also be read as a supreme example of the rhetorical manipulation of audience response. Orgon and his family have been brought to the point of despair and are then saved by Louis's seemingly divine intervention, even though they could in fact have been saved much earlier, since Tartuffe has a string of heinous deeds to his credit and could have been arrested at any time (see 5.7.1925–26). More important, although Louis never speaks a word on stage himself, the officer who represents him serves as his *orator*, his ambassador and spokesman, delivering a lengthy speech of praise that defines his master's Godlike qualities. Rhetoric here fabricates a compelling *ethos* for Louis, and it persuades his subjects not merely to accept him out of fear or duty but to submit to him freely out of love and gratitude. The play thus shows that it is not sufficient for Louis, as ruler, simply to eliminate Tartuffe and restore order in Orgon's house; he feels he must also be defined—created—as ruler by means of a carefully managed rhetorical transaction that simultaneously creates his subjects as subjects. Cléante indicates that Louis's maneuver has succeeded by telling Orgon to thank the king: "You will go on your knees to his goodness to render that which such a gentle [*doux*] treatment requires" (1955–56). Given the particular kind of rhetoric espoused by Cléante, Elmire, and Dorine, it should hardly be surprising that they would here characterize Louis's treatment of them as *doux*, that they would feel *obliged* to thank him, or that Orgon—converted at last to their way of thinking—should end the play by promising his daughter a "sweet wedding" (1961). Nevertheless, no matter how sweet or gentle Louis's actions may appear, that does not prevent them from being a matter of carefully calculated manipulation. L'Exempt's speech actually betrays Louis's real purpose when it praises the king for his ability, as he views the world beneath him, to *pierce* the hearts of his subjects (see 1919–20), for piercing the hearts of others is precisely what Renaissance rhetors are supposed to do to their auditors in an act that is synonymous with invading, seizing, and possessing them in a kind of imperial conquest. Such a conquest has clearly been made of Orgon and the others in the last scene of the play. Escaping the danger of being "tartuffified" has not prevented them from being, in the end—and, ironically, to their great contentment—"louis-fied."

To stop here, however, and turn the ending of *Tartuffe* into a simple celebration of the power of rhetoric, a celebration perfectly consistent with what defenders of the discipline claim about it throughout the Renaissance, is to stop a bit too soon. For the very fact that L'Exempt presents the king's speech can also be taken as evidence not of Louis's power but of his dependence, specifically of his dependence on rhetoric—which, as we saw in Chapter 1, the historical Sun King himself recognized he needed in order to be truly the emperor of men's minds. What is more, the fact that Louis manipulates others for his own benefit leaves him exposed to the charge that he is engaging in trickery of some sort, and the fact that he is able to pierce and penetrate the hearts of others makes him a kind of boundary violator just as surely as his *orator*, L'Exempt, becomes one when he crosses the threshold of Orgon's house. But to trick and manipulate others, to violate proper boundaries—doesn't such behavior make Louis seem uncannily, disturbingly similar to his opponent, Tartuffe? In the final analysis, what Molière's play suggests is that king and clown cannot be kept entirely distinct from one another. Being "louis-fied" may be preferable to being "tartuffified," but the result of the resemblance between the two processes and their creators is to make a solution into a problem, and to leave rhetoric no less troubling than it has been in reality from the start of the Renaissance to the end.

Bibliography of Works Consulted

Primary Works

Agricola, Rudolph. *De Inventione dialectica libri tres.* Foreword Wilhelm Risse. Cologne, 1528; rpt. Hildesheim: Georg Olms, 1976.

Agrippa, Henry Cornelius. *De Incertitudine et vanitate scientiarum et artium.* In *Opera*, vol. 2. Lyon, 1600 [?]; rpt. Hildesheim: Georg Olms, 1970.

Alciati, Andrea. *Emblemata.* Augsburg, 1531.

——. *Emblemata.* Ed. Christian Wechel. Paris, 1534.

——. *Emblemata.* Venice, 1546.

——. *Emblemata.* Padua, 1621.

——. *Emblemata.* 4th ed. Commentary Claude Mignault. Leiden, 1591.

——. *Emblemes en Latin et Francois.* Paris, 1574.

Alsted, Johann Heinrich. *Rhetorica.* Herborn, 1616.

Amyot, Jacques. *Projet de l'Eloquence royale, composé pour Henry III, roi de France.* Versailles: Ph.-D. Pierres, 1805.

Ariosto, Ludovico. *Satire e lettere.* Ed. Cesare Segre, intro. Lanfranco Caretti. Milan: Riccardo Ricciardi, 1954.

Aristotle. *The "Art" of Rhetoric.* Trans. John H. Freese. Cambridge, Mass.: Harvard University Press, 1982.

Arnauld, Antoine, and Pierre Nicole. *La Logique, ou l'Art de penser.* Ed. Pierre Clair and François Girbal. Paris: Presses Universitaires de France, 1965.

Artes Praedicandi: Contribution à l'histoire de la rhétorique au moyen âge. Ed. Th.-M. Charland, O.P. Paris: Vrin, 1936.

Augustine. *Confessions.* Trans. William Watts. 2 vols. Cambridge, Mass.: Harvard University Press, 1960.

Bacon, Francis. *Advancement of Learning and Novum Organon*. Intro. James E. Creighton. Rev. ed. New York: Willey, 1900.

———. *The Essays*. Ed. John Pitcher. Harmondsworth: Penguin, 1985.

———. *Selected Writings*. Ed. Hugh G. Dick. New York: Random House, 1955.

Barbaro, Daniel. *Della Eloquenza*. In *Trattati di poetica e retorica del Cinquecento*, ed. Bernard Weinberg, 2:335–451. Bari: Laterza, 1970.

Bary, René. *La Rhetorique françoise*. Paris, 1659. Microfilm.

Bersuire, Pierre. *Reductorium morale*. Ed. J. Engels. Utrecht: Instituut voor Laat Latijn der Rijksuniversiteit, 1962, 1966.

Boccaccio, Giovanni. *Genealogie deorum gentilium libri*. Ed. Vincenzo Romano. Bari: Laterza, 1951.

———. *On Poetry*. Trans. Charles G. Osgood. Indianapolis: Bobbs-Merrill, 1956.

Bocchi, Achille. *Symbolicarum quaestionum, de universo genere, quos serio ludebat, libri quinque*. Bologna, 1574.

Bodin, Jean. *Les six Livres de la République*. Paris, 1583; rpt. Aalen: Scientia, 1961.

Breen, Quirinus. "Giovanni Pico della Mirandola on the Conflict of Philosophy and Rhetoric." *Journal of the History of Ideas* 13 (1952): 384–412.

Bucoldianus, Gerard. *De Inventione & Amplificatione oratoria*. Leiden, 1534.

Bullough, Geoffrey, ed. *Narrative and Dramatic Sources of Shakespeare*. Vol. 5. London: Routledge & Kegan Paul, 1964.

Bulwer, John. *Chirologia: or the Natural Language of the Hand and Chironomia: or the Art of Manual Rhetoric*. Ed. James W. Cleary. Carbondale, Ill.: Southern Illinois University Press, 1974.

Butler, Charles. *Rhetoricae Libri Duo*. London, 1598.

Capella, Martianus. *Martianus Capella and the Seven Liberal Arts*. Trans. William H. Stahl and Richard Johnson with E. L. Burge. New York: Columbia University Press, 1977.

Castiglione, Baldesar. *Il libro del cortegiano*. Ed. Bruno Maier. 2d ed. Turin: Unione Tipografico-Editrice Torinese, 1964.

Caussin, Nicholas. *De Eloquentia sacra et humana*. 3d ed. Paris, 1630. Microfilm.

Cavalcanti, Bartolomeo. *La Retorica*. Ferrara: Gabriel Giolito, 1559. Microfilm.

Cervantes, Miguel de. *Don Quijote de la Mancha*. Ed. Martín de Riquer. 10th ed. 2 vols. Barcelona: Editorial Juventud, 1985.

Chappell, William. *The Preacher, or The Art and Method of Preaching*. London, 1656. Microfilm.

Charron, Pierre. *De la Sagesse: Trois Livres*. Ed. Amaury Duval. 3 vols. Paris, 1824.

Cicero. *De finibus bonorum et malorum*. Trans. H. Rackham. Cambridge: Harvard University Press, 1914.

———. *De inventione, De optimo genere oratorum, Topica*. Trans. H. M. Hubbell. London: William Heinemann, 1949.

———. *De oratore*. Trans. E. W. Sutton and H. Rackham. 2 vols. London: William Heinemann, 1959.

———. *Tusculan Disputations*. Trans. J. E. King. Cambridge, Mass.: Harvard University Press, 1950.

[Cicero]. *Rhetorica ad Herennium.* Trans. Harry Caplan. Cambridge, Mass.: Harvard University Press, 1989.

Coxe, Leonard. *The Arte or Craft of Rhethoryke.* London, 1524; rpt. Amsterdam, Walter J. Johnson, 1977.

Dante Alighieri. *Inferno.* Trans. Charles S. Singleton. 2 vols. Princeton: Princeton University Press, 1970.

Day, Angel. *The English Secretary.* Intro. Robert O. Evans. Gainesville, Fla.: Scholars' Facsimiles and Reprints, 1967.

de' Conti, Anto Maria. *De eloquentia dialogus.* In *Trattati di poetica e retorica del Cinquecento,* ed. Bernard Weinberg, 2:141–61. Bari: Laterza, 1970.

Denores, Giason. "Breve Trattato dell'Oratore." In *Trattati di poetica e retorica del Cinquecento,* ed. Bernard Weinberg, 3:101–34. Bari: Laterza, 1970.

Du Pont, Gracien. *Art et science de rhethoricque metriffiée.* Toulouse, 1539; rpt. Geneva: Slatkine Reprints, 1972.

Du Pré de la Porte, J. *Le Pourtraict de l'Eloquence Françoise.* Paris, 1621.

Du Vair, Guillaume. *Traitté de l'Eloquence Françoise.* In *Oeuvres,* 389–410. Paris: Sebastien Cramoisy, 1641; rpt. Geneva: Slatkine Reprints, 1970.

Erasmus, Desiderius. *Ciceronianus.* In Erasmus von Rotterdam, *Ausgewählte Schriften,* ed. Werner Welzig, vol. 7. Darmstadt: Wissenschaftliche Buchgesellschaft, 1972.

——. *Moriae Encomion.* In Erasmus von Rotterdam, *Ausgewählte Schriften,* ed. Werner Welzig, vol. 2. Darmstadt: Wissenschaftliche Buchgesellschaft, 1975.

——. *Opera omnia.* Ed. J. Clericus. Vol. 5. Leiden, 1703–6.

Fabri, Pierre. *Le grand et vrai art de pleine rhétorique.* Ed. A. Héron. Rouen: A. Lestringant, 1890.

Farnaby, Thomas. *Index Rhetoricus.* London, 1625. Microfilm.

Fenner, Dudley. *The Artes of Logike and Rhethorike.* London, 1584. Microfilm.

Fraunce, Abraham. *The Arcadian Rhetorike.* London, 1588. Microfilm.

Furetière, Antoine. *Nouvelle allégorique, ou Histoire des derniers troubles arrivés au royaume d'Eloquence.* Ed. Eva van Ginneken. Geneva: Droz, 1967.

Fuscano, Giovanni Berardino. "Della oratoria e poetica facoltà." In *Trattati di poetica e retorica del Cinquecento,* ed. Bernard Weinberg, 1:187–95. Bari: Laterza, 1970.

George of Trebizond [Trapezuntius]. *Oratio de laudibus eloquentie.* In John Monfasani, *George of Trebizond: A Biography and a Study of His Rhetoric and Logic,* 365–69. Leiden: E. J. Brill, 1976.

——. *Rhetoricorum libri V.* Venice: Aldine Press, 1523.

Gerbiers, Sir Balthazar. *The Art of Well Speaking: A Lecture.* London, 1650. Microfilm.

Gower, John. *The Complete Works.* Ed. G. C. Macaulay. Vol. 3. Oxford: Clarendon Press, 1901.

Granada, Luis de. *Ecclesiastica Rhetorica.* Cologne, 1582. Microfilm.

Guzman, Joan de. *Primera Parte de la Rhetorica.* Alcala de Henares, 1589.

Haddon, Walter. *De laudibus eloquentiae.* In *Lucubrationes passim collectae,* ed. Thomas Hatcher, 1–9. London, 1567.

Harvey, Gabriel. *Rhetor.* London, 1577. Microfilm.

Hawes, Stephen. *Works*. Intro. Frank J. Spang. Delmar, N.Y.: Scholars' Facsimiles and Reprints, 1975.

Herbert, George. *Works*. Ed. F. E. Hutchinson. Oxford: Clarendon Press, 1941.

Horace. *Opera*. Ed. Edward C. Wickham and H. W. Garrod. 2d ed. Oxford: Clarendon Press, 1901.

Hoskins, John. *Directions for Speech and Style*. Ed. Hoyt H. Hudson. Princeton: Princeton University Press, 1935.

Hudson, Hoyt H. "Jewel's Oration against Rhetoric: A Translation." *Quarterly Journal of Speech* 14 (1928): 374–92.

Isidore of Seville. *Etymologiarum libri*. Ed. W. M. Lindsay. Oxford: Clarendon Press, 1911.

Isocrates. *Works*. Trans. George Norlin. Cambridge, Mass.: Harvard University Press, 1929.

Jewel, John. *Oratio Contra Rhetoricam*. In *The Works*, ed. John Ayre, 4:1283–91. Cambridge: Cambridge University Press, 1850.

Jonson, Ben. *The Alchemist*. Ed. Alvin B. Kernan. New Haven: Yale University Press, 1974.

Keckermann, Bartholomew. *Systema Rhetorices*. Hanover, 1608.

Lactantius. *The Divine Institutes, Books I–VII*. Trans. Sister Mary Francis McDonald, O.P. Washington: Catholic University of America Press, 1964.

The Later Renaissance in England: Nondramatic Verse and Prose, 1600–1660. Ed. Herschel Baker. Boston: Houghton Mifflin, 1975.

Latini, Brunetto. *LI Livres dou Trésor*. Ed. Francis J. Carmody. University of Califonia Studies in Philology, 22. Berkeley: University of California Press, 1948.

———. *Il Tesoretto*. Ed. and trans. Julia B. Holloway. New York: Garland, 1981.

Latomus, Bartholomew. *Summa totius rationis disserendi*. Cologne, 1527.

Lazarillo de Tormes. Ed. Francisco Rico. Barcelona: Planeta, 1980.

Le Grand, M. *Discours*. In René Bary, *La Rhetorique françoise*. Paris, 1659. Microfilm.

Lipsius, Justus. *Politicorum sive civilis doctrinae libri sex*. In *Opera Omnia*. Vol. 4. Wesel, 1675.

Livy. *Books I and II (of Ab urbe condita)*. Trans. B. O. Foster. London: William Heinemann, 1967.

Machiavelli, Niccolò. *Istorie fiorentine*. Ed. Franco Gaeta. Milan: Feltrinelli, 1962.

———. *Il principe e Discorsi*. Ed. Sergio Bertelli. Milan: Feltrinelli, 1960.

———. *Il teatro e tutti gli scritti letterari*. Ed. Franco Gaeta. Milan: Feltrinelli, 1965.

Marlowe, Christopher. *The Complete Plays*. Ed. Irving Ribner. New York: Odyssey Press, 1963.

Melanchthon, Philip. *Elementorum Rhetorices Libri Duo*. Wittenberg, 1519. Microfilm.

———. *Encomion eloquentiae*. In *Werke in Auswahl*, ed. Robert Stupperich, 3:43–62. Gütersloh: Gütersloh Verlagshaus Gerd Mohn, 1961.

Milton, John. *Complete Poems and Major Prose*. Ed. Merritt Y. Hughes. New York: Odyssey Press, 1957.

Molière. *Le Tartuffe*. In *Théâtre complet*, ed. Robert Jouanny. Vol. 1. Paris: Garnier, 1962.

Montaigne, Michel de. *Oeuvres complètes*. Ed. Albert Thibaudet and Maurice Rat. Paris: Gallimard, 1962.

Müllner, Karl, ed. *Reden und Briefe italienischer Humanisten*. Vienna, 1899; rpt. Munich: Wilhelm Fink, 1970.

Nashe, Thomas. *The Unfortunate Traveler*. In *Elizabethan Prose Fiction*, ed. Merritt Lawlis. New York: Odyssey Press, 1967.

Ovid. *Metamorphoses*. Trans. Frank J. Miller. 2 vols. London: William Heinemann, 1932.

Pascal, Blaise. *Oeuvres complètes*. Ed. Jacques Chevalier. Paris: Gallimard, 1960.

Patrizi, Francesco. *Della retorica dieci dialoghi*. Venice, 1562. Microfilm.

Peacham, Henry. *The Garden of Eloquence (1593)*. Intro. William G. Crane. Gainesville, Fla.: Scholars' Facsimiles & Reprints, 1954.

Petrarca, Francesco. *Le familiari*. Ed. V. Rossi. Vol. 1. Florence, 1933–42.

Picinelli, Filippo. *Mundus Symbolicus*. Cologne, 1687.

Pico della Mirandola, Giovanni. *De Hominis Dignitate, Heptaplus, De Ente et Uno*. Ed. Eugenio Garin. Florence: Vallechi Editore, 1942.

——. *Epistola Hermolao Barbaro*. In Giovanni Pico della Mirandola and Gian Francesco Pico, *Opera Omnia*, intro. Cesare Vasoli, 351–58. Basel, 1557; rpt. Hildesheim: Georg Olms, 1969.

Prosatori latini del Quattrocento. Ed. Eugenio Garin. Milan: Riccardo Ricciardi, 1952.

Puttenham, George. *The Arte of English Poesie*. Intro. Baxter Hathaway. Kent, Ohio: Kent State University Press, 1970.

Quintilian. *Institutio oratoria*. Trans. H. E. Butler. 4 vols. London: William Heinemann, 1963.

Rabelais, François. *Oeuvres*. Ed. Jacques Boulenger and Lucien Scheler. Paris: Gallimard, 1962.

Rainolde, Richard. *The Foundacion of Rhetorike*. London, 1563; rpt. Amsterdam: Da Capo, 1969.

Rainolds, John. *Oratio in laudem artis poeticae*. Ed. William Ringler and Walter Allen, Jr. Princeton: Princeton University Press, 1940.

——. *Oxford Lectures on Aristotle's "Rhetoric."* Ed. Lawrence D. Green. Newark: University of Delaware Press, 1986.

Ramus, Petrus [Pierre de la Ramée]. *Attack on Cicero: Text and Translation of Ramus's "Brutinae Quaestiones."* Ed. James J. Murphy, trans. Carole Newlands. Davis, Calif.: Hermagoras Press, 1992.

——. *Dialectique*. In *Gramere (1562), Grammaire (1572), Dialectique (1555)*. Paris; rpt. Geneva: Slatkine Reprints, 1972.

Readings in Medieval Rhetoric. Ed. Joseph M. Miller, Michael H. Prosser, and Thomas W. Benson. Bloomington: Indiana University Press, 1973.

Regius, Raphael. *De Laudibus eloquentiae panegyricus*. Venice, 1485.

Ripa, Cesare. *Iconologia*. Rome, 1603.

Salutati, Coluccio. *De Laboribus Herculis*. Ed. B. L. Ullman. 2 vols. Zürich: Artemis Verlag, 1951.

——. *Epistolario*. Vol. 3. Rome, 1891–1905.

Sambucus, Johannes. *Emblemata*. Antwerp, 1566.

Shakespeare, William. *The Complete Works*. Ed. David Bevington. 3d ed. Glenview, Ill.: Scott, Foresman, 1951.

Sherry, Richard. *A Treatise of Schemes and Tropes (1550) and His Translation of "The Education of Children" by Desiderius Erasmus*. Intro. Herbert W. Hildebrandt. Gainesville, Fla.: Scholars' Facsimiles & Reprints, 1961.

Sidney, Sir Philip. *An Apology for Poetry*. Ed. Forrest G. Robinson. Indianapolis: Bobbs-Merrill, 1970.

Soarez, Cypriano. *De Arte Rhetorica Libri Tres*. Verona, 1589. Microfilm.

Speroni, Sperone. *Dialogo della rettorica*. In *Dialogo della lingua e Dialogo della rettorica*, intro. Giuseppe De Robertis, 85–140. Lanciano: R. Carabba, 1912.

Sturm, Johann. *De universa ratione elocutionis rhetoricae libri III (De Elocutione)*. Strassburg, 1576. Microfilm.

Susenbrotus, Johann. *Epitome Troporum ac Schematum*. Zürich, 1540.

Tacitus. *Agricola, Germania, Dialogus*. Trans. M. Hutton et al. Cambridge, Mass.: Harvard University Press, 1970.

Tesauro, Emanuele. *Il cannochiale aristotelico*. Ed. August Buck. Turin, 1670; rpt. Bad Homburg: Gehlen, 1968.

Thireau, Jean-Louis. *Les idées politiques de Louis XIV*. Paris: Presses Universitaires de France, 1973.

Three Medieval Rhetorical Arts. Ed. James J. Murphy. Berkeley: University of California Press, 1971.

Tirso de Molina. *El burlador de Sevilla y convidado de piedra*. Ed. Joaquín Casalduero. 6th ed. Madrid: Cátedra, 1982.

Valeriano, Giovanni Piero. *Hieroglyphica*. Leiden, 1579.

Valla, Giorgio. *Rhetorica*. Venice, 1514.

Vida, Marco Girolamo. *The "De Arte Poetica."* Trans. Ralph G. Williams. New York: Columbia University Press, 1976.

Vives, Juan Luis. *Opera Omnia*. Ed. Francisco Fabian y Fuero. 6 vols. Valencia, 1745; rpt. London: Gregg Press, 1964.

Vossius, Gerard. *Oratoriarum Institutionum Libri Sex*. Leiden, 1606.

Wilson, Thomas. *The Arte of Rhetorique (1560)*. Ed. G. H. Mair. Oxford: Clarendon Press, 1909.

Secondary Works

Altman, Joel. *The Tudor Play of Mind: Rhetorical Inquiry and the Development of Elizabethan Drama*. Berkeley: University of California Press, 1978.

Anderson, Perry. *Lineages of the Absolutist State*. London: Verso, 1974.

Babcock-Abrahams, Barbara. "'A Tolerated Margin of Mess': The Trickster and His Tales Reconsidered." *Journal of the Folklore Institute* 11 (1975): 147–86.

Bakhtin, Mikhail. *The Dialogic Imagination: Four Essays*. Ed. Michael Holquist, trans. Caryl Emerson and Michael Holquist. Austin: University of Texas Press, 1981.

——. *Rabelais and His World.* Trans. Helene Iswolsky. Cambridge, Mass.: MIT Press, 1968.

Barkan, Leonard. *Nature's Work of Art: The Human Body as Image of the World.* New Haven: Yale University Press, 1975.

Baron, Hans. *The Crisis of the Early Italian Renaissance.* Princeton: Princeton University Press, 1966.

Bashar, Nazife, ed. *The Sexual Dynamics of History: Men's Power, Women's Resistance.* London: Pluto Press, 1983.

Boswell, John. *Christianity, Social Tolerance, and Homosexuality.* Chicago: University of Chicago Press, 1980.

Bouwsma, William J. "Anxiety and the Formation of Early Modern Culture." In *After the Reformation,* ed. Barbara C. Malament, 215–46. Philadelphia: University of Pennsylvania Press, 1980.

Bray, Alan. *Homosexuality in Renaissance England.* London: Gay Men's Press, 1982.

Burke, Peter. *Popular Culture in Early Modern Europe.* New York: Harper & Row, 1978.

Bushnell, Rebecca. *Tragedies of Tyrants: Political Thought and Theater in the English Renaissance.* Ithaca: Cornell University Press, 1990.

Cahn, Michael. "The Eloquent Names of Rhetoric: The Gardens of Eloquence." In *Anglistentag 1990 Marburg: Proceedings,* ed. Claus Uhlig and Rüdiger Zimmermann, 129–38. Tübingen: Max Niemeyer Verlag, 1991.

Carey, Douglas M. "Lazarillo de Tormes and the Quest for Authority." *PMLA* 94 (1979): 36–46.

Cave, Terence. *The Cornucopian Text: Problems of Writing in the French Renaissance.* Oxford: Oxford University Press, 1979.

Certeau, Michel de. *The Practice of Everyday Life.* Trans. Steven Rendall. Berkeley: University of California Press, 1984.

Chew, Samuel C. *The Pilgrimage of Life.* New Haven: Yale University Press, 1962.

Cheyfitz, Eric. *The Poetics of Imperialism: Translation and Colonialization from "The Tempest" to "Tarzan."* New York: Oxford University Press, 1991.

Clarke, M. L. *Rhetoric at Rome.* New York: Barnes & Noble, 1963.

Conley, Thomas. *Rhetoric in the European Tradition.* New York: Longman, 1990.

Cossutta, Fabio. *Gli umanisti e la retorica.* Rome: Ateneo, 1984.

Curtius, Ernst Robert. *European Literature and the Latin Middle Ages.* Trans. Willard R. Trask. New York: Harper & Row, 1953.

d'Ancona, P. "Le rappresentazioni allegoriche delle arti liberali." *L'Arte* 5 (1902): 137–55, 211–28, 269–89, 370–81.

Diccionario crítico etimológico castellano e hispánico. Ed. Joan Corominas and José A. Pascual. Madrid: Editorial Gredos, 1981.

The Dictionary of National Biography. Ed. Leslie Stephen and Sidney Lee. Oxford: Oxford University Press, 1921–22.

Dictionnaire de la langue française du seizième siècle. Ed. Edmond Huguet. Paris: Didier, 1946.

Doglio, Maria Luisa. "Retorica e politica nel secondo cinquecento." In *Retorica e politica*, Atti del II Congresso Italo-tedesco, ed. D. Goldin, 55–77. Padua: Liviana, 1977.

Dollimore, Jonathan. *Sexual Dissidence: Augustine to Wilde, Freud to Foucault.* Oxford: Clarendon Press, 1991.

Douglas, Mary. *Purity and Danger: An Analysis of the Concepts of Pollution and Taboo.* London: Routledge & Kegan Paul, 1966.

duBois, Page. *Sowing the Body: Psychoanalysis and Ancient Representations of Women.* Chicago: University of Chicago Press, 1988.

Elias, Norbert. *The Civilizing Process.* Trans. Edmund Jephcott. New York: Random House, 1978. 2 vols.

——. *The Court Society.* Trans. Edmund Jephcott. New York: Random House, 1969.

Enders, Jody. *Rhetoric and the Origins of Medieval Drama.* Ithaca: Cornell University Press, 1992.

Ferguson, Margaret. *Trials of Desire: Renaissance Defenses of Poetry.* New Haven: Yale University Press, 1983.

Florescu, Vasile. *La retorica nel suo sviluppo storico.* Bologna: Il Mulino, 1971.

Foucault, Michel. "The Subject and Power." *Critical Inquiry* 8 (1982): 777–95.

Franklin, Julian H. *Jean Bodin and the Rise of Absolutist Theory.* Cambridge: Cambridge University Press, 1973.

Fumaroli, Marc. *L'âge de l'éloquence: Rhétorique et "res literaria" de la Renaissance au seuil de l'époque classique.* Geneva: Droz, 1980.

——. "Réflexions sur quelques frontispices gravés d'ouvrages de rhétorique et d'éloquence (1594–1641)." *Bulletin de la Société de l'Histoire et de l'Art Français* 101 (1975): 19–34.

Garin, Eugenio. *Medioevo e Rinascimento: Studi e ricerche.* 2d ed. Bari: Laterza, 1961.

——. *L'umanesimo italiano: Filosofia e vita civile nel Rinascimento.* 2d ed. Bari: Laterza, 1965.

Giamatti, A. Bartlett. "Proteus Unbound: Some Versions of the Sea God in the Renaissance." In *The Disciplines of Criticism*, ed. Peter Demetz, Thomas M. Greene, and Lowry Nelson, Jr., 437–75. New Haven: Yale University Press, 1968.

Gilmore, Myron P. "The Renaissance Conception of the Lessons of History." In *Facets of the Renaissance*, ed. Wallace K. Ferguson, 71–101. New York: Harper & Row, 1959.

Ginzburg, Carlo. *The Cheese and the Worms: The Cosmos of a Sixteenth-Century Miller.* Trans. John and Anne Tedeschi. Baltimore: Johns Hopkins University Press, 1980.

Goldberg, Jonathan. "Sodomy and Society: The Case of Christopher Marlowe." *Southwest Review* 69 (1984): 371–78.

Grand Larousse de la langue française. Paris: Librairie Larousse, 1975.

Grassi, Ernesto. *Rhetoric as Philosophy: The Humanist Tradition.* University Park: Penn State University Press, 1980.

Graus, F. "Social Utopias in the Middle Ages." *Past and Present* 38 (1967): 3–19.

Gravdal, Kathryn. *Ravishing Maidens: Writing Rape in Medieval French Literature and Law*. Philadelphia: University of Pennsylvania Press, 1991.

Gray, Hanna H. "Renaissance Humanism: The Pursuit of Eloquence." *Journal of the History of Ideas* 24 (1963): 497–514.

Greenblatt, Stephen. *Renaissance Self-Fashioning: From More to Shakespeare*. Chicago: University of Chicago Press, 1980.

Greene, Thomas M. "The Flexibility of the Self in Renaissance Literature." In *The Disciplines of Criticism*, ed. Peter Demetz, Thomas M. Greene, and Lowry Nelson, Jr., 241–64. New Haven: Yale University Press, 1968.

——. *The Light in Troy*. New Haven: Yale University Press, 1982.

Grendler, Paul F. *Schooling in Renaissance Italy*. Baltimore: Johns Hopkins University Press, 1989.

Guillén, Claudio. *Literature as System*. Princeton: Princeton University Press, 1971.

Guthrie, W. K. *The Sophists*. Cambridge: Cambridge University Press, 1971.

Hallowell, Robert G. "L'Hercule gallique: Expression et image politique." In *Lumières de la Pléiade*, 243–53. Paris: Vrin, 1966.

Hamilton, Donna B. *Shakespeare and the Politics of Protestant England*. Lexington: University Press of Kentucky, 1992.

Hartung, Fritz, and Roland Mousnier. "Quelques problèmes concernant la monarchie absolue." In *Relazioni del X Congresso Internazionale di Scienze Storiche*, vol. 4, *Storia Moderna*, 1–55. Florence: Sansoni, 1955.

Holmyard, E. J. *Alchemy*. Harmondsworth: Penguin, 1957.

Howell, Wilbur S. *Logic and Rhetoric in England, 1500–1700*. Princeton: Princeton University Press, 1956.

Hudson, Hoyt H. "The Folly of Erasmus." Introduction to Desiderius Erasmus, *The Praise of Folly*, trans. Hoyt H. Hudson. New York: Random House, 1941.

Huizinga, Johan. *Erasmus and the Age of Reformation*. New York: Harper & Row, 1957.

Huon, Antoinette. "'Le Roy Sainct Panigon' dans l'imagerie populaire du XVIe siècle." *Travaux d'Humanisme et Renaissance* 7 (1953): 210–25.

Jordan, Constance. *Renaissance Feminism: Literary Texts and Political Models*. Ithaca: Cornell University Press, 1990.

Joseph, Sister Miriam. *Shakespeare's Use of the Arts of Language*. New York: Columbia University Press, 1947.

Jung, Marc-René. *Hercule dans la littérature française du XVIe siècle*. Geneva: Droz, 1966.

Kahn, Victoria. *Rhetoric, Prudence, and Skepticism in the Renaissance*. Ithaca: Cornell University Press, 1985.

Kelley, Donald R. *The Beginning of Ideology: Consciousness and Society in the French Reformation*. Cambridge: Cambridge University Press, 1981.

Kennedy, George A. *Classical Rhetoric and Its Christian and Secular Tradition from Ancient to Modern Times*. Chapel Hill: University of North Carolina Press, 1980.

Kennedy, William J. *Rhetorical Norms in Renaissance Literature*. New Haven: Yale University Press, 1978.

Kerferd, George B. *The Sophistic Movement*. Cambridge: Cambridge University Press, 1981.

Kinneavy, James L. *Greek Rhetorical Origins of Christian Faith: An Inquiry*. New York: Oxford University Press, 1987.

Kinney, Arthur F. *Continental Humanist Poetics: Studies in Erasmus, Castiglione, Marguerite de Navarre, Rabelais, and Cervantes*. Amherst: University of Massachusetts Press, 1989.

Kristeller, Paul Oskar. "Un 'ars dictaminis' di Giovanni del Vergilio." *Italia Medievale et Umanistica* 4 (1961): 181–200.

———. "The Humanist Movement." In *Renaissance Thought: The Classic, Scholastic, and Humanist Strains*, 3–23. New York: Harper & Row, 1961.

Kunzle, David. "World Upside Down: The Iconography of a European Broadsheet Type." In *The Reversible World*, ed. Barbara A. Babcock, 39–94. Ithaca: Cornell University Press, 1978.

Laqueur, Thomas. *Making Sex: Body and Gender from the Greeks to Freud*. Cambridge, Mass.: Harvard University Press, 1990.

Laroque, François. *Shakespeare et la fête: Essai d'archéologie du spectacle dans l'Angleterre élisabéthaine*. Paris: Presses Universitaires de France, 1988.

A Latin Dictionary. Ed. Charlton T. Lewis and Charles Short. Oxford: Clarendon Press, 1962.

McNally, James R. "*Rector et Dux Populi*: Italian Humanists and the Relationship between Rhetoric and Logic." *Modern Philology* 67 (1969): 168–76.

Makarius, Laura. "Le Mythe du 'Trickster.'" *Revue de l'Histoire des Religions* 175 (1969): 17–46.

Marcus, Leah S. *Childhood and Cultural Despair: A Theme and Variations in Seventeenth-Century Literature*. Pittsburgh: University of Pittsburgh Press, 1978.

———. "The Milieu of Milton's *Comus*: Judicial Reform at Ludlow and the Problem of Sexual Assault." *Criticism* 25 (1983): 293–327.

Martí, Antonio. *La preceptiva retórica española en el siglo de oro*. Madrid: Editorial Gredos, 1972.

Martines, Lauro. *Power and Imagination: City-States in Renaissance Italy*. New York: Random House, 1979.

Mazzacurati, Giancarlo. *La crisi della retorica umanistica nel cinquecento (Antonio Riccobono)*. Naples: Libreria Scientifica Editrice, 1961.

Meerhoff, Kees. *Rhétorique et poétique au XVIe siècle en France: Du Bellay, Ramus et les autres*. Leiden: Brill, 1986.

Monfasani, John. "Episodes of Anti-Quintilianism in the Italian Renaissance: Quarrels on the Orator as a *Vir Bonus* and Rhetoric as the *Scientia Bene Dicendi*." *Rhetorica* 10 (1992): 119–38.

———. *George of Trebizond: A Biography and a Study of His Rhetoric and Logic*. Leiden: E. J. Brill, 1976.

———. "Humanism and Rhetoric." In *Renaissance Humanism: Foundations, Forms, and Legacy*, vol. 3, *Humanism and the Disciplines*, ed. Albert Rabil, Jr., 171–235. Philadelphia: University of Pennsylvania Press, 1988.

Murphy, James J. *Rhetoric in the Middle Ages*. Berkeley: University of California Press, 1974.

——, ed. *Renaissance Eloquence: Studies in the Theory and Practice of Renaissance Rhetoric.* Berkeley: University of California Press, 1983.

Murphy, James J., ed., with Kevin P. Roddy. *Renaissance Rhetoric.* New York: Garland, 1981.

O'Malley, John W. *Praise and Blame in Renaissance Rome: Rhetoric, Doctrine, and Reform in the Sacred Orators of the Papal Court, c. 1450–1521.* Durham, N.C.: Duke University Press, 1979.

Ong, Walter J., S.J., *Ramus: Method and the Decay of Dialogue.* Cambridge, Mass.: Harvard University Press, 1958.

Orgel, Stephen. *The Illusion of Power: Political Theater in the English Renaissance.* Berkeley: University of California Press, 1975.

Parker, Alexander A. *Literature and the Delinquent: The Picaresque Novel in Spain and Europe, 1599–1753.* Edinburgh: Edinburgh University Press, 1967.

Parker, Patricia. *Literary Fat Ladies: Rhetoric, Gender, Property.* London: Methuen, 1987.

——. "On the Tongue: Cross Gendering, Effeminacy, and the Art of Words." *Style* 23 (1989): 445–65.

Pelton, Robert D. *The Trickster in West Africa: A Study of Mythic Irony and Sacred Delight.* Berkeley: University of California Press, 1980.

Plett, Heinrich F. *Rhetorik der Affekte: Englische Wirkungsästhetik im Zeitalter der Renaissance.* Tübingen: Max Niemeyer, 1975.

Pocock, J. G. A. "Texts as Events: Reflections on the History of Political Thought." In *Politics of Discourse: The Literature and History of Seventeenth-Century England,* ed. Kevin Sharpe and Steven N. Zwicker, 21–34. Berkeley: University of California Press, 1987.

Radin, Paul. *The Trickster: A Study in American Indian Mythology.* 1956; rpt. New York: Schocken, 1972.

Rebhorn, Wayne A. *Foxes and Lions: Machiavelli's Confidence Men.* Ithaca: Cornell University Press, 1988.

——. "The Metamorphoses of Moria: Structure and Meaning in *The Praise of Folly.*" *PMLA* 89 (1974): 463–76.

Rewriting the Renaissance: The Discourse of Sexual Difference in Early Modern Europe. Ed. Margaret W. Ferguson, Maureen Quilligan, and Nancy Vickers. Chicago: University of Chicago Press, 1986.

Rico, Francisco. *The Spanish Picaresque Novel and the Point of View.* Trans. Charles Davis with Harry Sieber. Cambridge: Cambridge University Press, 1984.

Ruggiero, Guido. *The Boundaries of Eros: Sex Crime and Sexuality in Renaissance Venice.* New York: Oxford University Press, 1985.

Saslow, James M. *Ganymede in the Renaissance: Homosexuality in Art and Society.* New Haven: Yale University Press, 1986.

Schalk, Ellery. "Under the Law or Laws unto Themselves: Noble Attitudes and Absolutism in Sixteenth- and Seventeenth-Century France." *Historical Reflections/Reflexions Historiques* 15 (1988): 279–92.

Schoenfeldt, Michael C. *Prayer and Power: George Herbert and Renaissance Courtship.* Chicago: University of Chicago Press, 1991.

Seigel, Jerrold E. *Rhetoric and Philosophy in Renaissance Humanism: The Union of Eloquence and Wisdom, Petrarch to Valla*. Princeton: Princeton University Press, 1968.

Shennan, J. H. *The Origins of the Modern European State: 1450–1725*. London: Hutchinson Universal Library, 1974.

Shuger, Debora K. *Sacred Rhetoric: The Christian Grand Style in the English Renaissance*. Princeton: Princeton University Press, 1988.

Shumaker, Wayne. *The Occult Sciences in the Renaissance: A Study in Intellectual Patterns*. Berkeley: University of California Press, 1972.

Skinner, Quentin. *The Foundations of Modern Political Thought*. 2 vols. Cambridge: Cambridge University Press, 1978.

Sloane, Thomas O. *Donne, Milton, and the End of Humanist Rhetoric*. Berkeley: University of California Press, 1985.

Smith, Bruce R. *Homosexual Desire in Shakespeare's England: A Cultural Poetics*. Chicago: University of Chicago Press, 1991.

Stallybrass, Peter, and Allon White. *The Politics and Poetics of Transgression*. Ithaca: Cornell University Press, 1986.

Stephens, Walter. *Giants in Those Days: Folklore, Ancient History, and Nationalism*. Lincoln: University of Nebraska Press, 1989.

Strier, Richard. *Love Known: Theology and Experience in George Herbert's Poetry*. Chicago: University of Chicago Press, 1983.

Strong, Roy. *Splendour at Court: Renaissance Spectacle and Illusion*. London: Weidenfeld & Nicolson, 1973.

Struever, Nancy. *The Language of History in the Renaissance*. Princeton: Princeton University Press, 1970.

Todorov, Tzvetan. *Theories of the Symbol*. Trans. Catherine Porter. Ithaca: Cornell University Press, 1982.

Verdenius, W. J. "Gorgias' Doctrine of Deception." In *The Sophists and Their Legacy*, ed. George B. Kerferd, 116–28. Wiesbaden: Franz Steiner, 1981.

Verdier, Philippe. "L'iconographie des arts libéraux." In *Arts libéraux et philosophie au moyen âge*, Actes du Quatrième Congrès International de Philosophie Médiévale, 1967, 305–55. Montreal, 1969.

Vickers, Brian. *Classical Rhetoric in English Poetry*. London: Macmillan, 1970.

——. *In Defence of Rhetoric*. Oxford: Clarendon Press, 1988.

Watson, Donald G. "Erasmus's *Praise of Folly* and the Spirit of Carnival." *Renaissance Quarterly* 32 (1979): 333–53.

Whigham, Frank. *Ambition and Privilege: The Social Tropes of Elizabethan Courtesy Theory*. Berkeley: University of California Press, 1984.

Williams, Raymond. *Marxism and Literature*. Oxford: Oxford University Press, 1977.

Wind, Edgar. "'Hercules' and 'Orpheus': Two Mock-Heroic Designs by Dürer." *Journal of the Warburg Institute* 2 (1938–39): 206–18.

——. *Pagan Mysteries in the Renaissance*. Rev. ed. New York: Norton, 1958.

Zedler, Johann Heinrich. *Grosses vollständiges Universal-Lexikon*. Graz, 1961–64.

Index

DATE DUE

DEMCO 38-297